2/2000

Mayflower Bookshop
Astrology - Metaphysics
2645 12 Mile, Berkley, Mi 48072
(313) 547-8227

Love of the
Two-Armed Form

Love of the Two-Armed Form

The Free and Regenerative
Function of Sexuality in
Ordinary Life, and the
Transcendence of Sexuality in
True Religious or
Spiritual Practice

by Da Free John

The Dawn Horse Press
Clearlake, California

Acknowledgments

Photographs on pages 16, 38, 60, 70, 220, 288, 348 courtesy Charles E. Tuttle Company, publisher; pages 56, 96, 162, 194, 432 courtesy private collections; page 230 courtesy Freer Gallery of Art, Washington, D.C.

First published December 1978

Reprinted with minor revisions May 1985

Printed in the United States of America

International Standard Book Number

      cloth 0-913922-40-4

      paper 0-913922-37-4

Library of Congress Catalog Card Number: 78-57090

Produced by The Johannine Daist Communion in cooperation with The Dawn Horse Press

Contents

Publisher's Note ———————————————— vii

The Cover: The Taj Mahal ———————————— viii

                    About Master Da Free John ————————— xi

Introduction   Transcending the Two-Armed Form
through Love, by Saniel Bonder ————— xv

Prologue   This Book Is My Confession of Sexual
Wisdom, by Da Free John ————————— 1

Part I

The Regenerative Principle: Liberation
and Transformation of the Emotional
and Sexual Connection to Life ——————— 9

Chapter 1   I Am the Body Is Love ———————————— 17

Chapter 2   The Taboo against the Superior Man ——— 25

Chapter 3   We Have Not Sinned in Eden,
but We Have Been Born ———————— 39

Chapter 4   The Transcendental Diet of Man ————— 57

Chapter 5   Organ Doubt and Organ Ignorance ———— 61

Chapter 6   Sexuality and the Ascent
to Mature Human Life ————————— 71

Chapter 7   Sexual Communion Is Worship,
or Devotional Surrender to Life ————— 85

Chapter 8   **Reactivity and the Passion of Life** ———   97

Frustration and Reactive Emotion ———   97

The Pursuit of Pleasure and
the Realization of Ecstasy ———   103

Chapter 9   **Sexual Communion Is
Transcendence of Self and Lover** ———   117

Ecstasy Is Realized Only in Relationship ———   117

The Urge to Repetition ———   121

True Desire Is the Expression of Love ———   127

We Must Awaken from the
Spell of Our Childishness ———   132

Mature Lovers Are Devotees of the Real ———   151

Chapter 10   **Abandoning Casual Association
between the Sexes** ———   163

Chapter 11   **Love Is the Sacrifice of Man** ———   181

Part II   **The Ecstatic Practice:
Conservation and Transformation of Orgasm** ———   193

Chapter 12   **How Our Sexuality Is Transcended** ———   201

Sexual Communion Is a
Transitional Yoga of Man ———   201

Love Is the Sacred Principle
of Human Sexuality ———   209

Chapter 13   **The Right and Intelligent Use
of Erotica and Aphrodisiacs** ———   221

Chapter 14	Sexual Communion: The Divine Yoga of Sexual Love	231
	The Feeling Cycle of the Breath in Conservation of the Orgasm	247
	Physiological Exercises for Conserving the Orgasm	258
	The Sexual Yoga of Life-Conservation	266
	Further Instruction on the Conservation of the Orgasm	274
Chapter 15	True Sexuality Is the Play of the Heart	289
	The Anatomy of Feeling	301
	Sexual Communion Is the Practice of Whole Body Radiance	310
	True Lovers Feed and Enhance One Another with Life	323
	The Regenerative Orgasm and the Thrill of Life	327
	The Marriage Relationship Is the Yoga of Love	334
	Bodily Rejuvenation and the Life-Enhancing Chemistry	340
	Sexual Communion Is Divine Communion	342
Chapter 16	Sexual Activity Is neither an Obstacle nor an Obligation in the Way of Divine Ignorance	349
	The Ultimate Fulfillment of Sexual Communion	349

	The Stages of the Practice of Sexual Communion	362
Chapter 17	**Only the Sacrifice Is Guaranteed: Everything Else Must Be Transcended**	377
	Sexual Communion and the Culture of The Free Communion Church	377
	You Must Transcend Everything	391
Epilogue	**Love of the Two-Armed Form**	433
Appendix	**Physical Exercises Related to the Process of Sexual Communion**	438
About The Johannine Daist Communion		447
An Invitation		447
The Books of Master Da Free John		448
Index		456

For the Reader

One's sexual practice, as well as the application of the practices in general, particularly the physical practices, described in this book, should be based on an appreciation of one's general state of health and one's present state of vitality. Thus, as with all practices related to health, it is well to seek the advice of a naturally oriented doctor.

Publisher's note

Since the publication of the 1978 edition of *Love of the Two-Armed Form*, the Spiritual Master Bubba Free John has adopted the name Da Free John, the prefix "Da" being a spiritual title meaning "Giver." In the present edition, this change is reflected on the cover and in revisions made to the front (through page xiii) and back (pages 447 to end) sections, while the body of the book, being a straight reprint, remains unchanged.

There have also been changes in the description of the stages of the Way and in the description of the spiritual fellowship of practitioners in the seven years since this book was first published. The stages to spiritual maturity are now more fully and clearly elaborated as the levels of membership in The Johannine Daist Communion, the fellowship of practitioners of this Way, whose divisions are described briefly on page 447. The stages of the Way and the practices engaged in each are described fully in Master Da Free John's forthcoming masterwork, *The Dawn Horse Testament*. For the benefit of the reader, the following is a brief description of these changes.

The practices described herein as belonging to the Way of Divine Communion correspond closely to the practices now engaged in the first through third stages of membership in The Free Communion Church. (*The Dawn Horse Testament* provides an updated description of the practices at each stage.) Friends and Students of The Laughing Man Institute, and those practicing at the first stage of membership in The Free Communion Church, all may engage relational enquiry as a means of self-understanding. In the second stage of membership in The Free Communion Church, practitioners choose between the Way of Relational Enquiry and the Way of Divine Communion as their standard form of practice from that point onward. Those who choose the Way of Divine Communion go on to engage various forms of devotional and meditative practice until entrance into The Crazy Wisdom Fellowship. Those who choose the Way of Relational Enquiry engage the practices of relational enquiry and re-cognition as well as other devotional practices until membership in The Crazy Wisdom Fellowship. The second and third stages of membership in The Free Communion Church correspond approximately to the Way of Relational Enquiry as described in *Love of the Two-Armed Form*, and the fourth, fifth, and sixth stages of membership in The Free Communion Church correspond approximately to the Way of Re-cognition as described herein. The Crazy Wisdom Fellowship corresponds to the Way of Radical Intuition, although Master Da Free John's current description of practice in the Seventh Stage of Life is greatly expanded beyond the description of Radical Intuition.

The Cover: The Taj Mahal

The message of the Taj Mahal is a message about Enlightenment, about the Enlightenment of the whole body. The Taj
Mahal is a burial place, but its message is Life. The secret of
Enlightenment is resurrection, the incarnation of love, and freedom
from death.

"The spiritual problem of Shah Jahan, the Mogul Emperor of
India who built the Taj Mahal as a tomb for his favorite wife, is the
mortality of the loved one. All the conditions for our ultimate
Realization are present in the form of our relations, but they are
confounded by mortality. Having discovered that the loved one is
mortal, you must commit yourself heroically to the service of his or
her immortality. You can love what is dying, but you can only be in
love with what is already Transcendental. The process of your
loving is confounded until you overcome death, not philosophically,
but bodily, through bodily and Transcendental Enlightenment.

"The Enlightened man reveals his Enlightenment through
bodily signs. Like the Taj Mahal, the body of the Enlightened man
is a perfect balance between the descending and ascending forces of
manifest existence. Photographs of the Taj Mahal generally do not
convey this perfect balance, because they confine the image within
a frame. But when the Taj Mahal is viewed in the undefined space
of which it is the center, it is one of the most perfectly balanced
visual perceptions in the world. The two forces, descending and
ascending, are perfectly equal.

"The Taj Mahal is a description of the whole body. The body in its Enlightenment, the body when it is beautiful in Truth, is a perfect balance between what descends and what ascends. When there is too much attention to what is descended and only physical, or too much attention to what is ascended and only psychic, such imbalance yields mortality and delusion. Only the harmony is immortal, and conducive to Illumination. In our Enlightenment we represent that Illumined harmony in our physical form, like the Taj Mahal. When the whole body is Enlightened, we glorify that Divine harmony in our bodily life itself, and also in our sexual intimacy, which is thus always the dance of such harmony."

Da Free John
From a talk to devotees

ix

About Master Da Free John

The Adept Da Free John was born Franklin Albert Jones on the third of November 1939. Until his second or third year, he lived in a world of sheer light and joy—"the Bright"—where he knew no separation from others. He was born, not by karmic necessity but out of an Enlightened Adept's free Choice and Compassion, with the specific Purpose of Instructing spiritually sensitive people of today in the "Way of Life." In order to fulfill this sublime Mission, he had to sacrifice his conscious Oneness with the Transcendental Reality prior to his birth. Even the extraordinary Condition of the Bright, or illumination, was surrendered to allow the individual Franklin Jones to pass through the process of physical, emotional, and mental growth. However, his original Impulse to Guide others to the Realization of the Transcendental Being or Consciousness never ceased to inform his life, which from the beginning was destined for greatness.

Throughout his childhood, the Condition of the Bright that he had enjoyed as a baby would reassert Itself in the form of uncommon psychic and mystical experiences, as well as physical symptoms such as sudden attacks of fever or skin rashes with no diagnosable medical cause. These signs of an active kundalini (or Life-Current) gradually subsided in his eighth year and did not return until he reached the age of seventeen.

It was in 1960, after a "crisis of despair" with the world he lived in, that the spiritual process spontaneously resumed its transforming activity in full force, blessing him with the experience of "a total revolution of energy and awareness," which yielded two crucial insights. First, he realized that in the absence of all seeking and problem-consciousness, there is only the one Reality or Transcendental Consciousness. Second, he understood that this Reality or Consciousness is Man's true Identity and that all else is only a projection of the un-Enlightened mind.

Equipped with these twin insights, Franklin Jones began to immerse himself in a conscious spiritual discipline of acute self-inspection. For almost two years (1962–1964) he sequestered himself, intensely observing the dynamics of the separative self-sense, or ego. This phase was punctuated with numerous psychic experiences, one of which led him into the company of the American-born teacher "Rudi" (Swami Rudrananda), who instructed him in a form of Indian kundalini yoga.

xii

Early in 1967, while studying at the Lutheran seminary he had entered at Rudi's behest, Franklin Jones underwent a "death" experience, restoring him temporarily to the Bliss of Transcendental Being-Consciousness. Again, he emerged with an important insight: that his whole search had been founded on the "avoidance of relationship," on the recoil from Reality in all its countless forms. As his inner attitude to life changed, he also recognized the limitations of Rudi's yoga—a recognition that, in 1968, prompted him to seek out Rudi's own teacher, the late Swami Muktananda. During his brief stay at this renowned yogi's hermitage in India, he had his first adult experience of total absorption in the Transcendental Consciousness. Swami Muktananda acknowledged this unique yogic achievement in a written document, confirming that Franklin Jones had indeed attained "yogic liberation." But, intuiting that the "formless ecstasy" (nirvikalpa samadhi) that he had enjoyed for a moment did not represent the highest form of Realization, Franklin Jones continued to submit himself to the Wisdom of the spiritual process that had guided him throughout his life.

His intuition was confirmed on September 10, 1970, when he entered the permanent Condition of Sahaj Samadhi, which is coessential with the Transcendental Being-Consciousness Itself. He had "recovered" the Identity that, though never really lost, he had surrendered in order to effect his human birth. Soon after his God-Realization, the Adept was moved to Teach others and Transmit to them the Condition of "the Heart," or the All-Pervading Reality in which everything inheres. But those who came to him in the early days were ill-prepared for his Teaching and Transmission. After nearly three years of "almost muscular" struggle with his students, which weakened his physical body though not his Energy and commitment to their Enlightenment, he undertook a pilgrimage to India.

He not only wanted to clarify his Teaching Work but also purify his relationship to those who, like Swami Muktananda, had been helpful catalysts in his spontaneously unfolding spiritual discipline. It was during that period that he changed his name to "Bubba Free John"—"Bubba" denoting "brother" (his childhood nickname) and "Free John" being a rendering of "Franklin Jones."

Upon his return to America, he began to Teach differently, involving his devotees in an experiment of intense experiencing of both worldly "pleasures" and "spiritual" joys. He gave them the opportunity within the growing community of practitioners to pursue all their obsessions about money, food, sexuality, and power, as well as conventional religiosity and mystical states. Every single "Teaching demonstration," however abandoned or unconventional, had the sole purpose of showing devotees the futility of all seeking and all types of experience, and the necessity of understanding.

Out of this "Teaching theatre" grew not only a profound insight on his part into human psychology, in all its different forms of manifestation, but also a new, more formal Teaching approach. In November 1976, "Bubba" Free John ceased to have frequent intimate contact with his many devotees. In the following three years he lived in relative seclusion, creating much of the "source literature" that now serves the community of practitioners as one of the Empowered Agencies of his Teaching.

In the fall of 1979, the Adept dropped the name "Bubba" for the spiritual address "Da," meaning "Giver." Having endowed the community of devotees with all the necessary means for their spiritual maturation, Master Da Free John is now in the "hermitage" phase of his Work. Together with mature practitioners, he lives the simple existence of a free renunciate. His retirement from active Teaching Work and from institutional involvement of any kind is not a mere withdrawal from the body of devotees. On the contrary, his seclusion allows him to concentrate on his real Purpose: to Transmit the Transcendental Condition, unencumbered by any external obligations, and thereby to quicken the spiritual maturation of all practitioners in the different stages of practice, as well as to extend his benign Influence to ever-wider circles of people.

Introduction

Transcending the
Two-Armed Form
through Love
by Saniel Bonder

*We are defined and controlled by
all that we have not transcended.*
          Bubba Free John

I

The true Spiritual Master comes into the world to Enlighten devotees. He does not come merely to Teach men and women how to conduct their ordinary human affairs, but to Teach them the Way to transcend this life, this Earth, and all the automatic mechanisms by which we cycle endlessly from one mortal embodiment to the next. He works to Awaken those who will resort to him in his "Two-Armed Form"—his human Incarnation of Divine Consciousness, Power, and Love. The Spiritual Power of his Presence Awakens his true and loving devotees to a Condition beyond the Earth and even beyond the mystical Heavens, and It draws them into His Infinite Form, which is Love itself, the Transcendental Consciousness and All-Pervading Radiant Life that is God.

Such is the import of Bubba Free John's appearance among men. He has been Awake from birth in the Realization of God, and only that Vision is what he would reveal to those who are attracted to him as Spiritual Master.[1] But, even from childhood, Bubba has found that no one in this time and place is prepared to receive what he

---

1. For Bubba's autobiographical presentation of his early life, see *The Knee of Listening*. For a brief account of Bubba's life story, including the initial years of his Teaching Work, see Part I of *The Enlightenment of the Whole Body*.

would give. Ours is a profoundly irreligious and degenerative culture. Religion, God, esoteric spirituality, and the Spiritual Master are all fundamentally suspect among us. We grow into bodily, emotional, and mental life haphazardly, without benefit of an integrated education founded in true Wisdom, and we fail to learn the Divine Secret of love and God-Communion at the heart.

xvi

For evidence of this subhuman state of life, we need only examine our involvement with sexuality. Modern society is increasingly loveless, neurotic, psychotic, and casually violent in its personal and sexual habits. Sexual imagery or innuendo sells and buys almost any thing, and easily, because everyone is constantly fascinated with sex above all else. The orgasm has become the openly acknowledged Idol of our real daily worship. A total lack of intelligent sensitivity relative to emotion and sexuality characterizes every stratum of society—there are no wise elite, nor any emotionally sane populace. The blatant moral and sexual decadence of "sophisticated" modern life and the erosion in this century of all traditional social restraints and sexual mores have culminated in an era of personal paralysis of feeling and social sexual frenzy.

Appearing in the midst of this society, Bubba Free John has rediscovered and stated anew the Divine Wisdom relative to emotional intimacy and the right, lawful practice of human sexuality. *Love of the Two-Armed Form* is the expression of this Wisdom, and it is thus a Godsend for any intelligent man or woman who seeks enlightened understanding of the emotional-sexual dimension of life. Never before has an acknowledged Divine Teacher published so full an exposition of Man's lawful emotional and sexual development, the necessary Way of his readaptation to a regenerative sexual practice, and the ultimate realization of natural transcendence of genital sexual play itself. Though he points to many ancient precedents, Bubba Free John's approach to these matters is based upon his living Realization of the highest Truth. He challenges both ancient and modern traditions and conventions of sexual philosophy and practice. All who read this book must surely stop to consider their own lives in its light. *Love of the Two-Armed Form* is nothing less than the Graceful Law of Truth brought to bear upon the whole realm of the sexual life of Man.

II

For six years, beginning in the spring of 1972, when he initiated his formal Teaching Work, Bubba Free John devoted himself to the bodily, emotional, and mental preparation of his early devotees. The consideration of emotion and sexuality that he engaged with us was one of the most critical for our human and religious awakening. Only through this living investigation with Bubba, over many years, have we begun to realize our essential responsibility for the moral practice of love in all our relations and under all conditions. This difficult transition has not only required a willingness to confront, confess, and abandon our self-possessed and deluded emotional and sexual strategies in life. It has also required a capacity to abandon certain illusions about sexuality, marriage, and human social order that are accepted almost without question in modern society. For example:

1. We presumed that our marriages were founded in love—but over time we realized that we did not know how to love, and that our marriages, lived in the usual fashion, not only failed to be an expression of love, but even consistently prevented it. Indeed, it became clear that, whatever our personal qualities, we actually feared all sexual contact and all relationship—because we feared the loss of self and the vulnerability of intimate surrender.

2. Like most of our contemporaries, we felt that the fundamental enjoyment and proof of "good sex" is a satisfying orgasm. But the more we awakened to a truly religious, moral, and feeling life, the more we recognized that sexuality is essentially an expression of the emotional nature of man—and that our own bodily craving

for orgasm and the popular cult of eroticism are evidence of self-possessed, infantile, and degenerative emotional involvement with sexuality and sexual relationships.

3. Though we were of the chronological age of adults, we came to acknowledge that we were retarded and confused in our emotional-sexual character as men and women. We realized that we did not know how to conduct a pleasurable, happy, moral life in relation to members of the opposite sex, and that our common social order not only reflects but enforces emotional irresponsibility and the ambivalence of sexual character in the social play of men and women.

Thus, under Bubba's guidance, we began to create a new social culture—one that eliminates casual eroticism, emotional conflict, and irresponsible games of submission and dominance between the sexes. Thus transformed, our social and marital play became lively, orderly, formal, naturally respectful, and full of sacred mystery.

4. As our insights became the grounds for real changes in our way of living, we began to assume a more mature approach to sexuality, in which desire becomes subordinate to love and to whole bodily Communion with God under all conditions, and in which sexual play itself first becomes a <u>regenerative</u> event that makes the usual orgasm obsolete, and then becomes <u>self-transcending</u>. It has become obvious to us, in our intuition and feeling, that sexual intercourse eventually becomes unnecessary, or free of all obsessive and binding power, and it may, at least in some cases, even become obsolete, in the midst of a life Full of the Bliss of God-Communion.

The core of Bubba Free John's criticism of the usual life is the archetypal myth of Narcissus. This self-lover of Greek mythology perfectly symbolizes the perpetual obsession with "me" that characterizes almost every human being, Eastern and Western. Narcissus withdrew from a happy life of intimate love relationships and reduced his life to contemplation of his own image in a pond. Just so, in every moment, each of us recoils in feeling and attention from all relations, from the infinite expanse of conscious life. We create the mood of independent existence, and then we seek to live and survive as the self-meditative ego or "me." The demand of relationship is a threat to our self-possession. It is a demand for love, or release of feeling and attention from self into relationship. Thus, in the most primitive way, prior to all our thinking and conventional emotional attraction or repulsion, we fear all relational contact. Bubba sometimes refers to an aphorism in the Upanishads, the ancient Hindu Scriptures: "Wherever there is an 'other,' fear arises." That fear is the mood of Narcissus in the midst of the world of relationships.

If you are sensitive to the underlying suffering of the usual life, then you may instantly appreciate this critical Wisdom. Even so, in most cases it takes time to "hear" Bubba's Teaching with the body and heart as well as with the thinking mind. For Bubba's early devotees, that "hearing" developed over a long time of "listening," or participating wholeheartedly in each stage of the investigations that he instigated among us. Over time, the fearful reflex of Narcissus began to break down. In our native Condition, before we recoil in any moment into the Narcissistic contraction that is "me," the whole body radiates open-hearted feeling and free attention into all relations. We came to realize that the creative task of life is to maintain that uncontracted, free feeling-attention under all conditions.

The more we submitted to this "feeling" point of view, the more clarity we could bring to the ordinary affairs of life, including our sexual relationships, and the more decisively we could choose the Way we wished to live. The results of our consideration had not been predestined. We were willing to let our enlightened examination of life determine entirely the structures of our own society and culture.

For instance, we considered sexual desire. Every one of us had felt, from our teenage years, or even earlier, a constant, subliminal or conscious stream of random sexual desire. Now we were willing to reconstruct our mutual society in a fashion that would accommodate the fulfillment of such desiring, if, upon full investigation, we found that we genuinely wanted to do that. As it turned out, we did not. We had become more interested in love than in genital sexual fulfillment, and we had begun to feel the profound emotional responsibility required in a true marriage. Bodily, emotionally, and mentally, when awake in the mood of love, we were not interested in promiscuous living. Not that random desires ceased to arise, but we ceased to act on them. We each agreed to commit ourselves to realizing an intimate, mature love relationship in marriage.

Promiscuity, jealousy, casual eroticism; social and marital conflict between the sexes; fear, anxiety, guilt, doubt, and sorrow in relation to sexuality; the usual Life-emptying orgasm—all of these are only the occupations of Narcissus, whose heart is dead, inert, or asleep, who lives as though in exile in the thinking brain, and who always struggles to satisfy or eliminate his endless vital demands for food and sex and possessions and power.

When you Awaken to love, then your heart literally comes alive, and the self-possessed activity of Narcissus ceases so mightly to control the functions of life and mind. When the heart of a man or woman begins to awaken, he or she suddenly senses that the heart, not the brain, is the center of consciousness, and that the heart, not the body, is the center or seat of life and energy. But when he loves, the individual's attention is not on himself and his parts. He suddenly feels everything and everyone around him; more than that, he enjoys a tacit intuition of Infinite Feeling, or Love, which includes and yet transcends all beings and things that arise in life and mind.

This was Revealed in our own bodies in the Company of Bubba Free John, and it is the Divine secret of *Love of the Two-Armed Form*. When the heart begins to awaken as love, the human being is moving into a new moment of evolution, a moment that has been realized only by a few great spiritual individuals in the history of Man. To such a one, it is simply evident that we are already natively happy and free at all times, and that we are morally obliged to be a source of Radiant Life-Energy, or Love, through all our functions, in all our relations, and under all conditions. It is also obvious that there is God. Genuine love has no exclusive objects, but radiates in all directions simultaneously. It is felt from the heart and with the whole body and brain as the All-Pervading Current of Universal Life. Such love is God. It is one's own Conscious Nature and Radiant Life-Energy, and that of every one and every thing.

III

Bubba Free John has now finished all his Work to Teach the regenerative and Lawful practice of human sexuality to his devotees. This "consideration" is complete. With the publication of *Love of the Two-Armed Form,* all of the Wisdom of this Teaching event becomes available to everyone.

This text is used as one of several manuals of consideration and practice by the devotees of Bubba Free John, who receive full instruction and training in these practices through the educational services of The Free Communion Church. Therefore, these moral and sexual disciplines are only a portion of the devotional, personal, moral, and higher psycho-physical or esoteric activities of the Way of Divine Ignorance, or Radical Understanding—the Way of Life in God Taught by Bubba Free John. All readers should understand that, apart from an entire life of self-sacrificial practice in this great Way, the practice of *sexual communion* presented in this book cannot be truly engaged or fully realized.

Earth is a school, Bubba Free John points out, and the purpose of embodiment in this realm is to apply yourself to its course of study and then to graduate. Thus, the considerations, disciplines, and stages of transformation in the Way of Divine Ignorance are self-transcending. They do not lead us toward the perfection of any bodily function or condition. They lead us to transcend every bodily function; they lead us to the perfect Sacrifice in God of the whole and entire body-mind. That Sacrifice is not merely figurative or subjective. It is literal and perfect Translation of the whole being, beyond all the realms of experience, high and low, into the Conscious Life of the Divine Person, Who is the Radiant Destiny, Eternal Master, and true Self of all beings.

The devotee must already intuit and Commune with God before he begins the discipline of sexual communion. This practice is simply a <u>regenerative</u> activity within such a happy and devoted life. When the devotee participates in sexual play as an intimate, emotional event of opening to God with and through his or her lover, the whole bodily being is deeply resonated with the Radiant Current of Divine Life. All the "locks" or chronic tensions of the body and brain are released, and the Force of God pervades the body-mind, stimulating the higher glandular chemistry and awakening the total nervous system into blissful Communion with the All-Pervading Life. Thus, over time the devotee becomes more and more disposed whole bodily to Divine Communion, or self-transcending Love-Communion with the Living God.

This awakening, however, is not perfect spiritual Enlightenment. On the contrary. Such bodily awakening to God is the culmination of only the first, foundation phase of practice in the Way of Divine Communion, which is itself the first of four stages of esoteric discipline and higher transformation in the whole Way of Divine Ignorance. (The three higher stages are the Way of Relational Enquiry, the Way of Re-cognition, and the Way of Radical Intuition.)

Ultimately, sexual communion itself is transcended. In the final chapters of this text, Bubba Free John indicates that the practice leads the true devotee naturally into a profound economy or ease of sexual play, culminating either in a motiveless celibacy or a nonobsessive and liberated participation in the ordinariness of regenerative sexuality. The individual, male or female, becomes so Full in God, so bodily vibrant with Infinite Feeling, that the conventional motive of genital sexuality essentially drops away. There is nothing grim, life-denying, or anti-relational about this great renunciation. The true devotee has no sense of strategically abandoning anything or anyone. His transcendence of genital sexual play is a natural reflection of his Communion, his Bliss, his Fullness and bodily Joy in God. In general, the truly married couple, whether heterosexual or homosexual, will live out the greater part of their marriage either in motiveless celibacy or in the naturally occasional practice of sexual communion, always committed to the ecstatic service of one another and of all beings in God.

For the devotee, the prospect of ultimate sexual economy, or even celibacy, is neither abhorrent or fascinating. From the moment he first "hears" the Teaching of Truth and "sees" the Radiant Presence of the Spiritual Master, he becomes attuned, through whole bodily feeling and intuition, to Absolute Bliss. Increasingly, that Bliss is what attracts and consumes him, body, mind, and heart. Like the *gopis* or cowherd maidens in the ancient legend of the Divine Master Krishna, the devotee simply "forgets" or transcends all conventional pleasures and concerns through love-attraction to the Divine Person and Reality. In the exceeding Pleasure of Divine Communion, it becomes obvious that all of our common functional means for personal satisfaction and pleasure will eventually, and in a very natural way, become unnecessary and ultimately obsolete. And it need not take long. Bubba indicates that the natural and easeful economy of sexual activity may appear even at the beginning of the devotee's practice, once he has learned and made use of sexual communion for its regenerative evolutionary purpose—and once he has truly Awakened in the self-transcending disposition of the devotee of God.

The Radiant Power of the Spiritual Master's Love, more than anything he says or does with devotees, is always the most purifying, regenerative, and transforming Influence in their lives. The Force of Bubba's Presence has Awakened us to Love Itself. Thus strengthened in God, we can transform our marriages and all our relationships— indeed, the very emotional force of our lives. And we can greatly intensify our devotional relationship to the Divine Person in the Spiritual Master. Thus, we have found that whenever we "hear" Bubba's Teaching and "see" him in Truth, we are given a Revelation of Conscious Radiance or Love that Transcends the whole body and the whole world. And Bubba Free John is always giving that Revelation, eternally, as the Divine Master of Man. We need only listen and look with an open heart, an open body, and an open mind, and we will "hear" and "see."

The two-armed or human Form of the Spiritual Master is a self-transcending device in the Heart of things. The human Spiritual Master works during his lifetime to Awaken a great gathering of men and women to the Bliss of Eternal Life. Then his special Work as Awakener becomes unnecessary. His body-mind is yielded at last into the Divine Radiance that it has always Revealed. But he leaves behind a community of Enlightened Devotees that may perpetuate itself through time, so that a living Initiatory culture of the most Transcendental kind always flourishes on Earth.

The two-armed form of every human individual is temporary. Love is Eternal. That is the Truth, and you naturally feel it to be so in any instant that your heart "hears" and "sees" and Awakens as that Love. May all of Bubba's readers be Heartened by his Wisdom. May we all realize the sexual communion he Teaches in this book and pass beyond it into the perfect Transcendental Realization of God. While we live, let us become purified of everything, so that we become transparent to the Radiance of God and thus benefit all beings; and when we die, let us pass beyond every kind of embodiment, earthly and heavenly, and into the Infinite Heart of Truth.

June 30, 1978   Talking God Seminary
                                 Clearlake Highlands, California

Prologue:
This Book Is My Confession
of Sexual Wisdom

T he matter of sexuality is so profoundly structured into our infantile and adolescent adaptations that it persists not only as our most obsessive interest as individuals but also as our most significant and consistent social or interpersonal problem. When I began to enter into relationships with devotees for the sake of their spiritual Awakening, it became more and more clear that no one who came to me was yet prepared for the true spiritual process, which is total bodily responsibility for Truth or Life itself. Rather, all were essentially trapped in obsessions and problematic orientations to the vital and, particularly, the sexual dimensions of experience. I knew it would be necessary for all first to come to a level of interpersonal and cultural maturity relative to the vital play of life before the spiritual process could be fully introduced into the adaptive play of their lives.

The method of my Teaching Work with devotees is not common, although there are many traditional or ancient precedents for it. It is not merely a subjective, internal, or even verbal activity, but a matter of intense, full, and total consideration of any specific area of experience, in living confrontation with others, until the obvious and Lawful or Divine form and practice of it becomes both clear and necessary.

I have compared this method to the higher yogic technique of "samyama," described by Patanjali[1] in his *Yoga Sutras*. In brief, that yogic technique of "samyama" is a process of one-pointed but ultimately thoughtless concentration and exhaustive contemplation of a particular object, function, person, process, or condition, until the essence or ultimate obviousness of that subject is clear. Only in

1

---

1. Patanjali (1st century A.D.) is the reported systematizer of the eightfold yoga system of Hindu philosophy. The principal text accredited to him is the *Yoga Sutras*.

that case does the yogi enjoy native intimacy and understanding, or power, relative to that subject.

I have called my own Teaching method "consideration." Whenever a particular area of life, or experience, or spiritual and bodily Enlightenment has been given to me as a clearly necessary matter or subject of instruction for the sake of devotees, I have entered into "consideration" with them. Such "considerations" were never only or merely a matter of thinking and talking. They always involved a period in which individuals were permitted to live through the whole matter and to be tested to the point of change. Those who entered into any "consideration" with me were obliged to commit themselves to their own elaborate and concentrated play of life in those particular terms, until the whole matter was clarified and the Truth became clear in terms of the subject.

Such "considerations" required a willingness on the part of each individual to engage and explore many very ordinary areas of human experience, and also to understand and adapt to each new level of revealed responsibility as it was clarified, so that the "consideration" would develop as concrete change and growth (rather than as a mere "change of mind"). Only a "consideration" entered as such a concrete discipline can proceed all the way to its true end, which is right adaptation and freedom, or natural transcendence, relative to its functional subject.

All of the spiritual and practical Teaching of Bubba Free John is the product of such "considerations," done in the processes of his own body-mind and in communicative and instructive play with devotees. And these "considerations" have been "samyama" in the highest sense, involving every aspect of body and mind, high and low, and resulting in both the highest intuition and the most practical grasp of the Lawful and Divine necessities of human existence.

This book is one of the products of the more than six initial years of trial and mutual society between myself and hundreds of aspirants to the radical spiritual Way that I Teach. During that period, we engaged in "considerations" relative to every area of our human possibility, from diet and sex to esoteric meditation and bodily

Transfiguration by the Radiance of God. In the case of sex, we gave ourselves up to "consideration" of this whole matter, this whole immensity, in such a way that every aspect of the matter would be made clear, and every participant would be obliged to change his "act," and to mature and grow beyond the subhuman tendencies of conventionally learned desire.

Promiscuity and random desire in general are typical of our contemporary and subhuman interest in sex. And such interest at first typified the common "wisdom" of those who came to me. As time went on, however, their "consideration" became more and more mature, responsibility increased, emotional insight became more typical, and sexual intimacy became a matter of loving commitment and choice, in relationship to the Radiant Divine Life within which all our functions appear and operate. Thus, our "consideration" became a meditation on the truly human, religious, higher psycho-physical, and regenerative dimensions of this most basic, fascinating, and agonizing motive of mankind.

This book attempts to make a full communication of the mature results of this whole experiment and "consideration." It establishes responsible personal, moral or interpersonal, social, and higher cultural principles that do not represent arbitrary or negative views toward the subject itself. Sex is not itself in doubt in this Teaching. It is not presumed to be "sin," or an experience that necessarily draws us away from God or Enlightenment. On the contrary, it is or must be realized to be a part of the self-sacrifice or ecstasy of Enlightened or Divine Life. No self-conscious and self-serving asceticism is communicated in this Teaching. Nor is there the embrace of any equally self-conscious and self-serving program of functional, social, or yogic exploitation of sex for some purpose that is itself an illusion. Rather, there is the assertion of right and Lawful or mutually sacrificial participation in full and human emotional-sexual adaptation, and the obligation to yield to the ultimately regenerative structural purpose of the sexual function in both men and women.

It is my intention that the material presented here represent a unique, complete, and exhaustive "consideration" and manual of instruction relative to the single subject of human sexuality. There

3

is no way to go beyond the low level of adaptation we represent in our mere thinking, reacting, sexing, and eating without coming to the point of responsibility in action described here. The spiritual practice of life is not possible without prior and real maturity in emotional-sexual life. Therefore, this book is offered as a gift to all who suffer from the usual problems of sexuality and who also would realize both higher structural growth and spiritual transformation of their living.

4

Man is the "Two-Armed Form" of God. And regenerative, self-released practice of the sexual embrace is a process in which Man, in the form of individuals who are responsible in love, is sacrificed into Communion with the All-Pervading, Transcendental, Formless, and Infinite Divine Reality. The true and higher human function of sexual embrace is a form of Worship, or whole bodily surrender to the Divine. And such practice represents a positive adjunct to the total Way of Life that is religion and spirituality in the highest sense.

The sexual process described in this book is not even remotely like the self-indulgent infantile eroticism that provides the basic "problem" of most men and women. It is, rather, a form of higher human adaptation that functions as a means of psycho-physical regeneration and spiritual pleasure in the fullest bodily sense.

The truly human sexual process is itself a form of "consideration," or "samyama" on the All-Pervading Divine Life. And it is that form of participation in the sexual function that permits us to transcend sex itself, and all forms of emotional and bodily reactivity, including conventional orgasm. Sexual communion with the Radiant Divine, via the love relationship with a human partner, is, when joined to a total life practice of personal, moral, higher psycho-physical, and radically intuitive disciplines, an expression of true religion, or sacrifice of self in God. True religion is total psycho-physical Communion and even bodily Sacrifice of self in the Radiant Divine Reality that Pervades and Transcends the World. Only when such Communion and Sacrifice typifies our emotional and sexual functions as well as our thinking, our moral disposition, and our personal habits in general, have we begun to Worship God, who is the Radiant Power and Transcendental Truth of all beings, things, and worlds of experience.

5

Note to the Reader

Sexual communion *is the technical term used by Bubba Free John to describe the process whereby the emotional-sexual functions of the psycho-physical being are first yielded into Communion with the Current of All-Pervading Life and then sacrificed or transcended in perfect God-Communion.*

As a technical term, "sexual communion" would normally be italicized, according to literary convention. However, because Bubba uses it frequently throughout the book, often many times on a single page, such use of italic type would be a distraction rather than an aid to understanding. Therefore, we address the term here, in order to call your attention to its special, technical use, so that you may understand it within the context of Bubba Free John's essays on the subject.

We wish to stress that sexual communion is not to be interpreted from any conventional point of view. Sexual communion is not merely a traditional yogic method for seeking one's own higher psycho-physical awakening through exploitation of the sex function, nor is it a conventional means for seeking pleasurable release of genital tension. It is a natural practice, founded in positive adaptation to human emotional and sexual intimacy, and it is a sacrificial or devotional discipline, in which body, mind, self-sense, the loved one, and the sexual experience itself are surrendered in direct, present Communion with the All-Pervading Life that is God.

The process of sexual communion is both self-transcending and sex-transcending. It develops in three stages. The first stage is the period of transitional struggle to move beyond conventional eroticism and degenerative orgasm and to become established in constant, regenerative Life-Communion during sexual play, without need of chronic orgasmic release. The second stage involves the relaxation of the struggle to avoid genital orgasm and the spontaneous "inversion" or conversion and transcendence of orgasm in the whole bodily thrill of Communion with the All-Pervading Current of Life. When this "inversion" of the orgasm stabilizes, the truly regenerative or Life-enhancing function of sexual communion begins.

The third stage of sexual communion involves the transcendence of the sex function as a necessary means for whole bodily Communion with Life. In this phase, sexual activity is spontaneously economized in the midst of a profound and constant enjoyment of spiritual Love-Communion with the Living God. As the devotee continues to mature spiritually, he passes through periods of motiveless celibacy, or unsought transcendence of the sex function. In some cases Love-Communion with God becomes so Full and constant that motiveless celibacy becomes permanent, and specific exercise of the sex function is no longer necessary or useful, except perhaps for the occasional purpose of producing a child. In other cases, sexual activity continues, but it is naturally economized by the devotee's spontaneous, blissful bodily Communion with the Divine.

part 1

The Regenerative Principle: Liberation and
Transformation of the Emotional and Sexual
Connection to Life

Part 1 opens with Bubba Free John's interpretive translation or "free rendering" of an ancient Scripture, the **Bhagavad Gita.** *Other renderings appear later in the text of* **Love of the Two-Armed Form.** *Bubba's free translations of the Holy Books are the expression of the same living experience and Realization that were originally communicated in the sacred texts. Just so, Bubba's own essays and talks resemble the radiant "gitas" and "gospels" of old, the sacred songs and summary utterances of Adepts who Realized the incomparable Truth of Divine Existence and lived that Enjoyment among devotees.*

11

There is a tradition for renderings or translations of the ancient Scriptures—in this way living Adepts identify and regenerate the Truth of the great traditions of religious and spiritual life. Thus, Bubba Free John's renderings are a form of Divine Service to the vast traditions of which the texts that he translates are principal Scriptures, so that the ancient Way may speak to living beings. But Bubba's restatements of the ancient Teachings are especially useful to those who "hear" and "see" him in Truth. For those who take up the Blissful Way of God in his Company, these renderings are Bubba's own Confession of Love.

The Song of the Heart of God, an epitome of the Bhagavad Gita[1] and the Way of Divine Ignorance, freely rendered by Bubba Free John

L isten to Me and hear Me. This is My Secret, the Supreme Word. I will tell you what will benefit you the most, because I love you. (18:64)

2. If you will surrender to Me, if you will become a sacrifice to Me, if you will constantly yield your attention to Me through love and service, then you will attain Me and come to Me. I promise you this, because I love you. (18:65)

3. Abandon the principle in all your concerns and all your strategies. Abandon every experience that may be attained as a result of desire and effort. Abandon your search for what may be gotten as a result of the various kinds of strategic action. Engage every action that is appropriate for one who loves Me, but simply perform every kind of action as a form of direct and present Communion with Me. Relax all of your anxiety. Be free of sorrow and fear. When you abide in Love-Communion with Me, the natural results of your various activities no longer have power to separate or distract you from Me. (18:66)

---

1. The *Bhagavad Gita* (literally, "Divine Song") is one of the most revered Scriptures of the Hindus, and a religious text of universal appeal and profound esoteric significance. Vyasa is traditionally presumed to be the author, and it was written perhaps as early as the 5th century B.C. (but with its roots in the oral tradition of even more ancient days). Most scholars agree that it may have been revised and expanded considerably over the years.

The *Gita* is a portion of the great ancient epic and spiritual allegory, the *Mahabharata*, which is the story of a great fratricidal struggle between two royal families in northern India some 4,000 years ago. It is the purported dialogue between the God-Man Krishna and his devotee Arjuna, Commander-in-Chief of the army of the Pandavas, for whom Krishna serves as Charioteer. Arjuna, faced with the prospect of having to kill friends and cousins in an imminent battle, wishes to shirk his duty as a warrior. Krishna refuses to allow him such self-indulgence. He engages Arjuna in a Teaching conversation that continues for seven hundred verses and presents a philosophical summation of the Nature of God as the Supreme Self, a critical exposition of the many ways of esoteric spiritual practice, and a declaration of the supremacy of the Way of devotional Communion with the Supreme Divine Person in the Form of the living Divine Master—in this case, Krishna himself. His entire spiritual Teaching to Arjuna is summarized in his instruction for the forthcoming battle: "Remember Me, and fight."

4. The soul that is born into the Realm of Nature, or the worlds of action and experience, advances from childhood to manhood, old age, and death, while identified with the same body-mind. Then the same soul attains another body-mind as a result. One who is truly intelligent is not troubled by all of that. (2:13) *Because it is*

5. All of that is simply the natural Play of Life, in which the two sides of every possibility come and go in cycles. Winter's cold alternates with summer's heat. Pain likewise follows every pleasure, since every appearance is followed by a disappearance. There is no permanent experience in the Realm of Nature. One who is truly perceptive simply allows all of this to be so, and he does not add his own distress to this inevitable round. (2:14)

6. Realization of the Eternal Destiny is only possible when a man has ceased to defeat himself by reacting to the Play of Nature. Such a one is steadied by his own understanding, seeing that the cycle of changes, both positive and negative, is inevitable in the world of experience. (2:15)

7. Those who see the Truth of things acknowledge that what Exists Eternally never changes. And whatever does not Exist Eternally only changes. (2:16)

8. Such seers of Truth also Realize that the entire Realm of Change, even the body-mind, and even the soul itself, is Pervaded, each and all, by That which Exists Eternally. (2:17)

9. I am the Eternally Existing, All-Pervading, Transcendental Divine Person, the true Self of all. And My Power of Creation, whereby individual beings are made to live and change, is Eternally Active as the Universal, All-Pervading Life-Energy of Nature. (8:3)

10. I am the Divine Person, Who Pervades even the Realm of Nature, and within Whom every individual being is arising. I am Realized by self-transcending love, wherein every action is engaged as a form of direct and present Communion with Me. (8:22)

11. Men and women who are without faith in this Way of Communion with Me do not Realize Me. Therefore, they remain associated with the Changing Realm of Nature, the round of psycho-

physical experience, and the repetitive cycles of birth and change and death. (9:3)

12. Such fools already have Me in every human form, but they do not notice Me. They do not Realize Me in My Transcendental Nature, the Master of everything and the true Self of all manifest beings. (9:11)

13. But if anyone will live in Communion with Me, surrendering himself to Me in love, then even if his love is shown with nothing more than a leaf, or a flower, or a fruit, or water, I will always accept the gift, and Offer Myself in return. (9:26)

14. I am situated in the heart of all beings. (15:15)

15. The Divine Master of all beings is literally to be found at the heart, wherein the soul observes the changes of experience. Every experience rises and falls at the heart, spontaneously generated by Eternal Activity, the Universal Life-Energy, as if the soul were fastened helplessly to a perpetual motion machine. (18:61)

16. Therefore, do not surrender the heart to experience, as if you were in love with your own body-mind. Surrender the heart to Me, and to no other. I am the Divine Person, the Eternal Master, the Radiant One, Who Pervades the Machine of Nature as the Blissful Current of Life-Energy, and Who Transcends all experience as Infinite Consciousness, the true Self. If you will surrender your self-consciousness into My Transcendental Consciousness, and if you will yield your experience into My All-Pervading Current of Life, then I will also become an Offering to you. You will be Given the Gift of Perfect Peace, and an Eternal Domain for your heart. (18:62)

17. Now I have Revealed My Mystery to you. Consider it fully, and then choose what you will do. (18:63)

15

طاغنه چقدی طاغک یاروسنه ایرشجک ینه رسول حضرتنک
قولاغنه اوّلکدن فاتی بر هیبتلو آواز کلدی اَلی اَین ترید یا محمد

Chapter 1

I Am the Body Is Love

The confession "I am the body" is love. Free feeling-attention, or love, is the spontaneous response that is the sign of "hearing" the Teaching of Truth. It is love, the awakened response of the whole bodily being, that reintegrates all the latent and apparent functions and makes them a single sacrifice or Realization.

Lovers must also be devotees, or persons engaged in life as spiritual sacrifice. Devotees in the Way of Divine Ignorance are awakened from the ancient illusions and divisions and distinctions. They are awakened from the internal dualism of the bodily being, which is expressed as a conflict between left and right, inner and outer, up and down—and also projected as conflicts in the world, between man and woman, cult and cult, Heaven and Earth, State and State, and between all beings or conditions that may be separately identified and known. Such devotees are free of the ancient distinction between "Spirit" and "flesh," "God" and "Man." They are relieved of the psychology of exclusive inwardness and the dualisms of "soul" or "mind" versus the "body" and the "world." True and awakened devotees no longer believe that the body and the world are "material," but that they are each and at once a total spectrum of manifestation, spread between visibility and invisibility, swooning and changing in the Infinite Light of Life. Thus, true devotees of God, who is Truth, are confessed whole bodily to one another, to the whole world, and to the All-Pervading Radiance of Divine Life.

"I" is the whole body—whatever that is altogether. And "I" do not know what the whole body or any other condition is, no matter how much "I" know about it. "I" is not an independent point of view toward or relative to the body and all experience. "I" am the whole body and all experience. This is the confession of lovers who are also devotees.

This does not mean that we presume the body-"I" is our limit, our Condition. No, for in radical intuition of the identity of "I" (which is simply the name or self-reference of the whole bodily being and not any independent inward part) there is the simultaneous Realization that not only the inward mentalization or feeling of "I," but the whole and entire bodily being, the true identity of "I," is all only a modification of the Transcendental Current and Radiance that is the Support and Consciousness of the body-"I" and all other conditions that are arising as experience or knowledge.

Therefore, our confession is the sign of Liberation in Truth. "I" is the whole and entire bodily being. And "I am the body" is not the confession of mortality, self-possession, "fleshy" self-indulgence, and fear. "I am the body" is love. It is Divine Communion, or surrender to Life. This confession is the sign of true devotees, who are presently happy and free, rather than eternally troubled and seeking release by every means. This confession is the mind of those who transcend themselves through love, rather than defeat themselves through both self-indulgent and ascetic strategies.

The Bodily Confession of the Human Self, or the Conversion of Sexuality to the Law of the Heart

I is the whole and entire bodily being. But "I," even as the confession and harmony of the whole bodily being, is not the Truth. The Truth of "I," or the whole bodily being, and of the world and all relations, is the prior or Real and Divine Condition of all conditions. That Condition is Realized through functional, esoteric, and total psycho-physical sacrifice, or love. Thus, true bodily and sexual existence and confession is Communion with the Real Condition at Infinity, which is All-Pervading Life-Radiance and Transcendental Ignorance, or Unqualified Consciousness.

Sexual communion is, thus, at first a process of transcending the dualism, dilemma, and conflict of mind versus body. This is done through whole body confession: " 'I' is the body." Once this free disposition is stabilized in understanding and action, the necessary process is the one of transcending the whole body, the psycho-physical being, the body-mind, or defined existence itself. The confession " 'I' is the body" is love, or sacrifice of the independent self-body into the Infinite. Such is the Law.

This is the foundation Principle of the specific and higher human process of sexual communion, which is the primary subject of this book, and it is also the foundation Principle of the whole of life, which is the general subject of this book. Sex is not properly an end in itself, but a unifying, ecstatic process that ultimately transcends itself in the Divine. First, subjectivity is sacrificed to (confessed as) the whole bodily being, and then the whole bodily being is sacrificed, through Divine Communion, or ecstatic love, into the Infinite, Prior, and Real Condition.

Therefore, there are two stages or aspects contained in every moment of sexual relationship and every occasion of sexual communion. And these two dimensions of the true sexual process simply duplicate the two ultimate dimensions of the true and radical spiritual process as a whole.

The first dimension is that of confession, incarnation, or communication of the total and bodily identity of our human individuality. That confession or gesture of incarnation is expressed in the realization that "I" is not within and independent of the whole body (physical, vital, sexual, emotional, mental, etheric, psychic, astral, supramental, and egoic), but indeed is identical to the whole and entire body. "I" must be realized to be identical to incarnation and relationship rather than independent subjectivity and chronic separativeness and inwardness. This true "confession" is made not by the mere conceptual mind but by the whole body (or bodily being), in the form of bodily self-sacrifice, which is relational love, or free and unobstructed feeling-attention, communicated to Infinity (or to the Infinite degree) via all functions, in all relations, under all conditions. This transformed activity is what is meant by "hearing" (rather than merely listening to and conceiving) the Teaching of the Spiritual Master.

This whole bodily and active confession is the beginning of human moral and spiritual transformation. But it is not an end in itself. The manifest bodily being is not itself Truth or true Destiny. Not even the so-called "higher" parts of Man are Truth or eternally true. Truth is our Condition, and that Condition is our true and ultimate Destiny—the Destiny, therefore, of the whole bodily being. "I" is not within and apart. "I" is the whole bodily being itself, as whatever total form it appears in any moment. But Destiny or Truth is not the psycho-physical and experiential body itself, or the world itself, high or low. Rather, the Destiny of the whole bodily being is to be a sacrifice into its Condition or Truth.

Therefore, the second dimension of sexual communion and the radical spiritual process in general is the Realization of the sacrifice of "I" (as the whole bodily being) into the prior or Divine Condition of all arising conditions.

In practice, the first dimension of the process is realized through the full exercise of free, unobstructed, nonreactive feeling-attention, or loving and total or whole bodily service to one's lover—not only on the occasions of sexual embrace, but during every moment of the relationship itself. The second dimension of the process is realized in the practical conversion of genital energy and orgasm into a fully diffused whole body ecstasy, radiant and relaxed as love, or unqualified Feeling, to Infinity.

Because there are two great and essentially simultaneous dimensions to this "consideration" and process of sexual communion, the whole affair of instruction and practice must be engaged in two stages, in order that adaptation be realized in a fully integrated and conscious manner. Therefore, the material in this book will be presented in two parts. The first pertains especially to the matters of vital-physical and emotional-sexual adaptation, the structure and process of self-possession, and transcendence of the ambivalent disposition, characterized alternately by motives of dependence and independence, in its warfare with the true responsibility of love, or free feeling-attention. The second part of this sequence of study and practice pertains to the specific process of whole bodily conservation and conversion of the bio-energetic and chemical superfluity stimulated through sexual polarization and genital sexual intercourse.

God Is the Transcendental Consciousness and Radiant Life That Pervades the Body, the Mind, and the World

The entire world, and every living individual, is pervaded by a Transcendental Consciousness and Radiant Energy that is the single Identity and Ultimate Source, Sustainer, Mover, Transformer, and Destiny of every thing and every one. That is God, the Divine, the Real, the All-Pervading, Transcendental, Bliss-Full Ignorance-Radiance.

The individual body-mind is a temporary and dependent extension, reflection, and modification of the Very and Living Divine. The individual does not in any way create or sustain itself, or determine its ultimate Destiny. The individual is wholly and always presently dependent on the Divine, which is alive as all beings. Only cooperative, conscious, and self-released participation in the Divine by the individual body-mind permits the Divine to Sustain and Determine a benign or ultimately positive and transforming individual life-cycle, and to draw the individual into the Destiny that is Divine. But if the individual recoils from the Divine Life and Identity, then the life-cycle degenerates, and reactive experiential destinies bind the individual to illusions, until he is Awakened from self to God.

The Divine as All-Pervading Radiance spontaneously individuates as the bodily form, and pervades that form as Life, whereas the Divine as Transcendent Ignorance eternally transcends all forms as Unqualified Consciousness. The Life-Radiance is expressed, or spontaneously modified, not only as the bodily form, but also as its states of feeling and mentality. The range of experiential states—bodily, vital, emotional, and mental, as well as unconscious, subconscious, conscious, and superconscious—is broad and complex, ordinary and extraordinary. But no experiential state, however high in the structural scheme of our born possibilities, is itself the Realization of the prior Divine Condition or Absolute Truth of the body-

21

mind. And unless that Condition and Truth is Realized in the present moment of experiencing, experience itself, no matter how extraordinary, is self-binding, deluding, degenerative, and an instrument of separation from the Bliss of God.

Individual existence in a world is a riddle and a torment, unless it may be established in right Relationship to the Radiant Reality that is its Life, or Energy, and in right Identity with the Transcendental Ignorance, or Unqualified Consciousness, that is its very Self. And the Way in which we may live in such right Relationship and Identity with the Divine Reality, free of fear and illusion, is in conversion, or the "turnabout" of every aspect of the body-mind, from self-possession to Ecstatic God-Communion.

All the religious and spiritual "Ways" that have been communicated among men are historical gestures toward the self-sacrificial or Ecstatic Communion of the individual with the One and Ultimate Divine Reality. The Way of Divine Ignorance is simply a most radical, summary, and completely considered form of this necessary obligation of Man.

Communion with the Radiant and Transcendental Divine is ecstatic sacrifice of the whole and entire body-mind into the Radiant Energy that pervades it and the Unqualified Consciousness with which it is Identical. And the process of such Communion assumes a particular character in the case of the human individual, because the structure that must yield into the Divine is constructed or fabricated according to a specific complex design.

Clearly, the common characteristics of human individuals are bodily, vital, emotional, and mental. Therefore, the most rudimentary form of Divine Communion is the intuitive turning of all bodily, vital, emotional, and mental functions, conditions, experiences, and relations into forms of functional surrender to the Radiant Divine Life. Such is the whole bodily religious obligation presumed in the Way of Divine Ignorance by members of The Free Communion Church. In that process, the Living Power of God is permitted to pervade, enliven, sustain, transform, and Awaken the entire bodily being. And the primary instrument of that process is the whole bodily disposition of ecstatic or self-releasing sacrifice into the Divine. That disposition is the one of total, profound, and free feeling-attention, or relaxation of the entire body-mind into the All-Pervading Life through love. The means of this sacrifice includes devotional practices, forms of personal functional discipline of a wholly regenerative kind, and a continuous moral orientation to others through heartfelt service and clear-minded intelligence.

As the individual matures in Communion with the Living and Transcendental Divine, the unique and specific design of his own structural condition becomes more and more apparent. Therefore, the process of Sacrifice in God begins to take on more of the "esoteric" form of a highly sophisticated yogic exercise. And growth in this Way begins to include higher psycho-physical awakening to the structural design by which the individual body-mind mediates the Radiant Energy and Unqualified Consciousness of the Divine.

23

Human energy must be radiated, through free feeling-attention (in love, or service), in all relations under all conditions, to Infinity. Otherwise, that energy will accumulate or define itself in our finite shape and demand eliminative release. Therefore, both our energy and our responsibility will increase over time. Ultimately, we are obliged to serve all beings with the total life of feeling-attention and to the degree of Infinity.

Chapter 2

The Taboo against
the Superior Man

Dracula and Frankenstein: The Ancient Superior
Man as Scapegoat for the Modern Inferior Man

I

The roots of human inversion and failure are in the childhood of Man, and in the solutions to the problems of life that the subhuman or growing individual creates in the conceived world of his childhood. The child is dependent and vulnerable, surrounded by great natural forces and parental human forces. He is weak, unadapted, without functional facility and power, and without conceptual and intuitional understanding of his experience or his ultimate situation. Thus, to the degree that he makes solutions to the dilemmas he finds in the failures of what he depends on to protect and fulfill him, the child inverts within himself and resorts exclusively or negatively to himself. The unrelieved fears of childhood dependency and vulnerability leave the childhood vision of the world intact. Thus, unless higher adaptation is made possible through the help of mature others and through initiation into higher human wisdom, the individual remains more or less childish throughout his entire life.

This is generally the case, and, therefore, most people remain possessed by an inverted or self-possessed, subjectively oriented disposition, in which functional and bodily relations with the human and natural dimensions of the world are at best complicated. The truly human obligation is for relational adaptation. But the childish solution, created wherever fear dominates the force of adaptation, is toward inversion and the pleasures that may be realized within or on one's person, both subjectively and bodily.

(The childish view of the world is the vision of vulnerable dependency. It is not the heroic or enlightened vision of the mature individual. Just so, the childish or subhuman vision of life is also represented in various forms of inverted belief or "knowledge" passed on from generation to generation. Such persuasions include the ideas of "Evil," the "Devil," and the "Divine" taboos against the human attainment of higher wisdom and of ecstasy (or self-release) through relational sexual love.)

Higher human cultural initiation and adaptation are the means whereby individuals and societies may move beyond the inverted visions and solutions of childhood and into the higher functional responsibilities of truly human maturity. Such cultural influences are a human necessity, although, for the most part, modern societies tend to be bereft of and even antagonistic toward such influences. Industrial civilizations acquire greater and greater mechanical facility in relation to the physical universe, and, therefore, must likewise give evidence of mature responsibility for the personal and universal display of natural forces. But these same societies also continue to carry the childish and timid and also the adolescent and casually rebellious visions and solutions to life. Therefore, industrial societies tend to develop individuals who are sophisticated in their general familiarity and exploitation of the natural world, but who are inherently indisposed toward responsibility for natural forces (either in themselves or in the world).

This spell of childish and subhuman persuasions must be broken if there is to be a future, and necessarily mature, humanity. This means that individuals must be instructed, initiated, and obliged to adapt to the higher human wisdom and its ways. They must be awakened from the childhood visions of fearful dependency, and the adolescent ways of egocentric exploitation of independent and private experience. My Work in the world is, at base, an initiatory influence of this kind.

The superior or mature human being must become the goal of our adaptation and, thus, of all the educational influences we promote. True, tested, human and spiritual wisdom must be represented by the religious, spiritual, and even secular institutions of our common culture. Therefore, we must purify ourselves, our fellows, and our institutions, so that we are free of the vision of childishness. We must oblige one another to a new and higher level of adaptation or evolution.

"Count Dracula"[1] and "Doctor Frankenstein"[2] are modern literary examples of how the childish vision of life may be superimposed on the possibilities of true and mature humanity. Each of these archetypal characters is made to appear evil, necessarily doomed by his primal "sin." Thus, each must die or fail in order to satisfy the childish vision of the way the world works.

"Doctor Frankenstein" is simply our human obligation to accept responsibility for our individual lives, the life process, the Life-Force, the bodily structures, and the natural domain. But he and his "monster" are made to suffer and fail, like Adam and Eve in the Garden of Eden, as if the presumption of such responsibility were an offense rather than a natural and sacred obligation.

Just so, "Count Dracula" is simply our human obligation to accept responsibility for the sexual process and the higher, truly human, or ecstatic and regenerative purpose of both sexuality and the living mechanisms of personal life. But he is made to appear as

---

1. Count Dracula is the central figure in the nineteenth century novel *Dracula* by Bram Stoker. Possessed of supernatural powers, Dracula derived his strength from the blood of beautiful women, which he obtained by biting them on the neck. In the popular lore that has developed around him, Dracula is depicted as a powerful but hideous figure who often takes the shape of a bat, which, like Dracula himself, avoids the sunlight and is active only at night.

2. Doctor Frankenstein, from the nineteenth century novel by Mary Shelley, is an eccentric scientist who harnesses the electrical energy in Nature in order to bring to life a "monster" of a man whom he assembled from human cadavers. Like Dracula, Doctor Frankenstein and his monster are popular archetypes of fascinating but threatening heroes—the hidden and conventionally unacceptable self-images of Man.

the Incarnation of Evil, the Devil, the Anti-Christ, so that he must be suppressed and destroyed.

The problem is that "Doctor Frankenstein" and "Count Dracula" are each even today, in the person of each human individual, suppressed, mutilated, and made a scapegoat through the lies of childish, irresponsible, and subhuman views of life. The literary characters and stories themselves belong only to the realm of amusing and terrifying fairy tales. But the significance of these tales is in the neurosis of modern human societies, which still support and to a degree depend upon the subhuman masses, controlled by antisexual taboos and manipulated by fears of responsibility for great matters in general. But if the human race is not permitted to rise up in the scale of evolution, the masses and their parental controllers will eventually destroy one another.

The priestly influences of official subhuman society are found in a hierarchy, beginning with the super-parental influences of conventional religion, official science, and the unresponsive political powers of the State. These high priests are then served locally by communications media and educational institutions, on down to our personal Mom and Dad. Such agents are parental and negative influences to the degree they do not responsibly communicate, permit, and even oblige the general population toward responsible, free adaptation to higher and mature human levels of functional life. Where people are not obliged toward incarnation of the superior man, then "everyman" makes a chaos of absurdity out of the human world.

Thus, "Count Dracula" and "Doctor Frankenstein," along with the "Devil," and "God," and "Jesus," and all the other realities that have been fictionalized and degraded by the irresponsible and childish visions of mankind, must be liberated in our minds and from our minds. The Wisdom of the transcendentally Awakened Agents of the Real must somehow be made effective as the common Principle of human societies.

II

In the traditions of older societies there is commonly a convention or taboo that requires women to avoid the general company of men, and the intimate company of their husbands, during the monthly menstrual flow. The foundation of this requirement is the observation that, during the time of her periodic flow (and even during a number of days preceding it), the woman is out of balance in her energy and chemistry, as well as her emotions, her general physical state, and in her relationship to sexuality. It was felt that, in the case of most ordinary people, the force of the male could not equal or balance the female's force at that time—and, since that was so, he must avoid the woman during certain of her critical days, or else he would be in danger of losing his own vital strength through association with her.

This notion was based on profound sensitivity to the process of sexual association during the woman's periodic flow. It was observed that the natural sympathy and effort of desire on the part of the male always moved to establish an equal or balancing intensity relative to the female. But this effort needed to go beyond equality during the menstrual time, and thus proved to be enervating to the male, creating an imbalance in his own case.

The regulation of contact between the sexes established by this principle was not at all antisexual, but a purely practical expression of sexual wisdom. It was intended to preserve harmony and pleasure between the sexes. However, in more recent, complex societies, encompassed by "civilized" demands on the individual, certain antisexual taboos and conventions have been made to proliferate in our lives and obstruct our sensitivity to natural bodily processes. At the present time, particularly in industrial Western societies, the prohibition against social and sexual contact between the sexes during the woman's flow is barely perceived. But the general antisexual taboo is pervasive in its force.

In the progress of Western societies that led to the present state of affairs, men and women have moved from sexual sensitivity, and a valuation of both the relations and the relative independence of the sexes, to sexual insensitivity, or the general inability to inspect and be responsible for and engage the sexual process with free delight. This loss or suppression of sexual sensitivity has also been accompanied by a general devaluation of sexual relations (which came to be regarded more or less as "sin," or at best as a vulgar personal indulgence) as well as a devaluation of the relatively independent character and way of life that pertains to each sex. As a result, we have produced a society where the norm is casual relations (both social and sexual) between the sexes, an almost total absence of understanding of the higher or uniquely human function of sex, a persistent sense of the wrongness or vulgarity of sex in principle, an equally persistent obsession with personal or self-oriented sexual exploitation ("unseen" by the parentlike enforcers of sexual taboos), and a general tendency toward reversal of sexual roles (in either heterosexual or homosexual relations) as well as an androgynous equalization of the sexes in general (without the realization of higher and bodily evolution and Enlightenment, which is the necessary pre-Condition for the transcendence of sexual polarization and playful differentiation in the human world).

Clearly, we must realize a responsible level of awareness of human sexuality, free of the antisexual bias. However, we must likewise awaken to an understanding of the higher and often esoteric functions of the sexual mechanism (or the generalized bodily mechanism touched upon by our sexual practice). Such responsibilities do not characterize childish people or subhuman societies, but practical wisdom of this kind has been exhibited by superior men and women and by higher human cultures since ancient times.

The present book is an effort to help this full transition in our personal understanding of human sexuality. In the process, we must awaken from our gothic fears of sexuality, and our religious disinclination toward bodily existence.

III

The "Devil" is nothing more than the Divine Reality in its Function as the Destroyer and ultimate Destiny of the sacrifice of all beings and worlds. He is "Siva," the image of the Divine Person carrying a trident.[3] The free religious or spiritually awakened individual is not only himself restored to God, but his higher understanding restores aspects of God or the Godhead to Itself. When "sin" is forgiven, or when self is purified of its separative motivations, what was previously the "Devil's work" (by virtue of egoic, fearful, and self-possessed fascination) becomes a matter of ordinary responsibility and sacrifice.

In modern literature, one of the most potent Satanic images is that of Count Dracula, in the novel by Bram Stoker. But the pervasive evil of this character and his deeds is itself only an expression of an inverted sense of the sexual function in Man. And, curiously, the story itself represents a cultural memory of the whole taboo against the association between the sexes during the menstrual flow of the female.

In earlier times and places, men generally avoided social and sexual contact with women during the days of the menses. However, those who were mature and representative of the higher human type were often initiated by the elders into methods for transforming various "negative" sexual indications into positive and regenerative means. Such methods are reflected in the descriptions of sexual communion in this book. Among such methods or approaches was one regarding contact with a woman during her monthly flow. The man who was truly prepared could embrace a woman during the time of menses and not only avoid enervating imbalance but actually benefit from the increased available force of the female (or the

---

3. In the Hindu Trinity, Siva is the Destroyer aspect of the One Divine Person. (Brahma is the Creator aspect and Vishnu, the Sustainer.) The trident is associated with Siva, as it is also with Satan. (There is also a higher or perfect interpretation of Siva, as the Radiant Existing One, the Absolute Divine, Who Includes and yet Transcends the Trinity of Divine Functions.)

feminine, relatively passive, or "negative" and "left-sided"[4] pole in the polarized play of sex).

Male individuals trained in the greater arts and sacrificial responsibilities of sex knew not only how to compensate for and benefit by social and sexual relations during the menses of women and wife, but also how to use the force of the female in general, for regenerative purposes in the male body. And initiated females likewise knew how to use the force of the male for regenerative purposes in the female body. This yoga was common to certain classes in China, India, and elsewhere in more ancient times. In general, it was most often men who were trained in these methods, but there were frequent cases of women who were also trained in the positive regenerative sexual association with men. Whether ideal sex relations were considered to be polygamous or monogamous, the regenerative or Life-conservative practices related to sexuality were common throughout the ancient world.

In modern times, the positive, regenerative, higher, and esoteric approach to sexual relations and the sexual mechanism has become obstructed by dualistic and childishly inverted views of human life. The war of "flesh" and "spirit" has brought the world of mankind close to oblivion, and the last quarter of the twentieth century is perhaps going to be the ultimate test of our capacity to liberate ourselves from this profound lie and disturbance. The self-divided man is one in whom the psycho-physiological mechanisms of the left and right sides of brain and body are opposed to one another rather than polarized toward one another. Such a one originates Gods and Devils, Worlds and Heavens and Hells from his

---

4. The "left side" of the bodily being expresses and corresponds to the inward-turning, upward-moving, passive, receptive, emotional-psychic quality or force of bodily life. It is in opposition or play with the "right side," which expresses and corresponds to the verbally or analytically motivated, outward-turning, downward-moving or life-oriented, active, penetrative, vital-physical, expansive quality or force.

The left side is controlled by the right hemisphere of the brain, the locus of the psychic, spatial, nonverbal, holistic-intuitive mental functions (whereas the left hemisphere, which controls the right side of the body, is the locus of the intellectual, linear, verbal, analytical-deductive mental functions).

Bubba Free John criticizes both the objectively oriented ways of Western religion, philosophy, and culture and the subjectively oriented ways of Eastern religion, philosophy, and culture as imbalanced expressions of the whole body of Man.

own body-mind, and he lives his sexual character, male or female, as a principle of conflict with others and of independent satisfaction of self.

Thus, Count Dracula, the "Devil," is the product of our antisexual, inverted, self-divided psychology. In him, the ancient superior man is made to wear the guise of Evil, and our conventional psyche rejects him and all that he represents to us, both consciously and unconsciously. But if we understand ourselves and cease to be self-divided, antisexual, alternately at war with the body and with "Heaven," then we may also see the superior and even Divine qualities of Man underneath the superimposed vulgarities of Dracula.

Dracula—apart from the disgusting and negative disguise given him by the modern mind—is simply an ancient type of the superior man. He is a man who is free to embrace a woman during her time of menstrual imbalance, or greater force. He appears in the form of a bat—a blackened or evil inversion of a bird, a dove, the mind or "soul" of Man. He embraces his lover with passionate intent, as a life and death matter—and mysteriously, suddenly, like the Holy Spirit descending on the future mother of an Incarnation of Truth. But he is made to kill, rather than to give and to receive Life in the positive sense. He seeks the vulnerable place of life and blood, at the throat, in the manner of an animal. But, truly, this is only an inverted acknowledgment of the yogic passageway between the trunk and the brain, and the necessity for the sexual force and the higher blood chemistry to rise to the brain and to the entire body of the regenerated individual. The white canine teeth, the eye teeth of Dracula, penetrate the vulnerable throat of his lover, again in animal fashion, but symbolizing in an inverted way the act of sexual intercourse. The pervasive presence of blood, the association of penetration or sexual intercourse with blood, is a sign of the ancient yogic practice of coupling during the menses. Dracula's own bloody mouth, with white phallic teeth exposed, duplicates the image of the sexual scene, while also symbolizing his own harmonization of opposites within himself, thus giving him the power of regenera-

33

tion or relative immortality. And Dracula is given life every time he enters into embrace—so that he even becomes perfectly regenerated, or immortal, as long as he continues his habit of sexual love. All the rest of the story is a pseudo-Christian accretion that mainly serves the whole notion of anti-sex and anti-Life.

Modern man, in the conventional guise of "Everyman," fears the idea of taking responsibility for his own life, and the Process of Life itself, as it is altogether and everywhere displayed. Thus, another Gothic tale, by Mary Shelley, about the Frankenstein monster, manages to express the same psychology that inverts the ancient superior man into the "Monster," Dracula. Doctor Frankenstein, in the ancient manner, takes bold responsibility for life, and, by acquiring the lightning power, or Life-Force, of a storm, enlivens a corpse. But Doctor Frankenstein is made monstrous, along with his "Monster," by the inverted, antisexual and childish, subhuman mind of modern Man.

Truly, we must awaken to the ancient responsibility for sex and all the ordinary powers of Life in our own bodies. We must do this fearlessly, and return to the culture of a superior humanity, organized via a moral and esoteric order of physical and superphysical sacrifices of the individual. We must again accept our responsibility for life and death, and fearlessly embrace the bodily process of our existence, so that we may live humanly, and so that we may Realize the true Destiny of Man, which only comes through literal sacrifice and Translation of the whole and entire and individual body-mind into the All-Pervading and Transcendental Divine Radiance wherein we all appear.

I n the *Old Testament* it is suggested that Man exercise dominion over beasts and growing things. This is an acknowledgment that Man, in the form of every human individual, is not only functionally or structurally more and greater than anything else in the natural or elemental world, but that his happiness and even his survival depend on his acceptance of responsibility for everything in himself that is common to the rest of the natural world.

Thus, it is not merely that he is naturally superior to cattle, snakes, vegetables, and the elements, and, therefore, should force all such things into degraded submission to his own aggressive and stupid will to eat and use and do everything, and wait for understanding to come in the future, while the Cosmic Parent meanwhile keeps everything in order. Rather, the superiority of Man is in his responsibility to acknowledge that he is not merely a natural or vital creature, like the rest of the natural world. Man is structurally more and greater than the vital processes, and, therefore, he must understand, and accept responsibility for a right and Lawful relationship to what is merely vital, in himself as well as in the world.

If the individual does not accept active responsibility for his vital-physical and emotional-sexual functions, then he is reduced to these. And if he is not responsible for these functions in his own case, he will inevitably deal irresponsibly and destructively with all vital creatures and the natural domain itself.

Our science, technology, politics, and social experience bear this out. Mankind is, at this stage, generally still in the subhuman levels of adaptation, wherein responsibility for the vital functions and the vital domain is largely absent, because men and women have not sufficiently differentiated themselves from a sense of exclusive identity with the vital and elemental dimensions of themselves and the world. It is not that we must, as religious and spiritual cultists generally suggest, identify exclusively with what is not at all vital and elemental. Such would lead us into subjectivist illusions. However, we must realize that we are structurally more and greater than what is merely vital and elemental, even while we also realize that what is vital and elemental is a part of us, and the very part for which we must assume immediate and intelligent responsibility.

In our subhuman and childish condition, more or less exclusively identified with vital and physical experience, we tend to fear and avoid responsibility for the lower aspects of experience and of the world itself. Hence, we "play" with everything, but we cannot fully control our effects. We slaughter, exploit, poison, and spoil. We achieve power over great natural forces in the environment, but we cannot be the loving master of sex, or population, or industrial wastes, or international politics. Therefore, we are a destructive influence in the natural world, where beasts and elements consistently demonstrate an instinctual economy and harmony that puts our human vulgarities to shame.

The old orders of religion are the cults of this same childish irresponsibility. They support fear, dependence, and subhuman levels of adaptation and awareness. They do not do this altogether intentionally, but they do so effectively, by making consolation, mythical belief, child-parent imagery, and personal survival the core of the religious way, rather than self-sacrifice, radical spiritual intelligence, and higher adaptation.

Thus, higher or superior Man is present in this world only in the case of the rare individual, rather than in the form of the human world as a whole. And such an uncommon individual is regarded suspiciously by all. The responsibilities and the Vision he presumes make him appear like a "mad scientist" or an "evil" man of mysterious powers, in league with the "Devil." All of this because the usual man refuses to be responsible for all that he must master if he is to be truly human and pass on to his Divine Destiny.

Sexual taboos and the generalized sense that antisexual views and habits are humanly and even cosmically obligatory and correct are passed on from generation to generation by many means. The most influential means are those of the withholding of bodily and sexual communications. We only show and tell our children what we ourselves are not afraid to be and know. The rest is hidden behind the withholding of bodily and emotional intimacy as well as the absence of positive verbal communication about the whole affair of incarnate human experience, including sexuality.

The entire social and cultural game of antisexual, "spirit against flesh" education is so monstrous, so opposed to incarnate happiness and human responsibility, as well as the ultimate transcendental sacrifice of the individual body-mind through moral and spiritual processes, that it must be considered the primary social and even philosophical issue of our time.

We must all awaken from our loveless one-sidedness. The deluded religious and spiritual cultists are perpetually at war with the bodily life, choosing the brain-mind as if it were the Infinite. And the equally deluded anti-religionists, salt-of-the-earth political fanatics, and worldly humanistic social mechanics or scientific technocrats are perpetually at war with the higher, psychic, and spiritual dimensions of human experience.

Children of parents of the "spirit" are deprived of the energy of their incarnation, fastened to inward nonsense and the vision of a self-divided mortality that has no pleasure except away from here. And children of parents of the "flesh" are deprived of the powers of higher adaptation, fastened to cycles of endless work and reproduction, and the vision of utopian solutions that only serve those who happen to be alive when the great Future State comes.

We must awaken and adapt to the conditions of the whole and entire body-mind, and to the Way of truly human existence, which is made through personal, moral, and higher mental or spiritual sacrifice, or love. Then we will not only live in Truth, but we will withhold nothing from our children, who must always be permitted a complete bodily understanding that corresponds to their level of functional awareness, and who must be included in a culture of truly human adaptation, in which not exploitation but gradual responsibility is the key to human growth.

Chapter 3

We Have Not Sinned in Eden, but We Have Been Born

The play of sex is simply a special version of the play of whole body feeling-attention that should characterize all human activity. There is no justification for assigning any unique negative evaluation to the sexual potential of the bodily being any more than to breathing, digestion, or any other potential. Indeed, if we do conceive of sexuality in problematic terms, via attitudes of guilt, self-consciousness, and the like, a suppressive contraction appears in that function and affects not only our sexuality but the whole form and state of the body, emotion, and mind. There must be a characteristically positive and pleasurable attitude relative to all the functional possibilities of the whole body. And we must be naturally and stably capable of <u>unobstructed</u> whole body feeling-attention via the rhythmic relational play of all our functions.

Therefore, the sexual function is right, pleasurable, and free in principle—and it must, on that account, have a right or appropriate and Lawful use. That is the use described in this book. It is sexual communion, founded in a full, present, and ongoing relational response rather than any subjective, self-possessed, reactive mental or emotional obsessiveness. It is sexual relationship, founded in the sacrifice of subjectivity.

The Right Religious, Spiritual, and Human Discipline of the Sexual Function

T he advocates of the various spiritual traditions commonly recommend that the sex impulse be controlled. Indeed, they most often warn that if the sex impulse is not controlled, there is no way to progress by any or all of one's other spiritual or life practices. But what is "control" of the sex impulse? Is it merely to do without sexual intercourse? If it is, then the dead, the impotent, and the naturally uninterested would be the first if not the only ones to realize the Truth and the One Life.

The strategy of celibacy is only factual nonperformance of genital sexual acts. Even if there is also restraint of hidden thoughts and feelings of sexual desire as well as casual speech about sexual matters, the "control" of the sex impulse thus established is merely nonperformance. Nonperformance of the sexual act is not in itself control of the sex impulse in the sense that makes the difference in a life of religious and spiritual discipline. Rather, true control means nothing more nor less than responsibility for the sexual function, and, therefore, right, regenerative, and self-transcending participation in sexual activity rather than self-possessed and degenerative exploitation of the urge of the genitals.

The call to "control," or responsibility for the sexual function, is a call to Man—so that he may turn from "sin" (or missing the mark through misdirected intention of motion) to "righteousness" (or right intention of the functional motion of living existence). Therefore, we must learn and practice right or Lawful (sacrificial) application of the whole body to all its functional obligations and possibilities. The Law of human life is conscious sacrifice, or love, as a discipline of the whole bodily being or the totality of our functions, in all relations, under all conditions. We are not obliged to sacrifice what is not one with us. We are obliged to be sacrifice. And the sacrifice of the whole body (elemental physical, etheric or living emotional, mental, supermental, and egoic) is not realized by killing any or all of its parts, but by coordination of all the parts and functions into the single radiance and release that is love—in all relations, under all conditions. And love is unobstructed feeling-attention. It is human relational intensity—free of the recoil of self-possession or self-meditation, reactive or negative emotions, and absorption in the subjective stream of thoughts and images.

Our Lawful obligation in Truth is to be love as the whole body—to be unobstructed feeling-attention, or radiant happiness, in all our relations, via all our functions, under all conditions, from birth to death and beyond.

The Way whereby this Lawful obligation becomes realizable by ordinarily adapted human beings has been described as the Way of Divine Ignorance in *The Enlightenment of the Whole Body, The Paradox of Instruction,* and other books. The present book is intended to describe the manner of right use or participation in the play of sexuality.

Many advocates speak of this matter in prudish and problematic terms. They see all sin and violence inside their underwear. Such people are in a dilemma relative to this bodily appearance whereby we are communicated to one another. They are striving to go elsewhere by identifying with the subjective part and denying or separating from the living and elemental aspect of the whole body. Such an inclination is a form of conflict, in which the natural polar opposites at play in all worlds and bodies are felt to be antagonists—light versus darkness, "God" versus "Devil," male versus female.

In Truth, we are not the mind to a greater degree than we are the flesh. "I" is the whole body, high and low, within and without. There is no separable inwardness. The whole body is obliged to be a sacrifice to Infinity—to be Radiance without a center.

Therefore, the true Way is not founded on the conflicts created by the inwardness of experience or knowledge. Rather, it is founded on the freedom of absolute, unqualified, prior, and present Ignorance. No matter what arises as experience and presumption founded on experience, "I" do not know what even a single thing is. Existence is not inspected, nor is it ultimately defined. We have no option within. We are obliged to exist as Mystery and to be and act free of all inwardness, all subjectivity, the whole egoic illusion or recoil into meditation on the notion of independent, defined existence or consciousness, its finite destiny, and its numberless desires or hopes. The argument of the Teaching of Truth is communicated to us in our problematic self-possession. And that Teaching obliges us to fulfill the Law—to be free of self and subjectivity, and to be love, free of qualification by any reaction, and expressed through all functions. The whole body must be a perfect sacrifice to Infinity, or else we only forever create an illusory destiny, in mental and physical realms, until Awakening comes.

The advocates of the avoidance of sexuality imagine the sexual function to be unique relative to the rest of the body. They think it especially "evil" in comparison to other functions. But it is only a particular functional version of the same life process that is elsewhere particularized as breathing, walking, eating, sleeping, feeling, and so forth. If there is a necessity to avoid the sex function, then all the other functions, including the inwardness of higher mind and psyche, must likewise be abandoned. All functions are expressions of the same life. Therefore, if this logic holds, all functions must be abandoned as the same evil. And such, indeed, is the extreme ascetic view at the root of conventional spiritual advocacy.

But this view is obviously false. When its logic is followed to the end, it demands an absurd profession. In Truth, the whole body stands in Light. It is not in any part condemned or evil. It is simply that it is obliged by a single Law, which is love, or self-transcendence, in presumption and in practice.

Under the Law, no functional dimension of the whole body is false or evil in principle. Therefore, guilt is only a superficial and childish reaction, founded in the primal fear at the root of our birth. We have not sinned in Eden, but we have been born. Our ultimate fault is not any act within the world, but the primal act or presumption of independent, separate, and separative consciousness—the attitude and strategy of Narcissus. Our ultimate healing and happiness is not in outward or cosmic forgiveness for outward or cosmic actions. No amount of granted forgiveness or personal effort can work perfect purification or release from the effects of our actions and presumptions. We must be perfectly released, and thus priorly and radically free of the principle that underlies our actions, which is the egoic presumption, the independent "I," and the fear of vulnerability and death. If we are not free of the illusion of confinement to a separate and mutable existence, then we will miss the mark and be obsessed in our dilemmas forever.

The Wisdom of the Way of Divine Ignorance is the Awakening from separation, metaphysical independence, dilemma, doubt, guilt, anger, sorrow, fear, and the strategies of fear. It is the Awakening from the illusions of subjectivity, of knowledge, of separate experience, unique consciousness, and the powers of the independent self. It is not annihilation or persuasion toward the sleep of salt-of-the-earth collectivism. It is Bliss. It is love and transcendental Awareness. It is an entire life of whole body sacrifice, radiant as love to Infinity, wherein the born being is translated from this dream of parts and persons into the Divine Domain beyond all knowing.

What then is "control of the sex impulse"? It is whole body responsibility, as love, in relationship to a true lover (one to whom one is intimately committed in time and space) and in Communion with the Radiant Life of God. It is the same as love under any functional conditions. Love is "conscious exercise"[1] of the body-mind, in all relations and under all conditions. And such love is the Lawful establishment of the whole body in a right, living, regenerative, or radiant functional order.

The right play of genital sexuality is occasional—however frequent. That is, it is not continuous, as is the breath or heartbeat. Nor is it casual, as is the stream of thoughts. But the occasional incident of genital sexual play is an incident within what is otherwise a continuous rhythmic cycle or display of experience. Such is the relationship or polarized play of feeling-attention between lovers. The relationship is continuous. But the incident of genital play is an occasion, appearing at random, founded in the rhythms of the vital evidence of love-desire.

43

1. Conscious exercise is the natural coordination of body (form) and feeling-breath (energy) through free and steady attention (mind). Thus, it is the science of the responsibility to be love, or unobstructed feeling-attention as the whole body. The principles and practices of conscious exercise are given in *Conscious Exercise and the Transcendental Sun*, by Bubba Free John.

Thus, lovers occasionally move to genital embraces. And this is an unexplainable pleasure or ecstasy. It is not an end in itself, nor does it ever have an end. It is merely evidence—the shown Life—of their continuous polarization or pleasurable and playful opposition to one another. Love is expressed via functional incidents of all kinds. Sex is no more evil than the polarizations or rhythms of Life itself. Sexual play is right, good, human, and a Divine inspiration.

Then why is there so much controversy relative to the genital theatre of man? Above all, it is because of fear and the presumed knowledge that each of us is an irreducibly separate, finite, or vulnerable consciousness, self, person, or soul. But, in Truth, such separation is only a conventional appearance in this dream of Life. It is neither a true nor a necessary point of view, as devotees in the Way of Divine Ignorance realize through hearing, initiation, and Direct Revelation. But when men in general suppose independence, vulnerability, and fear, they recoil upon themselves. They suppress and mutilate the flow of feeling-attention, or love. They accumulate habits of self-indulgence and consolation based on separation, vulnerability, and suppressed love. And they organize their collective existence in ways that seek to control, manipulate, suppress, and otherwise make our separate and individual actions predictable within a formal scheme that permits very little variation, ecstasy, or original insight.

Therefore, religious ecstatics and innocent lovers are a threat to the political order of our fears. We are usually busy protecting ourselves from one another, whereas ecstatics cross the barriers of all worldly knowledge. They commune with unity where the worldly-wise find parts and sequences and endings in a humorless void of fleshes and atomic slime.

When men renounce fear and childishness and accept the Law of love and egoless Communion with the Real, then they begin to make truly human lives and human culture for their generations. It is for the sake of such humanity that this book is written. It is about the human realization or right use of the process of love in the play of sexual polarization.

Not all madmen are enjoying the Divine Intuition. Nor are all who lie down together enjoying the ecstasy of selfless Communion with the Real Condition of all conditions via intimacy with their lovers. The difference is in the foundation: Is it fear and self-consciousness, or is it intuition of the Real Condition of self, subjectivity, body, world, and others? Where there is the foundation, through "hearing" the argument of Truth, then all our functions come under the obligation of the Law, and our span of manifest existence becomes a discipline of functional sacrifice. Thus, lovers become the servants and advocates of one another. And they cease to embrace one another in the conventional manner. Rather, they become a "yoga" of one another, a mutual sacrifice, wherein all subjectivity is yielded as free feeling-attention to one another, and the whole body of each and both is yielded as a sacrifice or Radiation of feeling to Infinity.

Thus, control, responsibility, or right use relative to the sexual function is a conservative process of Life-Energy, in which the bodily (or more solid part) and the mental (or more subtle part) are both yielded via unobstructed feeling into the Infinite plane of Life, Light, Bliss, or Consciousness. This means that conventional obsessions, loveless meetings, private indulgences, and even the orgasm itself, must be naturally disciplined, replaced, transformed, and transcended, through feeling, via a regenerative or Life-conserving and Life-conducting process, rather than a degenerative or Life-discharging process.

The purpose of this book is to describe the spiritual import and technical details of the Life-conserving, regenerative, even rejuvenating process of sexual communion. It is intended primarily for married or intimate devotees (heterosexual or homosexual) in the Way of Divine Ignorance, who enjoy mature responsibility for the life of whole body service, and who stably maintain right practices of work, daily association, diet, and so forth. However, the book may be studied with profit by anyone. It should nevertheless be mentioned that, apart from a whole life of practical devotional discipline and primary insight, the technical process of sexual conservation described in this book is only a limited or conventional functional observance. Anyone may apply this discipline with some benefit to their human maturity, but only true devotees may fulfill it in Truth and as a spiritual discipline.

46 Marriage and the Positive Sexual Destiny of Man

There is a presumption in the usual mind that bodily pleasure is, in some deep and fundamental sense, wrong. And, for this reason, sexuality is problematic. The reasons for the anti-pleasure presumption and the problematic attitude toward sexuality are cultural, philosophical, and broadly social. They all belong to the subhuman, even anti-human, levels of persuasion, and they are largely due to popular misinterpretations of the ancient Holy Wisdom.

The ancient and most Holy Wisdom is neither subhuman nor anti-human. The subhuman persuasions of Man are all his motives toward self-indulgent physical excesses, including all forms of libertinism and casual or worldly indulgence of the gross bodily aspect of the individual. The anti-human persuasions of Man are all his motives toward inversion, subjectivism, asceticism, and other-worldliness. These two kinds of persuasion combine in the popular mind and culture to produce emotional self-division, physical self-doubt, chronic but disturbed self-indulgence, and addiction to romantic illusions, bizarre entertainments, fanciful or "popular" religions, and all the absurdities of conventional politics, crime, and anarchy.

But the truly human persuasions of Man constitute a whole bodily disposition, a total and single psycho-physical disposition, in which Man is naturally and positively aligned to the Divine Person, the Radiant Transcendental Consciousness that is the Real Condition of all experience.

Therefore, from the whole bodily point of view, the right orientation of Man is not self-indulgent and self-possessed, but self-
transcending and ecstatic. However, that orientation, or Way of
Life, is neither anti-human and ascetic (or body-renouncing) nor
subhuman and bodily self-indulgent (or psychically and psychologically destructive and irresponsible). Rather, the Way of Life for
Man involves physical, emotional, mental, psychic, higher mental,
and spiritual responsibility, freedom, and ecstasy.

47

Man is not to be negated, but he is to be transcended—not only
ultimately but in every moment. But if the individual lives in a
responsible and self-transcending manner, he is also made whole
and free, and his psycho-physical existence is Transformed and
Translated in the Radiant Energy of Divine Ecstasy.

Thus, a right understanding of our conditions of existence and
experience draws us into a truly human and spiritual orientation to
the Transcendental Divine. And, in turn, the Living Divine Reality
releases us from self-doubt, self-division, self-indulgence, self-
glorification, and self-negation.

From that Liberated and truly human point of view, bodily
pleasure, or any other natural form of human psycho-physical enjoyment, is not wrong in principle. Nor, as an extension of such
self-doubt, is sexuality inherently problematic. But sexuality can be
problematic in fact—if irresponsible, self-possessed, or self-negating
tendencies are allowed to interfere with the right emotional-sexual
process of Divine Communion.

The clearest sign that sexuality has become a problem for human
individuals is the evidence that sexual pleasure has been divorced
from the generalized, relational, and inherent pleasure of the body-
mind in God-Communion and has become an obsessive, temporary,
and localized pleasure, associated with the genital region of the
individual. And this evidence is, indeed, commonly displayed in
the sexual experience of most people today.

Truly human sexual activity is not self-divided, or in doubt of
bodily pleasure, nor is it self-indulgent and obsessive. Rather, it is
positively self-transcending, or ecstatic. It is a form of direct
psycho-physical participation in the relational condition of human

existence and in the Transcendental Life or Bliss, which is Itself the only inherent pleasure of the body-mind.

Therefore, right human sexual activity is a process of full emotional and bodily sexual surrender, feeling, and pleasure. It is personal submission to Life via the bodily love-relationship to one's lover.

So much of conventional sexual energy is wasted in anxiety, guilt, loveless self-indulgence, and the avoidance of the truly emotional and whole bodily profundity of pleasure. We must understand all of this and transcend our self-limitations and our cultural limitations. We must Realize the Truth and the Real Character of God.

The conventional, self-indulgent, and self-doubting rituals of sex are implemented by many kinds of mental, emotional, gross physical, and mechanical devices that reinforce the genitally localized and superficial nature of sexual experience. We tend to busy ourselves defending the superficial sexual experience of genital stimulation and discharge. And we tend to be childishly disposed toward sexual experience that is self-indulgent, erotic, promiscuous or casual, and without consequences or effects beyond the moment of genital pleasure. To be sexually "mature" tends simply to mean that one has become "cool" relative to erotic stimulations, but true sexual maturity is a matter of awakening to the true profundity of sexual experience, so that what is superficial is transcended in the Divine commitment of the whole body-mind.

The casual commitment to self, superficial or genitally localized pleasure, and freedom from profundity and consequence in sexual activity is reinforced by the improper use or subhuman exploitation of birth control devices, erotic entertainments, abortion, divorce, casual relations between the sexes, and so forth. We may put birth control devices and methods to right and responsible use within marriage. Erotica may occasionally have some instructive right use. Abortion may have its occasional right medical application. Divorce may, in cases where one or both partners are committed to worldly rather than spiritual demands, be occasionally appropriate. And, apart from the right formalities of the general relations between the

48

sexes, there is an appropriate and passionate playfulness between married individuals, and there should also be a right, feeling, and often humorous quality in the relations between friends and intimates of both sexes.

However, the conventional disposition toward sexuality is self-divided and uses all mechanical and social devices, as well as all aspects of the psycho-physical being, to reinforce a superficial indulgence of genital pleasure, rather than a profound participation in relational, whole bodily, emotional-sexual communion with the Living Reality. Thus, birth control devices, erotic entertainments, casual relations between the sexes, abortion, divorce, promiscuity, fetishism, masturbation, emotional defensiveness (or absence of feeling-surrender), orgasm, and so forth are all commonly used as strategies of self-defense against the true and ecstatic profundity of human sexuality.

The process of sexual communion is the truly human emotional-sexual process. It is a matter of the transcendence of sexual superficiality and self-possession. It is a matter of profound emotional and bodily Communion with the Living Reality. The localized genital orgasm cycle of stimulation-release is transformed (not suppressed) through prior release of mental, emotional, and physical tensions, so that the orgasm becomes a whole bodily thrill, more or less continuous throughout the period of sexual play, and occasionally heightened within the period of sexual play.

The process of sexual communion is profound emotional-sexual, whole bodily, or total psycho-physical and relational submission, in the human sexual relationship, and to the Living and Radiant Transcendental Reality. It is a process that is the privileged enjoyment of committed or married lovers, who are mature in their understanding of the Condition and Process of Man.

And marriage is the seal of that profundity, for it is a positive social act, rather than a merely private act. Marriage is the outward or social confession of responsibility and intimacy. It is the proper forum for sexual communion, because sexual activity has not only a personal but also a social role. The prior act of marriage transforms every subsequent act of sexual intercourse. The truly married couple,

49

as exemplified by devotees in The Free Communion Church, not only choose sexual intimacy (which can be a superficial indulgence of personal bodily pleasures), but (1) they choose to confine their sexual intimacy within marriage, (2) they choose sexual intimacy in the form of sexual communion, (3) they choose the responsibilities of householders, or socially adapted human beings (rather than self-possessed sociopaths or secluded ascetics), (4) they acknowledge the higher or regenerative emotional-sexual and spiritual purpose of their relationship, and (5) they acknowledge the reproductive or generative function and responsibility of heterosexual marriage.

Heterosexual marriage is the generally or commonly appropriate form of human sexual commitment. (Homosexual marriage is also a true possibility, but only in cases where heterosexual marriage is naturally or biologically and emotionally inauspicious. Homosexual marriage is not appropriate when determined merely by negative emotional or neurotic and psychologically sociopathic tendencies.)

Unmarried young people may, for the time being, be somewhat frivolous and variable in their emotional-sexual commitments, if they do not indulge in sexual intercourse. If they do begin to engage in sexual intercourse outside the marriage commitment, then they begin to become vulgar. But once true marriage is presumed, then neither husband nor wife should any longer be frivolous or vulgar. Marriage is the condition wherein right sexual intimacy can appear. And right sexual intimacy is profound. The right role of true lovers is not frivolous, or self-defensive. It is self-surrendering, bodily and emotionally. And it is even bodily profound. The pleasure of sexual play is raised up from its problematic and vulgar localization or isolation in the genitals, and it is radiated to the entire body-mind and all of its relations. Just so, that bodily profundity or profound sexual role of married lovers is also founded in the acknowledged obligation of timely reproduction, or the birth and upbringing of human individuals of the highest human type.

Moving beyond Subhuman Sexuality
*A talk given by Bubba Free John
to his devotees*

BUBBA: Be aware that without having become truly responsible for the conventional reactive disposition of the body-mind you should not entertain the consideration of the esoteric matters of human sexuality. You may like the idea of applying esoteric principles to your sexuality, but it is complete nonsense. You are not responsible, not truly human. You will simply be using these techniques as a way of reinforcing the self-possessed motives of your ordinary and unillumined life. The esoteric sexual practices respected since ancient times are given to introduce the body-mind into the process wherein it is transformed through Communion with the Absolute.

All true religion and spirituality are about this Communion. They are not about ideas and subjectivism, but about adapting the body-mind literally to the All-Pervading Current and Consciousness that is the Divine. And religious and spiritual life is about practice. It is about what you <u>do</u>. It is about changing your action and adapting in a new way. These ecstatic and evolutionary adaptations do not involve the brain centers only. They involve bringing one's bodily life, one's vital life, one's sexuality into confrontation with the Absolute. Standing off at the level of the brain and watching one's genitals rise and fall is subhuman. Animals and other lower beings rise and fall with the genitals. We must realize truly human existence by bringing the whole and entire body-mind into Communion with the All-Pervading Life.

The Spiritual Master is not only an instrument for the Teaching about this Process, but he is also an Instrument of the Life Itself. His Function is to communicate the absolute Force, the consummate Radiance, of the Real to those who are prepared. Thus, he is an Instrument of the Divine physics of evolution and ultimate Transcendence. He communicates the Force of Life in order to quicken the process of transformation in those who are prepared and who approach him properly, so that ultimately they may realize their lawful Destiny, which is sacrifice or ecstasy in God rather than any self-preserving, self-possessed destiny that they might manufacture in their fear.

A person is not considered fit to enter into spiritual relations with the Spiritual Master for the sake of regeneration in God until he or she has become responsible, through insight, for the reactive, self-possessed, self-divided patterns of ordinary living. To the conventional mind, you see, it seems an immense transition, tantamount to Enlightenment, to have realized such responsibility. But it is not. It is only the ordinary obligation to become human. The propagandizing that appears in our common society seeks the continuation of subhuman ways. Thus, anything that is more than subhuman is considered extraordinary, and only a few great men, who are considered accidents of Nature, are permitted the Realization of Absolute Life.

Only a few can become stars in our society. But the purpose of the Spiritual Master and all truly spiritual communications throughout human history has not been to glamorize the unique state of a few individuals, but to communicate the truly human process that anyone may enjoy. The Spiritual Master is also the Agent of the Divine Power, and he Communicates that Power in his sacrificial relationship with those who will also sacrifice themselves, so that other individuals than the Spiritual Master himself may enjoy the Process and Illumination of Divine Life.

All of the forms of personal and moral and religious preparation must be realized before the individual is prepared to make use of the Spiritual Master in this truly spiritual sense. Making use of the Spiritual Master is not simply to feel a little glow in the body or listen to inspiring talks in his Company. It is to become responsible for the submission of specific psycho-physical functions, specific structures of the body-mind, to the All-Pervading Life, so that the All-Pervading or Divine Life can transform the whole and entire body-mind. The Infinite degree of that Realization is the moment of Transfiguration, or Divine Translation, in which the independent body-mind is itself no longer necessary.

The body-mind is self-transcending when it enters into sacrificial Communion with the Divine. Just as sexuality is ultimately transcended within the context of the body-mind, the body-mind itself is transcended in God-Realization. It is Translated. It Dissolves. It ceases to be necessary. The body-mind is Transfigured, Awakened into the Divine Existence. One's human life may persist for a time, just as sexuality may persist for a time. Even after sexuality becomes unnecessary for the sake of higher human realization, it may continue as an ecstatic expression of Divine Communion, until there is perfect self-transcendence in God. Just so, after Transfiguration in God, the devotee may continue to exist in the manifest plane. He or she may continue the transformation of the body-mind, and then show the signs of the Divine Force in the body itself, signs of Super-Regeneration, ultimately perhaps even to dissolve in Bodily Translation, leaving no physical or mental remnants to be contacted within or without by anyone. Once the realization of Transfiguration has occurred, the body-mind is obsolete, and death will occur whenever it will.[2]

That is the Divine Realization in its highest form, and it makes the repetition of any expression of the body-mind obsolete, unnecessary. This Realization is what is meant, therefore, by bringing the cycle of birth and death to an end. The cycle of incarnation is literally brought to an end by making the body-mind obsolete through Translation into God. It is not by suppressing tendencies that you cease to be born or cease to be bound to repetitive cycles of self-possessed experience. It is by sacrifice into the Living Divine that these patterns come to an end.

The process of truly human sexuality is a form of responsibility that is part of the cycle of Divine Transformation and Translation. It is also the key to the beginning of human evolution. Now creatures of the world are essentially subhuman, and Man is new. The Force of Life is locked in his animal orientation, his horizontal orientation, his generative sexuality, and his unconsciousness. Having stood up,

2. In this paragraph, Bubba refers to the three kinds of supernormal signs or psychophysical evidence of Divine Translation, the ultimate stage of God-Realization: Transfiguration, or pervasion of the body-mind by Light; Super-Regeneration, or the appearance of prolonged longevity, psychic or healing powers, mental genius, etc.; and Bodily Translation, or literal Disappearance of the body-mind in Light.

he must now Awaken the Force of Life from its entrapment, or the reactive, vital contraction of the bodily being itself, which is preventing the whole bodily communication of Life in him.

This Awakening is what spiritual life is about. It is not the warfare of spirit against flesh conceived in the self-divided view of Man. We are evolving, and in order to evolve we must unlock the genitals. We must unlock the vital center from its unconsciousness and its devotion to merely vital experience. Until we do that, we are aberrated and half-made. We are neither Man nor animal. We are self-divided. On the one hand, we want to fly beyond the body into the realms of the mind, and on the other hand, we want to become completely immersed in continuous sexual and personal bodily stimulation. This unique conflict is the sign that we are in transition from the animal dimension to the human dimension. In order to evolve into the truly human dimension, we must unlock, or bring to consciousness, the energies in our vital centers. We must become responsible for all the forms of recoil, reactivity, self-division, and contraction upon our separated selves, to which we awaken in our infantilism, when we feel vulnerable, separate, like Narcissus, devoted to self-protection rather than ecstasy.

Thus, the evolution from animal to Man does not depend on cutting off the animal part. It depends on awakening the lower bodily functions to Life, rather than allowing them to continue as a form of reactive separation from Life. Until we awaken, sexuality is going to be obsessive and a problem. We will alternately deal with it either positively or negatively, and always in the conventional ways that characterize Man previous to his Divine Enlightenment. But when we awaken to the Truth of our sexual problem and our sub-humanity, then we can enter directly into Communion with the All-Pervading Life through the mechanisms of the body-mind. Only in that process of Life-Communion do we realize the human stage of our structural potential. Only then can we begin again to evolve, because the Life-Force has become magnified in the body-mind. Then we can go on to grow through the structural responsibilities of this Way of Divine Ignorance, until everything Dissolves in Radiant Bliss.

Chapter 4

The Transcendental Diet of Man

If our diet, or the process of taking food, is consciously lived in Divine Communion, then the functions of emotion and sexuality begin spontaneously to harmonize and stabilize; they come under natural, easeful control. But the food process only secondarily involves eating solid and liquid elements. Our principal food is Love, or the All-Pervading Bio-Energy of Life.

Therefore, before engaging the emotional and sexual disciplines presented in **Love of the Two-Armed Form,** *devotees must be firmly established in the Divinely Lawful practice of "conscious exercise" of feeling, breath, attention, and action in Communion with Life, as described in* **Conscious Exercise and the Transcendental Sun.** *Likewise, they must be proficient in the regenerative and Life-giving practice of diet and true health as presented in* **The Eating Gorilla Comes in Peace.**

The bodily being of Man is constantly sustained by the Eternal, All-Pervading Force of Life. In our infantile recoil, reaction, and psycho-physical contraction toward self, we separate from the Eternal Reality and become self-possessed. Thus, we begin to starve and suffer. The body-mind becomes a field of tensions, devoted to the search for consoling experiences that release tensions pleasurably. Such experiences include pleasures of eating and sex, willful control of life circumstances, the acquisition of mental knowledge, and the mental contemplation of abstractions. Such pleasures preoccupy and degenerate the usual man, until he is restored to Life.

The All-Pervading Divine Life Itself lives as the individual body-mind and sustains it. If only the body-mind will open into the Current of Radiant Life, with full feeling and without thought, it will be liberated from the self-possessed games of tension and release of tension. Then there is only Fullness of Life. Such psycho-physical opening into the Current of Life is "faith" in the highest sense. It is bodily confession of dependence on Life, prior both to fear and belief. It is bodily cooperation with the Real, prior to all subjectivity and problem-centered efforts.

Our Food is Life itself, which we may breathe—but only when breathing is combined with unobstructed Feeling of the All-Pervading Force of Life. We must feed on Life, through feeling breaths, relaxing the entire body, including the brain, into that Current of Force. We must receive that Life through inhalation to the vital organs of the lower body. And then we must release that Force, through exhalation, to the entire body, and via the entire body to Infinity.

This is our native "diet." We are always eating and sustained by Life, through every truly and openly feeling breath. But if we contract in our feeling, we also contract bodily and mentally. Thus, we become self-possessed, suffering reactive emotions, bodily tensions, and chronic mentalizing. Through the "conscious exercise" of the wholly feeling breath, we are fed and sustained and healed and transformed by the Radiant Divine Life. This is the secret of Life and of the transcendence of all experience. This is the true and highest "regenerative diet." And all other dietary disciplines are simply extensions of the feeling breath of Life.

The right and regenerative solid and liquid diet of Man is one that is most perfectly aligned to the reception-release[1] cycle of the feeling breath. Whatever we eat must be taken with the feeling action of receiving Life. Therefore, only that food should be chosen which is pure and vital and not toxifying. The usable or Life-granting elements of the diet must be such that they can be easily and quickly assimilated. And, the unusable or waste elements of the diet must be such that they can be easily and quickly eliminated. (The high natural carbohydrate, low animal protein, wholly regenerative vegetarian diet is the best general dietary plan for human beings.)

Only a benign, pure, vital, and complete diet can serve the body's Communion with Life. Even the solid and liquid diet must be a feeling cycle of reception-release in the All-Pervading Current of Life. But our true and right and ultimate Diet is in moment to moment, unobstructed whole bodily Feeling-Communion with the All-Pervading Force of Life—enacted via the breath cycle.

59

1. In *Conscious Exercise and the Transcendental Sun*, Bubba explains "reception-release" in terms of expansion and contraction, the two principal movements of the body and all phenomena in the cosmos. And he shows how this process operates in terms of breath and feeling:

In the simplest terms, the living body is an expression of two tendencies, uses, or currents of life. And, again in the simplest or most basic terms, these tendencies are the two motions of contraction and expansion, or reception and release. There is a negative or exclusive and unbalanced expression of each of these tendencies. When reactivity, or reaction to experience, becomes stronger than the force of Life and unobstructed or free feeling-attention that we commonly bring to experience, then reception and contraction disable us. We become self-possessed, confined to subjectivity, negatively emotional, vitally weak, and self-defeating in action. Then expansion or release is confined to patterns of mere self-indulgence, so that we are constantly emptied until death.

But there is a positive or true functional development of each of these motions, when they are in balance, and when attention and bodily form and action are controlled by full central communion or feeling into the universal environment of the Life-Force. In that case, even each breath becomes a balanced cycle of reception-release, contraction-expansion, in the constant field of fully felt intensity or Life.

It has already been considered how the inhalation of breath, or Life, is associated with reception, infilling, and natural conductivity or movement toward the whole body. Likewise, the exhalation is associated with release of the wastes, the accumulated contents or old circumstances and adaptations of life (not the release or emptying of Life itself), and natural expansion, which is conductivity or movement from the whole body outward.

Chapter 5

Organ Doubt and
Organ Ignorance

There is a form of whole bodily recognition that necessarily must precede a right approach to the play of sexuality: We enjoy playing with our genitals. We intensely and natively can and do enjoy all forms of genital activity.

This recognition is basic to a right understanding and happy realization of human sexuality. We must make our peace with our structural conditions. Recognition of the native pleasurableness of genital play—quite independent of any association with the reproductive cycle—is as necessary for human well-being as recognition of the native pleasurableness of eating, defecating, and urinating.

Bodily existence is structurally necessary to us. The body-mind, or bodily being, is the form of our existence. The inability to recognize this is a symptom of dis-ease, self-division, or a problematic and confused view of human life. The given body-mind gives structure to function, pleasure, and desire. Thus, sexuality is inherently right and good and necessary. Conflict about the rightness, goodness, and necessity of sexual play in the life of a human individual is essentially an expression of retarded adaptation. The individual must learn the doubt of sex through repressive influences. Indeed, the sense that life is fundamentally a matter of fear, doubt, and conflict is rooted in anxious feelings and negative assumptions about specific bodily organs and processes.

Modern men and women suffer from acute organ-doubt relative to the vital functions of life. And they also suffer from acute organ-ignorance relative to the higher mechanisms of the body-mind, at the heart and above. Such individuals tend to struggle with chronic self-doubt, shame relative to the organs and functions of assimilation and elimination of solid food, and guilt as well as secret and obsessive fascination with the whole possibility of sex. Likewise, their will and general responsibility in relations with others (especially in intimate friendships and sexual relationships) is chronically unstable—at times weak and at times aggressive or even righteous.

Such people tend to be sexually troubled and sexually self-possessed. They wonder curiously and even simultaneously about eroticism and asceticism. The "problem" of sex and the therapeutic liberation of sex preoccupy them. And all because of a self-divided anxiety about bodily functions and bodily existence itself.

The essence of the "problem" of sexuality and human well-being in general is in the inability to confess: "I am the body." We are self-divided, subjectively rooted, and spiritually deluded. The doubt of functions is expanded into philosophy and daily life. We imagine we _are_, exclusively and presently, something nonbodily. But in fact we are simply the body as a whole, including all of its physical and psychic or mental attributes and functions.

Until we become so confessed relative to the lower and vital functions to which we are already more or less adapted, we cannot continue to grow or stand up as the entire human structure. Thus, most men and women are totally ignorant of the functions and the potential consciousness above the verbal mind, the ordinary and reactive emotional life, and the vital physical processes. Nor are such individuals fully aware and responsible for the dimensions of the bodily psyche below the verbal mind—in the dimensions of the subconscious and unconscious mind.

But if we are bodily confessed, then we are also inherently at peace, one with the bodily organs and functions. In that case "I" has no fear of being seen, of expressing love, of accepting help, or fear of any other form of our necessary sacrifice and voluntary death.

The native pleasurableness of genital stimulation is the foundation or bodily justification for the rightness and necessity of the human sexual function. However, this pleasurableness is, in itself, simply a characteristic of the independent bodily self. If made the principle of sexual play, our sexuality remains simply a vitalistic form of self-possession and the Narcissistic solution to our fear of mortality. It is only in the awakening to our unique sexual character or role in the polarized and relational play of life that the sexual function, as well as all other functions of the bodily being or self, becomes an instrument of a truly human disposition. It is only in the polarized play of ecstatic intimacy or love that the generalized potential of genital pleasure is drawn out into the form of a specific, human, sexually polarized and relational character.

63

Therefore, the ground of sexual freedom is recognition of the inherent bodily pleasurableness, necessity, rightness, and goodness of the genital sexual function. However, the function itself is realized in human terms only in submission to the polarized play of a specific relational character—male or female—in intimate love-desire commitment with another. In that case, the generalized personal pleasurableness of genital or organ-based sexuality is replaced by the mutual ecstasy of whole bodily love.

The play of opposites is the goal of personal and positive genital pleasurableness. And only in that case is the individual relieved of the double-bind of bodily and subjective self-possession and given up to the ecstasy of love, whereby the bodily self is surrendered and yielded to the pattern and the Source in which it is included and ultimately dissolved.

The mature individual must grow and adapt beyond a childish personal or self-body sexual orientation and pass into an ecstatic, interpersonal, and transpersonal or transcendental involvement in life as a sexually characterized and free person.

The mature individual must first realize the personal pleasurableness of sex and the inherent bodily and sexual nature of his or her entire psycho-physical existence. But then there must be release of the self-body orientation into the great pattern of relations. This transition is made through the awakening of the whole body or feeling disposition and voluntary fulfillment of the inherent Law of the manifest worlds, which is sacrifice, change, and love.

B ecause of the generalized antisexual taboo to which so-called civilized societies oblige their members to adapt, people today tend not to grow and adapt to full relational sexuality. Instead, the individual tends to remain more or less bound to the primitive and infantile sexuality of his or her own bodily self.

The pleasurable and sexual nature of one's own bodily being becomes clear in the earliest years of life. But the ecstatic or self-released fulfillment of bodily life is possible only in intimate and feeling submission in relationship. However, the antisexual influences that pervade our experience even in childhood suppress our relational adaptation and leave us self-conscious in our natural relations.

True human culture is initiatory culture. That is, all influences and habits that suppress functional life should be countered by specific learning episodes that oblige the individual to be free and strong in the face of what is negative and untrue. In such a culture, individuals would be instructed about sexuality within the intimate circle of their social lives. In the culture or Church of the Way of Divine Ignorance, such instruction is indeed given, in stages, as the individual matures. *Love of the Two-Armed Form* is a general manual for such instruction and initiation.

But when such cultural influences are not present to oblige people to sane, human, and higher use of their sexuality, the body of the individual tends to remain as the field of sexual practice. Thus, even when a sexual partner is available, the uninitiated and irresponsible individual tends to remain essentially hidden and self-possessed in his or her practice. Love and desire tend to be more or less crippled in such people. Indeed, love and desire even seem to be in conflict. But love-desire, the single force of sexual ecstasy, is the necessary foundation of sexual relationships and sexual embrace.

The individual who is more or less confined to his own body, unadapted to the relational pleasures and responsibilities of his own functional existence, is incapable of ecstasy, except in facsimile. Thus, such a one tends to become dependent on internal imagery, promiscuity, and his own orgasm for a sense of relationship (which is only fascinated distraction), excitation, and release.

Couples who have been suppressed in their bodily and relational adaptation use one another more or less as tools of their own independent satisfaction—or the facsimile and illusion of ecstasy. But true ecstasy is necessarily a matter of full relational surrender—with unobstructed feeling and bodily self-giving. Thus, each individual and each couple should, ideally, enter into participation in a whole initiatory culture, wherein they may grow into the fully human and spiritual life of ecstasy. If they do not, they remain more or less in childish and adolescent levels of adaptation, self-possessed, self-oriented, subjectively oriented, in conflict with bodily existence, and incapable of the human and transcendental ecstasy whereby we are Translated into the prior Divine Radiance of the world.

Narcissism vs. Ecstasy, or the Transcendence of Masturbation, Fetishism, and Other Obsessive Desires

Obsessive sexual patterns are generally fetishistic and ritual versions of the stimulation-tension-release cycle of "normal" sexual play and orgasm. These patterns or tendencies are methods whereby the individual, beset by reactive tension and critical self-doubt, seeks a sense of inherent enjoyment, or self-pleasure. Such obsessive rituals or ritual inclinations are generally learned or created early in life, as solutions to the "sexual problem" during infantile, childish, and adolescent phases of development.

However, sexual enjoyment is not truly an inherent or self-bound enjoyment but an ecstatic or self-transcending relational enjoyment. All attempts to create sexual enjoyment as an inherent or exclusive self-pleasure tend to be ritualistic (fixed in form and obsessively repetitive) and to demonstrate a fundamental fear of the relational form of sexual activity. For this reason, the indulgence of obsessive inclinations always leads to guilt, shame, more tension,

increased self-doubt, frustration, the lust for repetition, addiction
to fantasies, the loss of the emotional capacity for intimacy, the
increase of chronic problems (such as anger, jealousy, and even
physical diseases), and so forth.

Thus, obsessive sex rituals, or the inclinations toward them, are
essentially Narcissistic. They are created at an immature phase of
life, when there is felt to be a taboo against sexual pleasure and the
relational enactment of sexual desires.

The inherent pleasurableness of existence is realized only in
ecstasy, or self-transcending feeling and intuition, in and via the
bodily relational conditions of experience. The indulgence of self is
self-possession, and it is turned away from the conditions of relationship and the ultimate or Real Condition of the Radiant Transcendental Consciousness, the Living God. Therefore, the "cure"
for all sexual obsessions is relationship, communication, and intimate commitment in love. All sexual obsessions are expressions of
emotional reactivity, or the fundamental fear of making a full,
demonstrative, and feeling communication of natural sexual desire.

Every one who is born into contemporary societies suffers from
the lingering taboos against the body, or the relational fulfillment of
Man. There is, therefore, much psychiatric or analytical talk about
the taboos against bodily pleasure. And such taboos are certainly
factual in the common experience. But the root of these taboos is
emotional. It is the emotion of Narcissism. It is the inability to be
bodily engaged in the emotional and relational conditions of human
intimacy—not only in sexual terms, but in broad social and moral
terms.

The taboo against bodily pleasure is a taboo against full commitment to Life in this world. It is the taboo against love, sacrifice,
forgiveness, compassion, and relational or demonstrative pleasure of
existence. All such taboos are the reflection of a preference for an
inward, subjective, other-worldly experience. But all such motives
are simply a recoil from death, and, therefore, from this world, from
relationships, and from the active and feeling obligations of Man.

We must awaken from the spell of these taboos and resort to the
Ecstasy of Communion with the Living God, even bodily, in all

relationships, and with profound love. It is not that we should merely violate the obstructive taboos and resort to the bodily capacity for inherent or exclusive self-pleasure. That is an equally Narcissistic solution to the dilemma in our feeling. Truth and, therefore, pleasure are only in ecstasy, or self-transcendence. Narcissism, or self-indulgence, is a disposition in which pleasure, or Life, is inherently obstructed. If we merely resort to permissive bodily pleasure as a reaction to the taboos against pleasure, we remain self-involved or, at best, mechanically sympathetic with others. We must, instead, understand and <u>actively</u> transcend the entire process of self-possession, reactivity, and self-indulgence.

Chronic masturbation, fetishism, and all other obsessive desires are ritual means of self-pleasure. That is, they achieve a sense of sexual pleasure bodily, but they are deficient in the dimension of feeling, or relational enjoyment. They are all forms of eroticism, or bodily self-pleasure with the minimum of relational and feeling involvement. Eroticism is maximum bodily or personal pleasure with minimum intimacy.

The erotic context of human sexuality is essentially a dramatization of separativeness. It produces casual society, ultimate separation or loss of sympathy between the sexes, constant disturbance by titillations of sexual desire, violent and self-possessed methods of sexual and social fulfillment, and a depression of the sympathetic, feeling, serving, moral, and intimate order of human life. Therefore, we must observe and understand and transcend our loveless ritual eroticism, or else there can be no sexual or even human freedom.

Devotees in The Free Communion Church are obliged to enter into this consideration and to become responsible for the entire pattern of emotional revulsion or recoil from the bodily-relational context of human existence. All members of the Church should freely confess to one another the tendency of Narcissus in every area of their lives. Thus, they should all deal with one another compassionately, with understanding, and also with right demands. And every one who is awakening from the bondage to self, or the emotional and bodily avoidance of relationship, must accept the discipline of relationship and feeling communication.

Every individual who is adapting to the process of sexual communion must confess his erotic tendencies, or self-possessed inclinations and rituals, to his intimates, who must likewise be confessed in the same manner to him. This is done through various forums in our Church, particularly during the period of initial study of the process of sexual communion. Then each individual must enter into the discipline of intimacy, or the relational rather than the self-possessed or self-meditative play of natural desires. Thus, the intimate sexual relationship, or marriage itself, becomes the healing place or "cure" of the conventional sexual dilemma.

Couples are instructed to engage in their intimate sexual play openly, even verbally, full of communication of desire and love-feeling. They should persist in this discipline of relational and bodily communication of mutual pleasure, and by these means, all of the self-possessed rituals will become gradually obsolete.

As such couples grow to maturity, the various kinds of evidence of their erotic inclinations will appear. Thus, inclinations toward masturbation, sexual imagination, fetishistic interests in various body parts, bodily or emotional attitudes, roles and settings, dress, and so forth will remain, to one or another degree, in evidence. Married intimates should abandon all indulgence of promiscuous and casually flirtatious association with others. And they should also relieve one another of the method of private masturbation by openly confessing their desire for one another and their passionate interest in every kind of sexual pleasure with one another, including masturbation of one another or in front of one another.

The state of mutually confessed enjoyment between married intimates should be such that they relieve one another of all taboos. Everything should be permitted in their relationship itself, and, therefore, no private, hidden, or relationless exercise should be necessary, or at least it should become infrequent and then gradually obsolete. (Thus, intimates "cure" one another of masturbatory and promiscuous eroticism. No individual can truly cure himself or herself of such motivations.)

Such ecstatic intimates may otherwise play out their erotic interests with one another. There may even be some use of erotic art and photography, erotic dress, playful role-playing, stimulating devices such as vibrators, and so forth. But the very fact that all of this play occurs in relationship to one another, as a mutual confession, and with open love-desire, undermines the very principle of eroticism, which is relationless self-absorption in bodily and secret or merely subjective pleasure. Therefore, over time the erotic play of such lovers becomes more and more the direct play of intimate love.

69

The play of erotic and sexually obsessive activities is always at the service of genital discharge, or the conventional eliminative orgasm. But lovers who play in the manner of sexual communion transcend the merely genital motive of sexual desire. The key to this transcendence is the same as the key to the transcendence of Narcissistic eroticism in general. That is, conventional orgasm is itself the primary sign of eroticism, or exclusive self-pleasure. Thus, to transcend the emotionally reactive recoil from pleasure in relationship is to transcend the bodily obsession with the genital discharge. The more the Narcissistic motive comes under natural control, through open love-desire in mutual enjoyment, the more the degenerative motive and exploitation of the genital discharge gives way to the whole bodily thrill of the regenerative orgasm, or Ecstatic Communion with Life, which is the Love-Radiance of the Transcendental Reality.

Chapter 6

Sexuality and the Ascent to Mature Human Life

In the Teaching of the Way of Divine Ignorance, Bubba Free John has accounted for every stage of human life, from birth through death. And the "seven stages of Eternal Life" that he Demonstrates and Teaches account for every stage of function and religio-spiritual adaptation, from ordinary self-possession of Man to his most perfect Enlightenment or Sacrifice in God.

These are the seven stages of Eternal Life:

1. The stage of vital-physical adaptation, corresponding to the awakening of the root of the abdominal organs at the base of the body and generally occupying the first seven years of life.

2. The stage of emotional and primitively sexual, or relationally polarized, adaptation, corresponding to the awakening of the sexual center and occupying the second seven years of life.

3. The stage of the development of the thinking mind and the will, and of the integration of the vital-physical, emotional-sexual, and mental-intentional functions. This stage corresponds to the awakening of the navel and solar plexus, and it generally occupies the third seven-year period of life.

In the first three stages, the individual is incarnating, physically, emotionally, and mentally, as a human body-mind in the world. The Bodily Current of Life is naturally polarized from crown to toe, or from the subtle range of the being downward and outward into earthly life. And attention naturally moves with the Life-Current into the experiential and relational functions of the centers below the heart.

4. The stage of psychic adaptation, corresponding to the awakening of the feeling dimension of the heart, and the subtle mechanisms in the throat and the lower rear of the brain. The centers above the heart are awakened via the spontaneous placing of attention in the internal Life-Current of the body-mind, and the repolarization of the Life-Current and attention itself toe to crown, rather than crown to toe (which is the polarization of the Life-Current previous to the fourth stage of life). This fourth stage, and all the later stages, cannot be conceived within fixed periods of time. The duration of the higher stages of life depends entirely upon the individual's qualities and his or her spiritual practice of self-transcendence.

5. The stage of higher mental (mystical and superconscious) adaptation, corresponding to the awakening of the brain core and the higher functions of the brain-mind via the fixed establishment of attention and the internal Life-Current in the brain core ("third eye" or "ajna chakra").

6. The stage of transcendental intuitive adaptation, corresponding to the Awakening of the Free soul at the root of Consciousness in the heart, and culminating in the State traditionally known as "Self-Realization." Attention, or mind, dissolves in Divine Ignorance, or unqualified Consciousness, at the heart.

7. The stage of the Translation of Man into God, corresponding to the Sacrifice of the whole and entire body-mind into Infinite Conscious Life, and culminating in Divine Translation of the Free soul into the Identity and Life of the Divine Person. In "Self-Realization," in the sixth stage, Consciousness abides as Divine Ignorance in the root of the heart, excluding awareness of body, mind, and world. The seventh stage begins with the further Awakening Bubba describes as "open eyes," in which Consciousness is released into perfect Identification-Communion with the Divine Person, or Inherence in the Current of Radiance that Pervades all bodies, minds, and worlds. The bodily Life-Current, liberated from bondage to the mind's tendencies to experience and knowledge in the body-mind, is released into the All-Pervading Radiance via the upper terminal of the brain (above the brain core) and in all directions to Infinity. Thus, in this stage, Transcendental Ignorance and Infinite Radiance become the single Intensity of God-Realized Bliss, until the devotee is Translated, even bodily, beyond all the dimensions of the Realm of Nature, high and low, into the Divine Domain that is that Very Bliss.

Realization of the seven stages of Eternal Life involves two processes:

1. The "vertical" structural growth, or progressive awakening of the functions of body and mind; and

72

2. *The conscious <u>sacrifice</u> of the whole and entire body-mind, and of all the experiential evidence of growth, through heartfelt love, happiness, or unobstructed feeling and free attention under all conditions.*

The process of sacrifice, founded in Consciousness, is senior to the process of functional awakening, which is founded in the Realm of Nature, or the bodily and mental modifications of Consciousness.

This "map" of human development and self-transcendence not only expresses a new Vision of God and of the ultimate spiritual potential of Man. It also offers a new understanding of the human being. We do not truly realize our humanity until the fourth stage of life—but, as Bubba indicates in his talks and essays, very few men and women have ever entered stably into the fourth or fully human stage of life.

The passage into the fourth stage of life signifies the mastery of body, emotions, sexuality, will, and the thinking mind by the psychic, feeling heart. It does not imply the annihilation of the ego. The functional ego, or independent self-sense, is never annihilated in this Way of Life. It is a necessary function of the whole body, like a muscle or a thought. We cannot mature without having acquired the sense of autonomous functional existence, and we can never act without that function.

However, the autonomous ego-sense must be illumined and transcended through the power of love. The heart must awaken and mature in the feeling and intuition of God, until the soul Realizes its Transcendental Unity and Perfect Communion with the Divine Person. Even then the functional ego persists, since the ego is nothing more than the body-mind itself, until the entire body-mind drops away in perfect psycho-physical death, or Divine Translation, in the seventh stage of life.

The Fourth Stage of Life Is the Origin of the Truly Human Function in the World

74   Because the human being participates in the movements of the natural world via his vital mechanisms and elemental states, he is driven by the same motives as are demonstrated by all subhuman or nonhuman beings embodied in the elemental world. The basic motives of all vital (or merely living) entities are the feeding frenzy and the reproductive frenzy, whereby individual beings liberally sacrifice one another and even themselves for the ultimate survival of kind.

Human beings, to the degree they yield to their merely living motives, not only participate in the frenzy of food and generative sex, but they become degraded, enervated, and degenerated thereby, through excess and the abandonment of critical functions that are higher, special, and native to Man. Thus, food and sex are a frenzy in the merely living natural realm, as well as in the degenerate human realm, and, in both cases, individuals and species are not themselves the point, but only the means and the temporary attainment.

The Law in the natural, elemental realm is sacrifice of individual and species through the processes of food and sex. As a consequence of this, the human or higher processes of psychic individuation, self-consciousness, self-transcendence, and sacrificial Translation into higher and Divine Conditions do not appear in the vital and elemental order of living beings. Nor do they fully appear in the case of human individuals who do not become responsible for attachment to the frenzy of feeding and sexing.

The human entity must realize a transformed, higher, personal, and transcendental responsibility for the vital and elemental urges. His early, lower functional, and subhuman adaptations do not demonstrate such responsibility. Therefore, he must grow beyond autonomy in the sheer mechanics of physical activity, food-taking, and sexual intercourse. He must go beyond the frenzy of food and sex, learned in childhood, or the first two stages of life, and he must adapt these functions to practical and analytical intelligence and to informed will or intention. Such is the process in the third stage of life, the stage of transition to truly human autonomy.

But this third stage of adaptation is not an end in itself, or the completion of potential human growth. Indeed, it only marks the awakening of self-conscious intelligence and a movement toward personal and individualistic survival motives. Man in the third stage of life is not yet truly human. He only brings individual force and form to the vital and elemental experience and world. He tempers and also extends the frenzy of feeding and sexing by submitting these to the processes of the verbal and analytical mind. Man in the third stage of life is characterized by the frenzy of mind, the frenzy of problems and solutions.

The truly human being appears only in the fourth stage of life, wherein the vital, elemental, emotional-sexual, and lower mental functions come into the summary and unifying dominion of the heart, the psyche of the whole bodily being. Such is the awakened moral and spiritual disposition, in which Truth becomes the Principle in consciousness, and higher structural growth becomes a benign, nonproblematic possibility. Thus, the Law in the truly human realm is sacrifice as the individual, whole, and entire human body-mind, through love, founded in prior intuition of the Divine Reality. The human sacrifice is the spiritual practice of love and intuition of the Real under all conditions of experience and higher growth.

The first three stages of the structural growth of Man develop adaptation relative to the vital-physical, the emotional-sexual, and the mental-intentional functions respectively. The current evolutionary state of the human race is one in which the first two stages predominate and more or less exclusively occupy the total span of a lifetime. The adaptation of the functions of the first two stages to those of the third stage (thought and will) is still a matter of struggle and failure and lower order success for most men and women.

The religious and spiritual communications that most generally appear, and which are to the point for most people, are a prophetic demand that human beings not only master and become responsible for the vital-physical and emotional-sexual functions via intelligence and willpower, but that the race as a whole ascend to the fourth stage of evolutionary development. That stage is the one in which the whole bodily being of the individual is awake as the heart, the psychic wholeness, the moral or sacrificial disposition of love and of radiant fullness. If men can generally realize this stage of structural growth, then the denser and lower functional nature, which is controlled below consciousness, will cease to determine or disturb human history and individual destiny. Also, in the fourth stage of life there is the beginning of human growth in psychic, subtle, and transcendental dimensions.

The process of sexual communion, described in this book, is a responsibility that must arise in the third stage of life, and, ideally, previous to marriage or any other adaptation to sexual play. However, the process is also not truly or fully realizable unless the individual is also awakened to spiritual understanding and practice—in which case, sexual communion provides a bridge to the fourth and truly human or conscious stage of life.

The first three stages of human evolution or development relate directly to our participation in the phenomena of food, sex, and thought respectively. The key to our adaptation at any stage is to realize autonomy, or personal adaptation and facility, relative to the essential functions and extended phenomena encountered most profoundly at that stage. Thus, relative to food, we must become capable of finding, selecting, ingesting, assimilating, and eliminating. Each succeeding stage has its own unique requirements.

However, education, or learning toward right adaptation, is not fulfilled by the attainment of functional autonomy alone. Mere autonomy is Narcissism. In that case, we are equipped only to function in self-orientation, and we are too profoundly individuated to integrate sympathetically with the total relational or cosmic pattern in which we appear.

Education, or right adaptation, necessarily involves not only learning toward responsible autonomy, but the functional realization of the disposition of relational sacrifice, or love. Such is the right or true cultural way of human adaptation.

The usual education is bereft of higher understanding and spiritual culture. Thus, people commonly move from food adaptation to sex adaptation—but they rarely fulfill the Law of sacrifice in relation to food before moving on to sex. Thus, the food process remains problematic, casual, obsessive, and a dramatization of the anxiety of separation from Infinity and mother's love. The self-possessed or Narcissistic orientation to food is thus duplicated in the further adaptation to sex. And once food and sex develop their powerful egoic consolations in the lower being of Man, it is immensely difficult to move on to the higher order of human structural and moral potential.

Therefore, our education must be completed at every stage before adaptation to the next higher level of complexity or subtlety can become an expression of the free energy of the cosmos rather than the rigid and contracting strategies of the ego. If love and tranquility are not made central to our adaptation to food, and to our general sustenance by the powers of the universe, then sex will necessarily be engaged as an extension of our self-possession and also as an extension of the process of food-taking. Then sexual play becomes an instrument for acquiring experiences for one's own body and for eliminating the forces and substances that necessarily accumulate when there is no capacity to communicate Life through love and service.

Our movement from stage to stage of evolution must be an autonomous movement from stage to stage of love relative to new levels of functional experience. Otherwise there is no freedom and no true or full growth.

One who is self-possessed at the level of life itself, anxious about his or her ultimate sustenance or survival, and motivated by fear and the search for solutions or acquisitions, is disturbed at the vital-physical level, the first stage of human individuation, adaptation, and evolution. Such a one moves on to emotional and sexual adaptation as a Narcissistic extension of the trouble with food, or Life itself.

Thus, sex becomes a childish and even infantile extension of the process of being fed. Those who do not learn functional responsibility as love, or the positive expression of feeling-attention, present themselves in negative fashion to all relations. They do not characteristically or stably bring fullness, or love, or Life to Life. Rather, they seek to acquire fullness, love, and Life from outside, independent of their own native participation in Life, love, and fullness. They represent a childish and dependent demand in all their relations. They are always looking to be fed and to be guaranteed the comforts of immortals. They fail to incarnate the very Life they seek, and which always already pervades the world. And they tend, in their dependency, always to treat their relations casually, without realizing that the world needs from them what they always seek from the world.

The quality of our sexuality tends to dramatize anxiety relative to our Life fundamentally. We look to be satisfied, to be fed, and to be emptied of stress, but, as a result, we do not love happily. Our sexuality acquires pleasure, but it rarely expresses inherent pleasure. It tends to dramatize a sense of dilemma, or inherent pleasurelessness.

Our sexuality tends to be all about satisfaction, more or less mutually served. But as such it is a dramatization of self-possession or Narcissism. Our sex play is anxious, obsessive, looking for release. The pleasure it develops is itself something from which we seek release. The release through orgasm is its meaning, rather than a prior fullness. We cannot sustain prolonged desire. Nor is love enough for us. We must be satisfied, released of our fullness.

Sexual communion is the true or human form of our sexual adaptation. It is realization of the Lawful or sacrificial form of sexual play. It is not based on self-possessed needs, nor on neurotic dependency, or childish anxiety. In sexual communion, and in the relationship of true marriage or true intimacy in general, lovers enjoy the capacity for prolonged and fundamental Fullness of Life. Thus, desire and loving play are prolonged by this disposition, and there is no anxious or erotic obsession with quick, ritualistic, and inappropriately frequent satisfaction through genital self-emptying. Just so, bodily existence in general becomes a matter of inherent Fullness, rather than the alternating acquisitions of Fullness and Emptiness, for those who live the principle of continuous Communion with Life at Infinity, through devotional sacrifice or love.

Sexual Communion Leads to Growth beyond Sex and Thought

In the earlier stages of the development of a human being, adaptation essentially occurs relative to the general physical or motor system and the functions of assimilation, elimination, reproduction, and speech (or the verbal mind). Thus, the level of adaptation of the lower-adapted or subhuman individual is expressed primarily via the organs of the mouth, anus, and sex organs, as well as the volitional and gross motor responses of the muscular body, and the lower brain centers that control these organs and responses as well as the general function of speech and discursive thought.

At the present stage of general or common human development, the average individual barely even touches upon levels of adaptation that exceed the earlier, infantile, or subhuman levels of function. Indeed, the usual man or woman is commonly less than fully and harmoniously adapted to the lower functions. Thus, people commonly experience and dramatize obsession, shame, guilt, fear, confusion, self-consciousness, self-division, and tendencies toward neurotic inversion and self-destructive as well as other-destructive habits relative to the ordinary functions and organs of our common condition. Therefore, the average individual is retarded in his possibility of growth beyond the vital mechanical and mental stage of human development.

For this reason, people do not commonly grow or even respond to the possibility of growth by adaptation to the whole bodily, truly human, and functional moral position of the heart. Nor do they regard the higher psychic and superhuman psycho-physical levels of growth that belong to the organs above the heart to be real or even possible.

The process of sexual communion is not a subhuman activity of lower vital accommodation. It is a way of continuing to grow, by realizing responsibility and a harmony in terms of the lower functions, and by consciously adapting to the whole body structure through the feeling disposition of the heart. Thus, sexual communion is a way of sexual love that inevitably moves beyond sexuality itself (or in itself), and all of the childish obsessions, repressions, emotional reactivity, and self-oriented or anti-ecstatic rituals that bind us below the fourth and truly human stage of the structural adaptation to Life.

The confinement to lower organs and their independent functions for the sake of consoling pleasurable release or repetitive fulfillment of desire is the ritual of Narcissus, or self-possession. It is the usual life of waking, thinking, talking, eating, sleeping, dreaming, eliminating, moving, and sexing. It is the life in which self-release into relationship and the ecstasy of Communion with the Real is essentially retarded and in doubt. The "hearing" of the argument or Teaching of the Spiritual Master is a process wherein the relational force of the whole bodily being is reawakened and set into fullness of motion. In that case, the lower functional order becomes capable of readaptation and responsible application to the whole bodily principle of love, or self-sacrifice, which is ecstasy. In the process, the lower three or subhuman stages of personal adaptation are clarified and relieved of inharmonious and neurotic patterns, and the bodily being is permitted to grow into its truly human and even superhuman functional destiny.

This is the essential import of the process of sexual communion and the fourth stage of human life. It is a matter of growth beyond lower-functional problems and chronic anxiety, fear, shame, anger, and self-doubt relative to the vital functional processes. And it is a matter of growth beyond confinement to sexual obsession or repression through the contraction of whole bodily feeling, as well as growth beyond the chronically self-differentiating disposition and incessant chatter of the verbal mind, which constantly distracts and contracts the open force of attention. In the patterns of growth that appear in the fourth and higher stages of life, sex and the verbal or abstracting mind cease to be the chronic limits of human enjoyment or realization, and they yield their primacy to the selfless ecstasy of Communion with the Real.

There is not only a right, responsible, or uniquely human exercise of the sexual process, but a humanizing effect or purpose to such exercise itself. Thus, we must not only prepare ourselves in the responsibilities of the third stage of life and the beginnings of the fourth stage of life before we become sexually active—but we must then submit ourselves to the relational life and the ecstatic (self-sacrificing) obligation to be sexually oriented and active in the fullest sense. In this way we will remain constantly obliged to be relieved of the precious artifacts of loveless frozen energy and anti-relational independence, as well as the preposterous absurdities and abstracted illusions of the internal or purely subjective solutions to the problem or paradox of living existence.

Sexual activity, in the present, and in the form of emotional-sexual communion or relational self-sacrifice in love to Infinity, opens the body-mind from its own limits, establishes unity with free and ecstatic Energy, harmonizes and balances the personal and interpersonal polarities of human and vital elemental existence, and promotes intuitive sympathy with all that the defined self or body-"I" cannot or does not conceive or contain. Thus, far from being identical to "sin," sexual communion is a human right, a humanizing obligation, and a living instrument of our ultimate and pleasurable sacrifice or Translation beyond human psycho-physical structures and human limits of knowledge.

Chapter 7

Sexual Communion Is Worship, or Devotional Surrender to Life

85

The practice of sexual communion serves a critical transition in the stages of practice of the Way of Divine Ignorance: the passage from <u>religious</u> preparation (engaged through devotional, personal, and moral disciplines of body, mind, and life) into esoteric <u>spiritual</u> practice (engaged most directly through meditative disciplines in the Company of the Spiritual Master).

Thus, sexual communion has a special, sacred function in the lives of devotees. It is the culmination of the preparatory devotional, personal, and moral practices. Right practice of sexual communion magnifies the devotional ecstasy of Divine Communion; it opens the whole body to the heart's delight in the All-Pervading Radiance of God. For those whose practice is true, sexual communion is a form of bodily prayer, or whole body feeling-surrender, through the loved one to the living God, the Divine Beloved.

Sex and Enlightenment

The key to Divine Life is hidden in sex. The secret process hidden in the common knowledge of religion, spirituality, mysticism, magic, and all yoga is the Communion of the whole and entire body-mind with the All-Pervading Current, Force, and Presence of Life, or the Divine Spirit, that appears to be separated from us via the sex organs and the vital centers of the body.

What we feel and exploit as the Life-Force in the genitals is but a trickle of the All-Pervading Life. The entire body-mind is contracted upon itself, separating as itself by reaction to its born-condition. We are chronically and even bodily recoiled from Infinity, and thus we are self-possessed rather than God-Possessed.

This recoil of the entire body-mind is realized in the first and infantile stage of life. And as the infant feeds, it informs itself of its independence, its vulnerability, and its separation from any sense of an Absolute Sustainer-Reality. Thus, when the sense of bodily pleasure arises, it is accepted as the primary consolation or reward for egoic individuation. And that consolation by the personal or own-body pleasure of self is ultimately epitomized in the second or mid-childhood stage of life, in the form of sexual awakening.

86

The usual individual is fixed in this infantile and childish level of psycho-physical adaptation (or the failure of adaptation) to the All-Pervading Life in which we appear, continue and change for a time, and then disappear. Thus, each individual represents a chronic disposition, universal to all human beings at this stage of evolution, in which the body-mind is contracted upon itself at its elemental base. And each individual therefore consoles himself through fixation upon the primary bodily pleasures of food, sensation, and sex.

Even so, because of the root and fundamental contractedness of the entire body-mind, the Divine Life is not contacted directly and realized in its Fullness. Rather, the Divine Life is contacted and more or less hidden by the already contracted body-mind. Thus, even though the body-mind consoles itself through its own structural pleasure, and even though the primary bodily or structural mechanism of pleasure is felt at the genitals—the Force of Life is not felt or realized except as a relatively weak and private trickle of bodily energy.

People in general have no understanding of this and its implications. They live in an essentially mechanical, reactive, self-possessed, confused, and degenerative manner. And either Life, or the Radiance of the Divine, is not acknowledged or there is no understanding of how to adapt the body-mind to the Power of the Living Divine.

I am not speaking of things I merely believe. I am speaking with the certainty of a complete experience of all of the psycho-physical processes and signs of total Regeneration in God. And anyone can see the proof of all that I say if they will only consider this Teaching and take up the Way in my Company.

The usual body-mind enjoys only that trickle of energy that manages to pass through the reactive locks or closed doors of the genitals and the vital base of the bodily form. The limitless Power of Life cannot invade the body-mind and motivate its truly human and superhuman adaptation and growth. The process of such growth awakens only when the intuition of Life is regained, and the body-mind submits to the Spirit or Life in which it is appearing and by which it is sustained.

That process of whole bodily submission to Life is true religion and spirituality. It is most radically realized in the Way of Divine Ignorance, engaged in Communion with the Spiritual Master, through whom the Radiant Divine is Revealed most directly to human beings. And all of the practices in that Company involve literal and ecstatic, or self-releasing, love and surrender to the Radiant Divine. Such practices bring every function and feature of the body-mind into direct and disarmed contact with the Divine Life of the body-mind and the whole world.

Because of the primacy of the contraction generated at the bodily base, and most especially at the sexual center of the body, the release of these reactive contractions is the fundamental necessity for Whole Bodily Enlightenment, or Translation of the independent body-mind into Life. Such is the practical necessity of religion, spirituality, and all forms of higher human structural awakening in God.

The process of sexual communion described in this book is only one of many essential disciplines to be enacted in Communion with the Divine Life. But it is a primary process in the Way of Divine Ignorance, and it matures into a profound and esoteric capacity in the later stages of practice.[1] Once the locks of the perineum, anus,

---

1. There are four stages of religious and spiritual practice, adaptation, and realization in the Way of Divine Ignorance, or Radical Understanding.

The first is the preparatory stage, the Way of Divine Communion. Its first phase of practice involves devotional, personal, and moral disciplines of religious Communion with the Living God, Who is Transcendental Consciousness, Radiant as All-Pervading Power, or Life. The emotional and sexual disciplines communicated in *Love of the Two-Armed Form* are the culminating responsibilities of this initial and foundation phase of the Way of Divine

genitals, navel, solar plexus, heart, chest, throat, mouth, face, spine, and the entire brain are all opened to Life, the bodily Revelation of God becomes a Glory that few have ever enjoyed. In the process of that Transforming Revelation, the body is sublimed into the Ecstasy of Light, and the mind is raised beyond mere soul into the transcendental Genius of Wisdom and Sacrifice, by which it passes beyond itself to God. May you be Blessed to Awaken in this Understanding.

88

S exual communion is not in itself a method for Realizing God or Truth. Sexuality is simply an aspect of the functional theatre of Life, and as such it may either be exploited for its own sake—yielding the egoic delusions of mere experience—or it may be lived as a Lawful or sacrificial discipline, from the point of view of Truth itself. Thus, sexual communion is one of many functional disciplines that express a right or appropriate adaptation of human life. As devotees mature, their own functions thus become a theatre wherein the primacy of Truth and sacrifice itself is revealed. Therefore, right or appropriate use of any function yields transcendence of that function, whereas conventional exploitation or mere experiential use of any function yields either aversion or else addiction to repetition.

Communion (although the discipline of sexual communion may also serve the devotee's adaptation in the two following stages of practice). The second phase or stage of the Way of Divine Communion extends these initial responsibilities in the form of higher psychophysical disciplines of esoteric meditation: the "Breath of God" (reception-release in the All-Pervading Presence of Life, in coordination with the cycle of breathing) and the "Name of God" (the *conscious process* of intuitive and bodily recollection or attention to the Living Divine Presence, Who is the Transcendental Consciousness and All-Pervading Current of Life). These spiritual disciplines become the devotee's responsibilities after he has been thoroughly Awakened to the Presence of the Divine Person in the Company of the Spiritual Master.

The Way of Relational Enquiry is the fully humanizing stage of practice. It begins with self-observation and radical insight into one's contractive, self-meditative, or Narcissistic activity. In this manner, the devotee matures to the point of formal responsibility for the enquiry "Avoiding relationship?" In the second phase of the Way of Relational Enquiry, the practice of the "Breath of God" becomes *conductivity,* or breathing of the Presence or Current of Life, in a continual internal cycle of descent and ascent of Life-Energy. (The process of *conductivity* involves technical exercises, which are communicated privately to all devotees at this stage of practice.) Through these conscious and technical disciplines in Communion

Truth is not at last Realized in fulfillment of any function, but in sacrifice or release of the whole and entire bodily being, which is perfect transcendence of the limitations of birth and the manifest functions of independent or egoic existence. For this reason, many will pass from an undeveloped, childish, and Narcissistic involvement in sex to a full relational intimacy founded in sexual communion—but even then they eventually pass into a motiveless economy of sexual activity, wherein gross body-consciousness and mental absorption are constantly yielded, relaxed, or dissolved in the Infinity of Ignorance-Radiance.

89

with the Spiritual Master, or the Living Agency of the Divine Person, the Life-Current begins to show signs of regenerative, Life-conserving reorientation from toe to crown, rather than vice versa (which is the case in the usual man and in the devotee previous to this stage of transformation).

The Way of Re-cognition is the higher spiritualizing stage of the Way of Divine Ignorance. In the process of this stage, the devotee recapitulates and transcends the traditional esoteric awakenings of yogis, saints, and sages in the classic spiritual traditions. In the three phases of the Way of Re-cognition, the devotee re-cognizes, "knows again," or literally feels through and passes beyond the experiential contractions of the body, the ordinary thinking mind, the subtle or higher mind, and the ego. The Radiant Current of Life is first fully reoriented to the crown, and it is later dissolved in the centerless, directionless Bliss of Divine Radiance Itself, prior to the body-mind.

The final phase of the Way of Re-cognition Realizes exclusive Self-Realization, or Absorption in Transcendental Consciousness prior to all subjective and objective conditions. This Realization is followed by "open eyes," the transition to Whole Body Enlightenment, which is the first stage of God-Realization in the fourth stage of practice, the Way of Radical Intuition.

The Way of Radical Intuition thus begins when there is "open-eyed" transcendence of exclusive or internalized Self-Realization. As the devotee persists in the spontaneously God-Realized Consciousness of Whole Body Enlightenment, he is drawn more and more profoundly into Divine Existence Itself, prior to all phenomena, high and low.

In the case of Whole Body Enlightenment, there is tacit re-cognition, or "knowing again," of all arising conditions, which are thus realized to be only unnecessary modifications of the Divine Condition. Persistence in such Enlightenment ultimately becomes Divine Translation, in which there is no longer any problematic experiential or subjective noticing of anything arising in or as the independent body, mind, or world. Even though all possible phenomena are eternally arising, the independent experiential position is not presumed. Only the Divine Condition is obvious. No independent act of attention arises to associate with phenomena or to cause experience in the unnecessary and changing Realm of Nature. This is the perfection of radical intuition. It is the native State of Free and Unobstructed Feeling-Attention, or Love, in which the devotee has Realized Identity with the Transcendental Consciousness of the Divine Person—the true Self of all bodies, minds, and worlds—and Ecstatic or perfectly self-transcending Communion with the Eternal Radiance of the Divine Person—the Bliss which is the true Condition or Happiness behind all experiential phenomena.

For a full discussion of the four stages of the total Way of Divine Ignorance, see *The Enlightenment of the Whole Body* and *The Paradox of Instruction*, by Bubba Free John. For further consideration of the devotional, personal, moral, and esoteric or higher psychophysical disciplines of the Way of Divine Communion, see *Breath and Name*, by Bubba Free John.

The Way of Divine Ignorance
Is True Religion, or the
Sacrifice of Self in God

90   The Way of Divine Ignorance involves worship of the Divine "in Spirit and in Truth." It is total and radical worship, or most profound sacrifice of self, granted to the transcendental Reality, or Life, that is the Condition and Consciousness of all that is alive and appearing.

Worship is sacrifice. Worship in "Truth" is sacrifice of mind, or all knowledge, into the intuition of Divine Ignorance. The sacrifice of self-possessed knowledge ultimately becomes selfless Wisdom.

Worship in "Spirit" is sacrifice of bodily existence into the All-Pervading Divine Radiance. The sacrifice of bodily or formal independence of self ultimately becomes selfless Divine Existence.

Worship in "Spirit" and in "Truth" is sacrifice of all that is oneself and that one possesses, or by which one is possessed. It is not sacrifice of what is less or other than oneself, or that is only symbolic of oneself, or that is less than the totality of what one possesses. It is the sacrifice of Man in God. And such worship or sacrifice is true religion, or religio-spiritual participation in Life.

The Way of Sacrifice in God, or Eternal Life, is a matter of growth in responsibility for the awakening and the sacrifice of all the various structures of the body-mind. The first level of such responsibility is expressed through the <u>personal</u> conditions of practice.

The personal conditions of practice involve responsibility for the regenerative management and Divine Sacrifice of the vital functions "below the heart." Thus, the personal conditions involve regenerative or Life-positive responsibilities relative to diet and health, sexuality, exercise and common activity, work, transformative discipline of the verbal mind through study, and right exercise of the will through service.

The second level of responsibility in this Way is expressed through the central, most fundamental, and whole bodily dimension of the <u>moral</u> conditions of practice. The moral conditions of practice involve responsibility for the regenerative or Life-positive and self-sacrificial devotion of the "heart" itself, or the total and feeling being. Thus, the moral conditions of practice involve every kind of responsibility for the reactive tendencies of the body-mind—or the fundamental, self-defining reflex of contraction into self-possession, negative emotion, relational avoidance, and the subjective orientation. The moral responsibility in practice is ex-pressed through service in the fullest sense of love, or devotion of feeling-attention, via all relations, under all conditions, into the Infinite Divine.

91

The third level of responsibility for true worship, or sacrifice of self into Life, is expressed through higher structural, or <u>higher psycho-physical</u> conditions of adaptation. Thus, the higher psycho-physical conditions of practice involve regenerative spiritual, yogic, and transcendental responsibilities, or forms of esoteric meditation and mental transcendence. The regenerative or Life-positive struc-tural development of higher psycho-physical responsibility is a matter of growth into the dimensions of the body-mind "above the heart."

The Way of Divine Ignorance, or the Life-Positive Way of Sacrifice of the independent body-mind into the Divine, is finally or ultimately summarized in a single, total, and radical responsibility. It is the intuitive Sacrifice of every dimension of our structure below and above and at the heart. It is that Sacrifice that is made from and as the heart in Truth. It is Dissolution and Translation of the body-mind, or separately defined self, into the Paradox and Spirit-Radiance of Divinity.

Love of Life

The process of ecstatic or self-sacrificed Communion with the Radiant All-Pervading Divine is simple in its description. It is a matter of relaxation-release of the body-mind into the All-Pervading Life and unqualified Ignorance intuited to be the Truth and Condition of all existence and experience. This is a matter of the relaxation of all bodily, emotional, and mental contraction or reactivity, and release of the whole body into Life through intense and free feeling, or love.

Thus, Divine Realization is a matter of the always present feeling-surrender, to Life, of all forms of mental contraction or reactivity, all forms of chronic thinking and imaging and speaking. The consciousness that observes subjective and objective phenomena cannot observe itself. Even the thought "I" has no specific reference that is independent of the body-mind, or the complex mental, emotional, and physical states that all arise as objects to the observing consciousness. Therefore, when the body-mind surrenders into the Divine, consciousness is released from the context of the observer and what is observed, or subject and object. Instead, consciousness abides undifferentiated in the Radiant Formlessness and Bliss of Life. The natural state of consciousness is simple awareness of and as the Radiant Fullness and Unqualified Consciousness that is Reality.

Likewise, Divine Realization is a matter of the always present feeling-surrender, to Life, of all forms of antifeeling, or reactive, self-possessed, and self-divided or self-contradictory emotion. Reactivity is the mechanism of Narcissistic self-possession and all the illusions of inwardness and self-survival. The natural state of emotion is simple feeling, or love, abiding undifferentiated in the Radiant Fullness and Bliss of the Living Divine.

Just so, Divine Realization is a matter of the always present feeling-surrender, to Life, of all forms of reactive bodily tension or contraction. The body must be combined with the All-Pervading Life that lives it, or else the body becomes possessed of the illusion that it lives by its own power, and that it is an altogether independent and self-generated "I." The natural state of body is simple functional openness and right or regenerative functional association with the All-Pervading Radiance and Bliss of Divine Life.

Therefore, the Way of Divine Ignorance is the Way of specific structural or psycho-physical submission of self into Life, the true Self, which is not exclusively within or without, but which is All-Pervading. This Way of Eternal Life and Bliss necessarily involves not merely subjective "belief" in God, but literal sacrifice of self in God. And such sacrifice involves literal functional relaxation-release of all self-directed bodily, emotional, and mental states. And the means of that sacrifice is present intuition of the Radiant Divine and surrender of the entire body-mind in love of the Divine, via all relations, and under all conditions. Those who become such a sacrifice Grow and Dissolve in God.

Growth and Transcendence

To live by the Law is our worship, and Life itself is our God. Sexual communion is worship, or Communion with Life, through the love-transformation of the sexual function. Just so, all the devotional, personal, moral, and higher psycho-physical conditions or responsibilities of the Way of Divine Ignorance are forms of regenerative worship of Life, or sacrificial Communion between structure and Life.

Life, or the All-Pervading and Radiant Divine Reality, must be realized to be the Condition as well as the Content of the vital functional dimension of human existence. Then the human individual is released from the illusion of separation from Reality, and he or she may continue to grow, through true worship, or regeneration and ultimate sacrifice of the entire body-mind into Life. Such growth depends on the intuitive awakening of the heart, or the free and whole bodily response of love, to Life. And the human being grows through the acceptance of personal conditions for the functions below the heart, moral conditions for the whole bodily disposition of the heart, and higher psycho-physical conditions for the psychic and higher mental functions above the heart. But that growth, through personal, moral, and higher psycho-physical adaptation, is always itself a matter of free participation in the Law of God, which is true worship, or the sacrifice of the whole body-mind into Life. Therefore, we ultimately transcend our own structural growth, through Translation into the very Divine.

S exual communion, with full emotional and physical responsibility, does indeed conserve or regenerate the Life-Force and the bodily and mental integrity of individuals and their intimate relationships. However, such conservation and regeneration is not an end in itself. It is only part of the personal responsibility for the intuitive feeling sacrifice of self, or the whole body-mind, into the transcendental Divine Life.

Thus, sexual communion is itself a kind of initiation or instructive lesson. It demonstrates the mechanism or process of self-transcendence in God. Ultimately, the sexual process is itself transcended through the radical sacrificial process of Communion with Life.

Over time, Fullness of Life dissolves and displaces all separative reactivity, self-possession, subjectivity, and functional or structural contraction of the body-mind. Therefore, not only the sex function but every function of the body-mind is gradually transcended through the regenerative and sacrificial disciplines of the Way of Divine Ignorance. Those disciplines include personal, moral, higher psycho-physical, and radically intuitive responsibilities. As the devotee matures, each of the functions of the body-mind awakens, adapts to a regenerative or Life-positive cycle of activity, relaxes into a nonobsessive or natural economy, and releases into the prior Condition or Life in which it is arising. Thus, in the case of mature devotees, native Fullness has replaced reactive motivations toward degenerative self-fulfillment, and even the regenerative patterns of function are relaxed into moderation, or a natural, motiveless economy. The sexual function, then, as with all other functions, eventually transcends itself in the prior Fullness of the body-mind.

95

Chapter 8

Reactivity and the Passion of Life

2

97

True morality is not obedience to conventional ethics of right and wrong. It is participation in the superphysics of the Universal Law of Sacrifice. The moral man lives continuously in ecstatic Communion with the Limitless Conscious Life of God. He abides in that Life, he acts and breathes in that Life, and he expresses that Communion in his human relations through love, or unobstructed and free feeling-attention under all conditions.

Thus, he is constantly transcending the implications of all experience, which tend to cause him to react and contract upon himself, to abandon his Communion with God. He is constantly cutting through the Narcissistic motion of all his tendencies—the physics that binds him to the cycle of births and deaths. He is bright and alive with love, and his love quickly makes obsolete the inverted or Life-rejecting satisfactions of emotional reactivity and every kind of orgasmic release. To begin to love in this Way is to enter the higher range of the cycle of evolution in Nature, wherein we Awaken beyond self-possessed embodiment and, ultimately, are Translated even bodily into Infinite Conscious Life.

Frustration and
Reactive Emotion

Always Meet the Mark

I n the instant in which reactive states of mind, emotion, and body arise, then desires, motivations, and obsessive fascinations also arise, high and low, as methods of relief from the problems and tensions of the bodily being. Such is the origin of self-possession, temptation, and "sin," which means "to miss the mark." The reactive and independent body-mind is turned upon itself, and so it avoids or "misses the mark" of all relations—human, natural, and Divine.

The mature and truly human individual is able to inspect and understand this cycle of reaction, self-possession, and tension-release, in his own case as well as in the case of others. Therefore, he does not indulge the self-possessed sense of dilemma, nor does he indulge the tendencies that automatically arise to relieve him of his self-contraction. He only observes the whole pattern in every moment, and so resorts to none of it. He yields himself instead to ecstasy, or Communion with the Divine, in every instant of self-contraction or dilemma. He always bypasses the ordinary destiny of problems and solutions. He abandons the problems and solutions of the reactive and independent body-mind in moment to moment feeling-sacrifice into the Living Divine Reality. This is his Way—always to meet the Mark. Therefore, he remains creatively effective, whole, essentially simple, and utterly free of the illusion of separation from what is Real, Divine, Blissful, and Great.

The Creative Function of Life-Frustration in the Process of Self-Sacrifice

In relations with the world of mankind, "I" feels and observes itself to be easily and profoundly disturbed and distracted by mechanical, irresponsibly motivated, utterly self-oriented, and disturbing people. Indeed, this automaton, altogether subhuman, is identified by "I" to be generally present in the form of most people, or as the principal and casual expression of most people. The moral and intimate, sane and humorous, responsible, intelligent, creative, and spiritual expressions that would constitute real human companionship and society appear at the present time to be almost totally absent from our ordinary worldly possibilities. And they are only tentatively or partially contained even in the sphere of our own creative and local or private human relations.

As a consequence, "I" is, in general, a disturbed individual. But the disturbances granted by ordinary life move us constantly to realize levels of communication and effect that may transform the theatre of our own experience and that of others in general.

At times, however, the frustration is so profound that "I" feels nearly immobilized, unable to see the possibility of significant, immediate, or ultimate and permanent effect upon this unconscious world, so stupid and arbitrary in all its ways. There are times when true ecstasy seems impossible. There is frustration. There is resort to the caves of inwardness, abstract insight, consoling illusions, and mechanical states of personal psycho-physical pleasure and certainty. But delight, release, and sublime participation in the displayed existence of the total World seem at times to be impossible. Indeed, it is always a struggle, and never a permanent realization.

Life is a creative opportunity, motivated by frustration of the impulse of the living individual toward ecstasy, or self-transcendence. There is no factual end to the struggle. There is at best a human maturity, in which frustration is not permitted to become negatively dominant, permitting no change or motion. Rather, frustration is maintained as a positive or creative circumstance for motion, change, and, ultimately, ecstatic participation in the Transcendental Reality.

In any case, the Law will be fulfilled. We are obliged from birth to be a sacrifice. We are obliged to a participatory existence that is most truly and freely realized when it is ecstasy—self-release via love, or whole body feeling-attention to the degree of Infinity. Nonetheless, such a life of love, or creative participation in the theatre of life-frustration, is a purifying fire that moves toward release or sacrifice of self rather than fixed survival.

Frustration must begin to awaken us at the heart to a feeling sacrifice or release of self and attention from the reactive contractions experiences tend to generate in the body-mind. And that heart-generated responsibility, rather than any functional form of self-exploitation, subtle or gross, must become our essential means of ecstasy. Only then is "I" a human being, real, moral, and true.

Reactivity and the Passion of Life

When the individual is frustrated, it is the Life in him that is suppressed. The Force of Life is naturally expansive, moving, blissful, and undefined. But frustration or suppression of the feeling being, the whole body-mind, tends to create an equal and opposite reaction, in the form of reactive contractions of attention (into forms of thought) and emotion (into reactive forms, such as fear, sorrow, guilt, anger, and self-doubt) and body (into genital tension and organ and muscle tensions or dis-eases all over the body). The reaction to experience defines life and limits it to the individual body-mind, or born self, preventing ecstatic Identification or Communion with the Divine Reality.

Therefore, self-defining reactivity, or contraction of body, feeling, and attention must be radically transcended and made a matter of moment to moment responsibility. Otherwise, Life is reduced to self-meditative psycho-physical releases of functional tensions. When self-transcending responsibility characterizes the individual, the self-defining, contracting, tensing effects of experience will become less and less profound. And, in that case, daily existence will cease to be a constant effort to overcome obstacles and purify or save the self, but will instead become ecstatic self-sacrifice through relational love and selfless Communion with the Real.

Such a Way of Life is natively free of the conventional self-meditative solutions to the "dilemma of life." Such an individual is not obliged to exploit the internal experiential capacity of the independent body-mind or the consoling benefits of the exploitation of relational contact for the sake of releasing his own tensions. Instead, ecstasy is realized in Divine Communion moment to moment, and the reactivity of the body-mind is thereby undermined and made penetrable by the Force of Life. Thus, the devotee is not obliged to solve the problems created by chronic reactivity, but he penetrates reactivity with living force, and he lives a happy life of love and service and constant Fullness in God.

Such freedom from the reactive tendencies of the mental, emotional, and physical dimensions of the bodily being is not a matter of living as a strategically unresponsive and passive character. It is a matter of always abiding in intuitive Communion with the Divine, and creatively dealing with the self-defining power of every experience. Such an individual is profoundly responsive and alive. And he transcends the frustrating and reaction-forming power of experience by intensity of participation rather than unresponsive coolness.

Such a character is profoundly emotional, intelligent, and full of Life. He works creatively within the mechanisms of his present adaptation, as one who is lived and pervaded by Life. Thus, he is a creative force or ecstatic agency of Life, rather than a self-possessed, abstracted, chronically reactive or strategically nonreactive opponent of his own mortality. He grows, adapts, and cuts through. He is not weak, but strong. His freedom is shown in his aggressive, self-yielding resort to the Divine under all circumstances. He is not passionless. Rather, his passion is pressed to God.

Because of the mortal vulnerability of individual existence, and the constant encounter with forces or events that frustrate and suppress the egoic urges of self-extension, self-glorification, and self-survival, the motive of our lives tends to become that of release. We seek release from the tensions of body and mind that result when self contracts under the force of the frustration of its will to ecstasy, or the will to expansive sacrifice into the Condition beyond separation and contraction and self-survival. And we tend to pursue means of release that require the least amount of success at self-extension. Thus, we become attached to forms of pleasurable release that may be attained at the lowest level of our own body-mind. We become self-manipulative, and we tend to manipulate the most easily available others as a means of manipulating ourselves and achieving pleasurable releases of the tensions of our own body-mind.

102

In this manner, we become attached to the orgasm as a means of release, and we become attached to sexual partners whom we may acquire through essentially loveless manipulative games. And it is this subhuman strategy of manipulation and release that chronically occupies the majority of individuals.

Sexual relations, and life itself, cannot be realized in a human, loving, and ecstatic form until the mechanism of bodily, emotional, and mental reactivity is itself understood and made a matter of consistent responsibility. Only then do dilemma, tension, and obsessive contraction upon the self cease to be the chronic state of the individual. Instead, the feeling capacity of love, ecstasy, and self-transcendence in Communion with the Real becomes the characteristic of the individual in his encounter with the phenomena of experience.

The responsible individual is constantly moved to ecstasy, not self-possessed and degenerative release. Such a one may realize relationships through love and service, rather than through motives of self-protection or self-glamorization, and his sexuality is expressed through loving intimacy, rather than eroticism and manipulation of self and other toward orgasm.

Orgasm separates. In itself, it is a method of relieving mental, emotional, and physical tension by exploiting and destroying the force of desire. By itself, it results in separation, self-isolation, and exploitation of mental and physical states without the unifying force of true love. It commonly depends on self-possession, conflict, fear, tension, and infantilism. In the case of responsible individuals, the motive of orgasmic release is not the foundation of sexual relationship or contact. Rather, the motive is ecstasy, or sacrifice of self, of possession by contracted or reactive states of body, emotion, and mind. It is not a matter of trying to "cure" the pain of desire, or to release the tension within self. But it is a matter of the release of the entire self, through unobstructed feeling and loving contact.

Thus, sexual communion is not about attaining or preventing orgasm. It is about love, contact, and ecstatic communion with one's lover at Infinity. Thus, it is not fundamentally about orgasm, or release, in any sense. It is about fullness, not release. It is about the embrace itself, not the result of embrace. It is about feeling, and the transformation of body and mind through feeling. When orgasm approaches, it is transformed by the very disposition of love, or responsible self-relaxation into whole bodily Fullness of Life rather than self-emptying through tension-release at the genitals.

The Pursuit of Pleasure and the Realization of Ecstasy

The Fullness of Life Dissolves Body and Mind

All attachment to degenerate sex must ultimately pass, or else the body-mind remains addicted to its own tension-release mechanism of self-consciousness. Just so, all chronic stimulation of the independent and separate parts of the body-mind must pass, releasing the body-mind itself into the All-Pervading Current of Life. The "Sacrifice of Man," or Divine Translation, occurs only when the body-mind is stabilized in both wholeness and fullness.

Thus, all reactivity, self-division, self-possession, tension, thought, and chronic obstruction or emptiness of Life must be dissolved. The Way of such dissolution is in regenerative practice (in which Life is constantly permitted to pervade the whole body rather than stimulate each part to a different degree), founded in awakened intuition (in which transcendental Ignorance constantly undermines the self-binding force of experience and knowledge).

The Way in which the awesome binding power of sex is dissolved is not through strategic detachment, suppression of sex-desire, or manipulation of thought. Just so, the chronically exclusive stimulation of any part of the bodily being cannot dissolve through self-manipulative strategies. Rather, the dissolution of the tendencies and the effects of partial bodily or psycho-physical stimulation of every kind occurs as a natural event, when the Fullness of Life is permitted to be continuous in the whole and entire body. When the Fullness of the Current of Life pervades the entire bodily being, without obstruction, contraction, or reaction of a mental, emotional, or physical kind, then every form of the partial stimulation of the body-mind relaxes and becomes gradually obsolete. The imbalanced or partial and chaotic stimulation of the bodily being gradually ceases as chronic fixation of Life, and attention in separate organs, parts, or functions relaxes. Ultimately, the *conductivity* [1] of the bodily being becomes total, continuous, and profound, permitting radical sacrifice of self, or whole bodily Communion with the Radiant Reality that pervades the world. It is not a matter of inward concentration, strategic exclusion of bodily awareness, mental manipulation, suppression of sexual feeling (which is only Life felt more or less exclusively in the genitals), or suppression of feeling in any sense. It is a matter of total feeling into the Current of Life, and intuitive abandonment of attachment to every form of experience that arises as modification of that Current.

When the bodily being is whole, the Current of Life is equalized throughout the body, dissolving chronic thought, reactive emotion, and bodily tension. And the consciousness, in Ignorance, intuits the Current not to be within but to pervade in all directions to Infinity.

1. Conductivity is the specifically yogic or technical form of responsibility in each stage of the Way of Divine Ignorance. (Its counterparts, upon which it depends in every stage, are the various forms of the *conscious process* of unobstructed, transcendental intuition, or Divine Ignorance.)

In general, conductivity is the capacity of the body-mind to conduct, or be surrendered into, the All-Pervading Life-Current. Such conductivity or surrender is realized through love, or radiant whole body feeling to Infinity, and such love involves coordinated engagement of body, breath, and attention in alignment with the Universal Current of Life-Energy.

Therefore, the self, or body-mind, yields to Life and becomes ecstatic as Fullness of Feeling to the degree of Infinity. In that case, the whole body-mind is Transfigured in the Radiance of Divine Ignorance, and thereafter there is only Transformation and Translation in God.

The Transition from Pleasure to Ecstasy

Things done to seek release from the bodily, emotional, and mental tensions or reactive contractions of life tend to be repeated for the sake of the pleasure they produce. Thus, whereas frustration is at first necessary to motivate action that seeks release of reactive tension, the repetition of such action requires nothing more than the desire for the pleasure attainable by that action.

This is how degenerative patterns of sexual behavior, as well as antisocial behaviors of all kinds, are created and maintained. And analysis of the rituals of such behaviors, including recollection of the frustrating circumstances of their origin, cannot fully account for the patterns themselves, or make them unnecessary. Frustrating circumstances duplicate themselves from time to time, and so we occasionally approximate the reactive motivations that may have originally created a degenerative pattern. But the primary motivation for the repetition of any chronic pattern—however bizarre the pattern appears—is the pleasurable release of ordinary tension, rather than any attempt to continue to solve an original problem or circumstance. There is, of course, a likely degree of problem-solving relative to original circumstances, but the reactions themselves last long beyond the circumstances they reflect. And the pleasure attainable by ritualistic tension-release is more fundamental than the tensions themselves, which are purely mechanical and barely inspected.

Reactivity creates a machine in the form of a pattern of tension-release that is done for the sake of present pleasure. Therefore, the search for pleasurable release is the motive behind all patterns, whether the patterns appear "bizarre" and clearly "antisocial" or "normal" and "social."

This is why it is so difficult to bring an individual, even oneself, to the point of responsibility for breaking apparently negative behavior patterns. To the individual, all patterns are nothing more than structures for attaining pleasurable release of tension. Many such behavior structures clearly involve the individual in cycles of disturbed, secretive, negative, self-destructive, and other-destructive activity. But the individual holds on to all of that with a sense of its inevitability and necessity. And the pleasure moments of tension-release are the centers of his concentration, so that he does not see the relative force of a brief moment of release over against a lifetime of ritual obsessiveness. Perhaps this can be brought to his attention by others, or he may awaken to it himself. But the ultimate key to the abandonment of fixed patterns of tension-release is not the observation of any pattern or its causes in the past. Rather, it is a matter of full awakening to the sense and valuation of ecstatic pleasure, or happiness in the highest sense.

Truly, everyone is involved in rituals of activity and persuasions of mind that were created in reactive situations in the past, and usually at an age of relative immaturity. These patterns may even be acceptable as "normal" behavior and thinking. But they function in precisely the same way and serve the same ultimate purposes as fixed patterns of "abnormal" behavior and thinking. That is, repetitive patterns of action and thought reflect adaptations that originally appeared in circumstances in which we reacted, protected ourselves, and sought release from the reactive tension. Those patterns continued even after the original circumstances passed, and even though few if any circumstances up to the present have tended to bear any force or likeness to the orginal. This is because reaction is more or less permanent, whereas circumstances pass.

This is all a matter of the physics of motion. Circumstances, or active forces confronting us as experience, tend to be reflected in the form of reactions, equal and opposite—unless we are stronger than the circumstance is effective. But the child, or the relatively childish individual, fixed in childhood rituals, is not so strong. Therefore, reactions are typical of those who are relatively weak—and this includes most people. And reactions remain in place due to another law of the physics of motion (or the effects of one force on another): What is already set in motion—such as a reaction—tends to remain in motion, or effect, until it is redirected, usually by another force or influence.

The "normal" patterns in our lives are mostly frozen reactions. We do not hope to simply drop the patterns themselves. They seem necessary and inevitable to us—because no other influence is present to change the reactive or contracting motion of the body-mind. Therefore, we accept chronically reactive or contracted physical, emotional, and mental patterns in our lives as simply the given structures wherein we must move to find our pleasurable satisfactions. We do not often reflect on the patterns themselves or the circumstances of their origin. Nor do we fully consider the significance of the pleasure we attain through release of chronic tension of body, emotion, and mind.

The "normal" patterns in our lives are, therefore, as "abnormal" as any reactive fixation and solution. All of our patterns of personally pleasurable tension-release are of the same ultimate kind. They are self-possessed, degenerative, and effectively separative, even anti-social, but always relatively loveless. Such patterns are not patterns of ecstasy—or surrender of the entire self into the prior Reality—but they are only patterns that pursue an internal or personal sense of self that is at least temporarily pleasurable and that is derived from acts that discharge personal functional tension.

Our lives are filled with rituals of this kind. Indeed, such a way of life is considered "normal" and "human," as long as the rituals are not too bizarre or unpredictable. But, truly, the way of life that essentially seeks pleasurable tension-release is not human in the fullest or ecstatic sense of Divine Realization.

Thus, the consideration of Truth or God through the Teaching Argument and the Transcendental Demonstration or Influence of the Spiritual Master are the primary means of truly human change. And such change is not only from relatively "bizarre" patterns to relatively "normal" patterns. It is a change from repetitive sub-human patterns of reactivity and degenerative tension-release to truly human or superhuman responsibilities of ecstatic and regen-erative or entirely self-released Communion with the Divine Condi-tion of our existence.

108

The Way of Divine Ignorance is founded on a call to self-obser-vation and conversion of the entire direction or reactive tendency of our lives. It requires the consideration of the past circumstantial origins, reactive contents, and tension-release goals of our charac-teristic patterns of activity. And it generates the awakening of primary pleasure, ecstasy, and love as a force that transcends and transforms the reactive motions, past, present, and future, of the body-mind. Thus, devotees in this Way do not merely "normalize" their patterns of living (although this may be true in some ordinary sense), but they are moved in an entirely new direction. They move on from self-meditative patterns of contraction, and they move into the self-released ecstasy of Divine Communion.

This transformation of the motion and pleasure of the body-mind is effective in many areas of our living that we would never have otherwise considered changing. Thus, the "normal" patterns of self-indulgence in gross and degenerative diet and drink, or in casual social amusements that only reflect the reactive vulgarity of childish people, or in sexual addiction to orgasm—even all of these patterns are interrupted and transcended in ecstasy. And the matur-ing of the life of ecstatic love and transcendental intuition of the Divine, via all functions and relations, demonstrates both human and superhuman growth through adaptation beyond the vital and lower mental functions exploited in the childhood of Man.

The Secret of How to Change

True change and higher human adaptation are not made on the basis of any self-conscious resistance to old, degenerative, and subhuman habits. Change is not a matter of <u>not</u> doing something. It is a matter of doing something <u>else</u>, something that is inherently right, free, and pleasurable. Therefore, the key is insight and the freedom to feel and participate in ways of functioning that are right and new.

The tendencies and patterns of our earlier adaptations are not wrong. They were appropriate enough in their own moment of creation, and there is no need to feel guilt or despair about them. Likewise, efforts to oppose and change them are basically fruitless. Such efforts are forms of conflict, and they only reinforce the modes of self-possession.

What is not used becomes obsolete, whereas what is opposed is kept before us. Therefore, the creative principle of change is the one of relaxed inspection and awareness of existing tendencies and persistent, full feeling orientation to right, new, regenerative functional patterns. If this is done consistently and in ecstatic resort to the Living Divine, free growth is assured.

Have no regrets. Resort to the Divine in Truth and in the present. All that has been done by anyone had its logic in its time. Only God avails. Whatever is your habit in this moment is not wrong. It is simply a beginning. No habit is necessary, but it is only tending to persist, because it has not yet been replaced by further growth. Hear the Teaching of Truth, and understand what is the right, ultimate, and regenerative pattern of each function of Man. Feel free of all negative judgments about what you have done and what you tend to do. Turn with full feeling-attention to the creative affair of new adaptation in most positive Communion with the God who is Life, and who is Alive as all beings.

The genital motivation is a primary drive that causes the condition of life and mind constantly to phase and fall, through dramatization of the reactive tendencies of old adaptation, into problematic states and confusions. Therefore, the process of sexual communion is simply right adaptation to sexual play, but, as such, it is a process in which genital play itself becomes a graceful pleasure without necessity. Genital play becomes secondary to the general *conductivity* or whole body diffusion and effulgence of the Life-Force. Thus, a true and motiveless economy of sexual activity naturally follows in the maturity of the practice of sexual communion.

Three Suitcases

I know three jokes about surprises in a suitcase. Actually, they are three stories, each told to me by a relative or a friend who was personally involved in one of the incidents I will describe.

The first story is that one time my uncle and another fellow went hunting in California, and they set up a snare to catch a wildcat. Sure enough, a wildcat was caught in the trap. They decided to put the wildcat into a suitcase, and they put the suitcase out on the highway. Then my uncle and his friend hid behind the trees and waited and watched. Many cars approached the suitcase, slowed down, and then passed it by. But, finally, a big car drove up. The car had three rows of seats, and a complete family of three generations was in the car, including a fat grandma and grandpa in the back seat. The car slowed down as it approached the suitcase. And then the front door opened, and a hand reached out for the suitcase and pulled it in, as the car picked up speed and shot away!

The second story is that one time my aunt, who lived in New York City, had a dog, and the dog died. She had no place to bury the dog, so she put it in a suitcase and went to the subway station. She intended to travel to Long Island, where her nephew lived, and to bury the dog there. While she waited for the train to arrive, she put the suitcase down on the subway platform. When the train arrived, she reached down for the suitcase and discovered that someone had stolen it!

The third story is that one time my old landlady prepared a rabbit for Christmas dinner in Germany. And she decided to play a trick. She took all of the guts and leavings and put them in a suitcase—or was it a Christmas package? Anyway, she left the suitcase in the back seat of her car—which she left unlocked and with open windows. When she looked into her car the next day, someone had stolen the suitcase!

Somehow, I think these stories are all about life and death, and something we do to try to survive. Sex is about life and death and it is something we commonly do to try to survive. The three stories are about tricks or pranks people play on one another. And ordinary sex is a kind of trick or prank people play on one another. Ordinary sex is a way of stealing something that belongs to another, or that is somehow hidden in the secret insides of everything. It is Life. But when it is secretly taken, or grasped for one's private pleasure, it is like a wildcat, or a dead animal, or the dead and vulgar insides of something that is no longer alive. Then it is a form of deception, and cunning, and hoarding, and self-possession. Then it kills and corrupts and disappoints and makes us dull. But when sexual embrace is a matter of love and self-surrender, then Life is found most directly, and we are certainly Full. Then it is as if my uncle, and my aunt, and my old landlady opened up the suitcase, and it contained a precious suit of lights!

Conventional sex play is a vicarious participation in an ordinary or degenerate death. Death also has a regenerative and true form which coincides with enlightened sacrifice of the whole bodily being. Sacrifice is our obligation and our happiness, but we are by tendency turned toward obsessive repetition of concrete experiences themselves. We suffer a profound need for release, since we do not simply live as a feeling sacrifice. Release becomes the ritual moment of "sacrifice" in the unenlightened life. Therefore, sex play is an obsessive interest or concern of most people.

We must realize our position and obligation in Truth, and so live as sacrifice or love rather than as an entity merely struggling to survive and to accumulate experiences and consoling conditions of existence. In that case, we will abandon the sexual obsession and stop dramatizing the failure to love and to be a sacrifice. Thus, we must bring an end to ritual pursuit of genital orgasm.

112

Once we realize that feeling sacrifice is our Law and need, we will die through love with every breath. Then release is no longer a need to be fulfilled through obsessive repetition of egoic or self-possessed rituals of our born functions. We will move beyond satisfaction of the self-body to continuous sacrifice of self-possessed conditions.

What is sought through the ritual of sexual release can only be realized in the Lawful transformation of the disposition of the whole bodily being—from the self-possession of Narcissus to the sacrifice of love into Infinity. When nothing is held onto and fear ceases to motivate action, then the conventional functions of life are released of their ritual burden and become priorly released or established in the pleasure of Infinity. Give yourself up whole bodily to feeling or radiance under all conditions, and you will no longer seek a symbolic moment of fascinated death in obsessive sexual release. Once the native pleasure of sacrifice or love is realized, there is no need for the negatively orgiastic moment of oblivion to obtain the feeling of ease. Then sexual love becomes ecstasy, which is sacrifice of the self-position and of bodily and emotional contraction. In that case, the orgasm is translated into free, whole body delight, even as death itself is Translation into the Divine Domain or Destiny in the case of true devotees.

Why Can't We Feel Such Pleasure All the Time?
A talk given by Bubba Free John to his devotees

BUBBA: In our ordinary living we depend on the ceremony of sexual intercourse for a certain sense of energy, a certain ability to contemplate energy, that we do not allow ourselves on any other occasion, unless we are devotees of the Living God. For the usual man, the only ceremony wherein he can experience a heightening of pleasure is sex. Everything else is a side show, a pseudo-pleasure, a pseudo-heightening of awareness and energy. It is at the level of sex that the usual man truly feels the energy of Life.

Like all common men and women, you have not adapted to your existence beyond childhood. You have become aware of yourself physically and emotionally, but you have not yet become responsible for either body or emotion. Thus, you are simply subject to the influence of manifest existence. The only ceremony wherein your pleasure can be heightened to the point of ecstasy is sexual intercourse. It is the only moment of your <u>complete</u> attention and feeling. Of course, you entertain this ecstasy only very briefly. You work toward the moment wherein you feel completely consumed by pleasure, wherein your whole body feels pleasure, and then there is a sudden spasm and it is over. This is the only moment of ecstasy, of distraction from yourself, wherein the whole nervous system becomes involved, and you waste it in this spasm. You perhaps control the pleasure to a point, but the release is inevitable, in the orgasm or in whatever emotional contraction you engage, and that is the end of it. You fall asleep or you get up in your gentlemanly or gentlewomanly fashion and go about your business.

Why do we experience a heightened level of pleasure only through this liturgy, this exercise, this quite ordinary event? Sex is just the frictional stimulation of a piece of the bodily being. And yet the mind, the emotions, and all our functions are completely involved in it and fascinated by it. Have any of you observed this? Sex is not even absolutely satisfying. It does not bring your desire to an end. It is just a certain pleasure by association for a moment, and then it disappears. Then all day long you experience the same craving, the same urge toward pleasurable release. What is it? Is it mysterious or is it really very ordinary? If we can become fully aware of it, would we see that it is just a ritual? You are not now completely aware of what sex is. You are submitted to it, by tendency associated with it, but if you could become completely aware of the whole affair, the whole act, the whole experience, not just in the moment of genital contact but in all the moments that precede it, all the games by which you prepare yourself for orgasm and genital meeting—if you could be aware of the whole thing, is it really mysterious any more? Are we really cut off from blissfulness except in that moment? Is it really true that you can experience the stimulation of the nervous system only in sexual embrace? If it is so pleasurable, why can't you experience the stimulation of the nervous system under all conditions and without wasting the Life-Force? Why go through the crisis of orgasm? Why can't you be ecstatic and innately full of pleasure under all conditions?

Why can't you be happy? If you are already happy, prior to all events, circumstances, and stimulations, then sex is no longer an obsession. Your pleasure is no longer determined by the event of sex. Your pleasure is inherent. Why can't we then enjoy the stimulation of the nervous system, of the cells, of the physical body—why can't we be in that condition all the time? Do you think it is impossible? Do you have to see a sexual organ in order to be stimulated to a state of pleasure?

Why can't we be always in a condition of enjoyment, not just psychologically, but even physically? Why can't we be always radiant, like the Siva we see in pictures, sitting there all blue with a jet of milk pouring out of his head? He is always enjoying the pleasure of orgasm, yet he is losing nothing. He does not experience the depression that you experience when you release all of your energy, all of your pleasure, in a crisis of orgasm. He is always enjoying that moment of ecstasy. He is not dependent on any ritual in the daily mechanics of life for his pleasure. He is not dependent on anything for his pleasure. He is already in a state of pleasure. Thus, he is a lover, and not because he needs his husband or wife to feel pleasure. He _is_ pleasure, he _is_ ecstasy, he _is_ happy, he _is_ love.

How many of you enjoy sex from that point of view? No—you _need_ the pleasure of sex. That is why you are so trapped in it. That is why you bind yourselves to one another. That is why you are so full of jealousy and hatred and unlove. That is why you do not even love when you make love. There is no humor in your lovemaking, no real pleasure. It is a very solemn matter. You do not even smile. You very seriously move through the ritual, meditating only on stimulation. How mediocre! And the rest of your life is humorless and stupid, full of anger and fear. The only time you brighten up a little bit is in the old open-legged vulgarity, TV at night, the excess, the spasm wherein you throw out your life.

But none of you is a lover. You are barbarians. You make love in order to feel pleasure. Thus, your sexuality is not about love. You are only hopeful for love. So what are you doing? You are trying to be happy with one person, trying to realize the archetype in your husband or wife, struggling against your own native unhappiness and lack of pleasure, trying to find through this ritual some release, some consolation, some way to get up in the morning and do whatever it is you do from day to day, or straining against your sexual impulse to remain somehow inverted in your attention, to remain projected upon the inward magnificence, always struggling from the point of view of your own independence, trying to become happy.

The true devotee, man or woman, must pass far beyond the ritual of orgasm. Pleasure is inherent. Our Bliss is God-Communion. It is at the heart, not in the genitals nor in the third eye, but it pervades the whole body and even the world. It is essential. It is the Law. One who is already full of such pleasure, already happy, can be a lover of Man and of God.

115

Chapter 9

Sexual Communion Is
Transcendence of Self and Lover

People commonly think they cannot pass beyond guilt, fear, anger, sorrow, jealousy, and other reactive emotions. They feel that all these, and all other forms of emotional dependence or separativeness, are simply the "given" of human life, the necessary and unique emotional qualities of the individual human personality. They resign themselves to a lifetime of promiscuous inclinations and pornographic inward mentality. Perhaps they even try to believe all this is also good and true and right by glamorizing their "sexual freedom," emotional "honesty," and "rich" fantasy life.

But all of this is subhuman, totally unnecessary, and easily transcended, if only we will hear the Teaching of Truth and begin to awaken at the heart, as devotees of God. The awakening devotee neither suppresses nor exploits his subhuman emotional and sexual tendencies. He simply is obliged to love, to live in Divine Communion, to be happy and free as feeling-attention no matter what arises in life and mind. He does this consistently, under all conditions, and then, when he approaches his lover to engage in sexual play, he enjoys an intimate and bodily Revelation of God that is unknown and unsuspected in the common world.

Ecstasy Is Realized Only in Relationship

Self-Possession and Divine Communion

The conditions of experience, high and low, must <u>all</u> be transcended. This is the Law—every thing must be a sacrifice in God. In each moment we are confronted by a Divine Test, in the form of our experience. We may yield all conditions and Commune with God, or we may choose self and relations and things and experiential states, and thus turn out of the Infinite toward passing illusions.

It is not that we must forsake all relations, functions, and conditions of experience. Such only leads toward self-possessed inversion, and possession by the illusions of structural inwardness. Rather, we must transform all relations, functions, and conditions of experience into forms of Communion with the Radiant Consciousness that is the Divine, Present to Man in the World.

If we thus transform all our conditions, we ultimately transcend all our conditions in the Fullness of the Living Divine. The Divine is never known in itself, as an object of our own functional awareness. Rather, the Divine Reality is that Condition with which we may only Commune, through functional and literal self-surrender. And when we Commune with the Divine, we are relieved of self-consciousness and all sense of confinement to conditions of the body-mind. Therefore, to Commune with the Divine is to lose oneself, to be Ecstatic, to be emptied of all knowledge, forms, limits, and conditions.

The usual man or woman recoils from the Mystery of the Infinite by absorption in the reaction of mortal fear. Thus, fear produces self-possession and loss of Communion with the Divine. Such recoil produces psycho-physical adaptation of a reactive kind, and every function, every relationship, every condition of experience, high or low in the structure of the body-mind, becomes a reflection of the primal recoil toward self, away from all relations, and away from Communion with the Living Mystery that is Divine. The self-possessed individual is wound up in self-recoil, and every part demonstrates the reactive drama of relational avoidance, subjective bondage, and bodily dis-ease.

There must be Awakening from this reactive bind of self. That Awakening comes through sudden "hearing" and "seeing" of Truth. The Spiritual Master is Awake, and he, with all devotees in Truth, serves that same Awakening in others. But that Awakening is not only sudden and present. It is the seed of the ongoing Process of Life.

Those who are Awake must be a whole and total and constant and ecstatic Sacrifice into the Divine, or else they are Godless and self-possessed. And those who are self-possessed only acquire suffering, in the form of experience. How can we be such a Sacrifice? Only by Awakening from the entire experiential self, and thus passing into Divine Communion. And we must allow that Awakening to transform the habitual and reactive and self-possessed tendencies of every part of the body-mind, or else Divine Communion itself becomes only a consoling illusion of the separate self.

The psycho-physical self in recoil from Ecstasy is submitted to structural tensions at every level of the bodily being. And such a one obsessively seeks release from these tensions through the acquisition of consoling personal pleasures and forms of knowledge. Through pleasure and knowledge Narcissus controls the frightening world, until he dies alone. But one who Awakens into ecstatic or self-released Divine Communion abides and is Transformed in the Fullness of Life. The true devotee of the Divine is an ecstatic Sacrifice in the Divine. He is alive in Fullness, not dying through convulsive and repetitive cycles of tension and release of tension.

Devotees in the Way of Divine Ignorance are Awake to self-released or ecstatic Communion with the Radiant Divine, via all functions, in all relations, under all conditions. They gradually adapt to the Condition of Fullness of Life, in which the body-mind is priorly free and whole and disposed toward regenerative activity. They do this rather than submit to the conventional state of total psycho-physical tension, or reactive self-possession, in which the body-mind chronically seeks degenerative release of tension. In Divine Communion we breathe the Life of God from the heart, and the body-mind is dissolved at Infinity.

119

Life Is the Urge to Ecstasy

T he constant purpose of manifest existence is ecstasy. But there is nothing <u>within</u> us that can produce ecstasy. To be "ecstatic" literally means to stand outside oneself or to be released of oneself—to transcend oneself. Therefore, ecstasy is not produced by experience, or by any kind of higher or lower knowledge, or even by self-knowledge. Ecstasy is realized only through sacrifice of self—which is fulfillment of the universal Law. Ecstasy is realizable only in relationship, not in inwardness. It is realized through moral and esoteric spiritual or transcendental sacrifice of self, or the whole body-mind, via all the kinds of relations, into the Transcendental Condition and Life-Intensity that is Absolute. Ecstasy is realized through love, which is surrender of self-attention and reactivity via unobstructed feeling-attention in all relations and to the degree of Infinity.

T he whole bodily motive of our sexual "urge" is not toward orgasm, or bodily fulfillment of self-generated desire. It is toward ecstasy, or release of the independent, partial, and divided condition of the self, or body-mind. It is a motive that necessarily and only finds its fulfillment in relationship. All self-possessed or Narcissistic uses of this possibility (or any other human possibility) only reinforce the anti-ecstatic mood of self, enhancing its problematic complexities, and deepening the desperate sense that manifest existence is inherently a dilemma. Only in the play of Life does the dilemma of self become the paradox of ecstasy.

The functional fulfillment of the sexual motive and urge should awaken us to the primal sense of unity, wholeness, and fullness, both of the totality of existence and of our own person. The individual, of either sex, should be continually awakened as the paradox that is the ecstatic person—appearing and functioning in ordinary ways, but happily, and attuned via all relations to Transcendental Communion with the Radiant Reality and Truth.

Ecstasy Is the Means
of Self-Realization

The essential function of ecstasy is the entire release of feeling and attention from meditation on the psycho-physical limits and reactive contents of the person, the soul in manifestation. When ecstasy becomes the case, the soul is Realized as the Self, transcending manifestation, or all possible experience. Then we are released into all our possible relations and into the absolute Intensity or Reality that is the always present Source of everything.

People use sex obsessively, as a way of acquiring the illusion of ecstasy, because they are unable to realize true ecstasy through the whole life of love and intuition of the Real.

In the truly ecstatic life, sex is a profound intensity, a yoga of love, free of obsession, conflict, and all intentions that confine the self to itself.

The Urge to Repetition

The "problem" of sex may not be identified with any of its specific pleasures or associations. The problem of sex is not in sex itself. The problem of sex is the same problem that appears in the theatre of all our functions. It is attachment to the consoling, self-defining power of experience. It is the urge to repetition. The problem of sex is the problem of experience in itself, when experience is not submitted to love. The problem of sex is the problem in all experience. It is the problem of again-ness, or repetition of the thing itself. If sex is submitted to love, it is never repeated, but is always a <u>present</u> devotional discipline, sacrifice, and pleasure. Whatever is not submitted to love binds us to itself. Therefore, sex, which is our most intense pleasure below the heart, binds us to repetition and unlove—unless we are free to embrace one another while abiding in perpetual Communion with the Radiant Divine.

Whatever is personally pleasurable tends to console body and mind. Pleasure of any kind creates a temporary and thus illusory sense of ecstasy, or of freedom and release from the self-division or double-bind of the mind-body complex. Thus, whatever is pleasurable is well remembered, or stored up as impulse, desire, and general reinforcement of the hopefulness of self-possession. Likewise, what has proved to be pleasurable tends to be compulsively and ritually sought and repeated.

The urge to repetition of what has proved to be pleasurable is the primary source of uncreative, self-possessed, dull, enervating, and destructive habits of living. The fault is not in pleasure, since pleasure is only a possible and ordinary effect associated with the larger circumstance of any present activity. The fault is in repetition of past pleasure, in itself or for its own sake. The fault occurs when activity ceases to be generated as a creative, self-yielding enterprise of the whole body-mind in the present, and instead becomes devotion of self, bodily or mentally, to the specific goal of the personal experience of known pleasure, or the repetition of past pleasures.

When action is primarily devotion to a specific and self-fulfilling effect, rather than an expression of the Lawful or relational and sacrificial disposition of self in the moment, then it becomes a degenerative and ultimately antipleasurable exercise or habit.

Intentional repetition of any specific and known pleasure itself bypasses the creative and Lawful obligation of self. Therefore, only right orientation and action, moment to moment, is both pleasurable and ecstatic, or self-releasing.

Ecstasy may be associated with pleasurable states of body and mind in any moment. But pleasure is not in itself ecstasy. The repetition of what is known to create pleasure only frustrates ecstatic self-release, and obsessive habits of intentionally acquiring pleasure for its own sake necessarily dull the mind and enervate the body. The cycle of mere pleasure-seeking is childish. It reflects the childish sense of separation from what sustains and consoles, and the equally childish delight in the attainment of reunion with the parent-force in instants of the pleasurable satisfaction of vital desire.

123

The cycle of self-possessed, habitual, and obsessive repetition of known pleasures must be broken, or we remain dull or superficial children until death. Death itself is the great fascination of those who depend on the repetition of everything that death brings to an end. And, paradoxically, the habit of pleasurable repetition hastens death through progressive degeneration and dis-ease.

The only way the cycle of repetition is broken is to cease the chronic indulgence of the consoling pattern of repetitions and always do everything freely, as a creative gesture of self-release. It is not a matter of the rigid and self-conscious attempt to never do anything twice. Rather, it is a matter of growing, through moment to moment adaptation, into a disposition, in ordinary or common action, that is truly ecstatic, or self-releasing. This requires the total inspection of one's life, the awakening of transforming insight, and the intelligent acceptance of personal and moral responsibilities in the functional and relational patterns of experience. Then love, rather than repetition of pleasures or known results, becomes the principle of life and action. And the life of love is regenerative, and always free, whereas the life of repetition is degenerative and always bound by illusions.

V ital sexual desire and genital orgasm belong only to a part of the body-mind, and they serve the orientation to self rather than self-sacrifice. Thus, when these become the motive and result of sexual practice, the whole body-mind becomes separative through the self orientation. And patterns of sexual obsession and self-conscious fear tend to develop, since inherent pleasure of life is forgotten and true ecstasy becomes impossible.

Wherever love or relational sacrifice of self (the yielding of feeling-attention into relationship) is not the motive of our functional disposition and activity, then ecstasy is, by definition, frustrated, and there is neither tranquility nor creative force in our living. Therefore, love must become the principle that masters desire. Desire must be permitted to awaken in relationship rather than remain as a constant and subjective characteristic of self. And love must transform the process of desire in sexual play in order that sexuality involve the whole bodily being and liberate it from both internal and relational conflicts.

A ny process and any enjoyment that depends on the mechanics of experience (rather than on participation and ecstasy through feeling) may also be duplicated and imitated mechanically.

The urge to repeat an experience is an urge to the ecstasy of a previous occasion. Thus, it is not truly an urge to the experience itself, but to ecstasy. However, people tend not to discriminate between experience, or occasion, and ecstasy. Thus, they methodically seek and mechanically tend to seek repetition of particular experiences, circumstances, and so forth. As a result, over time, people have a lot of experience but realize very little ecstasy. They are fixed in mechanical association with habits, desires, fetishes, ideas, places, mannerisms, rituals, types of intimates, and so forth.

The mechanics of the manifest universe appear to conspire with all our repetitive tendencies, to reduce us to irresponsible, robotlike, serious, reactive, ridiculous, and feelingless people, fixed to repetitions, incapable of ecstasy—incapable of release of self and its mechanical demands or limits. Thus, we must realize the capacity to discriminate between the mechanical and the ecstatic processes of our living. And, having so discriminated, we must freely choose the responsible way of ecstasy, sacrifice, or love, in every moment. And we must likewise enjoy a moment to moment capacity to abandon or eschew mechanical urges or tendencies toward ritualistic repetition of patterns of past experience. "Karma" is acquired tendency, or the destiny of mechanical repetition of the past, without the freedom to release the whole and entire body-mind to ecstasy in the present. "Freedom" is the capacity for ecstasy, or conscious and responsible self-release, moment to moment, via all functions of the body-mind, in all relations, under all conditions.

Sexual intercourse realized as sexual communion in a responsible relationship is a way of living the sacrifice that is love and of intensifying the perfection of that sacrifice, not only in sex play or marriage, but in all one's relations and conditions of existence. Right adaptation to sexual intimacy purifies the tendencies of attention, and it acts as a theatre of preparation for the perfect realization of transcendental or whole body sacrifice.

Orgasm, or sex in itself, is not the purpose or principal value of sexual play. Sexual communion, with conservation of the bio-energy and chemistry stimulated in the process, is not an end in itself, but a way of adapting the sexual function to the Law of sacrifice. Thus, sexual play must be lived in Truth, or else it is not true. In sexual play, as under any other conditions, we must remain in perfect alignment, through the sacrifice that is free feeling-attention, or love, with the intuition and the process of our Condition at Infinity—the Condition of the whole bodily being and the world.

Self-Sacrifice and Self-Denial

The process of self-sacrifice is not to be casually equated with the activity of self-denial. Self-denial tends to reinforce the contraction, isolation, and emptiness of the body-mind. But self-sacrifice is always a matter of ecstasy, or release of the contraction and isolation and emptiness of the body-mind into the prior Fullness of Radiant Existence. Self-denial is at best an occasional purifying technique or, at times, a moral necessity for love's sake. But whenever it is applied it must itself be transformed through the disposition of love, of self-release, of ecstatic sacrifice of the independent self or body-mind in the Living Reality that pervades all beings and things.

Everything of which the individual is free, or of which he is the master, is the foundation on which his life stands and moves. And everything of which the individual is not free or the master stands and moves as him, essentially preventing his freedom and mastery.

The absence of freedom and mastery relative to one's entire person, including each unique function, and every area of experience, actual or potential, is the evidence, the substance, and the ordinary cause of the neurotic sense of dilemma and the persistence of life as if it were inherently a problem.

The true man does not destroy his life and sex, nor does he exploit it as one who is without understanding. Rather, he stands up as his life, the sexual character, male or female, and makes his life and breath and heartbeat an instrument of Translation from the lesser to the greater and Absolute speeds of Light.

Sexual stimulation until orgasm is the most readily available intense pleasure of the extended human organism. For this very reason, those whose adaptation is, for one or another reason, limited to the willful and self-possessed exploitation of the vital functions and the verbal mind are obsessed with the sensations and problems of sexuality.

However, human happiness is not realizable by exploitation of either the most common or the most extraordinary capacities for experience. Happiness, free of fear, is realized only in ecstasy, or total liberation from psycho-physical limits. Such ecstasy is realized only in true, higher, and radical religio-spiritual devotion and practice, in which the individual life is sacrificed, through love and intuition, into the Divine Life.

127

True Desire Is the Expression of Love

True desire is not lust. Lust is obsessive interest in the sexual opportunity represented by others, whereby the orgasm and the frenzy of erotic distraction may be acquired. True desire is an expression of love. It is a movement toward one's intimate friend, via sexual feeling, and its fulfillment frees attention and love, passing then beyond orgasm, release, and functional distraction into Communion with the Infinite Mystery wherein this play of lovers appears.

Couples should live their Life together as a continuous polarized play of feeling-attention. Such stimulates and communicates the Life-Force bodily and awakens the chemistry of the whole bodily being. They should gradually, however, come to a natural discipline of relaxing genital stress and releasing the communicated Life to the whole body, with feeling to Infinity. Thus, the occasions of genital play will probably become less and less frequent (or at least more and more true).

The same polarization must exist between all devotees and the Spiritual Master, except that the genital play is not enacted (but is reserved for the play between the devotee and his or her lover or spouse in the world). The relationship between the Spiritual Master and the devotee is a polarized play in the full spiritual sense, and it involves mutual sacrifice, realized more and more perfectly over time, in which there is release of higher and Divine Energies to and from the whole bodily being of the devotee.

The satisfaction of self-motivated and conventional "love" is in passionless or self-based, and therefore ultimately love-less, regard of others.

The satisfaction of self-motivated desire is in the discharge of the Life-Force, and the temporary elimination of the pain of desire itself, through self-indulgence and orgasm.

But love-desire is called into existence by the loved-one, not oneself. And its satisfaction is in self-releasing service and fullness of feeling for the loved-one.

Love-desire is the principle in action of the process of sexual communion. Therefore, as the process matures, the forms of self-possession dissolve in the Realization of whole bodily Fullness of Life. Over time, self-involved detachment, self-motivated regard of others, and self-emptying desire for release of reactive tensions are all dissolved in transcendental Bliss, or that unselfed Love and Fullness which is the very Radiance of Life.

Thus, as sexual communion matures, the quality of love-desire is relieved of the superimposed associations with conventional love and desire, and love-desire, or true Love, comes to characterize the relationship between lovers more and more absolutely. Ultimately, self-involvement, reactivity, casual association, and chronic conflict are transcended in the Intensity or native Happiness of Divine Fullness. The transformation is not toward inversion, inwardness, or passionless seclusion in oneself, but toward a profound relational intensity and freedom from the self-binding and limiting effects of bodily and mental reactivity.

E ven love-desire is a form of recoil, or differentiation at Infinity. It is a specific functional expression of manifest, differentiated existence. Therefore, as the process of reactive differentiation weakens, ultimately becoming an obsolete reflex, the functional play of natural differentiation becomes more and more simple and serene. In spiritual maturity, functional love-desire is transformed by love itself, which is itself Translated into Bliss. This occurs through radical sacrifice of the body-mind, the self, the experiential point of view.

The occasion of sexual communion may remain, until late in life, or until the end of life, but, even so, it is transformed, economized, perfectly mastered, and, ultimately, yielded at Infinity. In the case of devotees in the Way of Divine Ignorance, the transcendental Play of the whole bodily being inevitably consumes and transforms the piecemeal functional exercise of conventional interest or motivation. Thus, sexual communion expands into a transcendental spiritual occasion.

Transcendence of Self and Lover

I n sexual communion we realize the Way in which sexual activity may be made into Communion with the Divine Life. Sexual communion is not a method of superior sexual fulfillment of the need for orgasm, or degenerative release of tension. Rather it is the process of regenerative sexual surrender to the

All-Pervading Life, so that self and other and conflict and orgasm are all transcended in Divine Fullness. Sexual communion is the sexual love of Life.

Ordinary sexual activity is an infantile method for releasing personal psycho-physical tension, by manipulation of self and others. The conventional games of sex are thus erotic, romantic, exploitative, and ultimately degenerative.

And social taboos surround our sexuality like a thicket of prickly thorns. We do well to rebel against sexual suppression, which only reinforces our childish and adolescent self-possession. But, in the process, we must transcend conventional genital sexuality itself, and this requires that we transcend not only ourselves but our lovers.

Sexual communion, or Communion with the All-Pervading Divine Life through genital and whole bodily sexual activity, is the uniquely human form of sexual activity. The conventional erotic and romantic games of sexuality are essentially dramatizations of mutual conflict and self-division. Therefore, ordinary sexual "fulfillment" is itself only a subhuman and self-possessed attainment of temporary vital pleasure.

Sexual communion involves functional psycho-physical submission or ecstatic love-surrender of self into the All-Pervading Life, via one's lover. Neither self nor lover, the ordinary consoler of self, is the goal or meaning of sexual communion. Rather, the whole process of self and other is ecstatically released into and integrated with the Radiant Life of the Infinite.

Therefore, true lovers are always already free of themselves and of one another. They love and respond to one another through ecstatic Communion with Radiant Divine Life. But they do not bind one another through the separative and self-possessed games of degenerative eroticism and "cultic" romance.

One who is a lover in God sees only the Divine Life expressed in and as the one he or she loves. When Life is recognized to be the Truth of the loved-one, then Life becomes the Loved-One. Thus, it is just such recognition of Life in the form of one's lover and the process of sexual relationship that makes true love possible and relieves the relationship of morbid self-possession, jealousy, binding attachment, and romantic illusions. Those who embrace the Divine in psycho-physical ecstasy of all kinds transcend self and other and are always already free in God.

Every Kind of Action Must Be Engaged as Love-Communion with the Living God

S exual communion is not about "cultic" attachment and obsessive fascination relative to one's lover. It is about ecstatic or self-releasing Communion with the All-Pervading Force of Life, via every function of the body-mind, and via one's lover. Neither one's own body-mind nor one's lover is the goal or ultimate object of sexual communion, but the Divine Life is itself the constant meditation of every part and moment. Therefore, self and lover are both sacrificed in the Divine Life in the process of sexual communion.

Just so, regenerative diet, health practice, and other personal and moral disciplines of the Way of Divine Communion are not merely about "health food," the ideal of nonkilling, or any conventional economic, social, or political intention. All practices in this Way are about whole bodily ecstatic Communion with the All-Pervading Divine Life. And through each particular discipline a different aspect or function of the body-mind is literally adapted to the All-Pervading Life. Ultimately, by all these means and more, the whole and entire body-mind is Translated or Dissolved into that Life and Divine Destiny.

We Must Awaken from the
Spell of Our Childishness

132 Jealousy is a profound dis-ease of the sexual relationship. It is a reflection of our childish vulnerability to rejection, or the withdrawal of love. It is only when the individual realizes that love is the Law and Radiance of Reality and, therefore, his or her own most fundamental obligation, that there is freedom from jealousy—as well as all other reactive or recoiling emotions. If there is not love, or unobstructed, noncontracting feeling-attention <u>as</u> you, then it does not truly exist for you at all. In that case it is only an external or circumstantial possibility, either coming to console you or else leaving and rejecting you—just like a parent!

We do not own our lovers. We are intimate with them, committed to them, in love with them—as they with us. This is sufficient to keep us freely in one another's company for a lifetime. But even if your lover were to love another, it is not rejection. In that case, your lover, as ever with you, is simply doing his or her own pleasure. You are still obliged to love, to be full at Infinity, and to let him or her pass. Only one thus free to be separated from his or her lover is free to love his or her lover. We may be separated from lovers by changes and death, but love is only present or not in our own case—since its presence or absence in our own case is simply a sign of our degree of participation in transcendental Communion or Bliss.

We must be able to tolerate, through our spiritual responsibility in Truth, not only the appearance and continuation of our lover, but also his or her changes, death, and even withdrawal or separation from us. Only on such a basis can an intimacy have the strength and pleasure sufficient for a lifetime. And such strength and pleasure come not from childish dependence on the attention of another, but on our own responsible love and intimate commitment of attention to another. Such is true of marriages, friendships, and, ultimately, all relationships.

One who is responsible for love, or energy in relationship, is already fundamentally free of jealousy, and the old habits or tendencies of jealousy that may remain will gradually fall away if he or she persists in the practice of love rather than the drama of the fear of rejection.

I magine a pair of Siamese twins, joined at the chest, and with a common heart, so they can never be surgically separated. They are otherwise a rather attractive pair of individuals, and generally like any Siamese twins of which you may have heard, with one exception: One is male and the other female.

They will be obliged to be the lifelong intimates of one another. They are two, and yet the single heart makes them also one. They experience many things as if they had the same body. Many phenomena of the nervous system, the blood system, and the glandular system are experienced in common and simultaneously. Their sensual and psychic states of awareness often coincide. In many ways they are as one body, or at least the two halves, right and left, or back and front, of one body. And yet, they also relate to one another as separate individuals—while also experiencing a tacit and preverbal sense of their common identity.

The situation appears somehow grotesque. This pair is the ultimate "freak," because their mutual singularity and their mutual independence are both in equal evidence. And both their personal and their sexual intimacy with one another is also inevitable. How could even love lead them elsewhere, since they are always face to face?

This individual and pair is the ultimate archetype of the conventional and erotic embrace of couples. Each only serves himself in his inevitable contact with the other. And the underlying identity of all individuals makes incest out of every embrace. The self-serving union of individuals is not the truly human function of sex. Uniquely human sexuality is self-transcending or ecstatic. The truly human lover does not merely embrace another for the sake of pleasures that his own body may register. Rather, human sexuality is the embrace of another as a gesture or process of ecstatic Communion with the Divine Reality that transcends self and other. The ecstasy of true lovers is not in personal sensual stimulations and tension-releasing orgasms, nor in the mortal personal characteristics of the one they embrace. The ecstasy of true lovers is in transcendence of the body-mind of both self and other in Divine Communion.

134

We Must Consent to Become Agents of Life

We cannot ultimately depend on any of our objective relations (high or low in the scale of manifestation) for love, attention, support, sustenance, or their unchanging continuation through time and space. First of all, we discover that our relations are themselves generally dependent and undependable, changing or mortal, coming and going, and always changing the objects and the quality of their feeling and attention. Thus, if we depend on them, we will surely feel betrayed, and anxious about the line of love or Life that feeds us through our relations. Then we become possessed in our relations with the testing mood of "You don't love me." But, more than this, if we depend on love or Life to come to us through our relations, then we ourselves tend to remain irresponsible as love or attention and Life. Always watching to see if we are loved, fed, and our pleasure and existence protected, we never abide as love simply. Such is the error in our childish and adolescent adaptation to born existence.

We enter our maturity and our true humanity when we come to terms not only with the variability in the energy that comes through our relations, but with our own reaction to that observation. The child adapts to the energy that comes through relations and becomes dependent. Then, as experience becomes more objective and complex, the sense of betrayal (as possibility or actuality) begins to intensify. The mortal news is heard in the very time of children. Consequently, children develop strategies of survival in the midst of their vulnerable dependence. They look for more dependable relations. They sulk. They despair and complain. They break out. They learn to compensate for the variability and ultimate betrayal (by death) of all relations by discovery of private and inward consolations.

Thus, adolescence follows childhood. It is a time of critical awareness that all relations are changing and mortal, and that dependency is futile but yet a profound motivation (because of childhood adaptation). Thus, it is a time spent in testing the worlds of relations and the degrees of consolation or pleasure offered by both inward and objective sources. It is a time of struggle between the motives of absolute dependence and absolute independence, between commitment to self and commitment to the play of relations.

Human beings tend to waste their whole life in that struggle or early awareness of the conditions of manifest existence. The spell is broken only when there is awakening from both the burden of dependence (wherein mortality is still the last word) and of separative independence (which is limited to rituals of self-consolation and of exploitation of relations in a self-possessed mood).

Our human freedom and maturity comes only with the abandonment of the whole disposition of dependence-independence, or the ritual of "You don't love me" and "I don't love you." It comes when we are reestablished in and readapted to the prior Condition of our existence, which precedes all relations (even if the great pattern of human and cosmic relations is the agent of that Condition in the framework of conventional experience). Our parents never were our Food or Life. They were only agents, more or less capable. They were a connection to Life. They were not Life Itself. But in our childish fear, founded in our own bodily and psychic individuation, we began to depend on the agents themselves, to the point that they no longer functioned as a connection to Life, but were objects to which we turned in despair, seeking the Absolute in them, but not yielding enough to find It in them or through them.

Thus, we grow beyond the experiential limits of the parent domain, but we cling to all other relations, conditions, experiences, and objects, high or low, in the same ritual manner. And that pattern does not pass until a new and mature level of understanding, response, and adaptation appears in our case. Otherwise we live until death crying for love and safety, absolute pleasure and help, immortality and an unchanging world of glorious fulfillments of our ordinary functional needs. Such is the root of conventional religion, in which dependence on the parent agency is projected on all relations to Infinity, where we install the cultic Deity of our childhood, the archetypal and immortal Parent, and spend our days alternately pleading for the fulfillment of our needs and turning away, in adolescent fashion, to doubts and the consolations of functional fulfillments themselves.

We must awaken from the spell of our childish presumptions and become human. We must neither depend on (in the absolute sense) nor recoil from any relations. We must discover Life Itself, prior to all agents, mediators, or means. We must become established as love rather than the search for love via agents outside us. We must enter into most direct Communion with the Life and Truth that literally sustains us, and with which we are ultimately identical, in consciousness and even bodily. We must be free of the illusion that the ordinary agents of Life are necessary in themselves. We must come into the responsible disposition of stable love (unobstructed feeling-attention) toward all the numberless and ordinary agents of Life that appear in the universal pattern of our relations, but we must be free of all illusions that bind us to others apart from the Radiant Life Itself. We must ourselves consent to be agents of Life through love, and, through Communion with the All-Pervading Life, we must become less and less obstructed in that function.

The Teaching of Truth, the Way of Divine Ignorance, is an argument or consideration and a path of new adaptation whereby and wherein the childish and adolescent man or woman, of any chronological age, may be awakened to mature responsibility in Communion with the prior Divine Reality. That Reality is not objective, within or without, but the prior, absolute, and most

136

radical Condition of all conditions. It is not our Parent but our Condition, Truth, and Happiness. The Spiritual Master communicates the Teaching and Reveals the Way at every stage of our new adaptation. As such he is an ordinary agent of Life, to which we should turn with love, and not dependence, but responsible surrender. He is not a Parent, but the awakened Agent who abides as love to Infinity in all relations, and in relation to whom we discover the prior Reality as Grace, quickening our new adaptation and liberating sacrifice. He does not ultimately draw us to himself, as an objective and independent entity, but he serves our Awakening, through spiritual relationship to him (wherein we Realize Communion with the Real), to the very Condition that is his own Realization. He is the direct Agent of the Real Condition. He is not other than that Condition, because he is surrendered, beyond all agents or relations, to that Condition. Therefore, the Spiritual Master is the Advantage of all true men and women.

Childish and adolescent individuals also approach the Spiritual Master. Those who are still critically burdened by their childish dependency look to the Spiritual Master, and to the Divine, as an objective, independent "other" or Parent, a Source that is also a perfect Agent. Such individuals must be awakened to the egoic illusion in their own approach, since it will prevent their Realization of the Truth served by the Spiritual Master and his Divine Revelation. Adolescent individuals tend to be interested in and even fascinated by the potential in the Spiritual Master and the Divine, but they remain self-protective and, therefore, possessed by doubt and even critical denials of both the Spiritual Master and the Divine. Just so, they remain self-possessed in all their relations, since doubt and fear of dependency are at their hearts. Love, in its true form (which depends on direct Communion with the Condition prior to all conditions) is not in their capacity, but only seeking, temporary satisfaction, self-protective fantasies of independence, and a constant doubt of love and Bliss. Therefore, such individuals must be tested until they are awakened to love in Divine Communion, or else they will live until death in doubt of love, certain only of their mortal independence, and without connection to the prior Life.

This is the Way. Be converted to love. Be awakened from the illusory incident of independent incarnation and self-possession and be turned to the Real and Eternal Incident of Divine Bliss, existence as love in all relations, and transcendence of all conditions, within and without, high and low, now and then. Hear me and resort only to the prior Divine in my Company.

138

The True Man

The childish individual wants someone to save him.

The adolescent individual wants to fulfill himself, absolutely and independently.

The true man simply serves Good Company and surrenders to Truth, the Living God.

The Need Connection
*A talk given by Bubba Free John
to his devotees*

BUBBA: As a child, every individual begins to suspect or presume that he or she is unloved and betrayed. This sense of betrayal is more than psychological; it is even a profound physical sense of the loss of our unqualified connection to Life and security. No matter what the actual circumstances of his life, the child always experiences some degree of this sense of betrayal or unlove. Eventually, the child, this vulnerable individual, concludes that "you don't love me."

The life of the ego is based on this illusion of betrayal. And it is an illusion, whatever the facts of anyone's experience. It may be that as a child your experience communicated betrayal; perhaps there was someone who did not love you. On the basis of those events you presumed "you don't love me; I am not loved." Such a presumption defines the individual as the ego. To be a defined consciousness implies separation, and this separation is naturally projected into the scene of one's human experience. If an event of betrayal did not actually occur, you would invent it in your childhood in order to differentiate yourself. Children invent monstrous interpretations of otherwise ordinary events, because they are at an age in which they do not have much insight into experience. Their awareness of things is inherently incomplete. Some of the conceived events of betrayal may be relatively true; others really do not have any of the significance the child presumes. Nevertheless, presumptions of betrayal are the inevitable basis of our emotional learning, even from the earliest moments of life.

139

This sense of betrayal or "you don't love me" is the same as "me." It is ego. Ego is not an entity; it is an action, a process. It is the avoidance of relationship, the contraction of feeling-attention. The life of the ego is separation and "you don't love me." But we may be converted, we may be transformed, we may be rightly adapted, and thus we need not live as the ego, or the sense of separate self. Rather, we may live in Divine Communion, in Communion with Infinity. We may release the self-contraction, and we may love. When we are relieved of the ego we are also necessarily relieved of the emotional contraction in the midst of relationships.

Without this conversion of the contracted self, or ego, to Radiant love, there is no Enlightenment. They are the same thing, you see. Enlightenment is relief from the ego contraction, which is the avoidance of relationship. Therefore, if you desire to live a spiritual life, your childish presumption of betrayal, of being unloved, must be transformed. It is a childish presumption, but you are no longer a child. You are relatively mature. Yet you represent a history of the presumption of betrayal that developed in infancy and upon which you have built your whole life. Even now, in your relative maturity, you still represent that emotional presumption. In the years beyond childhood it is totally inappropriate to be obsessively watching to see whether or not you are loved. Such a strategy may be appropriate at the infantile stage of your life, but it is at least neurotic at any other stage. It is loveless and dreadful.

In order to be free to love and to be responsible in your intimacies, you must be free of your infantilism, your childish dependence, your independence, conflict, coming and going, looking for love, feeling certain it is going to disappear. The point to be considered in any moment is not whether or not you are being loved. What must be observed is that you are not loving. The feeling of betrayal, of not being loved, is a cover for your own failure to love, for the contraction that is the ego. You are failing to realize and confess that you are Narcissus, that it was you who abandoned your parents, your friends, your lovers. It was not their abandonment of you that caused you to cease to love, and to become a betrayer of all love. The reaction of unlove is entirely your own responsibility.

If you remember the story of Narcissus, you will recall that it begins with his leaving his parents to go off on his own because he feels betrayed by them. Like Narcissus, you also defined yourself. You left home. You are the one who presumed betrayal, and ever since you have been failing to love. Maybe your parents did not love you for a few minutes—who knows? In any case, whatever they did or appeared to do occurred under the stress of this ordinary human predicament, and they, unlike you, did not have the benefit of the service of the Spiritual Master and the Teaching of Truth to convert them from their childishness.

Clearly, our "sexual" consideration is not about sexuality in itself. We cannot address the consideration of sexual practice until we have first inspected the history of our emotional adaptation. The key to the consideration of your sexuality is how you have adapted as an emotional being. Sex is not an isolated function, nor are you controlled by the function of sex exclusive of emotion. Your relationship to sex is determined absolutely and entirely by your emotional adaptation. If you are emotionally responsible, if you are love, if you are no longer emotionally crippled, no longer constantly watching to see whether you are loved or not, then it follows quite naturally that you are also sexually responsible. But if you try to become responsible for sexuality exclusive of prior responsibility for emotion, you will never be able to do it. You must first confront the emotional adaptation that is responsible for your sexual pattern.

You will see—you must see—that you have lived as if betrayed in order to justify the egoic gesture of the avoidance of relationship. Having inspected the history of your life, you must confess that you are Narcissus, that you are unlove, that you are not loving, and that you have failed to love all the while. You could just as well have been a saint, full of love, when your parents seemed to betray you, but you were not, because you preferred to separate yourself from them. Perhaps that separation is necessary at a certain stage of life; we do need to differentiate ourselves functionally. But it does seem humanly unnecessary that functional differentiation must be associated with a bizarre emotional episode that can go on for many years, even many lives!

You must be converted from the irresponsible emotional pattern of "you don't love me" to emotional responsibility, or love in relationship. Through Communion with the Divine, through real understanding, you must live as "I love you." You must live the sacrifice that is love via all your functions, in all of your relations, under all conditions. That is the demand of real Life. Yet, even though you may respond to that demand, your functions themselves have not yet been adapted to the perfection of love. Thus, you must practice the principle of love and not dramatize the life of "you don't love me." You must adapt to the functional, Lawful order of existence. You must in every moment be positively oriented toward open-hearted, energetic, bodily service to the Spiritual Master and all beings.

You must at the same time recognize that acquired emotional patterns tend to remain in place, instigating the repetition of old patterns. You now know this very well, and you must not forget it. What is set in motion will continue, until it is deflected or replaced by another motion. That is the law of natural physics. Therefore, you must change your action on the basis of this understanding. And you must also recognize that you will temporarily continue to experience the subjective signs of your old adaptation. The "motion" of old adaptation will continue in your feeling, in the casual moments of desiring that may appear, and in reactions in the midst of the circumstances of life.

Even so, you must mature in your responsibility for old, Narcissistic adaptation. You must not dramatize the old pattern in any form—emotional, mental, or physical. You must simply not be concerned about it. If it appears, that is just the way it is. It is mechanical. It is just machinery. It will inevitably appear and continue to appear, until it becomes obsolete through non-use, or present non-reaction. Whatever is not used becomes obsolete. Therefore, you must not dramatize or become concerned for the old tendencies that arise. They will become obsolete if you remain oriented through understanding and devotional sacrifice to the Lawful practice of life.

The more firmly adapted you are as the whole bodily being to the Lawful order of Life and to the Principle of unqualified relationship, rather than to the principle of the ego, the avoidance of relationship—the more positively adapted you are to that true Principle, the weaker will be the subjective signs of loveless adaptation. Eventually, the motion you represent in life will be only love and Divine Communion. The subjective urges to loveless action will have disappeared. Until then, you will have to put up with a certain amount of kicking from the old order.

The Spiritual Master is your advantage in that entire affair of re-adaptation. When you enter into spiritual Communion with the Spiritual Master, the subjective evidence, the tendencies that are the egoic motion of the being, may be relieved through all the many forms of contact with the Spiritual Master—through instruction within the Church, through your sharing of Life with other devotees, and through the unseen spiritual influence of the Presence of the Spiritual Master. The immediate effect of the devotee's relationship with the Spiritual Master is the purification of the subjective tendencies or the motions of the being, in meditation, in dreams, in ordinary circumstances, and in subtle ways rather than exaggerated ones.

You must be committed to the Spiritual Master through most profound love or devotional sacrifice, which is the very principle of the life of the devotee. Otherwise, you are still just Narcissus struggling to be free of your tendencies. In your spiritual submission or Communion with the Spiritual Master, the evidence that is now within you will not be dramatized, it will not be a matter of your concern, and it will also be dissolved sooner and easier and surer than your new adaptation alone would have dissolved it.

143

The force of your tendencies is tremendous. It goes beyond this lifetime. It is the force of all tendencies, ultimately the force of all incarnation. Thus, a Divine Service enters the plane of human events through the Agency of the Spiritual Master, who makes it possible for apparent individuals to be released from mechanical destinies. We are not new. We are patterns, we are memory, these very bodies are memory. Memory is not just in the mind. All the forms that exist are conditioned by previous influences. These bodies are memory. And how are we relieved of these memories, these dreams? Through the mutually sacrificial relationship we enjoy with the Spiritual Master, who is the Agent of the Divine, and, in that Company, through transcendental Absorption into the Divine Condition that is prior to motion, memory, and objects. The process whereby we may be so transformed is the life of Divine Communion, in which we are converted in our action, from identification with the separate and separative ego, and to Communion with What is everything, What is not differentiated, What is untouched, prior, and perfectly Transcendental. That Reality is manifest as all conditions and yet is utterly beyond all conditions.

Thus, if you would be converted to the life of Communion with that Divine Reality, and if you would Realize the Living God now, in this moment, then you must go far beyond the consideration of the suffering of your childhood and your parents and your adolescence and your sexual obsessions and all of your problems and your inability to love. You must become responsible as love in all relations, under all conditions, and as early in your life as possible, so that you can transcend this repetitive destiny of the ego, of separation, of the avoidance of relationship, of unlove, of "you don't love me," that keeps you out by the pond, meditating on yourself like Narcissus. Then you can go on to fulfill the Divine Destiny of Life in God while alive.

The universal religion is a call to mankind to love, because all human beings are living as betrayed children, as unlove, justified by some memory or complex of memories, not only in the mind and the subconscious, but in the body itself. The eternity behind us in time is a limiting condition on our loving, on the heart, on our psychic awareness, our opening into Infinity. Thus, religion is the call to men to abandon their childishness and their adolescent rebellion in the face of conceived betrayal or reactive unlove. It is the call to turn to the Divine, which is eternally superior to men and to any single event. It is the call to be love again, to be fully in Communion again with the Source of Infinite Light, the Sustenance, Creator Power, and Absorber of our being and forms.

Once you have begun to practice true religion, rather than the childish and vitalistic religion that binds you to the cult of betrayal— once you have begun to practice true religion, which is the responsibility of love or free feeling-attention via all functions, in all relations, under all conditions—then you can grow beyond the human and gross world, beyond its necessity. Then you can begin to perceive what your higher nature is as an individual, as an ego-soul. You may perceive the subtle energy or light of the ego. It is the energy of which the physical part is just the outer, more superficial and solid percolation.[1]

Once the heart of love awakens and the attention of the being can move via the internal Life-Current to the throat and midbrain, you will enjoy an intuitive vision of yourself as energy, as light, which manifests as the physical but which is prior to physical form and awareness. You will see, from the point of view of that light, how the awareness of the physical comes into experience in this moment. When you have realized that process, then the body becomes secondary, an extension, a superficial and unnecessary aspect of experience. It becomes something you can live, something with

1. For Bubba's full description of the Awakening of Man to the Radiant Consciousness of God, please see *The Enlightenment of the Whole Body*.

144

which you can love, because it is no longer threatened with terminal death and annihilation.

But there is more to Realize than that. Even the subtle light or mind of the born soul is nothing more than a temporary and superficial contraction in the field of Universal Light, or Divine Radiance. We must pass beyond it to the Realization of the true Condition of the "covered" soul or the ego. That Condition is without qualification. On the basis of that unqualified Realization of the Eternal and Transcendental Condition of our own consciousness, we are able to be a Sacrifice into Infinity. We no longer need go through this round of betrayal and eventual transcendence. For what purpose? Why go through it again and again? There is nothing inherently desirable about it. This world is a place in which to learn. If you learn the lesson of this world, you can remain in the disposition of Infinity, or love, regardless of events. And when you reach that point, you will be Translated out of this dimension altogether.

For the childish individual, a high percentage of the pleasure gained through sexual activity is derived from the fact that his circumstances permit him to do the sexual activity. He has the same kind of relationship to the circumstances of life as he would with a parent. Circumstance as parent is the logic of his vital activities. Thus, instead of understanding his total life and responsibly choosing the forms of his action and responsiveness, he is generally irresponsible, minimally aware, emotionally reactive, and always, secretly or openly, seeking to attain a circumstance in which degenerative self-indulgence is made possible. Circumstance that makes self-indulgence possible is immediately embraced, through desire, as permission for self-indulgence. On the other hand, circumstance that requires love and responsibility tends chronically to be the grounds for reactivity and the dramatization of frustration.

There is no truly human and free way of life until the common individual is obliged to adapt beyond childish dependence and adolescent ambivalence in the vital functional dimension of life.

146

Until then, the individual is a subhuman and chaotic influence in the world—irresponsible, stupid, crazy, and unfit for common participation in the mature community of mankind. The pity is that the mature community of mankind is generally made up of a relative handful of humanity, largely scattered and, therefore, isolated in effect, whereas the immature mass of "everyman" comprises the great population of the Earth. When "children" multiply so greatly that human maturity is a relatively rare incident, then such human maturity itself tends to become obscure, entrapped, and even outlawed, and so-called human society tends to remain fixed along the lines of parent-child and totalitarian structures, alternating with anarchy, rebellion, social chaos, war, and pestilence.

Love Is Freedom from
Fear, Doubt, and Despair

Men and women are commonly childish and self-possessed. They fear relational commitment and marriage primarily because they fear the loss of the right of promiscuity, they fear the promiscuity of any other to whom they might become attached, and they fear that the sexual attractiveness of any individual, including themselves, is short-lived. Doubt of self and other, and despair of life itself, are the critically disabling factors that disturb and prevent lasting sexual relationships, as well as friendships, and the stability of life-circumstances in general.

However, all doubt, despair, and fear become insignificant once the intention of life becomes love, rather than the childish dependency on love. Childish dependency on the love and attention given to us by others is disabling because it cannot love or grant attention until it has already been granted a high degree of love and attention. The childish individual is always on the verge of feeling rejected and unloved, and he is bright and lively only when he is the primary object of love, attention, and good fortune from without. But the mature individual is active as love under all conditions. Such a one always primarily grants love and attention rather than seeking or watching for whether or not he is being given love and attention.

It is not that the mature individual does not enjoy or need the love of others and the Blessings of God, but the mature individual enjoys such love and Blessings as a happiness that arises in the midst of a life in which he is himself perpetually responsible to love and to be a personally, morally, and spiritually responsible sacrifice in God.

Thus, those who have been initiated into the human principle of responsible love are already free of the burdensome fears, doubts, and reasons for despair that plague the childish and subhuman world.

P romiscuity is simply the avoidance of establishing continuous relationship via the sexual function. It represents anxiety (or guilt and fear) relative to sexuality, and a tendency to continuous self-possession rather than commitment to feeling-attention in relationship. When the individual awakens from the childish and adolescent moods of his or her early adaptation, love becomes responsible in his own case, and sexuality in its truly free form can be made a functional basis for relational commitment or marriage.

Marriage should express commitment on the part of individuals who are responsible as love rather than irresponsible through childish and adolescent weaknesses. Only such individuals can tolerate the potential failures of feeling-attention in others and still persist in love. And only such individuals can freely adapt to the regenerative exercise of the sexual function through unobstructed feeling-attention and Divine Communion.

Monogamy, Polygamy, and True Marriage

Conventional sexual desire is inherently promiscuous. It is moved by worldly attractiveness, reinforced by romantic illusions, and both frustrated and stimulated by the factual limitations of bodily pleasure and mortality itself.

Marriage is not properly a means either for satisfying or confining the power of sexual desire. True marriage is well instructed in advance. It is founded on the understanding that transcends the power of the desiring self.

Such marriage is founded on relational self-granting, or love, in Communion with Living Divine Reality. It is not founded on the satisfaction of desire—or even the frustration of desire. It is founded on Divine ecstasy, self-transcendence, and higher human responsibility.

The usual man cannot understand true marriage, because he is motivated by desire. He is inherently promiscuous and self-possessed. All of his associations with sex are problematic and ultimately disturbed. Both his monogamy and his polygamy are closets of mortal things. He would indulge his desiring with many others, but he fears to do so, or he dares to do so. In any case, he is in doubt of Life.

Only those who are Awake in God may also engage in true and free marriage, which is self-transcending and sex-transcending. Such true marriages cannot be made by the State, although the State commonly gives and withholds legal sanction in relation to all marriages. Only the Holy Community, the culture of devotees, can properly regard and accommodate true marriage. Therefore, each man and woman should be Awakened by Divine Instruction and then marry in the eyes of others of like mind and intent.

Multiple marriage, or polygamy, whatever degree of responsibility it may represent, is conventionally regarded to be taboo, much like incest and homosexuality. It is considered to be a form of promiscuity. Truly, it is a situation in which the usual man or woman would be promiscuous. But the usual man or woman is promiscuous even in the case of romantic and sex-centered monogamy. Only those who are Awake in God also marry in Truth. They transcend self and sex in their responsible commitment.

Therefore, ancient sacred societies and traditional cultures commonly allowed and honored both polygamy and monogamy. One or more wives could be rightly married to a man, if all were established in a relationship that ultimately transcended degenerative sexual activity. Such responsible marriage was often engaged in polygamous terms by men of power, property, and spiritual prominence. And responsible marriage was otherwise engaged in monogamous form by most people—but neither in a romantic nor an erotic mood.

149

Men and women in the present time need to be Awakened to the Living God in sexual terms. Then they will be free of erotic and romantic sexual illusions, and they will marry responsibly. Such individuals will practice sexual communion to the point of self-transcendence and sex-transcendence. And their marriages will ultimately be chaste, or free of binding force. Nearly all such marriages should be monogamous, but an equally responsible and chaste polygamous marriage can also be understood in Truth, even if it is not commonly practiced.

The ancients, having become responsible for the sexual self, found that polygamy could serve a special purpose, either socially or spiritually. Men of power and property extended their domain and brought peace within it through multiple marriages and large numbers of offspring. And men of spiritual Power often married many women, in order that their intimate instruction be granted to many, and also in order to establish a circle of Energy, a gathering of "Shaktis" or "Feminine Powers," who would extend the spiritual Influence within the sacred Community through various cultural institutions. Occasionally, women would marry more than one husband, but this was generally found to be biologically, psychologically, and socially unworkable.

Thus, both polygamy and monogamy have, since ancient times, been found to be both workable and auspicious by free and sexually responsible people—whereas both polygamy and monogamy have also been found to be unworkable and inauspicious by self-possessed and sexually irresponsible people. Only those who can realize Divine Communion in marriage—thus transcending self and sexual exploitation—can marry truly and also Realize God Perfectly.

150   Incest may be said to be worth avoiding for any number of reasons, including genetic, psychological, and social reasons. But the primary reason is that sexual intercourse should occur only within the total process of sexual communion, and sexual communion can occur only within the context of total commitment and mutual responsibility, or true marriage. Incest can, in general, only represent the exploitation of sexual or erotic fascination.

The parents or siblings of any individual inevitably become the target of casual sexual interest in the years of growth. And there is no natural or functional reason why any individual, within the blood family or not, could not be the physically sexual partner of another. The point is that merely physiological and casual sex must be transformed into a whole bodily and feeling process, exercised within a relationship of continuous commitment. Therefore, casual sex with <u>anyone</u>, whether incestuous or otherwise, is the form of sexual activity that is to be avoided or overcome. It is not a matter of taboos and fears and avoidance of love between any individuals, but of the free human choice of sexual communion, and confinement of sexual contact to the intimate plane of such marriage or commitment. Therefore, promiscuity is inherently bypassed by the truly human realization of sexual communion.

"Confession" is typically regarded and used as a method of self-cleansing. When one confesses, one expects a kind of liberation to come as a result—a kind of magical release effect. Thus, when individuals consider together the history and pattern of their emotional-sexual adaptation, they tend to "confess" in this sense. But such is at best only a secondary and mostly childish aspect of intimate personal communication. The higher or true function of confession is to serve personal responsibility through self-knowledge. And responsibility is not important as a merely internal state. Responsibility is intelligent only relative to action. Thus, true confession should not only produce but should itself be change of action, responsible change of the whole form of one's self-presentation in the pattern of relationships. This is the form of confession that we should value and mutually serve in one another's case.

151

Most human beings are at present evolving into the third stage of life—the stage of the development of the verbal mind and the functional will, or the power of intention. For this reason, they tend to remain fixed or fascinated in the verbal level of subjective life, and find difficulty in translating this level of understanding into bodily action. And even those who learn the exercise of the will must learn to devote the functions of mind and intention to the Law of love and service, the intelligence of the fourth stage of life, or else all their actions become no more than self-improvement and an extension of exclusively lower or vital motives.

Mature Lovers Are Devotees of the Real

Eroticism depends on both general unavailability of objective sexual contact (or a general taboo against objective sexual contact) and present temporary or imaginary availability of objective sexual contact. It depends on the opposition games of offense and defense, conflict, the roles of opponents, reactive emotions, unlove (or fluctuations of feeling-attention), self-possession, and the aggravated search for release from the sense that manifest existence is a problem.

General availability of both lover and love tends to bore the immature man or woman, leading him or her to seek the erotic either promiscuously or internally. But life in love with one's lover permits peace to devotees, and permits even sex itself to turn into what is beyond sex.

152

Marriage partners should be obliged (or oblige themselves) to bring to their relationship freedom from childish and adolescent demands. Thus, each must be free of the need to depend on the attention and energy of the other (which is the childish demand for the parent). And each must be free of the casual demand for satisfaction of vital, reactively emotional, and lower mental desires (all of which represent the adolescent demand to be self-involved without interference by others). Each partner must have realized that the future growth of their individual existence is about the higher spiritual culture and sacrifice of Man in God. And each must, therefore, have a right emotional and functional understanding of the relative and secondary significance of vital, sexual, reactive emotional, and lower mental demands. There must be responsibility for the whole affair of reactivity, all obsessive demands for attention, and the tendency toward repetitive and always exotically intense fulfillment of mere and loveless vital desires.

It is also true that we should prepare ourselves in all kinds of ordinary ways for marriage. We should, above all, be mature and capable of freedom from the need that our partner fulfill us perfectly (which only the Divine Process can do) and offer us guarantees of constant or eternal attention. We must live by the Law, which is that our attention and feeling are perpetually demanded to Infinity and not ultimately consoled by anything finite or directed exclusively toward us. And we should give substance in action to this whole obligation by training ourselves to be of practical service, to be good company, and to be a center of intelligence and feeling for our lover. And we should be fully and previously acquainted, through study, with the whole process of sexual communion as the obligation we are to fulfill in the intimacy of our marriage.

People do not generally assume all of this preparation should <u>precede</u> marriage, but it is imperative that all of this be realized if a marriage is to represent a process or a culture in which each partner is able to continue to grow into the highest Destiny while yet enjoying a pleasurable and rightly ordered structure of ordinary living.

153

Sexual communion, or the sex function expressed via a love relationship, spiritually dedicated, is not a matter of mutual strategic opposition, or the sense of negatively designed offense and defense. In that negative design there is the absence of love and surrender. One is aggressively penetrating or avoiding penetrating, and the other is, aggressively or passively, avoiding being penetrated or seeking to be penetrated. In that case, orgasm is victory, and orgasm is its own reward.

The erotic struggle and chronic conflict between so-called lovers is devoted to degenerative exploitation of orgasm or release, without any other or higher view of the structural function of sexuality—except perhaps for the occasional conception of children. Such is an expression of subhuman dullness, and self-possessed fear. It is a loveless mutual strategy that reinforces chronic self-meditation, lack of intimacy, lack of pleasure, and obsessive fantasy and promiscuity. True lovers are also human devotees of the Real, awakened to the understanding of the ultimate structural destiny of the human bodily being. They are at play with one another, humorous in their mutual polarization. They approach one another ecstatically, as a bodily expressed, free intensity of desiring love. And they are mutually submitted or open to one another, feeling one another, without fear or need for victory, free of the obsession with release.

Mature lovers should release one another of the burden to fulfill one another absolutely, and to satisfy one another's childish dependency. Lovers should be free, transcending one another through love itself, so that their existence is oriented not primarily to the theatre of their relationship but to the Divine in the Real Process of Communion and transcendental Love-Sacrifice.

154   Conflict is the dramatic human expression of the "problem." It is produced whenever a polarized pair, which should be at play, live to one another as opponents in a game of offense and defense—thus producing war and separation rather than embrace and unifying love.

Emotional reactivity or recoil—such as fear, shame, guilt, sorrow, anger, jealousy, and doubt—is the root of all "games" of conflict or mutual opposition. Such reactivity produces the sub-human and independent self-orientation, rather than the native relational orientation of the fully incarnated bodily being. The self-orientation is always aligned with emotional reactivity and separativeness, and all of this together makes a perpetual conception of life as a problem, a dilemma, and a field of conflict.

But when there is release from the pattern of recoil and self-possession through "hearing" the Teaching and "seeing" in the Company of the Spiritual Master, then life may be lived through love, or responsive and free feeling-attention, rather than patterns of reactivity and conflict in a field of inherent problems.

Unless there is spiritual awakening to Truth and true practice, or right adaptation of the structures of experience, all functions become enslaved to a negative destiny. Thus, sexuality tends to become obsessive and degenerative, and the sexual relationship tends to become devoted to problems, warfare, conflict, and strategies of offense and defense, wherein there is no mutual surrender, but only mutual struggle for victory or survival.

Over time, when a marriage matures toward a naturally chaste or regenerative love and spiritual fullness, couples may choose to sleep in separate beds or, even better, separate rooms, and to meet for either sexual intimacy or simply to rest with one another occasionally and by choice. This permits the psychic singularity of each partner to become whole and rested in Divine Communion, undisturbed by the physical and psychic contact that inevitably comes with intimate association, both during waking hours and when at rest. Just so, each individual should surrender the "cult of pairs" more and more as he or she matures, and thus release the dependency and the psychology of exclusiveness that comes by intimate association with another human individual. More and more privacy and solitude should be found each day, and used as spiritual occasion. In this way marriage leads toward spiritual integrity, and mature lovers, by constantly surrendering the binding effects of one another's company, realize happiness, renewal, and blissful love in their free intimacy with one another.

Marriage based on obsessive attachment, immature dependency, and genital indulgence becomes less and less intense, and ultimately leads to boredom, conflict, infidelity, superficiality, and so forth. But a marriage based on responsibility, love, feeling intimacy, freedom, spiritual discipline, and surrender of attachment (through complete love or nonwithholding) is a great happiness and a great demonstration of the Teaching of the Spiritual Master.

The conservation or conductivity of the Life-Force in sexual communion serves the purification and regeneration of the individual. But the attention of the individual is not to be upon himself. Rather, there must be loving communion between the lovers. There must be constant relaxation of bodily tensions and fixations of attention—but all of this is secondary to the fundamental relaxation-release of self, through feeling-attention, via one's lover, to Infinity.

Sexual communion is not fascinated and erotic fixation on one's lover or on one's own subjectivity and sensations. Rather, it is a matter of whole bodily release of feeling and attention from all subjective and objective fixations and into heartfelt Communion with the Divine Reality. It is a matter of free feeling-attention, or formless love to the degree of Infinity. It is a matter of the release of all fixation or holding on to subjective states and objective forms— and the release thereby of feeling and attention, so that feeling-attention may move or dissolve to the degree of Infinity. It is a matter of the relaxation of body and mind in love. In the process, conservation of the Life-Force, via the regenerative exercise of attention, breath, and bodily action, occurs as a natural and secondary affair. But it does not truly and fully occur unless the self-manipulative and strategic self-attention is given up to Communion with the Divine through sacrificial love of one's lover.

Sexual communion is right or sacrificial adaptation to the sexual potential of the bodily being. But the body in itself is not Truth, nor is any kind of bodily harmony or fulfillment of the bodily being itself Truth or sufficient realization for Man. The whole and entire bodily being must be a sacrifice into its very Condition. Thus, sexual fulfillment of the Law ultimately transcends sex. Lovers must be devotees and pass beyond the forms of body and mind. When their sexual play becomes communion rather than egoic release, they serve one another and turn one another toward the ultimate occupation of Man, which is the loving communion or sacrifice of the whole and entire bodily being in its ultimate Source, Condition, or Primal Radiance.

As lovers mature in the practice of sexual communion, and in the total practice of the Way of Divine Ignorance, the genital embrace becomes more and more secondary to the process of their relationship itself. Thus, their awareness of one another, their communications, the time they spend in one another's company, and the simple closeness wherein they love one another become the primary circumstances wherein they enjoy Divine Communion in relation to one another. Such lovers may occasionally engage in sexual embrace, in the form of sexual communion, but their relationship itself becomes the constant form of sexual communion. In one another's daily company, they love and yield, breathe and touch. This process of living to God bodily in one another's company becomes senior to all forms of genital activity, and it ultimately transcends genital activity, so that genital sexual embrace is naturally economized.

157

S elf-doubting, weak-willed, promiscuous sex partners (real or potential) are erotic, attractive, and fascinating. One tends secretly to desire and even to become sexually associated with such partners. If one is married to a man or woman who is essentially strong, loving, and giving, then one tends to doubt, and manipulate, and test that one—in order to prove he or she is really tending to leave you and not to love you.

This is because of one's own self-doubting, weak-willed, and promiscuous tendencies. Thus, one tends to believe the same must be true of one's lover, and the opposite sex in general. And one's polarized life tends to become a dramatized dilemma, a seat of conflict, in which separation must always appear to be at stake. If the relationship fails to allow this sense of conflict—as in the case where one's lover appears too submissive, self-sacrificing, affectionate, and attached to oneself—then one creates it, or imagines it, and, ultimately, loses interest in the relationship.

Thus, sexual relationships founded in the erotic motive depend on conflict and the potential of separation. They also depend on self-doubt in both partners and fascination with degenerative orgasm and the general exploitation of sexuality and reactive (or separative) emotions.

There is no happiness in sexual love until tranquility and a whole bodily, sacrificial, and feeling orientation become acceptable to both partners. The erotic becomes the motive whenever separation becomes fascinating. Where separation is fascinating, partners constantly test one another and seek to prove the lack of love in one another. Then, when the play of conflict finally does produce separation, there is despair and the suffering of feelings of rejection and self-pity.

One must inspect the desire for loveless or potentially promiscuous partners. Only responsibility for one's own self-doubt and inability to commit oneself in love will relieve one of the whole drama or script of the erotic and separative fascinations in the process of sexual relationship. When one is responsible as love and capable of intimacy, then one desires via love, and the erotic motive, the motive toward casual and loveless sex via conflict and fears of separation, will come to rest.

Sex play should become sexual communion, which is sexual relationship adapted to love and service, and sexual functioning adapted to the regenerative rather than degenerative cycle of the body. Thus, the partner to choose in marriage should be one who is at ease with feeling and attention in sexual love, rather than one who is troubled, obsessed, demanding, childish, promiscuous, fascinating, self-involved, and devoid of intelligence, self-control, and spiritual commitment to the Living Divine and to the higher or perfect Destiny of man.

Love Is the Bodily Intuition of God

The desire connection to the world is self-motivated and self-possessed, and it leads only to experience, which is self. Experience itself is the ego, the separate one, Narcissus, the mechanical illusion.

The love connection to the world is motivated by God and toward God. The love connection is God-Possessed, and it always already transcends self, or all experience, in God. Love is transcendence of all experience, through prior God-Communion.

Therefore, love, serve, be free, master all desire, and transcend all experience, through God-Communion. Simply love, serve, abide in God-Communion, and do no more than what is necessary for ordinary, simple, and free bodily existence in Communion with the Radiant Transcendental Reality.

Establish no relationships or habits that are founded upon or dependent upon mere desire, or satisfaction of the self-generated needs of yourself or of others. Live to God in all relationships, surrendering all consolations, all self-indulgence, all exploitation. Live in the prior or inherent pleasure of Existence, ecstatic in God-Communion, or love, rather than live in bondage to the acquired pleasures and limits of psycho-physical experience, high or low.

If you choose this, you are free in God. Make this Way in the free community of devotees, those who value and understand and mutually serve the attributes of manifest existence thus moved in God. The Spiritual Master of such devotees wanders freely at Infinity and never looks back.

I n one's maturity it becomes clear that sex has been fully explored and is known as it is (in the functional sense). It becomes clear that sex is just what it appears to be, and that it does not become more than that by any repetition or increase of its practice. It is greatly pleasurable, and it also tends to become obsessive unless there is true sacrifice of self through love. In itself, it is a question, a mystery. It is merely another form of attention, whereas attention or objective awareness itself is the primal event, worthy of the consideration of one's whole being.

There is a moment when all obsessive and repetitive motivations toward finite pleasures become very clear and unnecessary. And it is also clear that, apart from such obsessive motivations, there is no ultimate cause or necessity of any further exercise in the usual way. Therefore, the conventional life falls away from the force of one's intention, and sexual indulgence goes with it all. What is to be gained, or learned, or felt? Only repetition. Now the Way of Life becomes primal existence and feeling itself. It is the great interest and moment. Passing beyond distractions, there is the peace of ultimate commitment to what stands out above all.

160   If you would be free and a lover in sexual communion with your lover, first learn bliss, happiness, and love. First hear the Teaching, and awaken to Ignorance-Radiance, or unobstructed feeling-attention. Then, in every moment, through the conscious process of intuitive understanding and spiritual initiation in the Company of the Spiritual Master, and in the face of every condition, high or low, abide as that bliss, happiness, or love and be free forever.

Chapter 10

Abandoning Casual Association between the Sexes

Abandoning Casual
Association between
the Sexes
*A talk given by Bubba Free John
to his devotees*

BUBBA: There is something about the social polarization between men and women that is at the root of all problems about sexuality. The problems seem never to come to an end. They are not resolved in an hour or any number of hours of conversation and insight. If something becomes clarified by our conversation and your insight, you feel more responsible for your problems, but when you leave this room, go out and mingle with others and carry on your daily activities, the same influences and the same tendencies appear. They do not seem to be reduced by your mere understanding. Suddenly, it becomes overwhelmingly clear that the problem is not subject to insight alone. Insight is only the beginning of a process that must become more concrete.

The root of sexual problems is not internal. In dealing with our human problems we tend to play the old game of concentrating principally on the subjective or internal dimension, expecting to become more and more clear in our understanding, and by understanding alone we imagine we are free. But the problems persist. This is the common error. <u>Subjectivity is not senior to the pattern of relations</u>. Rather, it is the other way around. The pattern of relations is reflected in our subjectivity. You cannot go deep into your subjectivity and get to the root of ordinary things. The root of things is in the process of relationships, or the total pattern of experiencing.

Therefore, we must become aware of the living circumstance of the problem in our sexuality. It is not principally subjective. It is social. If you observe our social order, you can see that the sexes tend to be obliged to associate <u>casually</u> with one another from birth. This permissiveness is contrary to the ancient traditional way of life that pertained all over the world. Traditionally, the sexes were clearly differentiated and formally related, but in our modern technological society the sexes mingle casually, and the differentiation between the sexes is always tending to break down. In our own time there is a great social movement toward greater and greater equalization of the sexes. It is not only a movement to acquire the right of women to equal pay for equal work. What is ultimately being sought or otherwise created is depolarization, a quality of equal character and function in both men and women that undermines the naturally polarized play of human life. These social impulses that are at work are a reflection of the casual association of the sexes.

The casual mingling of the sexes is actually an antisexual social activity. It does not take into account, at the level of the social order or the social play, the natural distinction between the sexes. That distinction is not just physical, not just a matter of a portion of the anatomy. We are naturally polarized in our <u>character</u>. Each of us is by birth structurally disposed toward a certain genital function, but also toward a specifically differentiated character that reflects a specific psycho-physical polarity.

In general, the female character represents what does not move, what is still, what is in place, what is receptive. And the male character represents what moves, what is active, what is creatively expansive. These distinctions are essentially true, though there may be individual variations. Obviously, the male individual can also in fact perform domestic functions within the home, and if necessary, or otherwise desirable, the female individual can function in various work roles or professions in the world outside the home. But the variations of character between men and women and the form of their relationship to one another still hold true, in general, to the ancient distinctions. And, therefore, as a general rule, the ancient functional roles will likely most often apply—with women at the center or household plane of daily action, and men at the periphery, outward bound, in the theatre of expansive activity in the common world.

The natural distinction between the opposites is absolute even at the level of the cellular life. And all of the manifest worlds are an expression of the play of duality, of positive and negative. The energy of the manifest universe is not a warfare but a play of opposites. Where the sexes are not formally and socially acknowledged in their independence, nor permitted to fulfill their uniquely different social and cultural destinies, we see the mingling and diffusion of characters, and the dynamic polarization of human life breaks down and becomes confused. Women tend to become more and more manlike, tending toward the gesture of transcending the world through conceptualization, and looking to dominate the affair of life through what have traditionally been masculine roles. Likewise, men, through their casual association with women from birth, tend to become confused in their clarity of thought, their ability to consider and make moral and spiritually oriented decisions. They tend to become confused by functional impulses below the mind. The role and destiny of the woman thus become part of the male character adaptation, so that men cannot fulfill the total psychophysical role of the true man.

Another result of casual association between the sexes is that people become promiscuous. When the sexes are not differentiated socially, and their relations cease to be essentially formal (or regulated by moral and cultural presumptions), people must defend themselves in their casual meetings from the random intrusions of sexual feeling, or erotic suggestion. This defensiveness produces an inverted view toward sexuality, a sense that it is dangerous, overwhelming, and omnipresent. One of the ways women reflect this tension that arises from casual association with men is to become openly promiscuous, apparently available to everyone. Their availability is a gesture of self-defense to protect themselves from the casual and constant intrusion of men.

In traditional orders of the past, people have taken care to maintain the social division of the sexes. In many cases the motivation was antisexual, as in certain social levels of Hindu India, and other cultures where the body and its ordinary life are inherently in doubt. But in the more ancient orders, in India and elsewhere, the absolute division between the sexes was not a reflection of an interest in depolarizing life or suppressing sexuality. Rather, it was an acknowledgment of the profound force of the character play of opposites, the play out of which human life is made. It was because people valued that play that they maintained a social differentiation of the sexes.

We must also discover ways to minimize casual association between the sexes and to develop natural formalities for our relationships with members of the opposite sex when we are required to meet them. The games of superficial familiarity and erotic playfulness to which we are now accustomed must be eliminated from the context of our social life, particularly within the cultural context of the community of devotees. In the past, a woman would never look into the eyes of a man who was not her husband or her Spiritual Master. This formality was not just a social nicety, but an acknowledgment of the natural polarization of the energies of Life. A kind of rigidity may appear when we become so formal, and I am not suggesting that we exaggerate our formality with one another. However, we must acknowledge the play of Life and value it, not suppress it. We must develop natural formalities, and we should avoid casual contact with members of the opposite sex entirely. If you can realize the logic of this consideration and have a positive feeling for it and begin to practice it—with a certain level of insight, of course—the whole dimension of sexual problems and obsessions and problems of character will be minimized and even disappear altogether very quickly.

In the play of worldly life, at work, for example, we consider it to be economically necessary and politically appropriate for everybody to have optimum freedom to find work and establish a career.

166

At the worldly level of life we should, therefore, not make distinctions of sex, race, age, and so forth. But in the culture of our truly human and spiritual intimacy we must choose a way of life that takes into account the polarization of sexual characters. We will choose not to promote casual associations between the sexes, because we regard the human play of life and character to be a very profound matter. The polarized play of human characters is the dynamic Play of Life itself. Thus, there is no justification for casual associations. We want the meetings between the sexes to be mutually full within marriage, and we want to formalize the relations between the sexes, and between human beings in general, outside of marriage. Some may think it is suppressive to prohibit or to fail to instigate casual flirtations. But the need for such casual associations is a sign of subhuman immaturity. It is casual association that is suppressive. When casual eroticism is the norm, individuals tend to be always sexually concerned, defending themselves, "looking good," always making sexual gestures with someone of the opposite sex, and never truly entering into the transcendental and spiritual functions of consciousness.

167

Having heard this argument, you must realize the actual culture of this understanding in your daily life, and especially in the company of your own sex. Men, when they are not casually related to women, know how to make demands on one another. They demand responsibility from one another, as women do from one another in their own circle. Men cannot and should not make that demand on women. Nor can women demand that men be responsible. It is not their business to do so. Men and women must no longer defend themselves against one another. There should be no war between the sexes. There should be no mutual self-defense between the sexes. And there should be no casual association between the sexes. Rather, there should be union between the sexes in appropriate intimate relationships, and the contact between the sexes should be formal on all other occasions.

Women must realize a culture among themselves. They must be free, from childhood, to realize an essential feminine character that is entirely that of a woman, and one that is free to be responsive to husband and to men of spiritualized consciousness. A man must also be free, from his childhood, to realize the male character. We can only realize our true sexual character by entering into the culture and trial of our own sex. Men must learn how to be men by association with men. And women must learn how to be women by association with women. Casual contact between the sexes, even between children and parents of the opposite sex, qualifies and limits our development.

168

Your own life histories are the proof of this. Consider your past. You are troubled, dominated by your casual association with the opposite parent. There are cases of feeling rejected by the parent of the opposite sex. A sexual orientation, at least through character play, with the parent of the opposite sex, was even quite common. Your lives commonly describe premature involvement with sexuality, as well as obsessive erotic and degenerative involvement with sexuality. None of this would have occurred, nor would your character development have been made ambiguous, if there had been a formalization of the relations between the sexes from your earliest experience. Having observed this now, in this moment, in your maturity, you must allow it to make a difference in your actual practice. Mere insight is not sufficient, if, after this consideration, you return to a pattern of living in which you survive only through old adaptation. The problems are not arising from within. Internal or psychological problems about sex are fundamentally a reflection of wrong adaptation within a chaotic social order.

Social Sexual Order and Personal Sexual Transcendence

Individuals who are becoming responsible for the casually self-indulgent and childishly degenerate habits of life that characterize the common or subhuman order of society must adapt to regenerative practices of a personal and moral kind. As the disposition of nonreactive well-being grows, individuals begin to consider new agreements with one another—agreements that reflect a free religious and spiritual understanding. Thus, a politics or intimate cultural order of life begins to develop among devotees, and that order or society becomes primary, whereas the superficial and subhuman order of the common world becomes a secondary territory that represents less and less of the Purpose and Truth of Life—until the whole world turns to God in Truth.

Among the characteristics of the cultural order of devotees is the accommodation of sexual character, or the relative functional and social differentiation of the sexes. In the common subhuman world, the sexes tend to be casually associated. Forms of eroticism, conflict, and games of dominance and submission thus tend to be the common demonstration of the casual society of men and women. For this reason, inequalities and forms of exploitation necessarily develop. And either the natural differentiation of the sexes is used as an excuse to maintain erotic social play and broad social dominance of one sex by the other, or else the movement toward "unisex," or the breakdown of the dynamics of sexual character, begins to suppress the force and play of human identities.

The community of devotees in the Way of Divine Ignorance must, first of all, grant value, acknowledgment, and accommodation to the natural sexual differentiation of human beings. Men and women are not merely different in their physical characteristics, but they are, in the natural order of their ordinary humanity, structurally disposed toward different emotional, psychological, and mental characteristics. And the higher cultural order of human beings must allow for the dynamic play of sexual character, both in private intimacy and in daily society.

However, the dynamic social association of the sexes should not presume that the social contact and play of the sexes in general is of the same kind as the private, intimate meeting between lovers. Casual society is a form of subhuman mingling that produces eroticism, conflict, and ultimate suppression of sexual character. The human social order of devotees should represent a sense of true valuation of sexual differences as well as the regenerative intimate play of lovers, and it should likewise represent acknowledgment of the need for the formalization of the meeting of men and women who are not the personal, sexual intimates of one another.

Casual society of the sexes is a form of childish erotic chaos, in which the sexes cannot differentiate into their independent fullness and wholeness, but are forced always into forms of casual opposition and superficial equality. In the sacred culture of devotees, men and women must be permitted to enjoy the unique force of initiation and help that only the community of their own sex can provide. And the social access between the sexes should be formalized, to eliminate the forces of conflict and erosion of the responsibilities that uniquely belong to each sex.

Thus, as devotees begin to adapt and mature in the Way of Divine Ignorance, they should have access to the refuge of the Church community and its cultural sanctuaries. The casual order of the common and subhuman world should cease to be the primary focus of their lives. Rather, the sacred and dynamic order of the religious and spiritual culture of devotees should focus and inform the higher-adapting energy of each individual. The society of devotees should not be sexually casual. Marriages should be acknowledged and honored. Relations between the sexes should otherwise be pleasant and humorous and Life-positive, but they should not be casual, or a field of secretly erotic oppositions.

In the community of devotees all human responsibilities must be accommodated, while access between the sexes must be prevented from becoming casual. Therefore, it is likely that men and women will often perform the roles of activity that are traditionally assumed. However, there should be no limit to the potential of any individual of either sex to perform creatively in the realms of service, institutional responsibility, education, and all of the other higher cultural processes that all devotees share in common.

Likewise, in the common world of work that all human beings share, both men and women should be permitted, by law and custom, to realize any level of productivity and income for which they demonstrate an equal capacity. (However, it is not the obligation of the common social order to create a unisexual "culture," and this should indeed be prevented by maintaining, or recreating, some of the customary "good manners" and other practical accommodations that helped create a formal and honorable rather than a casual and exploitative environment in the social relations of the sexes.)

171

Within the general community of devotees, each sex should maintain an independent culture. The casual society of the sexes is also a society of childishness in which the sexes are almost entirely dependent on one another for what are considered the ordinary pleasures, useful influences, and constant values of life. Thus, women tend to be at a loss without the constant opportunity to "play it" for men, and the social amusements and conventional culture of common society tend to be almost entirely the creations of men. Likewise, men in their ordinary subhuman mode are self-indulgent vitalists, gaming for odds and spoils, winning women by strength and stealth, and otherwise preoccupied with a verbal mentality that expresses a sense of alienation from Life and from all that is woman.

Thus, in the community of devotees, men and women must enjoy the culture of their own sex, and live and grow in their unique fashion, as well as in their independent wholeness, without dependence on the play of opposition with the opposite sex. In that case, the social and intimate meeting between the sexes will become more and more the meeting of priorly mature and whole individuals, who are not completed by one another, but who are able to complement one another in a pleasurable play of natural abilities.

More than this, as the individual devotee matures, whether male or female, he realizes more and more of the superhuman wholeness that awakens in the Fullness of Divine Life. The devotee in his human functional role is part of a dynamic play of opposites in the human social order. But the devotee ultimately matures beyond the differentiated character of his sex. It is not that he or she becomes a homosexual or bisexual as a result of spiritual practice. But the two-sidedness of the human body-mind becomes a unity, simply

Full, at the level of spiritual identity and higher human character. As the devotee matures spiritually, and even his sexuality matures beyond conflict and orgasm, he begins to incarnate the higher human characteristics of the <u>whole</u> body-mind.

Thus, when conventional sexuality is itself transcended, the role limitations of casual society are also transcended. Such is the inevitable expression of human evolution in the higher or superhuman processes. However, such is not the effect of the "unisexual" motive of casual and subhuman society. (The "unisexual" obligation is, in itself, like the obligation to live in a society of casual association between the sexes, a suppressive demand. Only the transcendence of sexuality, rather than the subhuman social suppression and manipulation of sexual character, produces the higher human and whole, or relatively "androgynous," type of individual.)

The higher human type is neither self-possessed nor self-divided. Neither is he in conflict with or reactively disposed toward his own existence or the play of the world. He animates the priorly whole, or sex-transcending, role under all circumstances of life. Just so, under any particular circumstance of life, he, regardless of his apparent sex, may act more or less via the character role of the male (expansive-aggressive) or the female (receptive-passive). The ultimate Man, therefore, while living essentially as a fully mature man or woman, is whole, Full, and an incarnation of every aspect of human and superhuman character.

172

The Independence of the Sexes and the Play of Human Society

Every individual must enjoy all the benefits of a culture of his or her own sex. Thus, each is to be tested, instructed, and supported by the cultural influence of the members of his own sex.

However, such cultural development of the unique character of each sex is not an end in itself. It simply provides a basis, in character and understanding, for the sexual or polarized play of human life.

Therefore, each individual must enjoy natural access to the daily play with human individuals of both sexes. That contact should not be casual, exploitative, or repressive. But the play of human characters is to be valued, and the independent culture of each sex should serve the development of each form of polarized human character, so that the human play may be enhanced, and the human energies of the world kept in balance.

173

The daily society of human beings of both sexes becomes a matter of maturity only when each individual is obliged by the culture of his or her own sex to adapt to full human maturity. Where such maturity is not commonly attained, daily society becomes chaotic, loveless, humorless, and subhuman. Then the sexes mingle as if erotic play were the significance of all meetings, whereas the common human play of sexual characters must transcend genital sexuality.

The genital play itself must be informed and mastered by love and spiritual adaptation. And the potential of genital contact should be implied only between true and mutually committed intimates. The common society of both sexes is itself a play of characters, or dispositions of human energy in action, not a play of genitals. And that common play must become a matter of responsibility on the part of every individual—which responsibility should be obliged upon him through the character demands of the culture of his own sex.

Male and female roles of character and sex are ultimately determined by the functional polarizations of the body-mind below the conscious mind—in the subconscious and vital functional dimensions of the bodily being. Social institutions and taboos cannot alter the truly determining factors.

However, both male and female should strive creatively toward the fullest realization of both their common human and unique sexual characteristics. Thus, certain fixed ideas may originate from personal experience or the social order in general, and these must be dissolved in the wisdom of the whole body-mind.

Among these ideas currently are the notions that the male "embraces" and the female "gets embraced." It is true that the female character, in the play of life and sex, is generally more passive or receptive, and more sensual, while the male character is generally more aggressive (toward penetration, but not necessarily toward sex itself) and mental. But in the play of sex, both sexes or roles tend to balance and fulfill one another. Therefore, true sexual intimacy tends to be an instrument for making each partner more whole or balanced as an individual.

In casual society, where the sexes mingle without discrimination or formality, sexual practice tends to become casual and desire-oriented rather than oriented toward intimacy and the commitment of love. Thus, sexual activity tends to reinforce the independent characteristics of each sex—leaving the male with only the one-sided role of "macho" aggressiveness and the female with the equally one-sided role of "catch me if you can."

But in the sacred society or culture of devotees, the play of the sexes is honored and also accounted for in the structures and formalities of daily life. And married intimacy and household integrity are constantly protected and aided by all. In such a cultural way of Life, the wholeness of the individual is as important as the polarized play between individuals.

Therefore, devotees who would practice their sexuality in the form of sexual communion must consider their fixed and one-sided ideas about their own character and disposition. The male devotee must consider if he is not only willing to embrace, but if he is willing to be embraced, to submit to the loving embrace of another. If he is not comfortable with this idea, he must experience a greater emotional liberation and wholeness. It is not that he must become a homosexual or a bisexual. Rather, it is that in the polarized sexual relationship with his wife he must submit to her, feel to her, and be able to be sensually rather than mentally sensitive to her and touchable by her. Maleness is not to be a thing in itself. It is only a platform for ecstasy, for surrender and turning from self to lover.

Likewise, the female devotee must consider not only if she is willing to be embraced, but if she is willing to embrace another. She must become whole, and thus wholly capable. She must be positively turned with great force of love-desire to her husband—not only to receive him and be penetrated in her body and feeling, but to cling to him, to embrace and touch him, and to create the circumstance equally with him. She must understand and be responsible not only for love but for the whole regenerative process of sexual communion, just as her husband must. She must make her unique sexual character a means for ecstasy through sacrifice of itself and all its independent limitations toward the wholeness realized only in ecstatic love, ecstatic embrace, and ecstatic life in general.

Thus, the human play of sexual character is a play—a dynamic play of differentiated and mutually attracted opposites. And the intimate cultural order should account for this in its structures and formalities. Human life is also a matter of the realization of whole and total responsibility for all that the human individual is by virtue of its structure. The human individual ultimately transcends the internal and sexual structures that create negative self-division. But if differentiation itself were to disappear, life would cease to be a play, and its dynamics would be frustrated. Thus it is that wholeness or integrity is a matter of creative realization moment to moment in the play of Life. There is no independence to what is whole. If we are to be whole or balanced we must become a sacrifice of what we are in our independence. Through sacrifice, or the functional realization of the relational force of love we are always released into wholeness.

Therefore, the male and female roles of character are not to be suppressed or confused or diluted. They are to be acknowledged and supported by right living and a right order of relationships. It is only that the self-divided and self-possessed and rigid differentiation of the sexes and of individuals in general must continually be transformed.

The Spiritual Transformation
of Sexual Characters

176 Whatever is expansive and descending in its action is attracted by what is already descended and passive. What expands is thus also destined to fall to rest. Thus, the male is chronically bound by his own expansive and spatially directed activity, and both its frustration and satisfaction. He therefore tends to become self-indulgent, angry, distracted. He must see this and become balanced, a <u>whole</u> bodily being rather than a divided or self-contradicting entity. He must, therefore, also take up the <u>role</u> of the feminine in himself, rather than seek her exclusively as object and waste himself in obsessive expansion into the world.

The feminine <u>role</u> or <u>action</u> is ascending and inward, temporal and mental and supramental, whereas, as <u>object</u>, she is passive and descended and attracting toward descent. The male must balance expansive and worldly outwardness with calming inwardness (meditative coolness and ease). He must regularly dissolve the tensions of his tendencies and return to the origin or epitome of his feeling through whole bodily prayer[1] and real meditation, relaxing the motivations toward outer fulfillment, frustration, and anger. He must realize the Truth position, the Heart, prior to descent and ascent, and be single and whole.

Whatever is contractive, inward, and passive is attracted by what is already ascended, creative, and generative—the male as object, the "bindu,"[2] the point of origin, the light, the head, intelligence, creative spirit. But the female is chronically bound to

1. Whole bodily prayer is the principal devotional practice for members of The Free Communion Church. In the Cycle of Devotions engaged by devotees daily, bodily prayer is associated with a specific formal activity, wherein the devotee Communes whole bodily with the Living God. But ultimately, every kind of action, including sexual play, must be transformed into bodily prayer, or total psycho-physical Remembrance of God.
2. The bindu is a psycho-physical center or point that is the locus of energies and transmutations of consciousness. A vision of a single or complex center of light, or several points of light, sometimes colored, is commonly referred to as the bindu. The term may also be used to refer to a sense of a locus infinitely above the thinking mind, and which is silent, beyond form and visibility.

the self-image of herself as object by attractiveness rather than her natural activity of harmonious integrity and spiritual fullness. She cannot make the gesture either of involution and ascent or of radical conversion and dissolution of the self principle, but she lives as the passive object of the descending and male act. The male is chronically obsessed with his <u>action</u> (as expansive and descending subject) whereas the female is chronically obsessed with her <u>position</u> or <u>status</u> (the passive and descended object).

177

The male and female both need to awaken to <u>the feminine action</u>, which is self-transcendence, and fulfill it. In that case, both will also come into union with the male role or action (the creative spirit or subtle intelligence and generative power). Both need to restore the balance of the halves or motives of the whole bodily being before their sexual play with one another can pass beyond conflict into love and truly human pleasure.

It is not that the female needs to imitate the male action, and so become more expansive and worldly. She needs to become active, but in the feminine way—which is free, truly spiritual, and world-transcending. The male needs to do the same.

The play of male and female in the world is where the universal trouble is dramatized. There is no cure at the level of sex or attraction itself. Men and women need to turn from one another (except in spiritual love and service, in which each is whole, already fulfilled and free) into the regenerative process of unification with the subtler structures of the human bodily being and the Divine Condition of all structures and conditions.

Once this is done, and the worldly, self-possessed view of each is dissolved in a harmony and clarity of spiritual regeneration and contemplation, free of obsessive desire, emotional reactivity, mental disturbance, and unrest, then the Heart[3] or Truth may be revealed, and the devotee, male or female, will penetrate and transcend the

---

3. Because the Divine Condition Bubba describes in this paragraph is intuited at the heart, Bubba refers to it as the Heart. The Heart is not located inside body and mind, nor located in any place in relation to body and mind. The body and mind arise within this conscious Condition, and they are modifications of It. The Heart is the true Self and Divine Soul of all beings. Bubba capitalizes this term to distinguish the Divine Nature from the three aspects of the psycho-physical heart of the body and mind: the physical organ; the psychic, feeling dimension of the being; and the functional seat of the soul.

egoic error that is the cause of all the power in limitations, subtle or gross.

Once the initiatory and spiritual function of the sexual play is fully realized in the Way of Re-cognition, a profound psycho-physical obligation must be presumed by the devotee. Thereafter, the yogic ascent (or awakening of the subtler human structures above the heart) is made, and the limitations of body and mind are ultimately transcended. This done, the egoic foundation of the heart is also revealed and penetrated.

In the Way of Radical Intuition, devotees are sexually free in the true or highest sense. They may enjoy occasional and responsible sexual union, but they are not bound up in the conventional play of opposition, separation, and degenerative release. They are free individuals, active in service to the world—even as married householders, if they choose. But they are no longer bound by any gross and worldly or psychic and subtle manifestation. They exist as the Heart, instantly re-cognizing or penetrating the limiting force of all arising phenomena. They live this until, by Grace, they pass from bodily and mental conditions, by Dissolving into the Perfect Domain, prior to all objectification and limitation of Consciousness, or of the undifferentiated Radiance and Life in which all conditions are appearing.

Chapter 11

Love Is the Sacrifice of Man

A talk given by Bubba Free John
to his devotees

BUBBA: The import of the Spiritual Master is not that he comes into the world and is love, or that God independent of man is love. The import of the Spiritual Master and the Divine Communication is that you, and every being, must <u>be</u> love. Every being must fulfill the Law, regardless of his or her past. It does not make any difference how difficult it is for you. The Law remains the Law. The Law is unobstructed feeling-attention under all conditions and in all relations to Infinity. If you are obstructed in feeling and attention, you fail to fulfill the Law. That is why you suffer, and why you stop growing.

Until now you have adapted in complicated ways to the three lowest stages of the development of the whole body—the physical, the emotional-sexual, and the mental. But the structural destiny of mankind is to move into the fourth stage of life, wherein the heart, the psychic core of the being, truly awakens. All religions are basically about the awakening of the heart, the function of love. This is the essential idealism of humanity in our time. Nevertheless, human beings now are developing casually, realizing only the sub-human stages of life. We become human only when we awaken at the heart. We are spiritual then, God-conscious only then. Thus, profound Divine Communion, the fully spiritual initiation of the Way of Divine Ignorance, begins in the fourth stage of life.

Until you are living as the awakened heart, every last one of you feels that you have been separated from the Source, your link to life, your food line. It is not that when you were a dependent baby your parents stopped feeding you. You, for whatever reason, recoiled from the source of food. Though you may not now remember it, you consciously chose to cut yourself off from relations, to contract as unlove rather than to live openly in relationship under all conditions. Perhaps, in your childish need to survive, such an action was necessary. But you are not a child anymore. I am here to tell you that you are always connected to the true food Source through love, through unobstructed feeling-attention via the functions in which you are presently awake. That is the Law. We are fed through the spine from the heart, in all directions, when we are love. When we are not, then we are cut off from the food Source, and in our relations we cut everybody else off from it too. When you love, you are connected with the food Source on which the whole bodily being depends. It radiates to you, in you, around you, and <u>as</u> you most especially.

You must become love. And you must enjoy integrated responsibility for the whole of the lower life, if you are to continue to grow into the psychic dimensions and into the Light itself. Therefore, you must accept the discipline of the Law of love, or sacrifice, and bypass completely all of your old and loveless ways. To love is not a matter of self-denial, which is self-directed effort, concerned for the so-called sinfulness of your lower life. Love is the transformation of self through Divine Communion, through pleasure, the inherent Bliss of the bodily being when it is feeling to Infinity. No matter how difficult it is—because you can still sympathize mightily with these old tendencies—you must enter into the heartfelt enjoyment of the Divine Reality, and be its agent.

The Way is the way of the heart itself, which you realize not by constantly manipulating the lower life, but by submitting the lower life to Divine Communion in a natural, intimate, orderly, full, and human life. Releasing your concern for lower life to the power of the heart, you become aware, through a native process in the midst of this Divine Communion, of the higher life. You are being fed again. By reconnecting with the Light, with the heart, with the Divine, you grow again and begin to develop in your awareness, just as a child naturally grows from one stage to the next.

The stages of growth through which your human functions may naturally develop are not available only to the most extraordinary beings who enter the Earth plane. They are available to all human beings who will release themselves into the stream of the process. For you, now, existence is basically material, elemental, vital life, emotional-sexual awareness, and thinking. When you become steady as the heart, however, the psychic dimension of the being opens, and it becomes quite natural to you to be psychic—to intuit the Divine and to be blissful because of that intuition, to enjoy a psychic awareness of your environment and other beings. This function becomes quite natural to you, just as now it is natural to think or to have a physical sensation. Now your attention is focused, by tendency, below the psyche, below the heart. If you exercise the psychic function at all, it is through a vague, temporary, and only occasional stability in love and intuition. When you commit yourself to it, however, it becomes more and more natural to you. The aberrations of the lower life become less and less significant, less and less forceful, because now they are simply noticed, rather than identified with. They are taken into account through a profound responsibility. Thus, your humor toward the tendencies of the lower life begins to return, and you realize that you are not at all in Truth what you are by tendency.

On the basis of this awakening of the heart, you begin to grow again and to move into the higher stages of development. It is in the maturity of the second stage of practice, the Way of Relational Enquiry, and in the third stage of practice, the Way of Re-cognition, that the esoteric aspect of this Way of Divine Ignorance begins. In these higher stages, dimensions of awareness become natural to the being that are not imagined to be true or even possible by the usual man, who is still struggling with the ideal of love, only occasionally coming close to it, and spending all of his time in the dilemma of sex and all the usual reactive emotions—anger, jealousy, guilt, fear, sorrow, doubt—that keep him in conflict with others.

The individual who constantly dramatizes reactive emotions is a profoundly dependent and childish person. He, or she, is suffering uncertainty about whether he is loved—rather than presenting himself as love at all times. The dependent person, who is always watching to see if he is loved, is subject, for example, to jealousy.

The secret to overcoming jealousy is not to try somehow to stop being jealous. The secret to being essentially free of jealousy is to stop being dependent on whether or not you are loved in this moment. As long as you are always sitting back and reading each situation for evidence that you are loved, you yourself are being loveless and contracted. Thus, you will always continue to find the evidence you seek. You will always find that you are already not being loved. The truth is, however, that in your watching for love, you are already not <u>being</u> love.

The way to be free of jealousy, as of all reactive emotion, all contraction of the feeling being, is to be love, to be the radiant feeling-attention that is the truth of us in Divine Communion. When you are that, then you will respond in the appropriate way to the circumstances of life, no matter what they are. And perhaps on some occasions you may not be loved or properly acknowledged. But the effects of the circumstances of life will not be critical any longer. Not only will you be able to survive, but you will be able to transcend all the effects of your experience. Abiding in Divine Communion, you will be greater than experience.

If you are love with your lover under all circumstances, jealousy is not primary any longer—it could fundamentally be abandoned. It does not have any significance, any real force, when you are love. It is only when you are always wondering whether or not you are loved that you become insanely jealous, debilitated by jealousy, always testing your lover. So there is never any real evidence of loving in you. There is always the wondering, always the testing, always the suspicion, always the relative certainty that you are not loved. But basically you are not loving in relationship.

Eventually your attention becomes scattered, and you become promiscuous. You cannot concentrate in your relationship with your lover if you are not love. If love is in doubt, you are promiscuous. Hence the religious dictum that you are an adulterer if you think casually about having relations with someone else. The reason that you think casually about sex is that you are not love. When your love is in doubt in your intimacy, then your attention becomes casual. It cannot be concentrated through loving, through commitment, through real feeling in the moment. Thus, you become very mental, full of imagination, tending to be promiscuous, tending to believe that something romantic is happening between you and every one, and approaching every person as if he or she were ready for romance. All of this instead of being strong and free.

A relationship of true marriage is created and lived by choice, if you are free. Your sexual intimacy is chosen, a matter of commitment, concentration, real attention, real feeling. But to love all beings is not to be seductive with all beings. Nothing like that is at all associated with real love. The love of all beings, which is native to us, has nothing to do with sexual indulgence or any other curious and specific function. It is the whole life. It is Divine Life. It is the natural Fullness that we represent in the midst of Infinity.

Therefore, in order for women, for instance, to be devotees and naturally to move through free feeling-attention in all of their relations, they need not be subject to the casual sexual advances of all men. The disposition of Truth has nothing especially to do with sex or the role that a woman plays intimately with a man. Truth has no such implication. It is a moral force, a spiritual force. It does not require any self-conscious attempt not to be sexual. It simply is not inherently sexual.

But the woman who is not responsible, who is childish and dependent on sexual attention, is tending in one or another way to be sexually related to all men. She will always tend to be that way to one or another degree, at least in feeling, perhaps even in action, until she becomes responsible in the spiritual sense for love. Then the lower life, including sexuality, becomes her responsibility, something that she uses lawfully through real feeling, real commitment, real enjoyment.

You will never realize truly human sexuality until you are responsible for love. There is more to sexual intimacy than not being promiscuous anymore, or having a husband or a wife. You must be able to live that polarized, intimate relationship lawfully and to transform it. Just as you became emotionally adapted to lovelessness and contraction, you have also become adapted, physically and sexually, to the discharge of Life through orgasm and all the other

185

emotions associated with sexual intimacy. You waste energy, you stimulate one another, you lead one another to orgasm together. Until you are free in the spiritual sense, reponsible in your intimacy, you will not be able to realize the lawful sexual aspect of your intimate life. You will perhaps remain physically true to one person, but you will tend to live that relationship as a dramatization of orgasm, separation, self-indulgence, loss of Life. You will degenerate through it, even though you are applied to it from the point of view of conventional morality. People may say of you, "A very good marriage. They are a very good couple. See how devoted they are to one another. Neither one of them has ever been with anybody else." In fact you spend all your time exhausting one another's energies and separating together from the whole world.

You must be instructed in and learn through practice the regenerative form of your sexual possibility. The regenerative form of sexuality is not like the generative or degenerative ones. It does not arbitrarily discharge the Life-Force through the terminal of the genitals. The Life-Force must not be thrown out through one of the body's organs by stimulation of that or another organ. To do so devitalizes the body, emptying it of energy and degenerating its functions. The Life-Force, along with all the essential chemistry of the body, is not to be discharged in that frivolous fashion. It is to be conducted to the whole body and expressed by the whole body through love to Infinity. Not only is orgasm degenerative in this way, but also casual indulgence of sexual interest, sexual exploitation of the body, and the many ways of discharging vital and emotional energy through the terminals of the body. Nor must sexual relations, actual genital play with your lover, be engaged casually, indulged when you merely feel stimulated externally or subjectively.

Sexual desire alone is not the occasion for sexual intimacy between devotees. The quality between lovers must be mutually loving and full of desire. Their mutual feeling must be love-desire in its truest sense. Then the time they spend together in intimacy is not the brief moment that most people indulge for the sake of the orgasm. Sexual play must be engaged fully and as a regenerative process. If you will practice your sexual intimacy in the regenerative way that will be described to you at the appropriate stage of your practice, in a relatively short time you will find that you are beginning to enjoy sexual intimacy with one another less frequently, because you enjoy the same Fullness of Life in the incidents of ordinary intimacy.

The regenerative practice of sexuality should not be merely repeated, nor does it require repeating. It is too strong, too profound, too full a matter for casual repetition. There is a time of learning, a time of adapting to this regenerative process, but when the individuals are mature in its practice, then the frequency of their sexual contact normalizes in an appropriate emotional and vital economy. They are liberated from their sexual obsession as the process of their spiritual growth develops. There may come a time when actual genital intimacy is very occasional, in some cases even very rare. But when it does occur, it will not be solid, stiff, or self-conscious, as if the purpose of having sex were to prevent the loss of the semen or the Life-Force. (The purpose of sexual communion is Love-Communion with the Living God via intimate sexual embrace. The conservation of biochemical energy is secondary and merely natural to such Love-Communion.)

The true practice of sexuality is a natural extension of regenerative living, through right diet, energetic service to all beings, and conscious exercise of all your functions. And it becomes natural to you to choose not to indulge in sexuality casually. Thus, devotees who enjoy sexual intimacy in this regenerative form free one another of obsessive involvement with sex and become strong. They are no longer promiscuous in thought and feeling nor in action. They have become oriented toward spiritual delight in the midst of the conditions of ordinary life. The occasions of their sexual intimacy may become less frequent, but those occasions are also very true and profound when they do occur.

Secondarily, the right practice of sexual intimacy is also regenerative in the literal sense, generally strengthening and improving the health of husband and wife (or of homosexual mates), stabilizing and harmonizing them. And their attention moves naturally into the plane of their relationship itself, the polarization, the spiritual awareness of one another, the spiritual regard for one another, the presentation of love to one another rather than childish dependence.

You can see that this process is a profound leap into the human realization of sexuality. Truly human sexuality is all I am talking about, not any super-esoteric sexual magic. This regeneration is the human realization of sexuality. What we have been led to adapt to in our emotional and sexual experience is nothing like this at all. We have been bereft of culture, reared by people who did not turn us to the Divine Life, but rather served and reinforced and in various ways created a degenerative and irresponsible life, a self-indulgent life, a curiously disturbed life that cannot be love.

This discussion of love, which seems perfectly ordinary to me, is extraordinary to the view of people in general. Very few people would consider it, yet it is the absolute obligation of human beings. It is not our obligation in the sense that the world becomes utopia when we fulfill it. We are projected into this world until we realize the principle of existence, but the fact is that when we fulfill this obligation we go beyond the world. Thus, the world is populated by people who have not yet fulfilled it. That is why they are here. That is why this world is the way it is, not particularly hellish, but a school, a plane of experience that schools us for as long as we may be stupid enough to have to stay, and insensitive enough or self-indulgent enough to be trapped here.

The wise man or woman will go beyond his (or her) humanity, beyond his physical, sexual, emotional, mental adaptation, even beyond being a moral or worthy being in this world. He will move to adapt to functions higher than the human psyche, so that he may be projected into a dimension that corresponds to his adaptation. The truly wise individual will become an absolute sacrifice to the Divine. The more conventional aspirant looks to climb the ladder of the body toward cosmic knowledge and visions. But the true devotee transcends all knowledge and experience and passes into perfect God-Communion. He passes to and beyond the sahasrar.[1] He does

1. The sahasrar is the highest center of Life-Energy and the terminal goal of the yogi. It is associated with the crown of the head, the upper brain, and higher mind.

not linger in any of the levels of knowledge, but, on the basis of the realization of the heart, discards the whole bodily being to Infinity.

Therefore, I instruct you, as Krishna did Arjuna at the end of the *Bhagavad Gita,* to renounce all "dharmas"—gross, subtle, and causal—all supports, all principles, all levels of experience, and resort to Me, not to any dimension of experience, none. Throw yourself into Infinity. Climb the ladder of the body and throw it to Infinity, and then you will come to Me. God will be your Destiny. If you look only to ascend egoically to levels of knowledge represented by the esoteric centers of the body, you may go to more subtle worlds, more heavenlike places, but you will not be there eternally. You will have to be born in the human form again and continue climbing the ladder until you lose your taste for heaven. But if you acquire a taste for the Divine through sacrifice, there is no ultimate release until the whole body is sacrificed into God. That sacrifice is what this Teaching is about.

And when we bypass the illusions of all phenomena, even the highest, and throw ourselves whole bodily, as the whole psychophysical condition of our manifestation, into the Unknown Being of Ignorance-Radiance, that gesture transfigures us, transforms us into Radiance itself, the Light of God. If we persist long enough, it even begins to change the physical body into light, making it relatively immortal and regenerating it, so that ultimately, instead of dying and being left behind, the body may disappear in space. It is not necessary to persist to that point, but it is necessary to persist to the point of transfiguration and sacrifice in Divine Translation,[2] or the Bliss of Perfect Sacrifice, so that you remain in that Condition even bodily during the conventional states of waking, dreaming, and sleeping. You remain one with that Light which is not seen but which you are.

It is complete madness and utter devotion to make such a gesture. The lesser wise man settles for seeing the planes, the heavens, the beings, while the weak, foolish, ordinary man spends his life indulging physical, sexual, and mental possibilities. Those who have sinned and repented are a little wiser, but those who throw

2. The ultimate Realization of the Way of Divine Ignorance.

themselves into God are absolutely wise, absolutely foolish. True wise men are like fools. And like a truly wise and foolish man, the devotee realizes that experiences, high and low, are nothing, that they are only modifications of the Absolute. Thus, he is not fixed on them. He lets them dissolve into the Absolute. This is the Way of faith, sacrifice, love, and terrible obedience. It leads beyond all the worlds. It does not lead to any conventional heaven or subtle dimension. Its Destiny is the Divine itself.

190

part 11

The Ecstatic Practice:
Conservation and Transformation
of Orgasm

The Free Standing Man
(a free rendering of portions of the eleventh chapter of the Bhagavad Gita), by Bubba Free John

The Master of Life said to His devotee: "Look and see. The entire Realm of Nature arises in Me. Whatever may be desired is experienced in Me." And He gave insight to the man, with mystical Vision to conceive the Form of God. (verses 7–8) 195

The man said: "Soul of all souls, how can any man fail to surrender in Your Company? I see You are the First, the Origin of all creative causes, the Master of all powers, the Ultimate Domain of the Realm of Nature, the Eternal Radiance, All-Pervading, prior even to what is and what is not, the Transcendental Self. (37) I bow down. I acknowledge my absolute dependence on You. Radiant Master, Have Mercy. (44)

"But when I stand again and see You There, stretched between Heaven and Earth in a Rainbow of all the colors blazing bright, everything arising in Your vast eyes, and everything disappearing in Your great devouring mouth again, my inward soul begins to shake with the great fear, my mind becomes unsteady, and I fail to be Your Heart in this moment of Vision. (24)

"Even so, I am thrilled to see what Man has never seen before! Now, Divine Master of this body-mind, be kind to me, and show me your two-armed Form again." (45)

The Divine Person spoke to His devotee: "Stop all of this unmanly trembling, and this mood of fear. What does it matter if you see this Vision of Me, projected in the Realm of Nature? It is only Me. I am the Radiant Heart of Love, Eternally Free of fear. Now see Me again in my human form, as Your Spiritual Master, your friend in love." (49)

Then the Great Person restored the true heart of His devotee, and set his breathing free. The Vision of his mind's eye dissolved in the Natural State of the heart. And the Master reappeared to this ordinary eye, in which the mind is resolved in Bliss, free of every kind of Vision or experience. Now the devotee beholds his Master from the heart. Now he only sees the Free Standing Man. (50-51)

196 *Introduction:* Ecstasy and the Natural Transcendence of Sexuality, *by Bubba Free John*

T he beginning of sexual communion, or right human exercise of the sexual function, is the awakening beyond arbitrary views, or casual social and emotional presumptions about sex—whether positive or negative. In this manner, one is able to enter bodily into the significance of sex, and so be established in sexual relationship without the mood of either aversion or obsession—which are both founded in self-imagery rather than self-knowledge.

This awakening is, therefore, a matter of direct self-observation and self-knowledge, which become responsibility for the relational force of the psycho-physical being. Thus, the truly human being is responsible for the reactivity and self-possessed motives of the uninspected life. In the case of such a one, the body-mind is not turned upon itself, to protect, console, or satisfy itself in self-manipulative pleasures. Rather, the body-mind is a constant offering, a perfect form of sacrifice, yielded into ecstasy, or absorption in the All-Pervading Life-Bliss of God, through love and service in love.

The independent body-mind is a bag of memory and excrement. But unenlightened individuals seek to bind others to themselves by pretending to be, in and of themselves, the supreme object of attention.

True self-knowledge transcends such self-imagery, the Illusion of Narcissus. Thus, the individual who enjoys insight into the processes of the body-mind is free of ultimate identification with the body-mind, or "I." And such a one sees his own body-mind, and that of others, as it truly is.

Therefore, such a one is free of both positive and negative self-imagery. Indeed, he does not meditate on himself at all. Rather, he—whether male or female—is capable of ecstasy, or love, which is the power of Life in relationship. The foundation of sexual communion is just such self-knowledge, or awakened responsibility for ecstatic love, or self-transcendence.

And the key to self-transcendence in action is the process of feeling-attention in every moment. Therefore, the true man or woman lives as the devotee of the All-Pervading and Transcendental Divine Person, Who Pervades all things and beings as their Life, and Who Transcends all beings as the Self, or the Consciousness that Transcends the inner consciousness or separated soul of every living being. Such devotees ultimately Realize all experience to be an unnecessary and Ecstatic Play of the Divine Person, with Whom they are ultimately Identical, and with Whom they are also in Eternal Relationship.

Therefore, sexual communion is a form of devotional sacrifice. It is the manner in which the human sexual function is allowed to be a form of self-transcending Remembrance, or whole bodily Communion with the Living God. And the primary instrument of this devotional activity is, as in the case of all other activities in the Way of Divine Ignorance, the primal whole body principle of feeling-attention, or love, joined with the body and the breath.

The Perfect Secret of such activity is self-transcending or Ecstatic Communion with the Divine Reality. Therefore, even the literal exercise of the sexual function in truly intimate sexual communion is a process wherein conventional erotic motives of all kinds are natively transcended. Thus, erotic mental obsession, reactive emotional states, and even the physical attainment of orgasm are all transcended. Every activity that pursues or attains the loss of Life, rather than abides in Ecstasy, or the present and eternal Fullness of Life, is transcended in this process of sexual communion. Thus, as individuals mature in their intimate relationship, or sexual communion, they become more and more at ease in a natural condition wherein the body-mind is transcended in God-Communion. Action that is inherently self-transcending ultimately also transcends the very functions of manifest experience.

Devotees in the Way of Divine Ignorance practice sexual communion as one of many forms of functional or practical activity, whereby life as a whole, or the body-mind as a whole, is made a constant and perfect sacrifice into Divine Remembrance, or Ecstatic God-Communion. Therefore, such devotees inevitably transcend all devotion to self, or concern for the independent satisfaction of the self-possessed body-mind. In that Process, the sexual function demonstrates a gradual economy, devoted to regenerative and generative purposes, but free of degenerative purposes. (The generative purpose of sexual communion is to produce healthy children, who will also find it congenial to be oriented to the Divine Reality, Self, and Person via the All-Pervading Current of Life, rather than to be bound to the phenomena of experience through self-possession.)

Therefore, a regenerative and generative sexual economy ultimately characterizes true marriage, wherein the relational force of love is constant, devoted to the service of one's spouse and children as well as all other devotees and all living beings. True marriage is primarily a human social relationship, which transcends self-possessed motives and provides an occasion for Divine Communion under ordinary human circumstances.

Chapter 12

How Our Sexuality Is Transcended

Sexual Communion Is a
Transitional Yoga of Man

What may be discovered through the play of sex is itself the ultimate, true, and right virtue of the entire and whole body. It is the right and virtuous condition and alignment of the physical structures, the nervous and glandular systems, and the primary disposition of nonreactive emotion and nonreactive mind (or pure attention). Therefore, we must understand and so free ourselves of our chronic warfare or self-divided conflict about sex, and about manifest existence itself.

The right sexual process, which is sexual communion with the All-Pervading and Radiant Life of God, is the principle and summary of the yogas of Man in his transition from subhuman entrapment below the heart to the truly human and whole bodily disposition of the heart. Sexual communion is not a spiritual or higher human process. It is a transitional evolutionary process that guides us into the human estate, or the sacrificial and truly moral disposition of love, wherein we may begin the fourth or psychic and spiritualizing stage of life. Sexual communion is a primary instrument whereby the elemental physical, emotional-sexual, and the lower mental and intentional (or will) functions are made the responsibility of consciousness, and so unified and raised up as a sacrifice to the whole and entire bodily being via the mechanisms of the heart.

Spiritual Practice Is the "Conscious Exercise" of Love

The key to practice in every stage of the Way of Divine Ignorance is whole bodily Communion with the Divine through unobstructed feeling. Thus, each specific practice must be done as a form of "conscious exercise," as described in *Conscious Exercise and the Transcendental Sun*. In that case, the practice itself is made into a form of ecstatic sacrifice into the Divine and Communion with the Divine through feeling-release of the entire body-mind. Every kind of practice must be devoted and performed via profound self-released feeling into the All-Pervading Radiant Life of God. Such is true sacrifice to God, and such sacrifice must characterize all practices and every moment of the devotee's experience.

The four great stages in which the practices of this Way develop involve specific functional responsibilities at every level of the body-mind. Each of these responsibilities takes the form of a personal, moral, or higher psycho-physical practice. And all of these specific functional responsibilities are mastered by one or another form of the radical or whole bodily *conscious process*,[1] in which insight makes a sacrifice of all experience in God-Feeling.

Thus, the Way of Divine Ignorance is one in which every moment of experience is made a form of psycho-physical love of God. When that love makes the body-mind into a whole and single

---

1. The senior or transcendental practice and responsibility of devotees in each stage of the Way is the *conscious process*. It is the foundation discipline of conscious surrender of attention in God. It is founded upon true "hearing" of the Teaching, or radical and continuous release of self, knowledge, and all experience into the Transcendental Condition of Divine Ignorance. In the first phase of the Way of Div...e Communion (which is the first stage of practice in the Way of Divine Ignorance) the conscious process takes the form of devotional "prayer" to God and the moral practice of feeling-attention (through loving service of others). In the second phase, it takes the spiritual or esoteric form of the Name of God, or heartfelt attention to the All-Pervading Presence that is God. The conscious process matures as the enquiry "Avoiding relationship?" in the Way of Relational Enquiry; as re-cognition, or knowing again, of body, mind, and self-sense as contraction from Infinite Consciousness, in the Way of Re-cognition; and in the Way of Radical Intuition, the conscious process is realized as radical intuition of Divine Ignorance-Radiance, or Realization of the Transcendental Identity and Bliss of the Divine Person.

gesture of Communion with the Radiant Reality, then the experiential body-mind itself is transcended, and there is only God. Such Ecstasy ultimately becomes perfect dissolution of the psychophysical entity in the very Radiant Divine, Who transcends all that may be experienced or known.

No experience, however high in the esoteric order of yoga, is Blissful or Ecstatic in itself. Any experience is, in itself, a form of confinement to the separated self, the independent and reactive body-mind, or "I." Only when the body-mind and the principle of experience itself are sacrificed in God-Feeling is there the Ecstatic Bliss of the Divine. Therefore, the Way of Life in God is not experiential attainment, but the feeling-transcendence of specific experience in every moment.

This is certainly true. And, therefore, in every moment of experience, or spiritual practice in the midst of experience, there is also the contrary tendency to contract feeling and attention upon the experience or the practice itself. Thus, we tend to become "dry" or frustrated as we practice, and we wonder why our discipline has become dissociated from Bliss. In that case we must Awaken, through "hearing" the Teaching and "seeing" the Spiritual Master, so that we again release the body-mind and every practice into unobstructed whole bodily feeling-Communion with the All-Pervading Divine, which is neither objective nor subjective to us. Then we are Full and Ecstatic again.

S exual communion is not a sufficient and independent process that produces Enlightenment or God-Realization. It is simply a foundation human responsibility in one who is adapting to the great affair of spiritual life. The ultimate Realization of Truth is not merely inward to any man, or woman, but it involves a total psycho-physical event, a perfect sacrifice of the entire structure of the bodily being. Thus, that Realization depends on (or ultimately coincides with) the perfect awakening and evolution of the whole structural existence of the individual. The Realization of Truth in any moment further awakens and obliges the apparent individual toward the next level of structural awakening and responsibility. Thus, sexual communion effectively appears as a responsibility at the lowest levels of our structural awakening. The individual must continue, entering into the higher or super physics of the mature relationship between himself (as devotee) and the Spiritual Master (or effective Divine Agency). Thus, he (or she) will continue to grow in experience and responsibility, yielding all conditions into the Condition that is Truth as he grows, so that he may ultimately be the total sacrifice of all that he may appear to be, and so be Translated into the Radiance beyond all worlds.

204

S exual self-indulgence is the product of the inability to feel, to live as unobstructed emotion in relationship, and to persist as such in spite of frustrating conditions and even death. Sexual self-indulgence is simply a way to discharge the accumulated or residual Life-Energy that builds in the lower parts of the living bodily being when it cannot otherwise achieve a state of whole body diffusion and balance of the polarities of the Life-Force.

The approach to sexuality described in this book is not a prescription for sexual self-indulgence but a discipline for right use or participation in the sexual play of Life. It depends on the point of view of love, or unobstructed feeling-attention, which any man or woman may value in moments of thoughtful consideration, but which is truly manifested in daily life only on the basis of profound spiritual insight and commitment. Therefore, anyone considering the application of this practice should be warned that, unless there is the moral and spiritual awakening of the heart, the sexual play described here will tend to be only a way of manipulating sexual desires and vital bodily states.

The practice described here is intended as a discipline for devotees who have engaged the orderly disciplines of ordinary life at the beginning of the Way of Divine Communion. Thus, it is part of a total Way of Life, founded in true "hearing" of the argument of the

Spiritual Master. The right practice of sexual intimacy is not possible apart from devotional life in general, and application of disciplines of prayer, service, study, right diet, and the like—including, ultimately, awakened meditation in the Company of the Spiritual Master.

Right practice of sexual intimacy is a fiery and intelligent pleasure that corresponds exactly to the disciplines of bodily prayer, meditation, and total practice that otherwise oblige devotees in the whole Way of Divine Ignorance. It is not self-indulgence, but responsible human intimacy. There are those who recoil into the subjective illusions of our born existence and who presume that enjoyment of sexual intimacy is always sinful or deluding. They would bind their hearers into every kind of strategic avoidance of human incarnation—in order to realize God or Truth or Reality as a result. But those who are growing toward true maturity in God-Communion realize that, until the Awakening of the soul is Perfect, right intimacy of a sexual kind can be as appropriate as love itself, and such sexual discipline can yield as much ascetic "heat" as any hermit's retreat.

As devotees mature in practice and enter the Way of Re-cognition or the Way of Radical Intuition, the Realization of existence comes to exceed the content or the lessons provided by the common processes of their lives. The esoteric disciplines pass through and then beyond sexual intimacy and the scripts of gross limitation. In the Way of Re-cognition the incident of orgasm must have become a matter of full responsibility, and sexual abstinence may also become appropriate for periods of time. In the Way of Radical Intuition, although it naturally remains to be sacrificially engaged in a manner comparable to that described in the present book, sexual activity may remain an occasional practice, unless motiveless celibacy becomes permanent due to the extreme Power of Transcendental Ecstasy. (In other cases such motiveless celibacy will appear only for temporary periods.) In any case, whether they remain sexually active or not, devotees in the Way of Radical Intuition are constantly involved in a process that transcends and instantly obviates the conventionally binding effects of not only sexuality but all forms of born activity. We are at last neither bound nor liberated by sex or any subjective science or yoga. But Transfiguration of the body-mind by the Radiant Bliss of God-Consciousness liberates us from the forms of experience and all the functional representations of our desire.

The Lover of Mankind, and How Our Sexuality Is Transcended

The functional psycho-physical discipline of sexual communion, practiced by members of The Free Communion Church, is the process whereby our sexuality may become truly human. It is also the process whereby our truly or uniquely human sexuality ultimately transcends itself in ecstatic self-sacrifice into the All-Pervading Divine Life.

The transcendence of sex is the only truly human fulfillment of sex. That transcendence is not realized by problematic avoidance of sex or self-possessed mental and subjective manipulation of our sexual and bodily structures. It requires a positive, free, and human understanding of sex, and a reorientation of the sexual impulse as well as a readaptation of sexual habits of action. Then, through direct psycho-physical Communion with the Divine, and by specific sexual communion with the All-Pervading Life of the Divine, a true and literal transcendence of degenerative sexual adaptation may be realized.

Sexuality and food-taking are the most critical links in the bodily chain below the heart. Therefore, the casual satisfaction of sexual desire provides one of the principal consolations that bind us to ourselves and separate us from the Divine and Blissful Realization of Life. It must not be mechanically and self-consciously resisted, since that is fruitless and as much a matter of self-possession as the exploitation of sex.

But our sexuality must be transcended, and right sexual practice is a process that naturally and inevitably transcends sexuality itself. Such transcendence is a matter of the regenerative readaptation of sexual practice, leading to a wholly regenerative economy in practice, free of the chronic necessity of genital orgasm. Only then will degenerative and unillumined self-possession cease to create the conventional subhuman pattern of life that characterizes most men and women. Only in the transcendence of our sexuality, through regenerative fulfillment of our sexuality, does the Divine become our constant Occupation and our true Lover.

207

We must inspect and awaken to responsibility for all the functions of the bodily being. Conflict with the states of our living must be replaced with right and sacrificial application or use of all functions.

Thus, sexuality must be raised from its merely generative use, which places Man on a par with simple vital creatures. And it must likewise be raised from its common or degenerative uses, which bind us to subhuman and destructive realizations of our own structural potential. Our sexuality must be realized in its uniquely human and ecstatic form—which is the regenerative play of sexual communion.

At the level of responsibility we represent in sexual communion, we adapt and evolve in a natural pattern of growth into the fourth stage of life[2]—wherein the heart, or nonreactive feeling-attention, epitomizes the whole and entire bodily being. However, if the disposition of reactive individuation, self-possession, self-division, fear and separativeness, and localized and degenerative exploitation of functions persists, then sexuality and all other forms of our living expression actually prevent our growth into the fourth

---

2. A summary discussion of the seven stages of life appears in the introductory commentary to chapter 6.

and truly human stage of life. In that case, we remain self-destructive, chronically troubled, and even violently separative in our relations with others and the whole world to Infinity.

208   In every stage of our growth, function must be adapted to the Law (which is sacrifice, or love). The tendency in subhuman individuals (those who are not stably adapted to the conscious, intuitive position of the heart, or the fourth stage of life) is to adapt to functions in themselves, or for the sake of their objects. Consequently, the contrary tendency—to separate or invert attention from functions and their objects and toward self, or the subject of experience—becomes the conventional technique of salvation or release for those who despair of the games of Life. But Truth and happiness are neither in the extroversion nor the introversion of our awareness. Rather, Truth and happiness are in the surrender and adaptation of our total existence to the Law, so that we are expressed as Radiance, love, service, and freedom from both the introverted and the extroverted self-position.

When function (whether introverted or extroverted) becomes the Principle of manifest existence—rather than the adaptation of function to the Law—then born-existence becomes chaos, and a dilemma in need of a solution. Instead, function must follow love.

The usual man or woman is eventually informed with observations of what love becomes when sex is allowed to be the principle of intimacy. The common history of our emotional-sexual adaptation is one in which love is subordinated to function and ego, mind and desire. Therefore, love is the true esoteric, hidden, or secret principle of human existence. We must be transformed in our habit or adaptation, and thus come to observe what sex is (as well as mind, ego, and all the functions of the bodily being) when love is the principle. Love is the form of emotional adaptation that is reflected in true sexuality, or sexual communion.

Love Is the Sacred Principle of Human Sexuality

Wwhat we commonly regard to be good sex is anything "sexy"—that is, anything that stimulates us toward intense genital orgasm. Sexual intercourse tends to be devoted to this motive. And sex relationships tend to be based on this model. Therefore, even marriage tends to be an arrangement of this same kind, but projected as an expectation extending throughout the remaining lifetime of the partners.

Sexual "satisfaction" is the conventional measure of intimacy, and such satisfaction is measured by the frequency, intensity, and general means of stimulating and attaining orgasm. But such a measure is the expression of subhuman involvement in sexuality. The whole matter of the stimulation of desire and sensation in any form is secondary to truly human life. To make stimulation the principle of life and relationships is to establish a vital or subhuman principle as the dominant factor in our living.

Stimulation or intensification of our vital and desiring mechanisms is a natural enough consequence of all kinds of experience. But the process set in motion by stimulation must be a matter of whole body responsibility, or else we are constantly brought to degenerative ends in life.

Stimulation is something we come to depend on in our childishness. Dependence on stimulation from without is the principal characteristic of the immature individual. He or she cannot easily generate positive influences in the world, but is frozen in place, essentially negative or self-possessed, and is only relieved of boredom and despair by encounters with more and more stimulating events or entertainments. For most people, even marriage is primarily a sexual entertainment, an erotic romance—or else an anti-erotic theatre of boredom and despair.

Human sexuality cannot be summarized in the genital play alone. The whole bodily being of the individual must be the structural guide to every kind of functional experience and every form of relationship. Parts of our total structure are always tending to be used by us as solutions to the frustrations and mortality of our living. Thus, the vital and genital sexual possibility for stimulated and temporary release has become a universal method. But it leads to loveless, self-possessed, and degenerative habits of living.

210

Likewise, various structures deeply internal to the body-mind, primarily in the nervous system and the brain, have become a less common but traditional resort for solutions to the dilemmas of mortal independence. Such structures are, consciously or unconsciously, the universal foundation for religion and spirituality.

No part of the human structure is independent of the rest, or separate from any other part of the external or total cosmos. The internal "self" of the nervous system and brain is not a separable reality by which we may be "saved"—that is, made immortal or relieved of the obligation to be a sacrifice. Just so, the genital sexual mechanism in man is not sufficient for the generation of the truly human or whole body expression of sexual experience.

Thus, the lower vital mechanism or cycle of stimulation and release is only a secondary and partial aspect of our ultimate and creative sexual enjoyment. We must in any case be responsible for that cycle and free of the obsessive need to exploit it and degenerate ourselves in self-possessed, self-emptying, and desperate searches for pleasure. But the lower or vital cycle must itself be dominated or monitored and controlled by the whole body disposition, which is free and unobstructed feeling-attention.

The true human being is characterized by sacrifice, or the life of love expressed through service and responsibility for reactivity. Therefore, it is this characteristic that must inform and transform our deluded and conventional sexual practice. This is the true characteristic of human sexuality, and it is the principle whereby the stimulation-release mechanisms of vital desire may be transformed into regenerative and truly intimate sexual practice.

When desire, or erotic fascination, exceeds intimate love, there is already a separation between two intimates. Therefore, genital tension results, and orgasm is inevitably entertained or indulged.

For this reason, sexual embrace should be engaged only when love and desire are intense, equal, and controlled by open, relaxed, and whole bodily Communion with Life.

True sexual fulfillment is not a matter of lower bodily discharge but of whole bodily Fullness of Life. Modern sexual theories are based essentially on the clinical cure of neurotic sexual contraction that prevents natural or generative orgasmic release. But the true sexual awakening is awakening beyond the egoic contraction of emotion and self-possessed bodily and mental states. It is ultimately a matter of transcending or transforming the genital orgasm (once it has become a natural capability) through a conversion of emotion—from childish and adolescent fears of being unloved to a mature responsibility for love as a whole body and relational confession. Mature lovers constantly see and are seen in love, so they do not give up (discharge) their lives in degenerative orgasm, anger, jealousy, or any of the contractions of body, feeling, and mind from Infinity. The childish and adolescent individual constantly withdraws from the obligation of attention that is love and turns in on self-attention. And he or she also turns from inherent bliss or regenerative pleasure to acquired and temporary and degenerative pleasure, through orgasm and other functional releases.

The breaths of true lovers are balanced and full, and such breaths even feed the brain. The breaths of the usual man or woman are weak, unequal in their parts (exhaling and inhaling), disturbed. Such individuals are anxious about betrayal, even while engaged in embraces. They are anxious about being seen at pleasure or love. And the brains of such persons are constantly starved for the Light of the Heart.

True sexual realization, or sexual communion within a daily life of true intimacy (or loving polarization), is the natural "asceticism" of love. It is free of genital orgasm in itself, and it is responsible as love. Such realized intimacy is the foundation of the spiritual transformation of the whole and entire bodily being.

212

Emotional reactivity and the resultant sense of self-possessed isolation and tension are the root-cause of conventional and degenerative sexual patterns. Emotional reactivity is the fundamental cause of the necessary association of sex with genital orgasm. When emotional reactivity becomes a matter of responsibility, so that true love-desire becomes the stable means of approach to sexual embrace, then the whole obsessive and degenerative affair of conventional sexuality begins to change. The change is realized through the positive orientation of sexuality toward sexual communion with the loved-one in the Living Divine Reality.

The conventional orgasm in itself is the physiological version or expression of reactive emotion. It is sexual function patterned after the model of the bodily functions of elimination. It depends upon stimulation, not whole body loving or release and sacrifice of self. It most often reflects childish dependency on outer or fascinating stimulation of Life-Feeling, rather than responsibility for the intimate and priorly full movement of love for another. It is a common bodily solution to bodily pain, mediocrity, sorrow, and fear. The mechanism of vital stimulation and ultimate release of genital tension through orgasm is common to both the whole body or loving expression of sexuality and the divided body or self-conflict games of sexual exploitation. But in the case of the whole body expression, the vital cycle of stimulation-release is mastered by love and the ability to relax or release the whole body tension at will. In the case of ordinary, self-possessed sexual play, the whole body is divided, chronically tense or pleasureless, and in need of involuntary genital release to achieve a sense, albeit temporary, of well-being and wholeness.

Sexuality Is the Physical Drama of Emotion
A talk given by Bubba Free John to his devotees

BUBBA: Feeding creates a pleasurable sensation in the body that the baby recognizes and that makes it feel comfortable, sustained, protected. The adult gets a similar satisfaction from sexuality. Sexual intercourse is a way of feeding on energy. It is a pleasurable sensation that you can identify. It makes you feel good, because it is a contact with Life. But, just as nursing makes the baby feel dependent for Life on what is outside it, so sexuality makes you feel that you have a very dependent relationship to the energy of existence. This feeling of dependence, however, is false.

In truth, you yourself are a representative of the universal Life-Energy, which you communicate through your feeling response in your relations, through love, not only through orgasm and occasions of physical contact. Therefore, if your life is to be true, the energy that now you identify exclusively with sex must be your consistent manifestation, under all conditions, in all of your relations, most particularly in the intimate, marital occasion of your life. But being able to have orgasms and being sexually attractive and athletic does not make you a true lover. Thus, even your relatively successful adaptation to the orgasm must change, because, like feeding, it is a way of being consoled and dependent.

The Teaching relative to sexuality is that you must go beyond the dependent orientation that seeks to acquire pleasure. You must realize the inherent pleasurableness and blissfulness of existence by connecting to the higher levels of the Food Source, the higher levels of sustenance, or spiritual energy. Thus, you must see your capacity to be released pleasurably through orgasm for what it is—at best a rudimentary way of feeling good, of acquiring pleasure.

You must already be full of pleasure. You must be love. If you live as love, then the purpose once served by the conventional orgasm appears to your understanding as an old adaptation, a form of memory like the aberrated emotions of guilt, fear, and anger. The orgasm is exactly the same kind of aberrated development as guilt or fear or anger. It is the expression of a primarily physical reaction, a physical recoil rather than an emotional one. It is a sign on the physical level of the same recoil that guilt and fear and anxiety and withdrawal from life signify at the emotional level.

We learn orgasm. Orgasm is itself a form of adaptation that we learn at an early stage of life, even earlier than we become genitally active. We learn orgasm in being sustained, in nursing. We learn it in the pleasurable bodily states that we may realize early in life, and we associate those acquired pleasurable states with a continual connection to Life. When we discover our capacity for orgasm, we identify it at the most rudimentary level, just as we identify the pleasure of nursing as an infant. It is a solution to the dilemma of life, to the sense of emptiness, of needing to be fed, of feeling that we are not inherently one with infinite pleasure or Bliss.

Emotion and sexuality are the same. If you are adapted only to reactive, negative emotions, then your sexuality will take a very similar form. Thus, lovelessness and the rejection of Life at the level of emotion are reflected as orgasm and the rejection of Life at the level of sex. The orgasm is precisely the rejection, or discharge, of Life. In later life, we become ritually addicted to this pleasure, this physical emotion of the orgasm. We constantly hope to acquire it again and again, and our lives become very complex in order to acquire that pleasure.

Unless you are private and a masturbator, you generally depend for your orgasm on sexual intimacy with another individual. But in general the life you spend with people with whom you have orgasms is like orgasm itself. It is loveless, a recoil from relationship. It is a

214

theatre of jealousy, anger, fear, mediocrity, subhuman energy, and mutual stimulation to the point of acquiring orgasms. It is a life of conflict, a life lived at a very low level. The fundamental function of marriage for most people is to satisfy this drive toward orgasm. But we cannot have the life of orgasm without the life of negative emotions, because they represent the same negative adaptation. Thus, we must not only become responsible for our negative emotions and be present as feeling-attention, in all relations and under all conditions. We must also become responsible sexually, because emotion and sexuality represent the same level of adaptation and responsibility. Sexuality is the physical drama of the emotional dimension of life.

You are all presently sexually active—and most of you have been sexually active since very early in your life. Even if you have not, your early emotional adaptation to the conditions of life determined your sexual pattern in the future. Thus, even if there are no overt sexual incidents in your early life, your childhood, your early teens, before you became regularly active sexually, there are emotional incidents that created a double-bind, an emotional dilemma of pleasure versus fear and guilt. This feeling obstruction then appeared when you became sexually active.

Emotion and sexuality are exactly the same thing. There is absolutely no difference between them. Whatever you are emotionally, you are sexually. Whatever you are sexually, you are emotionally, and whatever you are emotionally and sexually, that is what you are as a living presence. That is your relationship to the Life-Force, upon which spiritual development, at least in its early phases, depends. If you are obstructed emotionally and obstructed sexually, you are also obstructed in the energy of the being. You are obstructed in the psyche, in the feeling dimension of the being, and thus you are prevented from realizing the fourth stage of life and adapting to the functional levels of the bodily being above the navel. You may have occasional contact with the depth that is the heart itself, but you will not fulfill and mature at the level of the heart. Your whole life will essentially be spent below it.

So it is that, in becoming a loving presence in the world, we must not only cease to dramatize all the contractions of emotion— we must also transcend the orgasm. The orgasm, the conventional "hype" of sexuality, is loss of Life, the discharge of Life. It is the degenerative form of Life and of sexual intimacy. It is the craving for sustenance, because we have adapted to the loss of Life. There is a certain momentary pleasure associated with orgasm, but its effects are psychologically and emotionally degenerative. It constantly reinforces negative emotional states, not the life of love.

Orgasm is also physically degenerative. When there is conventional orgasm, the body also eliminates certain glandular chemistries, with the discharge of the Life-Force, that are absolutely essential to its own regeneration and growth. Likewise, orgasm reinforces the attention in its fixation on the lower bodily being. As long as the fixation of attention is reinforced pleasurably and with some consistency in the lower body, attention will not rise to the higher functional dimensions of the body. Thus, the orgasm represents the loveless orientation to Life whereby Life is lost and attention is trapped in negative emotion and the most descended or fleshy capacity for experience.

It is not the pleasure associated with sexual intimacy that is wrong. Sexual pleasure is not in principle wrong. However, our use of it, our relationship to it, is degenerative and an expression of a negative emotional adaptation. Pleasure is associated with the loss of Life. In our casual adaptation, pleasure and death, sex and death, eroticism and death have always been felt to be the same event. We must, in our right emotional and sexual adaptation, discover the pleasure that is inherent in Life. We must realize a regenerative form of the whole process of Life, including our sexuality. We must find the way of enjoying sexual intimacy whereby Life is not lost, we do not discharge Life in order to achieve pleasure, and we love one another, completely happy and free in our life together.

In the societies that exist in our time there are essentially two approaches to orgasm. The traditional spiritual societies, the remnants of which appear in the Orient, regard orgasm as sinful and ignorant because it is loss of Life. It signifies the confinement of

attention to the lower life, whereas in this traditional view attention
properly belongs to the ascended life of God-Realization and to love
in intimate relations. Thus, in the traditional Eastern societies,
sexuality properly has only a generative purpose and no other.

The alternative point of view, which is represented by our
Western society, acknowledges that one should be intimate and a
loving and caring person, and also that orgasms are good. In fact,
you should have as many of them as you like, casually and pleasurably and athletically, with as many people as you can care for, or
who can care for you—you are all familiar with all that psychiatric
nonsense.

But apart from either of these limited points of view, there is a
regenerative form of the sexual process, one that permits people to
live with one another and also to be sexually intimate not merely on
occasions when they want to produce children. The obligation of
such people is a fully human one. They must be spiritually responsible for their lower life through love, through intention. They must
not casually indulge themselves sexually with one another, but
embrace only on occasions of mutual love-desire. Their sexuality is
not aberrated by inwardness, self-possession, imagery, or loveless
physical contact. On the contrary, they are obliged, through esoteric instruction, to the conversion of the orgasm itself, so that in
moments of the crisis of pleasure that naturally appears in sexual
play, the Life-Energy is not thrown off, not merely used to create
explosive sensations in the lower physical body. Life is consciously
conserved and released into the whole body from its fixation in the
genitals, and via the whole body to one's lover and to Infinity.

If individuals who become capable of love through "hearing"
this Teaching will also adapt to this regenerative form of sexual
practice, they may very well, since orgasm will have ceased to be the
justification for sexuality, come relatively soon to a stage wherein
the occasions of actual genital intimacy are less frequent but more
profound than was previously the case. They will realize, in their
continued growth, the essential pleasurableness of existence that
transcends the conventional sexual motive. Even though sexual
contact may continue throughout the entire lifetime of such devo-

tees, they realize a higher adaptation, a higher pleasurableness, a spiritual blissfulness, wherein they no longer require degenerative release in order to feel emotional and physical pleasure.

218

The conventional orgasm, out of the control of love, thrives on relational conflict, since stimulation is the key to ultimate release, and the coming and going of self-possessed and separative lovers stimulates sexual interest via the violence of vital reactivity. Therefore, conventional marriages or sex relationships tend to persist as vital romances or sexual entertainments, and they tend to fail, or they achieve separation, when the stimulative value or effect of conflict and possible separation ceases to be erotic and becomes terminal.

We are lovelessly disposed to use all kinds of bodily and mental means, including the stimulating effects and services represented by other human beings, to achieve the temporary organ satisfactions and intense psycho-physical consolations that are potential in our sexuality. However, it is not necessary for our release from these tendencies that we abandon our sexuality in principle and cling exclusively either to religious hopes or actual and yogic awakenings of the higher human structures in themselves. Rather, we must simply become responsible for right and regenerative use of the sexual and other lower human functions through the sacrificial and moral disposition of love. In that case, we may also continue to grow and awaken into right use of the higher human functions, and to the process of the ultimate sacrifice of the whole and entire body-mind in God.

Sexuality incarnates emotion. How we each live in our sexual function depends on our state of emotional responsibility or irresponsibility. Sexual communion is the incarnation of love in the form of sexual intimacy. All other forms of sexual exercise more or less incarnate reactive, self-possessed emotions and dramatize the self-protective and mortal sense of dilemma, inherent contradiction, conflict, opposition, necessary separation, independence, loneliness, self-doubt, anger, guilt, shame, and fear.

The sexual dramatization of self-possession (which is the contraction of the native love or radiance of the bodily being) is the conventional degenerative orgasm, the momentary illusion of release that in fact empties and ultimately kills the bodily being. It reflects an anxiety that cannot tolerate intensity or Fullness of Life and feeling, and which finds release in emptiness, whereas it should find freedom in love and prior happiness.

In the case of intimates who are bodily confessed as love in relation to one another, the orgasm extends to the whole bodily being, and the whole bodily being incarnates as love. Such orgasm is regenerative, free, priorly happy, and an instrument of continuous intimacy rather than occasional separation.

Genital sexual activity is not truly about genital orgasm, self-body excitation, subjective or mental preoccupation, or emotional catharsis. It is about love. It is about feeling one another, and touching one another nakedly at Infinity. Such loving, feeling, and touching should be steady in daily or married life and continuous in sexual embrace. In that case, degenerative orgasm, preoccupation with one's own bodily states, internal and separative fixation, and the entire emotional and physiological preoccupation with release (as if sexual activity began with a problem and solved it at the end) comes to rest. True lovers, initiated and adapted beyond fear and bodily self-possession, embrace as a continuous expression of their always present union in love and their ecstatic feeling-meditation on one another, which draws them, breathes them, and lives them into the Divine Intensity.

Chapter 13

The Right and Intelligent Use of Erotica and Aphrodisiacs

There is a clearly observable tendency to betray one's lover on one's own body. This is done via all the loveless acts or sympathies of self-attention and self-manipulation, which include the performance of the sex act without love or desire, meditation on internal or mental images and sensations, and self-manipulation to the point of orgasm (using either the body of one's lover or parts of oneself as the instruments).

All ritualistic or repetitive indulgence of thoughts or memories, desires, and acts is in fact a self-possessed or nonecstatic activity, and it reinforces self-possession as well as self-division. Such a habit of existence becomes possessed of a sense of futility, or frustration that makes one motionless, incapable of ecstasy. The mechanical repetition of experiences prevents ecstasy, or the happiness of release from the fixed mechanics of individuated existence, and reinforces the sense of inherent dilemma, or the conception of existence as a problem and a process of solving problems.

Therefore, sexual rituals, the mechanical repetitions of pleasure-producing acts and events, must give way to thoughtless, imageless, sensual, and wholly feeling ecstasy in love. Only love-desire, or the bodily yielding of full feeling-attention, can control or dissolve the self-binding stream of thought, subjective-imagery, self-meditation, bodily insensitivity, and the loveless tedium or obsessive liturgy of degenerative orgasm.

I n general, aphrodisiacs are stimulants of the vital play of the body. They open, relax, and attune the elemental physical dimension of the body to the etheric, emotional-vital, and subtler chemical dimension of the body. Thus, the contracted and apparently or relatively unresponsive lover may be stimulated to open to the intensity of the functional and universal fields of Life-Force by the "medicine" of an aphrodisiac. But aphrodisiacs are not only generally unnatural substances, being either actual drugs or drug-like in their effects, but they throw the whole body out of balance, and they turn attention on subjective and personal conditions rather than into communion with one's lover and the Infinity in which he or she, as well as oneself, is appearing.

Thus, aphrodisiacs are simply a mechanical and secondary medical method for compensating for the constriction of free feeling-attention, the mediocrity of vital desire, and the absence of whole bodily availability for the play of sexual love. Instead of depending on aphrodisiacs (including erotica and fetishes), devotees must submit to the discipline of love through "hearing" of the Teaching of Truth. Then they will be awakened to one another, free of self-consciousness, and their play will be a harmony of mutual feeling in which the sacrifice that is love may ultimately become transparent to Love, which is Divine Bliss.

Note: The "aphrodisiacs" criticized in this essay include every kind of device that acts as a sudden stimulant of sexual desire, independent of the process of intimate love. Such stimulants exploit the urge toward orgasm and self-possessed bodily pleasure, and so have an ultimately enervating and deluding effect on the bodily personality and its relationships. There are other substances that may technically be considered to be aphrodisiacs, or enhancers of sexual capacity, but which simply vitalize and strengthen the bodily being. Such herbs as ginseng may have such an effect. And a regenerative diet in general has such an effect. Therefore, degenerative aphrodisiacs should be avoided, whereas regenerative aphrodisiacs, or natural dietary substances that do not stimulate imbalances or deluding urges, may be found useful.

Erotic art and literature communicate and legitimatize the view that sexual play is universal, normal, pleasurable, and, in principle, right, positive, and even religiously or spiritually profound. Therefore, sexually explicit art and literature, in which the subject is raised to a level beyond conventional taboos and fascinations, may be an appropriate art form for people to contemplate in their daily lives.

The contemplation of erotic art and literature, as well as manuals of practical sexual wisdom, is also of value to individuals who are relatively inexperienced and limited in their intimate sexual expression and communication.

However, there is also a wrong or degenerative use of erotic art and sexual description, and that is as a means of stimulating mental imagery and feeding self-possessed and obsessive sexual interest. As such, erotic descriptions only serve to reinforce subjective, separative obsessions and orient the individual toward orgasmic discharge as well as chaos in the intimate relationship to his or her lover. Imagery, obsessiveness, emotional suppression, and the inability to enter into intimate and sensuous bodily communication are all signs or instruments of the failure of love-desire and the whole bodily confession of love. And the wrong use of erotic and sexual arts and literature tends to create or reinforce such tendencies. Erotic and sexual descriptions should only increase the availability of lovers to one another, not separate them by establishing obsessive subjective meditations that prevent loving intimacy.

If, however, such communications are rightly used, they may contribute to one's natural intimacy by removing patterns of self-consciousness, guilt, and suppression of sensual feeling-communication. Lovers should be "erotic" (in the truest sense) for one another. This means they must be able to desire and embrace one another with mindless enthusiasm. And this requires them to yield as free feeling-attention to one another—free of subjective obsessions, fetishes, and inhibitions. Only then will lovers remain devotees of the Infinite in their functional movement toward one another and all other common relations.

Erotica, loveless subjective imagery, and degenerative aphrodisiacs, just as obsessive desire itself, tend to instigate or force the genital discharge. Only communion through love-desire brings natural control to mind and body.

The sacrifice that is love is not deranged and madly orgiastic, but profound, full, and intensely radiant. Sexual communion is a theatre of love's practice. But love, or sacrifice of the whole bodily being, is the Way. Therefore, those who embrace one another in love transcend the embrace itself, and their sexuality is relieved of all degenerative orgasmic obsessions.

Aphrodisiacs, and erotica in general, emphasize the rapid buildup and elimination of Life-Intensity through orgasm. Therefore, such devices are part of the conventional and traditional ritual of orgasm. The usefulness of such devices is generally restricted to the awakening and instruction of those who are yet sexually immature and weak. Others will, through fascination and dependency, tend to become self-involved and enervated by such things. Masturbation is the likely extension of loveless self-stimulation, and self-oriented lovers tend to use sex as a ritual of mutual masturbation without mutual feeling-submission. And private masturbation is an extension of infantile and childish motivations toward loveless and relationless pleasuring of the self-body. It is, therefore, generally separative, enervating, and founded in fear (including the fear of being "seen," or caught having sex), guilt, shame, and relational disability in general.

There is value not only in right participation in sex play, but in the feeling consideration and observation of it in one's own case as well as in the case of others. Thus, erotic art and literature may have a communicative or educational function as a form of observation, just as frank conversations between lovers as well as among friends in general serve understanding and release from the bogies of both inwardness and excessive or "cultic" privacy. The full variability of the play of human sexuality may thus be seen and so become psychologically and emotionally acceptable, and the ordinariness of the play—even its humorous quality—may also be recognized, which serves to take the pressure or force out of obsessiveness.

Erotic media may thus have an educational function, if used properly and on right occasions. But their wrong use is to indulge them casually and obsessively, as themselves a means of stimulation and gratification of sexual desire. Obsessive masturbatory fantasizing may thus be reinforced, turning one into privacy and inwardness, even during sexual intercourse, whereas right sexual play is relational, intimate, forceful, and imageless. The present display of the loved-one is the only natural, true, and perfect source of arousal.

There are ancient texts that visually and verbally describe the play of sex. Such texts are intended to be considered by true lovers, those who have been initiated into the true "yoga" of their union, in order that they may freely feel their way into the full display of their own imageless union.

Such texts may be read or viewed for the same purpose by lovers who live the discipline of sexual communion described in this book. Contemporary erotic photography, art, and literature may also serve the same purpose. But such media must be approached only occasionally, and usually with one's lover, and not for the sake of internalization of the images created by the media. The sexual play should be essentially imageless, and the stimulation should be provided by one's lover. (If one's lover is not sufficient stimulation on any one occasion, and the mind begins to turn to images, it is not appropriate to engage in sexual play at that time.) Thus, obsession with sexual imagery, either internally or in the form of visual and literary media, is only a liability that ultimately dissipates the Life-Force and prevents peace and fullness of feeling in the play of love.

Birth control devices should not only be safe for the users, they should be used only as an adjunct to the mature relationship of committed lovers. They should not be used in order to permit promiscuity or immoderate and self-indulgent exploitation of sex desire. Love must master desire and make desire its servant and friend. Thus, sex desire, or the impulse to achieve release of the force of life's frustration via erotic play and orgasm, should not determine the frequency of sexual intimacy, nor should birth control devices be used in order to be able to indulge sex and orgasm at random or irresponsibly.

Love-desire should determine the frequency of sexual occasions, and orgasm should become a matter of regular responsibility. Thus, contraceptive devices are to be used simply as a means of choosing the incident of conception. They are used because, even where frequency of contact and of conventional orgasm are responsibly chosen, those very occasions do not necessarily fall on days when the woman is infertile.

Thus, contraceptive devices (including the woman's regular observation of all the signs and cycles of her body rhythms) are to be used, in effect, as a means of responsibly choosing the event of conception, not of irresponsibly preventing conception. All other uses of contraceptive devices belong to the worldly and irresponsible realm of sexual choices based on self-serving and vital desire itself, rather than self-sacrifice or love, which is the master of desire.

Erotic stimulation of all kinds, including erotic art and literature, aphrodisiacs, fetishes, and even the self-indulgent use of birth control devices (as an excuse either for promiscuity or for immoderate and ill-timed sexual activity within marriage) all tend to relegate sex to the lower functional order of vital desire rather than love. Thus, sex becomes an indulgence of partial, one-sided, and conflict-oriented impulses. Unless sex is lived by the whole body-mind and as a sacrifice of the whole body-mind through love, it becomes a subjective and self-meditative activity.

Stimulation stimulates desire, not love. There is a possible right use of erotic devices, either as a method of initiation, learning, and dissolving of adherence to taboos, or as a secondary and free adjunct to the pleasure of true and loving lovers. However, attachment to the method of erotic stimulation rather than strict dependence on the whole creative and emotional process of mutual love becomes a depressive and separative motive in one's character and one's characteristic level of inherent pleasure. It leads to sex as little or nothing more than eroticism and the anxious search for orgasmic release. And it creates internal or subjective mental, emotional, and physical fixations that become the chronically necessary and prime movers of all one's sexual activity.

Therefore, abandon all but right use of all stimulating devices or methods, and surrender entirely to the motive and process of love in your intimate life. If you do not, sex will become self-motivated and self-serving rather than an awakening to the Infinite through relationship and through sacrifice in love.

Abandon sex in itself and all service to the principle of orgasmic release. Become tranquil through love, and allow desire to become the creative servant of love. If desire becomes the principle that love must serve, then love dies. Love will fall upon the self through its sacrifice to vital desire. Love awakens only in relationship, and it sacrifices self, the whole body-mind, at Infinity, or to the degree of Infinite Intensity.

The Law is sacrifice. Therefore, we are obliged to choose the way of love and service rather than the way of desire and self-glorification. This is the great and fundamental moral lesson of Man.

In general, masturbation is a strategy of Narcissus, a self-possessed display of attention to subjective, psychic, and other personal or bodily experiential states. The method of self-love implicitly contains the strategy of the avoidance of relationship, and, therefore, it is a reactive, contracting, ritualistic obsession, founded, like the mortal ego presumption itself, in the fear of death and the reluctance to be the living sacrifice that is love.

Those who feel addicted to this practice need not struggle with the impulse itself. It is simply the sexual urge, which is a positive virtue of Life, but it is trapped in a childish or adolescent level of adaptation. However, a positive orientation toward the life of relational feeling and open sexual submission to a true intimate must develop.

228

Those who have no sexual intimate should become oriented toward the life of service or feeling-sacrifice in the Company of the Spiritual Master as well as other devotees. They should serve others, study, and, while refraining from dramatization of sexual conflict through masturbation, move in a sensitive manner toward a real intimacy with a lover who is freely communicative of Life, and touch, and feeling.

Through readaptation of the sexual impulse in the real intimacy of sexual communion, the self-directed tendencies of masturbation, internal imagery, strategic sexual obsession (whether directed toward conventional orgasm or longevity or yogic transcendence), and all the rest of the lovelessness of mutilated sexual adaptation will gradually become obsolete. In the meantime, do not indulge or dramatize via Narcissistic, fetishistic, and obsessive sexual rituals, but remain persistent in the positive and newly adapting orientation of relational sacrifice, or service, through feeling.

Both masturbation and conventional eroticism are, in general, the expressions of inverted feeling-attention. The chronic and, especially, private resort to such means is resort to the stimulation-release mechanism of the reactive and independent or infantile body-mind.

Masturbation and eroticism tend to be forms of regression, or resort to the self, exclusive of relationship. Even though masturbation may involve the mental imaging of others, and even though eroticism may involve forms of sexual play with others, the primary and obsessive occupation is with the self, or the stimulation-release of the personal body-mind.

Such an occupation arises as a result of reactivity to conditions of actual or possible experience, past, present, or future. Masturbation and eroticism are attempted solutions to reactive problems. And these solutions not only fail to be responsible for reactivity itself, but they involve regressive inversion, from the plane of feeling and relationships to the infantile plane of personal sensation, exclusive of or only mechanically associated with the play of relationship.

Thus, sexual "problems," obsessions, and fixed patterns of stimulation and release are all a matter of regressive or self-possessed reactivity. It is not by self-manipulation and stressful concerns that we are liberated from our reactive functional solutions. Rather, it is a matter of insight into our reactive and regressive patterns and gradual adaptation to new patterns that oblige us to live primarily through feeling and into relationship.

The process of sexual communion is just such a process of growth through responsible feeling-adaptation in relationship. In that process, the bodily, emotional, and mental reactivity that causes reversion to the independent self-sensations is undermined through moment to moment self-observation, insight, and awakened commitment to transcendental ecstasy. And the feeling-attention of the whole and entire bodily being is thereby liberated from reactive contractions and made available as love in the Infinite pattern of relationships.

Chapter 14

Sexual Communion: The Divine Yoga of Sexual Love

In this chapter, Bubba Free John presents the fundamental psycho-physical disciplines of sexual communion. Those of his devotees who are prepared to apply this discipline engage in personal consideration of their practice in formal courses, lectures, and seminars with the educational staff of The Free Communion Church. But they do not thereby learn anything that is not essentially communicated in this book (except for certain modifications of the practice of sexual communion that correspond to various aspects of esoteric meditation in the later stages of the Way). This is the whole and entire practice. There is nothing fundamental that is hidden. Bubba has fully revealed the Teaching on sexuality in these pages, so that all may benefit from this Wisdom.

However, the practice remains secret in another sense. Only one who is already bodily Awakened in Divine Communion can fully appreciate this consideration and realize it in practice. Sexual communion is a Divine Yoga of sex and love. It is not a way of seeking to find God or "higher" states of life and consciousness via sexual exploitation of one's own or another's body and energies. Rather, it is a way of sacrifice of the whole and entire body-mind into the Divine Life of God, Who is already felt to pervade and to be one's lover and all beings and things. Sexual communion is an enlightened practice of Divine Communion, and it is accessible only to the devotee. Others may approximate its technical procedures, and derive significant conventional benefits. But they will not thereby enjoy the Transcendental Pleasure that is the real essence of the practice, and by which the practicing devotee evolves into a superior man or woman.

The Essence of the Process
of Sexual Communion

The primary function of the process of sexual communion is
to establish or consciously support a direct relationship of
mutual Communion (or mutual surrender) between the nervous
system (epitomized at the heart and extended throughout the body)
and the All-Pervading Current of Life (which is prior and senior to the
body-mind).

Secondary to this primary function or process is the bodily
conservation and internal or whole bodily conductivity of biochemical energy (including hormonal or glandular secretions, such
as the seminal fluid).

And the instrument for this total process, in both its primary
and secondary aspects, is the functional and relational surrender of
the body-mind, via (1) the direct physical and even verbal communication of love-feeling and sexual desire between the partners
(both during and apart from times of sexual intercourse) and (2) the
release of sexual tensions, in the genitals, the heart and lungs, the
brain, and even everywhere in the body, which are produced by the
erotic power of sexual stimulation, and which, if not transcended (or
released to the whole and entire body-mind) would tend to produce
the degenerative orgasm (which separates the nervous system, and,
therefore, the body-mind as a whole, from Life and discharges or
eliminates, to a critical degree, biochemical energy and vital
secretions).

Sexual Communion:
The Human and Conscious
Exercise of Sexuality

I

Ll human activities tend to concentrate life-energy, via attention and both physical and emotional feeling, in specific functional regions of the body. Conventional use of human functions tends to discharge life-energy through the bodily functions involved in every kind of activity. Devotees in the Way of Divine Ignorance, however, adapt to Lawful (sacrificial or loving) use of their various functional possibilities. They do not in principle avoid the total context of human functions, but they do apply themselves to "conscious exercise" of every functional aspect of their possibilities.

The principles of "conscious exercise," which are applicable to every functional condition of life, are described in the book *Conscious Exercise and the Transcendental Sun*. These principles are to be applied to every condition of life, every function, every process of activity. In essence, these principles involve the voluntary and intentional direction of free attention, via unobstructed relational feeling of and as the whole body, into the conscious performance of appropriate relational action in the present. The core of the process in every case is primary, unobstructed, psycho-physical feeling, or love. And feeling is directly related to the pattern of breathing, which is a cycle of inhalation-reception-retention and exhalation-release-permeation.

Therefore, all truly human activity is fully felt relational action conceived via the cycle of breathing, or reception-release. The breath cycle is itself the living cycle of feeling, or Life-Force. And the root functional activity that most obviously involves the total pattern of Life-Force, feeling, and breathing is the play of sexuality.

For this reason, the sexual function, in the case of human beings, is the epitome or paradigm case of all functions in the gross material sphere. It is in our sexual communication and activity that we are most profoundly revealed, instructed, and tested relative to our participation in the Power and Process of Life.

If the sexual function and play epitomizes the gross life play as a whole, the orgasm epitomizes the function and play of sex itself. And it is precisely in the incident of orgasm that we demonstrate either our conventional or our free, spiritual, and regenerative response to the Life-Process.

The conventional orgasm is genital discharge. It is a form of bodily elimination. It is sexuality lived after the model provided by the organs of digestion and elimination. It empties us. It is a form of reactivity or recoil. It separates us from others and from Life. It makes sexual play a form of conflict rather than relational intimacy and mutual communion with Life. It reinforces attachment to subjectivity, inwardness, obsessive thinking, reactive or negative emotions, bodily contraction, and self-possession. It is, in its common form, not the result of the "conscious exercise" of the sexual function but of the conventional, reactive exploitation of the sexual function.

The right or conscious exercise of the sexual function is founded in intimate commitment or marriage and initiated by the human impulse of love-desire. It is to be responsibly enjoyed in the fullest sense. It is to be realized as a profound and feeling pleasure. And, therefore, it is to be realized as a process of conservation of the Life-Force.

Conventional orgasm is degenerative in its effects. It breaks or obstructs the cycle of Life. The cycle of the breath of Life receives and accumulates energy through inhalation, and receptivity in general. That same Life is released to permeate the whole body and all relations to Infinity via exhalation. But the impulse of conventional orgasm is a disturbance in this harmony. The Life-Energy is inhaled, received, and allowed to build to a certain point, and then it is eliminated through uncontrolled genital discharge. The right use of the intensification generated through sexual play is to consciously inhale, receive, relax, exhale, release, and so control the Energy of the approaching crisis, allowing it to move from the concentrated area of the genitals and to permeate or pervade the whole body, one's lover, and the whole world to Infinity. Such is the conservative or regenerative and conscious exercise of human sexuality.

As such, our sexuality is raised from the merely generative level of the sexual function in lower biological entities. Human sexuality is occasionally generative (for the sake of childbirth), but it is commonly to be regenerative rather than degenerative. It is to be embraced for the sake of Life, health, clarity of mind, service of true emotion, or love, and right preparation of the whole and entire bodily being for spiritual Communion and Realization of the Divine Condition of all conditions.

235

II

The process of sexual conservation is the process of responsible participation in the full cycle of feeling-breathing in sex play, so that it becomes sexual communion with Life—a positive and conscious exercise of the living being that serves both health and the ultimate disposition of spiritual intuition.

This process of sexual conservation involves full and right participation in both halves of the Life-Cycle of the breath, which are inhalation-reception-accumulation (or retention) and exhalation-release-permeation. Thus, it is responsibility for not violating or breaking this Life-Cycle through degenerative and obsessive bodily discharge.

In the process, both the Life-Force and certain critical bodily secretions are stimulated, or bodily communicated. They are stimulated in excess of the amount that would be stimulated if there were neither conservative sexual play nor yogic manipulation of the gross body. Thus, by this approach to sexual practice, the nervous system and the endocrine gland system are excessively stimulated— that is, stimulated beyond the degree necessary for ordinary and mediocre functional existence. Therefore, energy and glandular secretions are made available for heightened development of physical health and longevity, mental power, and spiritual processes of meditation and the like.

236

In both male and female, signs of heightened and reintegrated functioning of the whole body will appear if there is right sexual activity (avoiding excessive discharge of Life-Force and seminal or glandular fluids) as well as a whole life rightly and lawfully exercised and spiritually oriented.

It is not necessary to be sexually active, as long as some other means, generally yogic in nature, is devised to develop, conserve, and use the same excess stimulation of the nervous system and the endocrine glands. But it is both likely and appropriate that most individuals will prefer to fulfill the laws of human incarnation in the actual and pleasurable exercise of their sexual character. If sexual intimacy is chosen, rather than celibacy, then the sexual function must be exercised constantly as described in these essays, or else there will be no destiny but the usual mediocrity.

III

The orgasm, or the feeling-tendency toward the crisis moment in sex play, is a form of the exhaled breath. The conventional use of sex play, as of the possibilities of the functional organism in general, is to discharge the accumulated Life-Force. Therefore, the crisis of orgasm is sought, or not avoided, and the Life-Force sent out, emptying the whole body and creating a psycho-physical pattern of recoil that reinforces the sense of emptiness, unconsciousness, separativeness, and self-possession.

The right approach to sexual play is the one of communion with the All-Pervading and Divine Force of Life through loving intimacy with another human being. In that case, sexual union must necessarily become a conscious exercise of attention, feeling, and action. All the functional rules of activity described in *Conscious Exercise and the Transcendental Sun* therefore apply to sexual communion.

Thus, the play is to be one of unobstructed relational feeling (mental, emotional, and physical). Constant feeling and love in intimate contact with one's lover frees the mind from obsessive thinking and presents it as free attention in the process of the love play of sexual union. This free attention enables one to feel one's lover physically and with deep and sensual emotion.

237

In this emotional and feeling play, it is unobstructed Life and Love that are operative to reintegrate and harmonize mind, or awareness, and body. The instrument of that reintegration is the cycle of feeling-breathing, the cycle of participation in the Force of Life.

Therefore, through full feeling of the cycle of breathing, directed by free attention, and duplicated in bodily action, sex play becomes a regenerative Communion that heals and vitalizes lovers and clarifies their minds.

The inhalation of breath is the absolute feeling-reception and retention of Life from or within the Infinite. It occurs naturally, in sex play, with the passive motion, away from one's lover (the withdrawal of the penis or the hips and vulva).

The exhalation of breath is release of Life to permeate the whole body, one's lover, and the world to Infinity. It occurs naturally, in sex play, with the positive, aggressive, or penetrating motion, toward or into one's lover (the forward intention and motion of the penis or the hips and vulva).

Therefore, in the play of sexual communion with one's lover, breath and physical motion are to become a rhythmic unity of inhalation-reception-retention-withdrawal and exhalation-release-permeation-confrontation. The whole cycle is to be felt and lived by each partner. It is to be fully felt, without obstruction (either physical or emotional). And it is to be intended, fully observed, and controlled by constant free attention, through love-feeling, to one's lover and the whole process of the cycle of this play.

Such is the conscious exercise of sexual communion. If it is lived as such, it is a positive factor in one's entire and spiritual life. If it is lived otherwise, so that one is exploited and controlled by the functional possibilities and tendencies themselves, then it is a powerful liability to health and happiness.

238

The critical factor in this play of sexual communion is the potential of either conventional orgasm, which is bodily, genital discharge and elimination of the accumulated Life-Force, and regenerative orgasm, wherein the peak intensity of Energy is not discharged below but released to permeate the whole body, one's lover, and the whole world to Infinity.

The cycle of breathing, controlled via free attention, unobstructed feeling, and physical motion timed to the breath cycle, is the key to right or regenerative use of the orgasm.

As the feeling-intensity rises, so that genital discharge will soon occur, you must exercise the activities that relate to inhalation and exhalation. The whole body inhales, receives, and accumulates or retains a great charge of Life-Energy (and living chemistry) in the sexual play. That charge is received through intense feeling receptivity to one's lover and, via one's lover, to the All-Pervading field of Life. One's lover and the All-Pervading Life transmit or communicate Life through this feeling play, and it is received through one's sympathetic receptivity and inhalation. One's lover represents an opposite charge or tendency of Life than one's own. Therefore, in this communion, the balanced or total and whole Energy of Life is accumulated whole bodily in the case of each partner.

The tendency toward genital discharge is the obvious potential in sexual play, since it is a physical process that focuses on the genital intimacy. All the functions or forms of play or communion that we engage in our daily activities tend to accumulate and discharge the Life-Force at the point of the specific bodily regions or organs used in the action. If we exploit any functional play of Life, it ceases to be a conscious exercise. Then Life is lost through that function, and attention becomes controlled by obsessive thinking, while subjectivity and self-possession are reinforced, and feeling and body or action separate from one another, all creating a living disharmony. Therefore, all activity must become a form of "conscious exercise."

This being the case, the tendency toward genital discharge in sex play must come under control through conscious exercise of the entire cycle of sexual union. The key to this is control of the cycle of breathing, or reception-release, through unobstructed feeling-attention.

239

Through inhalation or receptivity, the Life-Force accumulates. When we begin to exceed our level of tolerance for Life-Intensity, a rhythmic functional process begins whereby the Life-Force is ultimately discharged, or exhaled, until the Life-Force is returned to a tolerable level for calm and balanced feeling, sensation, and action.

Over time, if we live every function as a total conscious exercise of Life, our level of tolerance for pleasurable intensity increases, and, therefore, the urge toward orgasmic or other kinds of functional, emotional, and mental discharge decreases. However, we must still be responsible for feeling-control over the automatic tendency toward discharge of Life.

In sexual play, the control of the breath, or the feeling cycle, is the key to the control of genital discharge. Genital discharge is the predominant liability of the sexual play. If it is permitted to occur casually, we are emptied, weakened, separated, and recoiled upon self and subjectivity. Casual orgasm leads to a search for its repetition, since it is a momentary pleasurable release and thus a solution to the relatively painful sense and pressure of Life-Force accumulated beyond tolerance in both sex play and the daily round of stimulation and frustration in common experience. But the addiction to conventional orgasm, or genital discharge, is a pattern of adaptation that represents an empty and self-possessed character, incapable of unobstructed feeling-attention, and thus, ultimately, incapable of radical intuition of the Divine Reality.

Genital discharge is a negative or reactive form of the exhaled breath. It is natural to release the Life-Force once it has been inhaled or received. That release should not, however, be in the form of expulsion but, rather, of whole body relaxation into the pervasive Energy.

Therefore, genital discharge must come under control through right application to the exhalation functions of the Life-Cycle. This means that, <u>each time the critical sense of approaching crisis appears, one must relax the entire body, cease or limit its outer motions, and exhale—that is, allow the feeling-intensity to pass from concentration in the genitals and to the entire body. There should be complete feeling-relaxation into the sensation and Energy and pleasure that immediately precede the actual crisis. When the entire body is relaxed and restored to a generalized condition of Feeling-Energy, no longer concentrated in the genitals and seeking to be discharged there, then inhalation, reception of Life, and the stimulative movements of love play may resume.</u>

The effect of this conscious exercise of both the inhalation-reception and exhalation-release aspects of the play of Life in sexual communion is to replace the generative orgasm (the genital discharge, which becomes a degenerative and obsessive orgasm when casually permitted) with a <u>regenerative orgasm</u>. When exhalation and whole body relaxation and permeation is applied previous to genital discharge, there is an intensely pleasurable release of Energy to the entire nervous system and the entire body. The Life-Force is not discharged. It is allowed to permeate the organism. This not only allows the sex play to actually increase our present level of vitality (rather than decrease it, as it does in the genital discharge), but it stimulates the entire nervous system and endocrine gland system in a manner that is intensely pleasurable, ultimately regenerative in its effects on body and mind, and also compatible with continuous intuition of the Divine Reality.

It is by such conservation of accumulated Bio-Energy in sexual play that Taoist and Tantric yogic adepts,[1] among others, have traditionally sought or achieved greater health, longevity, and

---

1. Sexuality has long been used as a traditional means of achieving salvation, most prominently in the Chinese Taoist and Indian Tantric schools. The Taoist sexual tradition flourished in the beginning of the Christian era. Taoist masters had a positive orientation to sexuality, not primarily for the sake of pleasure, but as a device for achieving health and immortality. They believed that the vital essence is stored in the sex organs of the male and female (the opposite poles of energy in Nature). The male sought to acquire the energy of the female through her orgasm during intercourse, and, through the prevention of his own

magical as well as mystical experience and power. The same re-orientation of Life-Energy has also been used by celibate practi-tioners, who awaken the process of excessive receptivity to and accumulation of the inhaled Life-Force by private yogic manipula-tion of the mechanisms of the gross body (including forms of con-centration, breath control, and poses, actions, or manipulations of the physical body, particularly in the region of the sex organs or the perineum). In doing so, they have then made controlled or inten-tional use of the excessively available energy and glandular chem-istry to produce extraordinary effects on either or both the body (as in Taoist yoga) or the mind (as in kundalini yoga).[2]

241

---

ejaculation, the vital essence was thought to be transmuted into an alchemical substance that eventually moved up the spine to the brain. This process was intended to imbue the brain with Eternal Life-Energy and to endow the practitioner with extended life and increased vitality. Ultimately, Taoists believed that this process enabled them at death to assume an astral or light body and therefore to live as an immortal in the astral worlds. (Some women learned this process and thus worked to prevent their own orgasm while absorbing the male energy, but, in general, the practice was learned by men, who did not instruct their female partners, but, on the contrary, encouraged their orgasm, in order to acquire their energy.)

The Indian Tantric tradition of sexuality began much later, probably around 600–700 A.D. in northeast India, according to the most informed speculations, and probably under the influence of Taoist ideas. The almost invariably male Tantric yogis, like the Taoists who influenced them, transformed the sexual act by manipulating the orgasm, so that the semen was retained and supposedly sent upward along the spinal line to the brain. There was a wide range of approaches within the Tantric tradition, and some of them sought bodily immortality and held a philosophical point of view similar to that of the Taoist practi-tioners. Most of the Hindu Tantrics, however, unlike the Taoists, had an essentially negative orientation to sexuality and bodily existence altogether. This was perhaps due to the ascetic influence of Buddhism. The more ascetic purpose of Tantric yoga was to use the energy of the sexual act to intensify the inversion and upward-turning of attention, in order to realize subtle conditions that transcend this gross world. Such yogis did not seek to immortalize the body, but to transcend it by attaining a higher, subjective, inward condition that they presumed to be the Divine Plane or God-World. Later developments of most schools of Tantric practice extended this ascetic approach toward achievement of the complete internalization of the sexual process through the techniques of yoga and medita-tion. In the later schools, literal sexual practice was abandoned, and practitioners sought to internalize the yogic process completely through physical and meditative techniques. (The schools of hatha yoga and kundalini yoga are, among others, the modern and ascetic evidence of the more ancient and body-positive Tantric tradition.)

2. The kundalini or kundalini-shakti is the "serpent power" of esoteric spirituality. It is the very Creative Power of the universe, but it also lies dormant in Man, coiled at the base of the spine. It may be awakened spontaneously in the yogic practitioner, after which it appears to ascend within him, producing all the various forms of yogic and mystical experience. Bubba indicates that the internal spiritual force is eternally awake, but Man is not awake. Therefore, he recommends no exclusive efforts to awaken this force itself, but puts all attention to our awakening to the prior, eternal, and always present Nature and Condition. In the course of such spiritual practice, internal force is awakened as a secondary event, but it is regarded and dealt with in quite a different manner than is recommended by the yogis.

242

The process that is recommended in the present book is simply the right and natural way of participation in sexual play as the positive communion of Love with Life. If sexual play is approached in this manner, there is no doubt that the general state of one's vitality will increase, the mind will become and remain clear and steady, and there will be positive benefits to health and longevity. This discipline also becomes extended in various esoteric ways (not described herein) as the stages of the Way of Divine Ignorance mature, and it, therefore, helps to provide a living foundation for the maturing of real devotional and spiritual life. By its means, devotees may lead an ordinary, pleasurable human life, rather than a conventionally ascetic life, and still mature toward the Fullness of unqualified Divine Realization.

IV

The conventional genital orgasm or discharge may and, in the earlier stage of one's adaptation to the process of sexual communion, even should be permitted on occasion. If one practices sexual communion in the manner described in these essays, continuous sexual play may, on any occasion, be prolonged for as much as an hour or even several hours. And it may, at least in the earlier stages of one's spiritual practice, be engaged with considerable frequency, if all positive factors are present. (In general, however, sexual intimacy should be occasional, allowing for periods of ordinariness or simple, loving contact. These periods also allow time for the intense accumulations of Bio-Energy to normalize. Frequent sexual intimacy tends to create a pattern of obsessive desiring, unless both individuals are able to make full use of the awakened energies through a highly developed life of service and spiritual practice.)

As a result of this "yoga of sexuality" a great and profound degree of Life-Force and super-chemistry is likely to be accumulated. The Energy and clarity realized in the conscious exercise of sexuality, through love-desire, should be used to intensify one's whole life of service, "bodily prayer," meditation, and study, as well as all other ordinary activities. However, if more energy is accumulated than we can pleasurably use in an harmonious life of spiritual and human practices, then the intensity will produce profound internal heat, which may tend to produce obsessive desire for sexual release.

243

Therefore, the individual who is beginning to adapt to the process of sexual communion must measure the intensity he or she bears in this practice. If health is good and stable, and the sense of bodily and sexual intensity has recently seemed to be excessive or tending to become obsessive, then the genital discharge can be permitted during the next occasion of love play. However, the genital discharge should never be casually and regularly indulged. It should, even at the beginning of adaptation to the process of sexual communion, appear no more than once a week in the most active individuals. Over time, the frequency of actual genital crisis should decrease to no more than once or twice per month, and the genital discharge should, in general, become subject to regular, natural, and spontaneous control.

Even so, on any occasion where genital discharge is permitted, it should be exercised in precisely the same manner as the pre-genital crisis is exercised in this conservative or regenerative approach to sexual play. That is, it should be associated with relaxation into full feeling of the pervasive Energy, and exhalation with the feeling that the Energy is spreading from the genitals, pervading the entire body, one's lover, and the world to Infinity.

There is also a middle ground in this. It is a matter of how closely one allows oneself to approach actual genital discharge. Normally, one should exhale and permeate the entire body just as the sense of the crisis originates. At other times, one can go a little further, even to the point just prior to the actual discharge. In that case, it is recommended that the male lover withdraw the penis, rest all motion, and relax, feeling-intending that the genital spasm will not occur. He may also press the genital region between the testicles and the perineum with the fingers of one hand. (The ejaculatory fluid will not be completely conserved by such means. A portion of it will enter the bladder in any case.)

Thus, over time, both male and female individuals should adapt to regular and naturally conservative participation in the cycles of motion, feeling, breathing, and transference of attention from the local stimulation of the genitals to the whole body ecstasy in love. The general recommendation is to practice the exhalation-permeation exercise prior to actual genital discharge as a regular rule. Then, occasionally, depending on one's general condition, the conventional orgasm may be more closely approached or even actually permitted, but, in any case, the conscious exercise of the exhaled and permeating breath should be engaged.

244

The Genital "Mudra"

The word "mudra" is a Sanskrit term that is used to refer to certain bodily "moods" or attitudes of a yogic kind. Various bodily movements or gestures associated with the distribution of the Life-Current in the nervous system are called "mudras."

The entire process of sexual communion could, in a sense, be called a mudra. And that process is also composed of a number of individual mudras. One of the primary mudras in the process of sexual communion is one that we might name the "genital mudra," because it involves a bodily attitude or gesture related to the movement of Life-Energy in the genitals.

The primary physical movement that produces the conventional orgasm—or the discharge of Life-Energy via the genitals—is a process of lower bodily relaxation, initiated by the brain and the spinal cord, and communicated via the circuits of the autonomic nervous system in the lower body. That relaxation is itself a mudra, for it is not only a physical process, but it is a process or movement of the Life-Current, toward discharge from the nervous system. The physical process involved is a downward relaxation in the entire lower body. That relaxation is extended downward and forward, along the spinal line, then through the anus and the perineum, to the genitals. The process of this relaxation is a form of reaction to a previous tension in the same area. And the process occurs in a spasmodic or rhythmic fashion, producing a brief explosive and generally pleasurable sense of the release of Life-Energy via the lower body, particularly the genitals. (However, the lasting result, particularly of frequent and repetitive exploitation of this bodily effect or negative mudra, are physical addiction, mental and emotional obsession, Narcissistic self-interest, a loss of the "tone" or flexibility of the body and nervous system, and degeneration of the body-mind in general.)

245

The process of sexual communion involves a positive or conservative mudra of the genitals and the entire lower body (or "lower coil"). This genital mudra is ultimately a natural whole bodily response to the degenerative tendency of the conventional orgasm (which is a form of bodily reactivity).

The conventional orgasm is a temporary relaxation of the body's natural tension or "tone." By this means, the reproductive organs are energized, and bodily fluids as well as nerve force (or Life-Energy) are communicated between the partners. But when this process is made frequent and obsessive, the lower body becomes more and more chronically relaxed, and the entire body-mind becomes addicted to the degenerative pleasure of orgasm. Thus, over time, the natural tension of the lower body, whereby the Life-Current is conserved and distributed to the total body-mind, is weakened and critically lost.

The positive responsibility or "genital mudra" is the reverse of the action of the conventional orgasm. Thus, it involves intentional upward tension of the bodily base, or a "pulling" tension, from the penis, or from the clitoris, urethra, and vagina, back through the perineum and the anus, to the spinal line, and up, via the abdomen and the spinal line itself, to the general region of the brain.

In the practice of sexual communion, this genital mudra should be exercised randomly and periodically, prior to actual orgasm. The action may be brief, and repeated several times in succession, in a rhythmic manner. But it must also occasionally be done as an intense, steady, and prolonged upward pull, for several seconds or more, particularly when any of the initial signs of the approaching crisis of orgasm begin to appear.

Associated with the genital mudra are also all of the other aspects of sexual communion, including the exercise of feeling and breathing, the drawing up of the abdomen (with exhalation), the application of finger pressure at the base of the genitals (near the perineum), the release of all thoughts into love-feeling in the All-Pervading Life-Energy, and so forth.

This genital mudra should be performed prior to orgasm, in order to conserve the Life-Energy whole bodily. However, on occasions when the crisis of orgasm is permitted to approach very near, the genital mudra should then be applied with great force. And even on those occasions when the conventional orgasm is permitted, the genital mudra may be applied afterwards, as a means to restore the natural conservative tension of the lower body.

Along with the physical application of the genital mudra (and its associated exercises), it should always be felt not only that the Life-Current pervades the entire body-mind with Fullness, but that the Life-Energy is literally being drawn back and up from the genitals, via the perineum and the anus, into the spinal line, and up to the brain. One of the signs that may be observed that demonstrates this occurrence is a kind of clicking sound or pulsation at the base of the brain. This sound or pulse is made when the cerebrospinal fluid is pressurized upward from the spinal cord into the brain via the fourth ventricle.

The practice of the genital mudra matures over time, as sympathy with the whole bodily Bliss of the Life-Current begins to dominate the urges toward the degenerative pleasures of functional and sexual self-exploitation. And, in practice, there are also times when the application of the genital mudra itself is profoundly difficult, or it may even add to the tendency toward conventional orgasm. Thus, on occasions when the crisis of genital orgasm is imminent, the immediate application of the genital mudra might

246

add to the tendency of genital discharge. Therefore, at the approach of the crisis, the genital mudra may be temporarily bypassed—although the exercise of exhalation, drawing up of the abdomen, and so forth would be immediately applied. Then, as soon as a feeling of control is restored to the genital region, the genital mudra should be applied steadily and firmly. (As individuals mature in the practice of sexual communion, the conservative application of the genital mudra more and more commonly replaces the conventional orgasm and all degenerative effects of sexual activity.)

247

The practice of sexual communion also involves the responsibility to randomly relax the genital and general sexual tension that eventually produces the urge to the conventional orgasm. The common orgasm is itself a relaxation-reaction to that tension. But if the tension itself is relaxed, prior to orgasm, the orgasm is naturally controlled and even bypassed. The periodic exercise of the genital mudra should thus be combined or alternated with the general relaxation of genital and bodily tension during sexual activity. In this manner, the Life-Energy is conserved whole bodily (by maintaining the "lock" or closed circuit in the bodily base), and the All-Pervading Life-Energy Itself becomes the lover and the loved one. Thus, the body-mind of each lover ceases to be an idol or an obstruction to Divine Love, and the body-mind of each one is transcended in self-surrendering Love-Communion with the Living God.

The Feeling Cycle of the Breath in Conservation of the Orgasm

Those who have been Awakened from self to the All-Pervading Life, through "hearing" and "seeing" in the Company of the Spiritual Master, and who regularly practice devotion to God through forms of "bodily prayer," and who have mastered the regenerative art of eating, and who have accepted responsibility for right association in every area of daily living, and who have committed themselves in true love to the service and embrace of another who is responsible in love like themselves—these, and only these, are fit to practice the art of sexual communion with the Living God.

Sexual communion is the process of sexual participation in the All-Pervading Force Field of the Radiant Divine Life, through free and full feeling, unobstructed breathing, control of the genital spasm, and relaxation-release of the whole and entire bodily being into the Force of Life.

The feeling cycle of the breath is the primary activity in this form of embrace. And the breath must be related to the All-Pervading Life, rather than merely to the chemical air.

The genital spasm is controlled by regulation of breathing prior to orgasm, by control of bodily motion, by submission of the bodily self, and all internal thoughts or images, into Life-Feeling, and by various combinations of relaxation of the genitals and upward tension of or pressure upon the bodily base (which includes the urethra, the genitals, the perineum, and the anus). The conventional orgasm is bypassed by these means, so that the stimulated Force of sex play, which accumulates at the genitals and the lower or vital region of the body, may be released or "conducted" to the entire body, rather than discharged through the genitals as a form of degenerative bodily elimination.

In this process of sexual communion, the regenerative processes that have already been set into motion by the responsibilities described earlier (in paragraph one) are extended into a higher human level of adaptation to Life. The conservation, or regenerative use, of the Life-Force contacted through sexual intimacy is the second level of practice wherein psycho-physical regeneration and growth is made possible. If sexual communion is not realized in practice, we may not ascend to higher human levels of structural growth—since the evolutionary Force is simply wasted in the Sleep of lower vital exploitation. But those who practice sexual communion with God become Radiant with Life and Full of Love.

The uniquely human function of sexuality is not reproduction but ecstasy. It is the unification of the separate physical, emotional, and mental functions through a total release of reactivity—and it is the sacrifice of the whole and entire bodily and independent being through the awakening of total psycho-physical feeling, or love.

Truly human lovers become a sacrifice to one another, and through one another to Infinity, in the very cycle of their breathing. All motion, all tension, all degenerative urgency, and all localization of feeling and attention in the genitals alone are mastered through awareness and feeling as the whole and entire bodily being. That free, unobstructed, nonreactive, and intense feeling is to be breathed to the entire bodily being in every cycle of breath, during sexual embrace and also in every moment of living.

The process of sexual communion expresses primary physical, emotional, and mental responsibility via the breath and via the utter sacrificial gesture of love, or feeling-attention, to one's lover. By these means, the lower body cycles of generative and degenerative exploitation of the sexual process are transformed into the regenerative or whole bodily and uniquely human sexual process.

Love and Breath

The process of sexual communion is a matter of the Lawful or sacrificial and conservative awakening, integration, and harmonious presentation of the <u>entire</u> bodily being. It is not merely a genital process, but a process that involves all the functions and raises them to a state of integrated singleness—a single force— which is yielded in relationship and to the Infinite degree.

There are two senior elements in this process. They are feeling-attention and the breath. The breath is the senior function whereby all of the mechanical bodily and mental or psychic functions are

250

integrated and related to the whole bodily being, or body-mind. But the force of feeling-attention is senior to the breath and the mechanical functions. Therefore, feeling-attention is the essential principle of sexual communion, and whole bodily conservation and sacrifice in general. Feeling-attention must first be free and unobstructed in the relationship between lovers. <u>Then</u> free feeling-attention, or love, is permitted to become the motive and the principle of the process of sexual embrace.

When love becomes surrender in sexual embrace, through true and intense mutual desire, the bodily process is to be mastered by love via the breath at every moment of the embrace as well as at the moment or near-moment of the orgasmic crisis.

Thus, sexual communion conserves the emotional and bodily process and makes it a form of sacrifice or surrender into the Infinity of Life, or the Condition prior to the contraction into loveless self-possession and problem-oriented self-meditation.

Free feeling-attention (or the relational sacrifice that is love) is made the master of the whole and entire bodily being via the cycle of breathing, as described in *Conscious Exercise and the Transcendental Sun*. Sexual communion is simply the "conscious exercise" of the whole and entire bodily being in sexual relationship and sexual embrace.

Feeling-attention must be mutually yielded between lovers. They must live with one another in love and as spiritual devotees of the ultimate or Divine Reality. And they should embrace only occasionally, when there is the fullness of uncomplicated and mutual love-desire.

During sexual embrace, the occupation of each partner should be in love, in present and intense feeling and attention to one another, expressed in fully and freely conscious bodily submission and sensitivity to one another. There should be no preoccupation with internal, subjective, mental, or self-meditative phenomena, nor with mechanical physiological phenomena. However, in the full bodily confession and play of love, or conscious, intentional and mutual bodily surrender, both the subjective and the objective psycho-physical phenomena come under natural and easy control.

Thus, lovers may enjoy control over subjective phenomena (such as internal imagery, casual thoughts, rigidity, fear, and so forth) via constant and intense feeling-attention to Life, via one another, made natural by their loving feeling and their presently highly vital desire for one another. Therefore, they should not engage in sexual embrace casually, but only on those occasions wherein love-desire is mutual and intense, to the degree that the inversion of attention and emotion toward self and subjectivity will not occur. Where love-desire is not mutual and intense, the partners are separated from one another by a chasm that mere genital contact cannot bridge. Therefore, they should deal with the condition of their relationship and their individual states of life rather than indulge in sex for its own sake or as a solution to their loveless, lonely, and obsessed problems.

251

The process of the whole and entire bodily being is naturally conservative, regenerative, and sacrificial. But it lives as such only via the responsibility of awakened and spiritualized intelligence and the transforming or moral force of relational love. Where love is not the motive of action, we are self-possessed, separative, Narcissistic, and bound to the illusory subjective order. Thus, obsessive involvement with internal phenomena of mind and reactive (rather than relational) emotion, and equally self-possessed involvement with the mechanics of the bodily or psycho-physical mechanisms themselves, are both, under all conditions of experience, signs of a degenerative and loveless or recoiled disposition. In sexual play, in the sexual relationship in general, and in every ordinary or extraordinary moment of the process of living, the self-possessed, self-meditative, subjective, separative, and degenerative use of functions must be transformed or made Lawful via the force of free feeling-attention, or love, made bodily active via the cycle of breathing, or the circulation and conductivity of the Life-Force.

Thus, in sexual communion, intense and mutual love-desire not only controls or dissolves inwardness, but it controls the physiology—via the breath, in its association with the whole nervous system, the endocrine gland system, and every aspect of the lower elemental, muscular, and vital bodily being, including the All-

Pervading Current of Life-Force. In sexual communion, free feeling-attention, as present love-desire, controls and unifies mind, emotion, desire, Life-Force, bodily motion, and orgasm. The play of sex naturally generates attention, feeling, tension, modifications of breathing, motion, crisis, and eventual stasis or rest. The key to the process is feeling-attention, or love. And such love, or mutual bodily confession, controls and integrates all the mechanics of the sexual process via conscious participation in the breath cycle. Thus, love transforms every act or function of the bodily being into love, and it monitors this process of transformation via the breath.

Our right emotional-sexual adaptation (or re-adaptation) is made possible when emotion ceases to be locked into uninspected patterns of contraction or reactivity, wherein we are ourselves irresponsible as feeling-attention and dependent on the feeling-attention of others. Then we are free to engage in mature or responsible intimacy. When such an intimate relationship has been created by us, we may begin to enter into occasions of loving sexual embrace. But our right participation depends on consistent control over the patterns of psycho-physical self-possession. Thus, our right adaptation or re-adaptation to sexual intimacy depends on present love-desire and our ability to monitor and participate in the true psycho-physiology of sexual communion via the breath cycle, or the cycle of the communication of the Life-Force within and via the whole and entire bodily being. We must abide in love-desire, or the bodily confession of free feeling-attention, and we must permit relational love-desire to awaken and master the whole process via the vital link of the breath.

Throughout the incident of sexual play, the breath must be permitted to be full with feeling, or open love and desire for one's lover. The breath cycles naturally as inhalation-retention-exhalation-retention. Each inhalation is the inbreath of Fullness, filling the genital region and the entire vital region of the lower body with Life. And each exhalation releases that Life-Fullness to the whole and entire bodily being universally. The brief retention ("kumbak") or cessation of breath motion at the end of inhalation is the cresting moment of lower or vital Fullness, and the moment of the turnaround of the breath cycle toward exhalation. The brief retention or cessation at the end of exhalation is the cresting moment of whole bodily Fullness, the moment in which the entire bodily being radiates to Infinity, and also the moment of the turnaround of the breath cycle toward inhalation.

The breath cycle is a feeding cycle. It involves acquisition and assimilation of chemical substances through the lungs on inhalation, and further assimilation as well as elimination of chemical substances on exhalation. Thus, to breathe is to eat, and our breathing reflects the state of our emotional and physical orientation toward what sustains us. Sexual play naturally stimulates this breath cycle, and, therefore, sexuality tends to reflect the state of maturity or immaturity relative to the first stage of life—wherein we must learn to be autonomously related to the sources of sustenance. (For many, sex play is essentially an extension of an anxious search to be fed, and sustained, and parented.)

However, there is a higher function to the process of breathing. The breath cycle is not only a process of biochemical feeding via the lungs. It is simultaneously a rhythmic extension of the total nervous system, the glandular system, and the emotional and sexual functions. Therefore, changes in the nervous system, or the glandular system, or variations in the emotional state, or the awakening of sexual desire and activity, all—among other kinds of psycho-physical change—affect the breathing process.

The lower function of the breath cycle belongs to the realm of feeding and the first stage of life. The higher function of the breath cycle belongs to certain of the higher stages of life and to the realms of the nervous system, the Life-Force, emotion, sexuality, glandular processes of growth and purification and rejuvenation, brain development, and central control of the entire psycho-physical mechanism. Thus, in the process of sexual communion, the breath cycle becomes the agent of love, to awaken and harmonize all the functions of the bodily being as a single Force that is then Radiated to Infinity through total feeling-sacrifice.

Breath, Feeling, and Orgasm

There are two principal moments of the application of the breath cycle in sexual communion: one before the crisis of orgasm and one at the threshold or coincident with the crisis of orgasm.

1. The application of the breath cycle previous to the crisis of orgasm is the primary and mature form of the use of breath. The genital play, engaged with open feeling as well as complete and whole bodily attention, awakens or stimulates the Life-Force and living chemistry of the entire bodily being. The process of sexual communion is one in which that stimulated or "excess" Life-Force and biochemistry are conserved rather than eliminated. Thus, what is added to the living bodily being through polarized sexual play is retained and also circulated in the bodily system, to serve regenerative or rejuvenative purposes.

Therefore, the application of the breath cycle previous to the crisis of orgasm is the most important, since it effectively regains the balance of the bodily processes, and thereby prevents the eliminative crisis of the orgasm. The genital play itself not only stimulates the Life-Force and biochemistry, in both partners, but it also tends toward a temporary bodily imbalance, in the direction of the expansive and "right-sided" states. Therefore, by virtue of this imbalance, the bodily conditions tend to approach the instant of eliminative spasm or discharge, in order to regain the balance of the left (the passive or contractive) and right (the active or expansive).

But the conventional or eliminative orgasm in fact eliminates both Life-Force and biochemistry, as if these were bodily wastes. Hence, the conventional orgasm is ultimately degenerative and enervating, particularly when practiced frequently over time or by those who are relatively devitalized or otherwise beyond the time of early youth.

The process of sexual communion is the human way of sexual union. It involves emotional and mental responsibility, true intimacy, relational commitment, regulation of occasion through the monitoring of mutual love-desire, and regenerative or rejuvenative responsibility for the total physiology of the sexual play. And the central and senior function in this process is the breath cycle.

The breath cycle is made to incarnate the entire bodily being as a whole or single Force in the play of true sexual communion. The breath cycle is the function through which each partner should organize sensitivity to the entire play. The breath cycle is thus not only the medium of chemical ingestion and elimination of the air, but the cycle of reception and release, or rhythmic coordination of the physical body, the Life-Force, and the full force of free or unobstructed emotion (or love feeling) and attention.

255

Thus, during the entire course of any occasion of sexual communion, each partner periodically comes to a moment of profound intensification of life and feeling—a sense of imbalance which, if permitted to continue, would produce the crisis of orgasm. Each partner must be sensitive, through intentional and emotional play with his or her lover, to this sense of imbalance or impending crisis. As often as it occurs, the individual should inhale fully and relax deeply all over the body. Then exhale fully, relaxing deeply all over the body. This should be done one or more times, until a generalized feeling of fullness, balance, and natural control over orgasm is enjoyed. Then the play may resume as before. By this practice the crisis of orgasm may be prevented or detained indefinitely. (Indeed, the crisis of orgasm itself should not be casually permitted but intentionally chosen, and only on relatively infrequent occasions, and when the feeling of Life-Force or vitality is strongly in evidence.) The whole matter is not one of frustration of orgasm but of undermining its necessity through the continuous return to a condition of bodily balance, fullness, integrity of feeling, and mental freedom from recoil on self through concepts, images, or exclusive sensuality.

2. The application of the breath cycle at the threshold or coincident with the crisis of orgasm is the secondary form of the use of breath in sexual communion, and it is most commonly practiced by individuals who are only beginning to adapt and mature in this

process of sexual communion. It is more of an emergency matter, since the eliminative spasm of the genitals has in that case already begun to be indulged. Whenever the critical imbalance of the bodily being is allowed to be prolonged (in either the contractive or the expansive mode), enervation is the eventual result. In the case of genital stimulation, prolonged expansive excitation leads to orgasm. But it should be clear that such orgasm is, when casually indulged, more of a disease, or a symptom of imbalance, than it is a "natural" bodily event. Thus, the event of such eliminative orgasm should be controlled through right application of feeling, through the breath cycle, previous to orgasm. Occasionally, the crisis may be approached and even permitted, but if that event is to serve a positive, regenerative, loving, and nonseparative effect, there must be responsible application of feeling, attention, and Life, via the cycle of the breath as well as other physiological means.

Thus, on occasions of loving sexual communion, the crisis of orgasm should be either prevented or delayed in the manner previously described (i.e., the primary application of the breath cycle). If, after prolonged embrace, the genital orgasm is to be permitted or approached, the moment of the rising crisis should be met, via the breath, in such a way that (as in the primary application of the breath cycle) the whole bodily balance, fullness, relaxation, and loving polarization between the lovers, is quickly regained.

In the case of the application of the breath cycle previous to the crisis of orgasm, the inhalation was to be engaged first and primarily. However, in the case where the crisis is immediate, inhalation or infilling will only tend to promote the eliminative spasm in both male and female. Therefore, on occasions when the crisis of orgasm is approaching or inevitable, there must first and primarily be the exercise of full exhalation, with the sense of releasing and relaxing the intensified and local genital Energy to the entire body. When the sense of fullness, balance, and natural control over orgasm returns, then infilling and relaxing via inhalation may be done.

In the case of such application of the breath at the point of crisis, the genital discharge generally does in fact occur to one or another degree. But the primary Force of orgasm, as well as the biochemical secretions, internal or external, of both male and female, will, by right application of the cycle of breath and whole bodily feeling-relaxation, be to a high degree conserved. Thus, the regenerative use or application of the intensified Life-Force and biochemistry of sexual play may also occur on the random occasions of genital orgasm. Through right application, the orgasm is converted—the bodily balance is restored in the instant of the crisis—and far less of Life and chemistry and mutual feeling intimacy is lost in the process. Such orgasm becomes whole bodily orgasm or regenerative orgasm. Over time, the individual learns, bodily, how the thrill of orgasm may become a conservative whole body thrill rather than a necessarily degenerative moment of pleasure gotten by elimination of chemistry and Life via the genitals, or the heart, solar plexus, and vital or lower body region in general.

In the response that should develop as the routine at the point of the crisis of orgasm, the exhaled breath and release of both tension and attention in the genital region may also be followed by a period in which the exhaled breath is held out. During that period there should be whole bodily relaxation of sexual tension, feeling, and sensation. When it is felt that the involuntary urge to genital orgasm is essentially at rest, then the inhalation may be resumed.

If too long a period passes or must pass before relaxation of the genital spasm occurs, then the breath cycle may be resumed, but only short and shallow inhalations should be engaged, in order to prevent the intensification of genital pressure and the general state of bodily tension and attention that would tend to produce conventional orgasm.

Until there is complete rest from the tendency to genital spasm, repeat the cycle of inhalation (shallow) and exhalation (full and held out as long as is comfortable). When there is relaxation into whole bodily Fullness and natural sexual attention, then the motions and play of sexual communion may resume.

If, however, there is an individual or mutual preference for genital separation, then the lovers should simply rest with one another in close bodily embrace, with or without genital contact, until an appropriate moment to depart from one another lovingly.

258

Physiological Exercises for Conserving the Orgasm

T he pressure of the fingers, applied at the base of the sexual organ (near the perineum), should often be used even when the genital spasm is not immediately approaching, and certainly when it is. Then the emission of semen and/or Energy may be minimized. Even when the spasm is allowed to begin, it may be made brief by this means, along with the general discipline associated with exhalation-relaxation of the Life-Energy to the entire body (and thence to Infinity).

The application of finger pressure should always be firm, not only in order to prevent the ejaculation of semen, but also to prevent the rhythmic muscular contractions that lead to the genital and general lower bodily elimination of the Life-Force in the case of both male and female individuals.

The Uses of Tension, Pressure, and Relaxation of the Bodily Base in the Conservation of Orgasm

W hole bodily feeling and breathing are the primary means of conservative or regenerative Communion with the All-

Pervading Life and the relaxation-release of that Life to the entire body, and via the entire body to Infinity.

The secondary means are essentially:

1. The control of bodily motion, so that excited motion does not produce the genital crisis, and

2. The exercise of either tension, or pressure, or relaxation at the bodily base—or the region from the urethra to the entire genital region to the perineum and the anus

259

Feeling, breathing, Communion with the Radiant Life, and control of motion are thoroughly discussed in other essays. In this essay, we want to consider the various forms of exercise that relate to the bodily base.

It has already been described how the male lover should, when the crisis of orgasm is actually in motion, apply pressure to the lower base of the penis, behind the testicles, and just forward of the perineum—while, at the same time, relaxing all genital tension and exhaling the Force of Life to the entire body. However, this is only one example of the kind of discipline that may be applied to the bodily base.

In general, as the individual matures in sexual communion, the orgasm is more often bypassed than indulged. Therefore, the exercise of sexual communion becomes less and less one of response to the genital crisis and more and more one of ecstatic play, in which the crisis is bypassed. In that process, the intensity develops, and the bodily bliss that would otherwise tend toward orgasm does indeed appear, but the form of relationship to the intensifying Force of Life is such that orgasm is at most only approached. As the Energy builds, the cycle of inhalation and exhalation, or whole bodily reception and release, is engaged, so that the genital crisis does not fully develop. And, at random, as the hint of the crisis appears, genital tension in itself is to be joined to a deliberate upward tension of the entire bodily base (urethra, genitals, perineum, anus). Thus, the bodily base should be tensed upwardly as one inhales fully, then continued while the exhalation-release to the entire body begins, and the tension of the bodily base is itself relaxed as the exhalation grows toward its completion. Also, during sexual communion prior to orgasm, there may be random upward tension alternating with relaxation-release of the bodily base. This exercise may be done in multiple cycles, quickly or slowly, as a means of restoring equilibrium to the lower body, and, in association with cycles of feeling-breathing, to the entire body.

Tension and relaxation of the bodily base should be done by both men and women, prior to orgasm. If the crisis of orgasm is definitely in motion, then upward internal tension and relaxation of the bodily base will not be sufficient to achieve equilibrium and avoid orgasm. Thus, as the crisis approaches, external pressure must be applied. In the case of the male, ejaculation is to be prevented and, through the exercise of the feeling-breathing of the Force of Life, it is to be minimized even as it arises, and equilibrium is to be restored quickly. But in the case of the female, even though ejaculation does not occur, genital discharge of the Life-Force does occur in the event of orgasm. Thus, as the crisis approaches, the female lover should also make use of finger pressure on the bodily base, at the perineum, or at the very base of the vagina—in order to obstruct the outward flow or loss of Life and to interrupt the spasm that may be felt in the bodily base.

In the case of both male and female, finger pressure may be applied to the bodily base during the crisis of orgasm and also prior to it, as a general aid to the prevention of the spasm. And such pressure should always be accompanied by either the slowing or the cessation of motion, and by exhalation.

The internal tension on the bodily base is not only insufficient at the point of actual orgasm, but it tends even to reinforce the genital tension that is moving toward orgasm. Therefore, only external finger pressure is useful, until the basic force of the spasm has relaxed. Then internal tension, or cycles of tension and relaxation, may be resumed.

Just so, in addition to internal tension (or tension and relaxation) and external pressure on the bodily base, there is the method of relaxation of the bodily base, particularly the genitals and the perineum. This may be done randomly and even for regular and prolonged periods during sex play. It has the effect of allowing the

Life-Force to move immediately to the entire body, and it prevents the buildup of tension in the genitals and the bodily base.

The application of external pressure on the lower portion of the genitals, as a means of minimizing and shortening the orgasm, may become less necessary as practice matures in sexual communion. And, over time, conservative and regenerative control of orgasm becomes more and more natural and easy, so that the exclusively genital form of the crisis is commonly bypassed, and conventional genital orgasm is converted into the regenerative whole body thrill. However, whether or not the use of external pressure becomes less common, the alternation of internal tension and relaxation of the bodily base will remain the common exercise.

261

The application of finger pressure on the base of the genitals, near the perineum, is simply an external version of the natural upward tensing of the anus-perineum-genital region that should be periodically and intentionally performed by both the male and the female. Such upward tensing should be done at random (along with full inhalation-exhalation cycles of Life-Feeling to the entire body) throughout every occasion of sexual communion. The application of finger pressure by both the male and the female may also be done at random, and for the same purpose. (Both the upward tensing and the finger pressure simply emphasize the natural lower bodily mechanism that reverses and conserves the flow of Bio-Energy and bodily secretion from the genitals toward the environment.)

On occasions when the genital crisis of orgasm is permitted (or not fully bypassed), finger pressure near the perineum may be applied by the male and the female. But in that case it is essentially an emergency procedure, and a degree of loss of Bio-Energy and body chemistry is inevitable. Just so, both sexes may exercise the upward tension of the anus-perineum-genitals, along with the breath and the cessation of motion, but once the crisis of orgasm has been entered, such procedures are only an emergency measure, to minimize rather than prevent loss.

Therefore, as maturity in sexual communion develops, the actual crisis of genital orgasm should be bypassed more and more commonly and naturally. The entire occasion should involve full intimacy, but also continuous responsibility, exercised via control of breath, motion, and upward tension of the bodily base. In this natural or nonemergency exercise (in which the genital crisis is not suppressed but simply bypassed), both the male and the female may at times use external finger pressure as an extension of internal body-base tension. And many individuals may simply rely on the natural whole body exercise, including upward internal tension of the bodily base, without external finger pressure.

Until such mature ease begins to characterize the practice of sexual communion, the individual should adapt by degrees, and, at least for the time being, the male and the female should make use of finger pressure as an emergency measure whenever the genital crisis arises or even approaches.

When preventing male ejaculation or female genital spasm with the fingers, the traditional recommendation is to use the passive, negatively polarized, or "yin" hand. Right-handed people would, therefore, use the left hand, and those for whom the left hand is dominant would use the right hand. This corresponds to the idea that, in the moment of crisis, the passive or inversive influence, rather than the expansive or orgasmically positive influence, should be presented to the sex organs. In practice, however, the individual may choose to perform this action with either hand. The action should be performed in as natural and comfortable a manner as possible, but always firmly and effectively.

The mature practice of sexual communion is one in which degenerative orgasm, or genital discharge of Life from the body (rather than inspiration of Life from the genitals to the whole and entire body), is consistently bypassed, or made unnecessary.

The process of gradual adaptation to this practice is one in which the individual learns <u>bodily</u> control and regenerative conservation of the impulse of orgasm. Mature control involves a process that is free of mental or emotional or physical armor, or negative effort. Only when forms of thought and imagery, reactive emotion, and physical contraction or recoil are all naturally yielded in full and free feeling of Life is there maturity in the practice of sexual communion.

263

Adaptation to the process of sexual communion should develop by stages, toward a total conservative and regenerative economy of the Bio-Energy and living chemistry of the bodily being.

In the first stage, practice is largely a matter of intentional application of certain physiological exercises. The primary exercise is the one of consistent and bodily love-feeling in relation to one's lover and, via one's lover, to the Infinity of the All-Pervading Life. Associated with this responsible exercise of love-feeling, or Communion with Life, the primary physiological exercise includes:

1. Random application of fully receptive inhalation of Life and whole bodily relaxation into Life via the exhalation

2. Control of bodily motion as the genital crisis shows any signs of its approach

3. Upward "drawing" or tensing of the anus-perineum-genital region, or bodily base, in order to reverse the current or flow that is tending to pass outward from the genitals

4. The application of finger pressure at the base of the underside of the penis, or at the base of the vagina, just forward from the perineum, whenever the genital crisis approaches or actually appears

In the second stage of the adaptation to the process of sexual communion, the entire emotional and physiological exercise should be quite natural, and more a matter of spontaneous bodily response than a willful exercise. Just so, it should be quite natural and easy to bypass the degenerative or casual and exclusive genital orgasm as a matter of regular practice. Thus, the process should fundamentally involve a naturally conservative and regenerative control of feeling and breathing. The pacing of physical motion should occur quite naturally, but it should become less and less a factor determining whether or not the genital crisis will appear. The application of finger pressure along with natural upward tensing of the bodily base should also be done at random, but they are also likely to become less and less of a determining factor in the genital crisis. (Application of finger pressure should, if and when it is done, generally be an extension of the upward tensing of the bodily base prior to orgasm, more than an emergency response to orgasm.) Conventional genital orgasm should naturally and commonly be bypassed, through conversion of the play of bodily energy (including feeling and breathing). The awakened sexual energy should be accompanied by minimal genital, emotional, and mental tension—so that any tendency to the "crisis" is easily converted into the regenerative whole body thrill.

In the fully mature practice of sexual communion, exclusive or degenerative genital orgasm should become obsolete as a matter of casual indulgence. And the bodily being should be at ease in the native Fullness of Divine Life rather than chronically tense, reactive, self-possessed, and in need of degenerative release.

The basic and essential instruments of sexual communion:

1. Free and unobstructed feeling-attention in intimate relationship

2. Present and mutual love-desire, fully and bodily awakened

3. Understanding and sensitivity relative to the physiology and psychology of the entire bodily process of sexuality

4. Freedom of attention from the verbal mind, or concepts and images

5. Freedom of feeling, free from chronic reactivity and bodily or emotional self-possession

6. General responsibility for the rhythmic or periodic relaxation, conservation, or whole body conductivity and release of genital, sexual, emotional, mental, and other forms of bodily tension—a process of regenerative release of stimulated Bio-Energy to and via the whole body rather than degenerative elimination of chemistry and Life-Force through the genitals

265

The aspects of practice to be applied near or at the point of the genital crisis:

1. Relational attention, free of inwardness in the form of thoughts and images

2. Relational feeling, free of bodily contraction or self-possession by bodily sensation

3. Control of personal bodily motion and intentionally or casually stimulating contact with one's lover

4. Control of ejaculation in the male via finger pressure at the base of the penis near the perineum, and control of orgasmic spasm in the female via finger pressure at the base of the vagina, near or at the perineum

5. Control of the genital discharge or spasm of Life-release in both male and female via:

a. Intentional use of the breath cycle (inhalation-reception, exhalation-release, and retention or interruption of the breath cycle itself) to control the genital discharge and to release or conduct the stimulated Life-Force to the entire body

b. Relaxation of the genitals, the lower body (including the anus and perineum), and the entire body, until equilibrium is regained

c. The use of a drawing tension at the perineum as well as the anus and sex organs, as the sense of equilibrium increases, in order to limit the sense of energy flowing in the genitals

d. The temporary exhalation-emptying of energy from the abdominal region to the entire body, particularly to the heart and above the heart

6. A general orientation toward pleasurable whole body full-ness, or loving radiance, founded in the sense of prior continuity with the Living Force of Reality, rather than the remedy of bodily or lower organ discharge of the Life-Force because of the chronic sense of separation, tension, self-division, and conflict

266

The Sexual Yoga of Life-Conservation

Even if sexual intercourse is engaged to the point of the crisis of orgasm, the conservative and feeling responsibility of whole body ecstasy should be intentionally performed. This respon-sibility and process is generated primarily via the exhalation and relaxation-release of the genital energy to the entire body, until stability returns. Secondarily, there may also be cessation of motion, relaxation of the genitals, genital separation, finger pressure at the base of the underside of the penis or the vagina (near the perineum), release of attention from one's own genitals as well as particular and arousing body regions of one's lover, turning the attention to the upper body, rhythms of relaxation and upward tension of the bodily base, and so forth. In any case, the exhalation gesture and the relaxation-release of the stimulated sexual Force from the genitals and the places of concentration in the lower body should at first be directed to the upper body rather than to the entire body.

At the point of orgasm, bodily energy is concentrated below and seeks release through the lower organs, particularly the genitals. Thus, in the immediate gesture that should be generated as the orgasm begins, the bodily energy must be relaxed-released to the body as a whole. If this is to be done, the attention and the feeling-energy should at first be exhaled and internally relaxed-released into the entire body <u>above</u> the genitals, and especially above the heart. The energy should be felt primarily in the trunk and head, essentially bypassing the arms, hands, and fingers, as well as every part from the genitals to the legs and feet. This should continue, allowing the focus of the attention and feeling-energy to be the tops of one's ears, until the bodily force is again generalized or equalized, and the urge to orgasm is under control. At that point, the full sense of inhalation and of exhalation may again be felt to include not only the genital region but the entire region below the genitals, including the legs, feet, and toes, and all of the total body, including the arms, hands, and fingers.

If the process is not generated in this fashion, the orgasm will tend to occur as a full local or genital spasm, emptying the body of the <u>extra</u> or stimulated Life-Force as well as a degree of its basic store of Life. Such orgasm is enervating and self-possessed, or separative. Thus, at the point of crisis, first exhale and relax-release the attention and feeling-energy via the trunk to the two ears. Then, as equilibrium returns, inhale the feeling-force of Life even to the genitals, legs, and arms. And exhale that balanced, whole bodily Fullness to the entire body, and via the whole body to one's lover and all of manifest existence, to the point or degree of Infinity.

On the more frequent occasions when the conservative process is exercised again and again just prior to the crisis of orgasm, the inhalation and general relaxation-release of energy may immediately be to the entire body. If, however, the slightest tendency to the actual crisis is felt, the procedure should be as in the case of the actual crisis—or at least the infilling of energy should at first bypass the genitals and the legs as well as the arms.

The crisis of orgasm should not generally be permitted to go to its full degree. Rather, as it approaches, the process of conservation should begin. Otherwise, most of the Energy and, in the male, the seminal fluid, will be lost. (Even if the fingers were to be held to prevent the seminal flow, a significant amount of the essential chemistry would pass into the bladder and out with the urine.) Thus, the permeation of the entire bodily being to Infinity (including all relations) should generally be done no later than the moment just before the crisis begins—even as soon as there is any heightening toward it.

268

The basic process whereby the rejuvenating Energy and chemistry is conserved, or drawn from concentration in the sex organs to pervasion of the entire bodily being, is through exhalation and a series of psycho-physical events that tend to duplicate the design and effect of the "uddiyana bandha," "nauli kriyas," and "vajroli mudra," including deep breathing with abdominal motion, described in the system of hatha yoga. (See *Conscious Exercise and the Transcendental Sun*, as well as "Physical Exercises Related to the Process of Sexual Communion," the appendix of the present book.) Thus, as the crisis approaches, there should be a full or complete exhalation, with the sense of "blowing" localized genital energy, feeling, and attention to the entire bodily being, which then should radiate that Energy with feeling to one's lover and via one's lover to Infinity (or to the Infinite degree). The breath Energy, feeling, and attention should be thrown and released up and out from the sex organs to the rest of the bodily being, all the way to the ears, the finger tips, and the toes. With the exhalation, all attention, feeling, desiring, breath, Energy, movement, and sensation should be released from the sex organs—from the tip (the tip of the penis or the clitoris), and from the root at the perineum, to the spine and the solar plexus, and then upward, downward, and outward, not leaving the bodily being (except, at first, the sex organs), but pervading it as a whole.

As soon as the exhalation begins, there should be a feeling of the Living Energy passing in a thrill or a pleasant rising fullness into the spine and the solar plexus, upwards to the face and ears, trunk and arms, and fully outwards, including the legs and one's lover and everything to Infinity. The stomach may even be drawn up slightly with the initiation of exhalation, but there should generally be no tension at the perineum until the genital urge to orgasm has begun to subside. There should be "kumbak" (or retention of breath) at the end of the exhalation (which should be sudden, fully intentional, and complete) until it is felt that the Energy has been released to the entire bodily being and that inhalation may now return Energy fully below without stimulating the orgasm. If it becomes necessary to breathe before this occurs, breathe in very shallow, quick, partial breaths, then blow out (exhale) again and hold, etc., until the crisis is passed. Then the play of feeling-attention may resume in normal sex play.

In this manner, Living Energy and chemistry are stimulated, conserved, and conducted in the entire bodily being. And the capacity for continuous unobstructed feeling-attention is served, rather than obstruction of feeling and reinforcement of self-possession and obsessive localized feeling-attention (in the genitals, in the mind through ideas of sex, etc.). The play of sex must become sacrifice of oneself, not merely of what is outside or not oneself. Thus, sex may incarnate love. Otherwise, sex is only a cycle of self-emptying and a dramatization of the illusory separation of body and Life and feeling and mind.

If a male lover permits sexual play to attain a point very near or even into the crisis of genital discharge, but the force of the crisis itself is dissolved in whole body diffusion in the manner described (perhaps including the application of the fingers to the base of the sex organs), at least a portion of the ejaculatory fluid will back up into the bladder and later be released with the urine. However, the erection will generally remain (as long as the process of whole body diffusion has indeed taken place, and the external ejaculation prevented), and a sense of strength and intensified energy and pleasure will also remain (unlike the case when genital discharge is indulged).

A s orgasm approaches, the male may:

    1. Withdraw and cease his movements

    2. Withdraw, cease movements, and press the base of the underside of the penis, near the perineum

    3. Remain inserted, but press deeply to the cervix, womb, or inner depths of his lover, and remain motionless

270

    In all three cases, the general process relative to the breath, feeling, and attention must also be done.

S exual awareness tends to locate itself in the regions and organs below the heart. Therefore, the heart must be made the principle of the sexual relationship and sexual intercourse. Feeling-attention must be granted continuously, and by this means genital sexuality becomes sexual communion.

    Just so, during the several times in any occasion of sexual embrace when the crisis of genital orgasm nears or fully approaches, the accumulated energy below the heart should not only be permitted to fill the heart as loving feeling, but it should be released to the regions and organs above the heart. Raise your attention briefly from the genitals and feel as if it is located in your ears, particularly the upper part of the ears. Thus, relax and release the sexually awakened energy to be <u>bodily</u> felt in the chest, neck, throat, and head (with attention particularly pressed to the physical ears, allowing the energy to pervade the entire physical head). Then let the energy pervade all the rest of the body, including the arms and legs. Do not empty the body—not even the lower body—but allow the energy to spread to the upper body, then to the extremities, as well as the lower body in general. When the whole body is radiant with or as Energy, love, and blissful sensation, relax and release it to and via your lover to Infinity (or to the unqualified degree). In doing so, do not empty your body, but radiate as the whole body in love.

The stages of sexual maturity:

1. The sexual function is, first of all, to be realized in relationship, in an ongoing commitment of love-desire (rather than suppressed as no-sex, or exploited degeneratively as masturbation or promiscuity).

2. The sexual play, in that relational intimacy, is to express itself as conscious control of the Life-eliminating orgasm.

The principles of the conscious exercise of sexuality:

1. Sexual intimacy is good, if relational, that is, a matter of ongoing commitment and love-desire, and if mutually enjoyed as a conservative or regenerative discipline.

2. Frequent sexual communion is good, if the orgasmic crisis is controlled and conserved, and if both partners remain free of obsession and can make full physical, emotional, mental, human, and spiritual use of the awakened chemistry and Energy.

3. Sex play with regenerative control of orgasm conserves Life, or vitality, improves health, promotes longevity, grants clarity and strength of psyche and mind, and the like. It balances the two Life-tendencies, expansive and passive, male and female, at the level of human bodily relations. They become a mutual sacrifice. Each shares the opposite quality of Life-Force through loving, feeling communion—whole bodily.

When the male individual is first adapting to the process of sexual communion, he may learn the factors involved in sexual conservation by moving near or to the point of the genital crisis, but not applying the fingers to prevent the flow. He should otherwise apply all the other factors that release the concentration of energy from the genitals to the total body. Thus, he will observe what factors truly must be applied if the conventional orgasm is to be obviated. The tendency to the flow will be his sign.

When he has observed and experienced the new or conservative process of regenerative orgasm, then he may use the fingers as a conservative device near or at the point of crisis. However, this device is not to be casually exploited. It is not commonly to be used as an "emergency" measure, forcefully to stop the flow of seminal fluid itself, but, rather, as a naturally conservative extension of upward tension at the bodily base, to firmly hold the muscles at the base of the sex organ in a calm, nonspasmodic state, prior to the actual flow. By these means, we effectively communicate to the sex region of the nervous system and brain that the spasm of genital discharge is not necessary or appropriate but, rather, that the diffusion of the biochemical Energy from the sex region to the total body is the open and pleasurably correct channel.

If the fingers are applied after the spasm has already begun the process of discharge, the conventional orgasm has already begun, and at least a portion of the seminal fluid will pass into the urinary system. Therefore, the moment to apply the fingers is anytime prior to the spasm rather than just prior to or coincident with the appearance of ejaculation and after the spasm has begun. Such use of the fingers may generally be done as often as one chooses and is not likely to produce negative physical effects over time.

During the entire occasion of sexual love play, both partners should balance the awakening of tension, infilling of Life, and approach to genital discharge with an equal degree of relaxation, releasing the Energy of the tension to the entire body, and thus allowing genital diffusion to the entire body rather than forcing the localized genital spasm.

In this way, the love play will be prolonged, and orgasm may be approached by choice and controlled by feeling and relaxation, thus becoming regenerative rather than degenerative. Likewise, if this compensating factor of continuous relaxation is applied, the awakened or stimulated Energy and chemistry will be constantly (rather than merely at the point of approaching crisis) relaxed-released to the total body.

The factor of prolongation of sexual communion is significant for the same reason. The more Energy and chemistry is released to and via the total body rather than thrown from the body, the more profound the regenerative force of the sacrifice.

During sex play, genital stress or contraction should be constantly relaxed (rather than increased). Genital stress leads to orgasm. Concentration in the genitals is natural, but it must be randomly and pleasurably relaxed—particularly at the point of crisis. Exhalation and release of the stimulated genital energy to the entire bodily being should often accompany the genital relaxation, even when the crisis is not near. Genital relaxation, rather than the cycle of genital stimulation, tension, and eventual release, should be central to one's sexual practice. Upon this the whole matter of sexual communion rests. Attention and feeling should concentrate in one's lover, and genital stress should be relaxed to the entire body. Thus, the demand for orgasm will gradually come under a natural control or economy. Just so, the pattern of relaxation into whole body feeling-energy should more and more characterize one's general state, under all conditions—rather than reactivity, stress, and functional release or dissipation of Life-Energy.

With exhalation, relax all stress, energy, and attention from the stimulated genital and general vital region below the heart, and release that energy to the entire bodily being. Likewise, relax and open the entire bodily being to receive and accept that Energy and radiate it as unobstructed feeling-attention to all relations to Infinity.

At the point of crisis, and, in general, throughout the play and in all the hours of the relationship: Relax, release, and allow the heartbeat to pump or radiate the accumulated and concentrated Life-Force from the region of the genitals and the abdomen to the entire bodily being, and thence to one's lover and via one's lover to Infinity in all directions. In that event of surrender or love to one's lover to Infinity there is no independent and exclusive sense of self or center or separate soul.

274

This may be done quite naturally when, through the practice of love, or free feeling-attention, sexual play is engaged without fascination and identification with imagery, memory, and the fixed or obsessive vital demand for ritual repetition of previous experiences of pleasure.

The appropriate end of any occasion of sex play is when a sense of whole body fullness and diffusion of Energy begins to replace the sense of concentration in the genitals. If sex play continues beyond that point—even if the male erection remains (and it usually does), or both partners desire the play to continue—then it will tend to be enervating, a search for repetition, and the dimension of love-feeling will cool, leaving only the mental and vital desire and the tendency toward imagery and mechanical repetition of remembered moments.

Further Instruction on the
Conservation of the Orgasm

The couple should freely embrace one another in a dance of postures and "mudras"[3] and patterns of breathing, looking at one another, closing their eyes, gazing into one another's eyes,

3. Bodily poses, especially of the hands and face, that signify and symbolize the movement and transmission of spiritual force.

moving toward intensity, moving toward calm fullness, and the like. At the end, or at any moment, place like body parts to one another—not only genitals to genitals, but hands to hands, forehead to forehead, eyes to eyes, breast to breast—every like to every like. This establishes balance and ease.

Likewise, when opposites are placed to one another (as when the male enters the female from behind), or when there is a separation and opposition of parts in general (one partner with eyes closed and the other with eyes open; or one active, one passive, etc.) tension or excitement will tend to be created.

The combination of opposition and likeness is the technical dance of the play of lovers.

A t the moment of release and diffusion of the sexually stimulated Energy, it is of primary importance that there be no debilitating self-consciousness, but only mutual intimacy, love, desire, and absorption in the pleasure of one another. Otherwise, the process of diffusion of the genital Force to the entire body will be inhibited, and, although the genital spasm may be avoided, the energy will, to one or another degree, be diffused only locally relative to the genital region.

This points to the whole dilemma of "being seen." Each lover is only free to be released in feeling to Infinity if his or her lover fully loves and desires and is pleasurably absorbed in the whole appearance and activity that is his or her lover. Otherwise, one's lover's attention traps one in one's own place—the effect of "being seen."

W hen conservation of orgasm is engaged over a prolonged period (of weeks, or even days), or if there are frequent occasions of sexual communion with full conservation over a short period, an excessive or at least uncomfortable accumulation of stimulated Energy and glandular chemistry may be developed. In general, there should be only slightly more stimulated Energy and chemistry than can be tolerated with complete ease. In other words, there should be an intensification that exceeds one's common mediocrity or emptiness, but it should not too much exceed the use one has for it through nongenital activities. If the excess is too great, an obsessive desire and need for release through sexual contact may arise. In that case, one becomes driven to sexual embrace independent of feeling sensitivity. Such embraces may begin to become obsessively frequent and repetitive—and also self-defeating. Since orgasm is not permitted, each embrace becomes a kind of intentional frustration.

276

When such a condition of excessive stimulation appears, it may be best to permit the conventional genital orgasm during the next occasion of sexual embrace. The conventional orgasm is better than critical or intolerable imbalance, but it should not be permitted repetitively, casually, or frequently. Rather, one should measure the frequency and the period of the occasions of intimacy so that the stimulation is not excessive, and one should develop more and more the tolerance for whole bodily Fullness of Life to the highest degree, free of the reactive recoiling of self that necessitates the tension-release cycle of degenerative orgasm.

Over time, one's tolerance or capacity for the whole body awakening stimulated through the conservation of orgasm increases. Thus, the frequency and period of intimate occasions may increase. Likewise, whole body wisdom arises in the practice, so that the process revealed in sexual communion becomes available under all conditions, even independent of sexual embrace. This is the case in the various stages of the Way of Divine Ignorance.

When the crisis of orgasm occurs, the yoga of conservation should be enacted as described, and it should be maintained until the crisis is completely past (that is, bypassed). In the male, if the sequence is not maintained sufficiently long, or with sufficient intention, reserve involuntary motions will cause some of the ejaculatory fluid to pass out to the tip of the penis, or else more than is necessary will pass to the bladder. In the case of both sexes, insufficient application to the conservative and regenerative process and sequence, at the point of crisis as well as at every other moment in the sexual play, may at best defuse the genital orgasm, but it will fail to trigger the endocrine system and the nervous system all the way to the brain. Superficial application of feeling-attention in this process relegates it to the lower dimension of the bodily being and makes the whole affair only slightly superior to conventional degenerative sexuality.

S exual communion is a rhythm of two whole body attitudes: concentration and relaxation.

Concentration in sexual play is the complex of feeling-attention in which Life-Energy is inbreathed, accumulated via the genitals, and constantly intensified by every kind of regard between the lovers. This attitude and play eventually brings the bodily being to a state of genital accumulation that can no longer support further accumulation without discharge through orgasmic spasm. Thus, when this pleasurable accumulation approaches its crest or crisis point (generally before the crisis or orgasm fully appears) the second attitude (the attitude of relaxation) must be adopted, or else there will be only emptying of the entire bodily being of its Life and vital chemistry, and there will be psychic separation between the lovers as well. Therefore, near the point of orgasmic crisis, as often as it occurs in the play, the entire bodily being must be released from the forms of concentration of feeling-attention and permitted to enter a period of diffusion of feeling-attention. Thus, there must be relaxation from the forms of feeling-attention that stimulate and accumulate Energy at the genitals, and relaxation of the feeling-attention of the entire body—allowing the accumulated intensity of the Life-Force to pass from the genitals to diffusion in the total bodily being, and thence, via love feeling, to one's lover and all things to Infinity. Thus, the Life-Force and stimulated chemistry of sexual communion is conserved rather than discharged—leaving both partners in a continued or continuous union of feeling and sensation, clear in attention, and full of the attributes of vitality.

278 The Intentional Discipline of Adaptation to Sexual Communion with Life

1. Realize the sex-function as a process in relationship, rather than a manipulative exercise of your own body-mind. Love and serve others, become responsible for emotional reactivity, maintain a regenerative discipline of diet, and a general health practice that relaxes the bodily being into the All-Pervading Life and feeds upon that Life. Become intelligent through consideration of the Teaching of Truth and the observation of self and others, and bring order to your household living. When an intimate commitment truly appears, then account for it in the form of a responsible household agreement, or marriage, in the community of your friends. Then engage in sexual relations with your lover on occasions of intense mutual love-desire, and practice regular intentional application of the functional design of sexual communion until the "inversion" or bodily release of the motive of casual or degenerative genital orgasm.

2. Practice sexual communion as a form of "conscious exercise" (see *Conscious Exercise and the Transcendental Sun*). This involves the primacy of free or unobstructed and nonreactive feeling-attention—or full and sensitive psycho-physical feeling in love with one's lover. And it involves the cycle of reception and release, of the All-Pervading Current of Life (realized when feeling is permitted to the degree of Infinity), via the process of breathing.

3. If and when the crisis of orgasm approaches, slow or stop all sexually stimulating movements, and exhale the force of Life from the genitals to the entire body, and thence to Infinity, via your

lover. (All of the technical elaborations of this process are described in the extended text of this book.)

4. As long as orgasm is not immediately approaching, receive and release the force of Life to the entire body, via the cycles of inhalation and exhalation.

5. Practice sexual activity as a discipline in which the entire bodily being is expressed as a single force of feeling-attention, via your lover, to the Infinity of All-Pervading Life. In this manner, all emotional reactivity is bypassed. Likewise, all bodily tension and urges toward degenerative release or discharge of Life are relaxed—at the genitals and at every other part. And the brain-mind is relaxed of all its contents, including thoughts and erotic images, by its relaxation, through feeling, into Life.

279

6. If and when the crisis of orgasm approaches, the exhalation of Life from the genitals to the entire bodily being must be done, using any or all of the bodily techniques described (such as pressure at the base of the sex organ, cessation of motion, and so forth). However, when the orgasm is not approaching, the process is the simple one of whole bodily Communion with Life through feeling, and the force of Life is breathed whole bodily—primarily via the heart and solar plexus.

7. If, on occasion, your lover passes into genital orgasm, inhale the Force of Life that is radiated to you thereby. Allow it to pervade your entire bodily being, and to radiate therefrom to your lover, and via your lover to the Infinity of Life. If, however, your lover shows signs of approaching orgasm, and he or she makes indications of preferring to bypass the orgasm, then relax all efforts on your part that might stimulate or exploit the crisis.

8. The proper end of the play of sexual communion is not mutual orgasm or the attainment of orgasm by either partner. It comes to an end naturally when both partners enter into a sense of whole bodily Fullness of Life, so that the motive of orgasm relaxes and the motive of sexual intercourse itself comes to rest in Ecstasy. In that case, simply rest in close and affectionate bodily contact until natural physical (but not emotional) separation occurs.

9. Through a total discipline of the right adaptation to Life, liberate the vital-physical, emotional-sexual, and mental-volitional aspects of the body-mind from reactivity and the self-possessed games of tension-release. Bring your vital-physical and "vital person"[4] characteristics to Life through right diet and health practice, right and intimate association with others, right occupation, and true religious devotion to the Divine and the Spiritual Master. Bring your emotional-sexual and "peculiar person"[5] characteristics to Life through consideration and abandonment of reactive emotional patterns and reactive, degenerative, romantic, and conventionally erotic sexual patterns. Renounce petty and chronic conflicts, and commit yourself to intimacy. Bring your mental-intentional and "solid person"[6] characteristics to Life through study of the Teaching, sensitive and intelligent observation of self and others, and commitment in practice to the constant exercise of the disciplines of right and regenerative adaptation to Life. Realize a living harmony and equality of physical, emotional, and mental functions, and release all of these, through the moral disposition of the heart, or love in the service of others. Thus, be purified, and realize a harmony of the lower functions of Life, and submit all of that to the disposition of the heart, or Communion with Divine Life, whereby the subhuman evolves into the truly human.

10. Through the regenerative conservation of the tendency to orgasm, submit to orgasm less and less frequently. Require the frequency of the occasions of sexual communion to be determined entirely by daily observation of the mutual intensity of both intimate love-feeling and fullness of desire. And, through adaptation to the process of sexual communion, prolong these occasions more and more, and transform them totally into the process of sexual communion with Life. Grow in the process, so that orgasm occurs less

4. The vital person's attention and self-image are focused in the gross physical dimension of life.

Please refer to *The Eating Gorilla Comes in Peace* for a complete discussion of the three types, or qualities of life—the vital person, the peculiar person, and the solid person.

5. The peculiar person is one whose principal focus of attention is the emotional-sexual dimension of life.

6. The solid person is one in whom the lower mental or willful and conceptual functions are the focus of life and attention.

and less, until it rarely even approaches. At last, the motive of tension-releasing orgasm dissolves in the Fullness of Life.

11. Adapt to sexual communion gradually. Do not even begin it until you are firmly based in the understanding of this process and its relationship to higher and evolutionary psycho-physical adaptation as well as the ultimate sacrifice of the body-mind to the Divine Life. Also, do not begin it until you are firmly based in a nonreactive, full, and mutually intimate relationship that is mature in the ordinary sense, and that involves the full creative commitment of marriage and daily household living. That relationship can be workable, whether heterosexual or homosexual, providing both partners are committed in love, sensitive and intelligent in their daily association with one another, responsible for their individual reactive patterns and old or childish adaptations, and rightly oriented to the Divine Life that is the true and ultimate content of sexual intimacy.

12. The entire body should be free of reactive tension and reactive feeling. The brain-mind should be relaxed into Life, and so permitted to be entirely and constantly free of thoughts and images. And the entire body-mind should be expressed as unobstructed and nonreactive feeling, altogether responsive to one's lover in the Field of All-Pervading Life. This is the only disposition that can make true and ecstatic sexual love.

13. During sexual embrace, many mini-crises or near approaches of genital orgasm may occur, without indulgence of the full genital crisis. As each such near-crisis approaches, inhale and exhale with full feeling-relaxation to the whole body, control bodily motion, and tense the "bodily base" (including the genitals, perineum, and anus) upward, until the tendency toward the genital crisis dissolves in Fullness of Life-Feeling.

14. Natural "kumbak," or spontaneous holding in of the inhaled breath (or holding out of the exhaled breath), may occur at times in the pleasurable exercise of sexual communion. In such a case, simply relax whole bodily into the Bliss-Fullness of Life.

15. Thought forces genital orgasm. When the brain is allowed, with the rest of the body, simply to feel into the All-Pervading Life,

then thought relaxes and dissolves. Chronic thought and compulsive internalizing toward images and memories are a compulsive contraction of the verbal and sensory centers of the brain. When the whole body Communes with Life, there is no self-binding process of thought. Likewise, orgasm ceases to be forced, and it is, therefore, bypassed by the naturally conservative mechanism of the sex function. We must allow the Life-Feeling to become Full, whole bodily. When this is done, genital orgasm ceases to arise. When Fullness replaces emotional reactivity, or the recoil toward self, the bodily signs of tension and degenerative release of tension (including genital orgasm) are naturally bypassed. Thus, as we mature in the process of sexual communion, genital orgasm must be created by an act of will, or intentional permission, whereas, in the initial stage of our adaptation to the process, genital orgasm must be prevented by such acts of will.

16. Relax all efforts, all thoughts, and all tensions that are methods of creating orgasm. Over time, this relaxation of the intention toward orgasm makes orgasm a natural matter of the body's own control. Then, as you mature, enter into Fullness of Life-Feeling in sexual communion, free of the whole strategic and reactive search for release. In that case, the genital crisis may often be approached, but it is readily controlled by the whole body, so that genital orgasm is bypassed. If genital orgasm is approached at all, let it be created by relaxed or open bodily and feeling responses in love-desire, and not by thoughts or tensions that seek release. And if the crisis approaches, abandon all tension in the lower body, and allow the stimulated Life to pass to the entire body, and thence to your lover and the Infinite Divine.

17. Sex is not wrong in principle. The body is structured for sex. Therefore, sex is not in doubt, nor a process to be suppressed, or feared, or exploited. The question is, what kind of responsibility does the sex function represent in the mature individual who lives in Communion with the Divine? What is the optimum, most enlivening, auspicious, free, loving, uniquely human, and ultimately pleasurable form of sexual participation in the Play of Life? Sex is not itself "sin." It is not inherently shameful, hidden, antisocial,

destructive, separative, or Godless. Therefore, the right question is not, how can we avoid, suppress, or manipulate sex? The question is, what is the right human practice of sexuality, and what kind of specific responsibility does that involve?

18. Every occasion of sexual communion should be a profound but natural discipline of feeling-attention. It should never be casual, obsessive, subjectively oriented, reactively motivated, devoid of intimate feeling-surrender, or separate from conscious communion with the All-Pervading Force Field of Life.

283

19. There are two ways to breathe.

The conventional breath cycle is unconscious of Life. It receives very little, suffers chronic contraction of feeling and of the trunk and belly, and does not exhale fully. Such unnatural or contracted breathing expresses an emotionally reactive personality, self-possessed, self-protective, and separated from Life. The results of such breathing are a chronic buildup of tension in the lower body, particularly in the genitals. And such a personality is generally either obsessed with genital release through orgasm, or else is so rigid that even degenerative contact with the pleasurable feeling of Life is chronically avoided.

The true form of the breath is founded in freedom from chronic reactive recoil, and it is consciously established in Feeling-Communion with the All-Pervading Life. Such breathing receives much Life in the vital region of the body (at the solar plexus and below). Such breathing involves full exhalation of the waste products of the lungs, and it involves full relaxation-release of the Life-Fullness, from or via the vital region to the entire body, and thence, via all relations, to Infinity. Such breathing of Fullness expresses an emotionally free and loving personality, self-released into the All-Pervading Life on which it depends and which is its ultimate and true Identity.

fter sexual communion has been practiced in the full feeling manner for some time, genital and other bodily tensions,

284

reactive emotions, and mental concepts and images tend to disappear from one's intimate living. Thus, the factors that commonly motivate sexual intercourse and sex play in general all tend to be dissolved in whole bodily and relational feeling-communion with the All-Pervading Life of the world. For this reason, orgasm, which is the product of physical and emotional tensions as well as mental fixations, tends to be less and less a factor in the process of sexual communion.

Over time, through feeling-communion, linked with the breath and other bodily factors, the whole and entire body-mind tends to relax its reactive tensions and contractions and its subjective self-possession. Thus, Fullness of Life is communicated in the body-mind, whereas previously the self, or body-mind, was in a chronic state of recoil from Life. As this begins, the urge to orgasm begins to relax, as a result of the relaxation of all aspects of body, emotion, and mind. Thus, the motive for sexual intercourse gradually ceases to be orgasm and becomes, instead, the bodily-magnetic or truly desiring force of love. The body breathes as free feeling, or love, and the brain and mind likewise relax into the feeling of Life, so that thought and imagery are replaced by simple and heartfelt attention.

Eventually, the bodily reactive urge to orgasm disappears. This does not mean that sexual communion ceases, but only that it becomes wholly devoted to the bodily awakening to Life and the whole bodily Communion with Life. The process becomes the simple awakening of the high or free and intense Energy of Life through loving contact. And the awakened Life is breathed and felt whole bodily, Radiating to Infinity via one's lover.

In such a case, there should be no anxiety that one has become sexually "dead." Rather, the conventional and reactive basis for sexual activity has been transcended. Bodily contraction or tension, emotional reactivity, the loveless dramatization of relational conflict, and all erotic concepts, obsessive designs of the will, and chronic imaging cease to be the necessary accessories of one's sexuality. Instead, forceful loving contact becomes intensified, and the regenerative process of the bodily conservation of the Life-Force and internal chemistry becomes more and more stable and profound.

Therefore, devotees who practice sexual communion should eventually observe the signs that accompany the Fullness of Divine Communion. That Fullness is contacted via the total complex of practice in the Way of Divine Ignorance, but the discipline of sexual communion itself is a primary element of that practice. When the natural conservation of orgasm thus begins to appear, this is one of the signs that determine the devotee's readiness for instruction and responsibility in the more esoteric aspects of sexual communion and bodily *conductivity* of Life. Such instruction is given in the later or mature phase of the Way of Relational Enquiry and also in the Way of Re-cognition.

Both partners should embrace with profound feeling-attention or love-desire into the great Life-Sensation of their bodily loving. However, they should <u>know</u> one another continuously as they embrace, and not turn away and into their independent and internal feeling-sensations and thoughts. This turning away into the independent bodily self is the commonly learned method that leads to orgasm, or bodily discharge of the Life-Force.

The conventional orgasm is the primary physical expression of the egoic emotion associated with the avoidance of relationship, or the contraction of feeling-attention. The "betrayed ego" of the childish and adolescent individual, bound up in the dilemma of the mutually exclusive desires of dependence and independence, is the incarnation of Narcissus. If such an individual adapts to sexual relationships and intimate practice before he or she is free of the betrayed ego principle and is responsible to persist as unobstructed feeling-attention under all conditions, in all relations, and via all functions (including the genital function), then the orgasm, or the stimulation and discharge cycle of sexuality, will bind him in the dilemma of loveless sex. Casual genital orgasm is identical to ego, contraction, dilemma, the obstruction of feeling-attention and relationship.

Therefore, lovers must approach one another only when free, even bodily, of the egoic principle of contraction and self-possession. In that case, they will not turn from one another to discharge their Force of Life. They will embrace one another and hold to one another, fully feeling one another in love. Their bliss will increase, and they will constantly release and relax all contractions that are tending to turn them away, to be unseen and unloving, for even a moment. As a result, orgasm may not even be approached for prolonged periods while they embrace. There is heightening, but not the crisis. (If, in learning to adapt to the relational rather than the egoic form of sexual love, the crisis approaches, it should be dealt with as described elsewhere in these essays.) The full form of true sexual or love embrace is one of full and continuous relational feeling and awareness, both of and by one's partner. The eyes may often meet, to see and be seen in love. And instead of the crisis of orgasm, a blissfulness and heightening will appear as the essence and consequence of the embrace. The bliss will constantly be breathed to the entire bodily being, and via the entire bodily being (not merely the genitals) to and through one's lover to Infinity. Thus, after a time of this play, the straining impulse of desire simply relaxes. The lovers rest in mutual bliss and love-feeling. (The male erection does not necessarily subside, or at least does not do so until the point of separation, or complete relaxation of the embrace.) The end phenomenon is not necessarily discharge, and certainly not recoil and separation, but fullness of love and whole body intensity, or bliss in a condition of complete relaxation. It is not a matter of passive or empty relaxation, but of living, blissful, radiant Fullness of Life. True lovers rest in attention and feeling to one another, rather than stimulation of one another to the point of separation from that feeling-attention in degenerative and self-possessed orgasmic discharges.

Lovers who are responsible for reactivity and recoil toward self are able to be responsible for pleasure beyond genital orgasm. It is the inherent pleasure we enjoy in Communion at Infinity, rather than the acquired and brief pleasure we inherit through exploitation of ourselves in loveless self-possession. Those who do not realize the first step, which is responsibility for reactive emotion, bodily tension, and positive conversion to love and spiritual Communion, will not truly be able to realize the sexual responsibility of a mature human being. They will be unable to adapt fully to this instruction, but they will need and demand release through genital orgasm. Such individuals are constantly interrupted in their inherent pleasure, blissfulness, and loving by the contraction of the heart and all the extended functions of the bodily being.

Therefore, first learn love, by unlearning the recoil of self. Be restored to the Infinite Life and Bliss through the responsibility of present love. Then you will be able to be responsible for turning away to self in your sexuality as well as in the continuous emotional context of everyday life. Betrayal and degenerative genital orgasm are a single reflex. They are the presumptions of the loveless ego. Be free of betrayal, or the presumption that you are not loved and that you are weak, separate, starving, and never full or inherently blissful. Be free of your infantile philosophy. Bring an end to the perpetual adolescence of seeking in dilemma for the absent Bliss. By existing as love, be free of the search for love. Then you will love in sexual embrace as one in love, and you will be transformed bodily and mentally to the full confession of happiness.

When obsessive and mechanical exploitation of genital orgasm is truly transcended by love, the fourth stage of life, the life of the opening heart or psyche, has begun.

Chapter 15

True Sexuality Is the
Play of the Heart

Sexual Communion versus the
Sexual Yogas of the Ancients
*A talk given by Bubba Free John
to his devotees*

BUBBA: I would like to discuss the Taoist and Tantric traditions
relative to sexual practice and esoteric spiritual transformation.

Since ancient times, spiritual life has been associated with the
capacities of men to realize an alternative experience, an "Alternative Reality," that corresponds to their psycho-physiological
orientation. For thousands of years, spiritual life on Earth has been
essentially a "male club," and esoteric spiritual philosophies and
practices reflect certain habit capacities that pertain most naturally
or commonly to men. The practices of Tantric and Taoist yogas,
which are at the root of the yogic understanding of the purpose of
sexuality, are extensions of this male orientation toward salvation
through the particular physiological and psychological disposition
of men.

Religious dogmas would lead us to believe that sin is fundamentally a matter of sex. Sin, in the usual mind, means enjoyment
of sex, or exploitation of sex, but the line between enjoyment and
exploitation of sex is felt to be very fine. Merely to be involved in sex
is, therefore, somehow to involve yourself in doubt and sin. We
receive this communication as a kind of bald social reference, a part

of our conventional self-image, but the origin of this doubting of sexuality (and therefore of bodily life in general) is in the ancient practices and philosophies. It did not originate in the notion that the Deity judges sex to be fundamentally wrong. It originated in the more sophisticated idea that you must turn to God and that, to do so, you must turn within, above, and beyond the body. Conventional religion is a kind of metaphorical, man-on-the-street communication that reflects the very technical philosophical persuasions of ancient times. In their mentalizing habit, the males in traditional cultures have been the chief originators of conventional spiritual life since ancient times. They have been fundamentally committed to this notion of the inversion and upward-turning of attention. Because he is relatively right-sided, fiery, expansive, the male feels his mortality in the form of his bodily experience. He comes to doubt bodily life itself, and he looks for ways to be saved, to be immortalized, or to be raised to the God-Condition, or the "Alternative Reality," through the exploitation of an alternative dimension of his physiology. Thus, he becomes left-sided, cool, and inward in hopes of being saved.

The sexual process exists in the gross, expansive dimension of pleasure and bodily life. Therefore, since ancient times, it has fundamentally or most often been in doubt in the male consciousness. The Taoist point of view represents one original solution to this sense of doubt. It is perhaps more ancient than the Hindu Tantric point of view, which is even more left-sided or classically Oriental, and which represents the further evolution of this disposition. Thus, when men discussed spirituality in ancient times, they were not just discussing inward, subjective, metaphysical subjects. They were referring to a bodily disposition of inversion, in which we turn attention away from outward expansion and back toward the center, toward what is within and above rather than what is external and below.

Previous to these developments, in the most ancient times, the critical division between left and right, in and out, and up and down was not absolute. Through magic, rituals, and certain kinds of yoga, men sought to invoke What is above in order to gain benefits in life. In the most ancient disposition of male philosophy, which tended to doubt the gross, apparently mortal dimension of life, there was an inversion of attention certainly, but it was not an attempt to leave the world. It was rather a matter of turning the attention to what is subtle and what is above in order to gain blessings in the gross world and beyond after death. In these ancient times, even in India, human beings engaged in magical rituals and invocations of the elemental powers and other practices in order to gain blessings that would change ordinary human life.

As time went on, however, the critical doubt of life became profound in male philosophy, and spiritual men turned exclusively to what is above and within, rather than remaining content simply to be helped by It. Later on, in the Upanishadic period and later times, all kinds of ascetics begin to appear, not only in India, but all over the world, people who were oriented exclusively toward what is within and above. Such individuals no longer sought the transformation of gross life through blessings that could be attained by the invocation of higher powers. Rather, they sought to leave this world and to incarnate in the dimensions or worlds of the subtle, inward, and higher powers.

The tradition of Taoism represents a primitive, most original form of this philosophical disposition of inversion. The disposition of Tantra, whether Hindu or Buddhist, represents more of the Upanishadic and later ascetic philosophical disposition. Both the Taoist and the Tantric philosophies reflect this male philosophy of the inversion of attention. As I said, this process of inversion is not simply a matter of thinking and metaphysics and inwardness; it is a matter of how you manipulate the body. It is matter of yogic physiology, of psycho-physical inversion. And one of the primary dimensions of experience wherein this yoga was manipulated was sexuality.

In most ancient times and, to a large degree, in the Taoist tradition, men did not have an entirely negative orientation toward sexuality. In other words, they did not attempt to avoid sexuality, but they manipulated sexuality for esoteric spiritual purposes—to transform the gross life, and also to insure a desirable future beyond death. In the Tantric tradition, however, even though there were many classes, tribes, sects, or cults, they all were more or less fixed in the later, Upanishadic, ascetic disposition that looks to attain what is within and above more or less exclusively. Tantra yoga still maintains a certain positive orientation toward sexuality and the things of life, but it does so only ritually. And further along in time, even this liberal disposition of the Tantra is lost, and we find only the more modern ascetic tradition, which does not make use of the things of the gross life but turns away from them altogether.

In any case, all of these ancient traditions of the male philosophy are based in the dilemma of gross life, and they are reflected in a similar physiological point of view toward sexuality. This physiological point of view is also reflected in the moralities of the great religions that have survived to the present day, which are in some sense always antisexual. They are not antisexual because of a belief that sexuality is bad or wrong in principle. They are antisexual because of a fundamental doubt of life, which in turn is based on this ancient male reaction. And the physiology or yoga of the male consciousness since ancient times has involved not only the inversion of attention, but the inversion of sexual experience, and particularly the inversion of the process of the orgasm, or ejaculation. In this yoga, instead of moving down and out, the orgasmic impulse is reversed and made to move in and up.

Therefore, in the present day, when you all think about realizing a rejuvenating yoga in your sexuality as well as in all of the ordinary physiology of your life, you tend naturally to move to a relatively negative and manipulative disposition toward sexuality. The physiology with which you are sympathetic, therefore, is the inversion of the orgasm. The Taoists, who represented a more primitive and ancient version of this consideration, were not in any sense antisexual. They were not in doubt about having sexual relations, but they were certainly oriented toward a conversion of their sexual relations, toward the manipulation of the sexual act so that the ultimate event of orgasm was not a downward-outward movement, but an inward-upward movement. By controlling the ejaculatory moment they sought to draw the semen and the Life-Force up through the spinal column and into the brain centers. They felt they would thus rejuvenate the body and achieve an ultimately immortal body, moving out of the physical encasement at the point of death into an astral or light body. The specific yoga of sexuality was one of the primary means for attaining this result.

The purpose of achieving longevity or immortality in the physical is more or less absent in the Tantric disposition. There are some Tantric sects that look toward immortalization and that are very similar to the Taoist tradition, but for the most part the Tantra is about the ritual use of sexuality for the sake of the inversion of attention, not for the sake of physical immortalization.

293

The later ascetic cults also look to exploit the physiology of sexuality, but through hatha yoga practices rather than sexual intercourse. They specifically seek to avoid sexual intercourse.

In all of these traditions there is a specific manipulation of the physiology of sexuality, particularly the physiology of the male body, just as the whole of this philosophy in all its forms is essentially a male creation. The principal concern is the manipulation of the moment of ejaculation. In the Taoist tradition, for instance, where longevity and immortalization of the body were part of the positive consideration of life, the Taoist male philosophers looked to have sexual intercourse with as many young female virgins as they could. They did not only sit in a room and meditate. They tried to have sexual relations with as many women as they possibly could. The women had to be essentially young, virgin, and possessed of a great deal of stored energy of the opposite kind to that of the male. The Taoist males sought to acquire this energy for themselves.

These philosophers, you see, were very physiological in their orientation. They would try to make the women have orgasms as many times as possible when they were with them, but the men tried to prevent their own orgasm as much as possible, even to the absolute degree. For this purpose they made use of various physiological devices. Seminal discharge was prevented by contracting the perineal muscles through the withholding of the breath, by deep inhaling and grinding of the teeth. Another method of preventing seminal discharge and, it was supposed, of sending the seminal fluid up the spine, was to exert pressure with the two middle fingers of the left hand on the urethra, between the scrotum and the anus, at the time of ejaculation.

This aspect of the physiological understanding of the ancients was not altogether correct. If the man prevents the actually arising ejaculatory discharge by manipulating the breath or by pressing the fingers to the base of the penis, what actually happens is that, yes, the ejaculation is stopped, but the seminal fluid is only forced back and emptied into the bladder. So the ancient belief that the ejaculated seminal fluid could be sent up the spine to nourish the brain and to create rejuvenating effects or ultimately to create a light body was a false understanding from a physiological point of view. If the man does come to the point of ejaculation and simply prevents it mechanically, it is true that at least a portion of the seminal fluid is not even introduced into the eliminative tract of the penis. Some of it is withheld sheerly by the pressure. But what seminal fluid does enter into that tract is inevitably emptied into the bladder and then eliminated via urination. For all practical purposes, then, the individual does not send that fluid into the brain or into the rest of the body. Therefore, from a purely medical point of view, some students of these matters think that this ancient practice was entirely false.

But such thinkers are also not completely correct. The Taoist yogis were very practical individuals. They did not just believe that something would happen if they manipulated themselves in this way. They did in fact observe that certain processes or effects occur in this practice. They appear only to have misinterpreted some of the physiological phenomena.

I have also spoken to you about the inversion or conversion of the process of sexuality. In our own orientation, in the Way of Divine Ignorance, there is no philosophical disposition that is strategically opposed to the world or founded in the reactive "male" doubt of life and of sexuality. Nor is our realization of rejuvenation, or the natural law of enlivenment of the body, based on this conventional male philosophy, or any doubt of life, or any strategic, problem-oriented manipulation of attention. But in the whole bodily process of love, of unobstructed feeling in sexual communion with our consort, there is a natural transformation of the whole process of orgasm, the whole affair of sexual love. In the process of the love relationship between true lovers, in the total feeling relationship between men and women, there is a natural conversion of the genital process of sexuality. Pleasure is no longer felt exclusively in the genital region. The total psycho-physical body is stimulated. The orgasm is converted from a downward and outward, vitally exhausting spasm to a thrill of the whole body that stimulates all of the glandular centers in both the man and the woman. Therefore, the process of sexuality, fully realized, is indeed rejuvenating. Not only is the chemistry of the genitals stimulated—and certainly most of it is also retained if there is no ejaculation at all—but the entire nervous system and all of the glands of the body, including the glands in the brain, are also stimulated. And when this occurs, sexual activity is not a process of loss, separation, or the emptying of Life, but it is inherently rejuvenating. It is rejuvenating completely independent of any self-involved physiological manipulation or dualistic, doubting philosophy; it is rejuvenating, but purely on the basis of surrender in love. In such a case, the usual results of sexual intercourse do not appear. In general, the man's erection does not disappear in some moment of crisis. In general, there is no loss of strength, no loss of vitality in either the man or the woman. There is no subtle sense of emptiness or depression. In fact, there is even a continuing or unending capacity for intense sexual activity.

Thus, the ancients were right, at least on a certain level. The semen is not mechanically drawn up the spine, as they sometimes taught, but the total nervous system and all of the glands are certainly stimulated, and the glandular chemistry is absorbed into the bloodstream, thus nourishing the body and the brain, and producing higher evolutionary growth of the body-mind. If you simply submit to the downward and outward trend of the orgasm, the glands above the sexual center are not stimulated and the regenerative chemistry is not introduced into the plane of the body. Vulgar sexuality is an obsessive, more or less exclusive stimulation of the lower vehicle of the nervous system and the glands of the sexual center, and an elimination of vital force and chemistry through orgasm. But if there is natural conservation—not through the strategic manipulations of the ancient yogas, wherein self and world are in doubt, but through love—the total nervous system is stimulated. All the glands are thereby stimulated in both man and woman, and a rejuvenating process is realized to be native to the body. We are initiated into that process through sexual communion.

DEVOTEE: Is this process related to the act of retaining the semen or to some more esoteric practice?

BUBBA: The semen is retained and absorbed—not by mechanical suppression of orgasm, but by natural transcendence of the urge to orgasm itself. In that process, the total nervous system and all of the glands, including the sex glands, are stimulated.

DEVOTEE: I can certainly associate the physiological drain in the lower body with the loss of semen. But I also experience a shock to the rest of the body. The glands, particularly in the throat, underneath the arms, in the head, even the legs, feel depleted of vitality.

BUBBA: In our obsessive orientation toward sexuality, only the sexual center is stimulated; through the sexual center all of the vitality of the body tends to be spasmodically eliminated. We regard this process of elimination to be the essential pleasure of sex, but it is ultimately degenerative in its effect. In right orientation, through love, to the process of sexuality, and to human relations altogether, the entire nervous system and all of the glands of the body are stimulated beyond the capacity of experience to empty us, and therefore we enjoy abundant Life, which works to rejuvenate us and to keep us healthy by counteracting the effects that would make us unhealthy or devitalized.

There is a principle of the ancient yogic practice that remains true, if we can set aside the body-denying and male-oriented philosophy of such yogas. What is true about it is not that only those who retain the seminal fluid and send it up the spine to the brain can be saved! Women cannot do that, for instance, but women can engage the process of regenerative sexuality through their own unique bodily functions, which involve the conversion of their own bio-chemical substance and psycho-physical force of Life. What remains true about the ancient yoga is that the orgasm as an exclusive genital occasion must be conserved, but through love, through whole body feeling-attention in the Infinite Field of Life. The usual man or woman engages in sexuality through exclusive stimulation of the sexual center, not only losing the sexual chemistry but devitalizing the entire body-mind. Sexual intercourse is thus a degenerative process that, engaged throughout a lifetime, becomes more and more degrading. Not only is the usual man or woman oriented to the ultimate process of the loss of Life, but all ordinary functions—all of breathing, feeling, thinking, and all of the acts of attention—are associated with partial-body stimulation and chronic loss of Life. In love, however, there is natural conservation of the Life-Force.

297

Our capacity to be stimulated and enlivened whole bodily rather than degenerated and emptied is the key to Fullness of being, to pleasure of existence, to health, well-being, and ultimately longev-ity. The principle of that regenerative process, however, is not the self-divided point of view of the ancient yogas. The principle of that process is the whole body disposition, or love. In that disposition there is natural conservation of the Life-Force, the chemistry of the body, natural stimulation of the total body, of all the glands, and of the entire nervous system. The life of love in Truth, in its Fullness, involves total transformation of even the body. If we could live long enough we would see that even the cells of the body are transformed. The body itself is converted into something more subtle than the elemental physical form. Ultimately, the body can even be changed into energy and disappear.

However, for true devotees of the Living God, the esoteric sexual process is not an end in itself. It is not the Way whereby we perfectly Realize our Unity with the Transcendental and All-Pervading Divine Person. But it is an instructive incident, wherein we may observe the whole body process that must become our responsibility and enjoyment under <u>all</u> conditions, not only in sexual activity. Thus, we must understand our sexuality and parti-cipate in it Lawfully. Sexuality is simply a moment in our transition from ordinary life to Communion with God in right relationship to the Spiritual Master, in whose Company we enjoy the same Life-enhancing physiological process, but without the dogma of sexual experience. Now you may enjoy brief association with the Bliss of Existence in ritual moments of sexual exploitation. But you must realize the ultimate process of the whole body in loving responsibility. Then, in this life of Divine Communion, and in the Yoga of the relationship to the Spiritual Master, you may enjoy that perfectly transforming process under all conditions.

298

Ordinary people confine the virtue of the whole body to sexuality, but Blissfulness must be lifted out of the ritual degradation of sex. The Bliss of God must be released in the body-mind, and made available to human relations through ordinary contemplation, breathing, feeling, and acting. You are not required to go to the bedroom in order to be rejuvenated or to Realize God or to find pleasure. You certainly do not Realize God there. And whole bodily pleasure is not exclusively the province of sexual intercourse; otherwise we would have to be yogis in bed twenty-four hours a day! Through right understanding, however, sexuality may become an incident of initiation into the process that we always already represent in our structural potential, and that must become our constant, native Enjoyment under all conditions.

The whole body is only put to sleep through conventional sexual confrontation. Now, in your ordinary adaptation, you depend on erotic stimulation for the pleasure of existence. You know no greater pleasure than sex. But the same pleasure that is isolated in moments of sexuality is native to you bodily and in your ultimate Consciousness. The Radiant Energy of the great cosmos is available at all times. Once initiated into this process of bodily God-Communion, then you can move beyond sexual obsession into spiritual life, wherein the same mechanism is awakened and is actively heightened under all conditions. Through right understanding, through the life of love, the native Pleasure of Existence is released from bondage to sexuality, and it is restored to the whole body and to all of your relations. This process, which is sexual communion, normalizes sexuality and releases it from obsession and degrading insanity. Sexual communion does not make us sexless at all. It makes us capable of sexuality in truly human terms, and it releases us from all limitations of a sexual nature, in order that we may continue to grow and engage in the higher and ultimate affair of Life.

It is through our whole body orientation to Infinity that we continually exist in the disposition that is enlivening, that is rejuvenating, and that enables us to continue to grow, to realize not only the faculties but the experiences that are structurally potential in us above the vital or lower human functions. In your experience up to this time, you have been basically oriented to the lower life below the heart, to food and sex and ordinary conceptual thinking and aggravated willfulness. But if the whole body is your point of view, if love is your disposition, if the Living God is your Condition, the true occupation of body and mind, then the total structure of the whole body is also your potential, and you may continue to grow. This is true of both man and woman. It is not that women have to reverse the seminal ejaculation. Obviously not! But, through love, both men and women must enjoy the *conductivity* of Life throughout the body, rather than the discharge of Life and the elimination of higher chemistry in a continuous cycle of degenerative actions. Such petty habituation leads throughout a lifetime toward awful death, via not only degenerative sexuality but the irresponsible exploitation of all ordinary activity.

In our loving, in our whole body disposition, we are not involved in a dualistic confrontation with the Earth and with the elements and with sexuality. We must realize a disposition that is totally free of guilt and free of that nagging sense that sexuality and life itself are somehow in principle sinful. We must become oriented not toward a promiscuous and self-indulgent sexual life, but toward complete loving responsibility for Life. Such responsibility is not in any sense divided or negative in its orientation toward the functions below the heart. If you can become so clarified in your disposition, then you may also continue to grow. And you will not pursue what is above the heart as an "Alternative Reality," but as a further expression of your whole bodily enjoyment and ultimate Sacrifice.

All I want to indicate in this discussion is that there is a negative or inverted philosophy at work in the ancient esoteric sexual practices, but that the physiology of the ancient yoga does, on one level, belong to the physiology of our natural or Lawful disposition. There is a process involved in sexuality and the whole affair of living that is regenerative, that is whole bodily in its nature and orientation, and that overstimulates the mechanism of the bodily being and therefore enables the being to enjoy an excess of Life, so that the process of existence may be essentially regenerative. This does not mean that we must seek to become immortal. But the process of death becomes natural to us, as it is natural to the flowers. Right responsibility for the body-mind in relation to Life is inherently self-transcending. Therefore, the devotee ultimately transcends the body-mind, its experiences, and its death. And death itself need not always be preceded by some overwhelmingly negative, degenerative disease. This does not mean that no true devotee will die from such degenerative disease. All have lived degenerative lives up to a point, and such practices have their consequences. But, even so, devotees can be oriented Lawfully toward the whole affair of existence in such a way that they may be transformed by a Process of infinitely greater strength than the mere experiential or degenerative cycle of the body-mind.

In the form of your sexuality, then, you must be a lover. You must be in love in a completely positive way, free of negative, fascinated, obsessive orientations towards sexual experience. Your sexuality will then be positive in the psychological sense, and also positive in the physiological sense. Your practice will not develop quite as the ancients described it, but the same mechanism that they were stimulating or exploiting through their strategic means will also be awakened in you through love.

The Anatomy of Feeling

The Bodily House
of Narcissus

301

The true psycho-physical "root" or "center" of the human body-mind is the entire body-mind itself, rather than some center within the body-mind. Thus, the reactive contraction that separates the body-mind from the All-Pervading Life is the reactive contraction of the entire body-mind, which curls upon itself in every part, toward self-possession and problematic commitment to the survival and fulfillment of the independent "I."

However, the characteristic signs of that self-defining reaction to Life in the case of the usual individual may be read in a specific organ and function complex. Thus, the usual individual displays chronic psycho-physical tension at the perineum, anus, genitals, navel, solar plexus, heart, lungs, throat, mouth, face, spinal line, and brain.

The bodily "base" or "floor," which includes the anus, perineum, and sex organs, is the common functional "lock" that separates the individual or whole body from the foundation that is Life. Likewise, the bodily "ceiling," which tends to be created by reactive "locks" or chronic tensions at the mouth and the visual, verbal-mental, and speech centers of the brain, creates a continuous and unpassable barrier to aspiration and intelligence. All the rest of the body-mind composes the "four walls" or self-enclosure.

Only when the "door" or "window" of the heart awakens the whole and entire body-mind in the intuition and spontaneous love of Life, or the Divine Ignorance-Radiance, does this house and hedge of Narcissus dissolve in the ecstatic Regeneration of Happiness.

T he heart is the center and the epitome of the whole bodily being. It is the integrator and the Energy control center of the gross bodily form, and it also contains the root of the subtle dimensions of awareness as well as the "doorway" to the Truth of our existence.

302

In sexual play, the heart not only represents the center from which love radiates from and as the whole bodily being, but it also regulates the process of desire, excitement, sexual responsiveness, and orgasm.

At the heart, Life and Light and Consciousness are reconciled and made one. The body and feeling and mind, or attention, are also unified and projected into action as the single principle of love at and from the heart. The heart is the ultimate seat of waking, dreaming, and sleeping, of ego, of attention, and of absolute, unqualified Consciousness. The heart is the soul and Spirit of the whole bodily being. The heart is the Mystery of our Condition, of the Cosmos, and of God, Truth, or Reality.

In true sexual play, excitement is generated in or via the lower coil of the bodily being (the vital base, the realm of functional organs below the heart). The mind of thoughts becomes the pure intensity of attention to one's lover via the feeling force of the heart. Then the whole body is projected as love-desire.

As the play progresses, the heart intensifies the condition of the whole body—physically, emotionally, and mentally (not as imagery but as free or relaxed brain attention). Thus, the All-Pervading Life accumulates, particularly in the lower body, where the genital stimulation originates. Even if the devotee continually releases the awakening Energy to the entire bodily being (thence to his or her lover, and on to Infinity), it is possible and often likely that the intensification will yield a lower body or genital accumulation of Force that will approach genital discharge.

The process of sexual communion is a natural play of feeling-attention, as love-desire, in which the intensification worked in the total bodily being through love play is maintained as a nonsubjective and whole body condition. That is, the separate interior of imagery, emotional recoil, distraction, and insensitivity to one's lover is not indulged. Rather, there is sacrifice of the subjective position to the position of the total bodily being, in relational play with one's lover. In that case, the Energy stimulated and accumulated in the play will not be thrown away through some spasm of pleasure that takes place in only a portion of the body and effectively disturbs or breaks the Energy connection with one's lover. Rather, the Energy is diffused, from the genitals to the entire bodily being, and kept in play with one's lover to Infinity.

303

The process by which this takes place is one of the natural regulation of the whole body stimulation generated from the heart region. Through the discipline of maintaining feeling-attention, free of subjective recoil and imagery, in continuous communion with Life via one's lover, the activity of the heart comes under a natural economy. That is, if attention is stably held in the play rather than in distractions or images, and the connection of feeling rather than mere perception and sensation (but not excluding these) is maintained, then the stimulating activity of the heart is easily regulated via the breath cycle.

If, however, subjective distractions (images, fears, thoughts, and the like) or lack of present desire (permitting outer and inner distractions) disturbs the sexual play, the stimulated Energy will turn in on the body itself, independent of one's lover. Two things may take place in that case—both due to the failure to be responsible for present feeling-attention. In general, the heart stimulation will be permitted to move such a one toward genital discharge and a willingness to indulge genital discharge. In the more rare case, subjective distraction in the form of fear or disinterest and the like (rather than erotic distraction in images, and so forth) may create a temporary or chronic impotence or frigidity.

The failure to enjoy full erection, in the male, or the failure to enjoy a progressive state of sexual stimulation in intercourse, particularly in the female, is generally due to the inability to enter into intimate sexual play with full and free feeling-attention in the present. In that case, the heart is not awakened to its energizing role, but is inhibited. Then, no matter how much mental interest there may otherwise be in enjoying sexual play, the interest will fall short of full pleasure.

The case of impotence or frigidity is equally as negative a condition as erotic self-possession, or sexual distraction that cannot be responsible for feeling-attention, and, therefore, for conservation of the orgasm to whole body diffusion.

304

The process of sexual communion is not merely a process of conservation of orgasm, but of conservation of the Life-Force and chemistry stimulated throughout the whole event of every occasion of sexual play—even throughout the whole life of polarized human and emotional relationship between lovers. Indeed, the whole of spiritual life, in terms of responsibility at the gross or physical level, is a way of life in which the entire bodily being is maintained as the continuous response and responsibility of love, or radiance, and the Life-Force and other psycho-physical essences stimulated in that manner are constantly conserved or diffused to the entire bodily being, and thence to Infinity.

Therefore, the devotee must in general become responsible for whole body feeling-attention, and, in the sexual relationship, he or she must likewise be responsible for love-desire in the specific functional terms of the sexual and polarized play. This means that the heart must govern the entire bodily being, and it must be the core of every discipline, every moment of experience, every moment of awareness in any condition, and every moment of sexual play.

Sexual play is not to be frivolous or casual, but a profound feeling-confession, bodily communicated. As such, it is able to become a field of Life-Theatre, in which ultimate or spiritual responsibilities may be demonstrated and recognized for the first time. Then the native pleasure of sexual play may also be raised to ecstasy, or self-release, and thereby we may be pleasurably adapted to our ultimate responsibility. That responsibility is to sacrifice the independent subjective being to the singleness of the total bodily being, and thence to be the sacrifice of the whole bodily being to Infinity, via all relations and functions, and under all conditions.

E motional responsibility is the key to sexual communion. When the reactivity of physical, emotional, and mental individuation, or separative contraction, becomes a matter of moment to moment responsibility—then whole bodily and non-reactive feeling-attention, or love, becomes the content of every cycle of the breath. And it is the nonreactive cycle of the feeling-breath that is the instrument of the mutual sacrifice of true lovers.

305

S exual communion is established via the maintenance of a constant sense of Life-Fullness through imageless relational feeling and sensation without thought.

Chronic Thinking Is Separation Anxiety, and It Motivates Us to Achieve the Sense of Reunion through Sex

B oth sexual obsession and sexual repression have their roots in the verbal and abstracting mind, the mind of speech. Thus, the mouth, the functions of food-taking and assimilation, and the sense of either relative connectedness or disconnectedness to what sustains personal and self-conscious existence have a direct influence or control over the lower bodily processes, including the functions of sexuality and of elimination.

Oral anxiety is the sense of separation from what sustains, and obsessive thinking is only an expression of primal anxiety, or the sense of separation from Reality. When oral anxiety and verbal anxiety come to rest, lower functional problems and chronic sexual tensions, which demand orgasm, also disappear.

Thus, the realization of sexual and bodily freedom and ecstasy is dependent upon release of oral anxiety and chronic verbal or mental activity. The self-defensive, Narcissistic, fearful, separated, knowledge-seeking tendencies must relax if the sexual function is to realize its natural form.

Thus, sex and thought correspond to one another, and thought, or separation anxiety, is the chronic source of sexual tension, obsession, repression, and the common patterns of erotic desire. When thought is released as simple attention in the All-Pervading Life, via whole bodily feeling, then all chronic contractions of the body-mind are released. Therefore, the realization of the disposition of the heart, or whole body feeling-attention in relationship and to the degree of Infinity, is the central principle of sexual communion. By virtue of unobstructed feeling-attention, or love in all relations to Infinity, the mind and body are released to the intuition of the Divine Radiance that Lives the world.

The process of sexual communion is an instrument of higher and truly human adaptation. In that process, the anxiety of separation and self-possessed independence is relaxed, and both the mind, with all its thinking and imagery, and the vital functional order, including the dimension of sex, are themselves released into a higher realization and integration of the body-mind.

As long as the separated and separative disposition that is the chronic verbal mind is dominant, the lower functional dimension tends to be problematic, or a battlefield of strategies and solutions, in the usual man or woman. Thus, the mind both controls and stimulates sex desire in the immature individual. And sex is either exploited or repressed as a strategy of the verbal mind (the oral and lower brain anxiety of separation). By such strategies, the sense of union, or reunion, is sought. Thus, sex is exploited to give a sense of self-release or release of the tension of the bodily self, and, thereby, an illusion of union with the sustaining Power of the Real World. Just so, sex is also repressed in other cases, in order to avoid the exercise that, it is felt, creates the sense of separation. Thus, some seek, by avoiding the sex function, to return to a native sense of union with the Life Power. But in either case, the root of the

306

True Sexuality Is the Play of the Heart

strategy is the sense of inherent or present separation from Life, or what sustains the individual. Thus, the oral and mental functions are the chronic roots of conventional sex adaptation. And only the release of chronic self-possession, separativeness, and contraction of the whole bodily or feeling-radiance of the body-mind will also release sex and all common functions to their natural fullness, free of tension-motivation and problematic strategies. Both thought and sex must ultimately relax into feeling and abide in the whole bodily Radiance of Life.

The fundamental principle of sexual communion is the conservation and transformation of orgasm (or of feeling-energy in general—throughout the whole act of sexual play, and not merely at the point of crisis). The process is a version of "conscious exercise" (involving free attention, unobstructed whole body feeling in relationship, appropriate bodily disposition, and appropriate bodily actions).

It is not that there is a <u>taboo</u> against inwardness, images, and so forth in the play of sexual communion. It is not that you are to watch yourself constantly, and react whenever subjective conditions appear. But you should constantly, in every present moment of the play, apply yourself to the Lawful exercise of unobstructed whole bodily feeling-attention, via the relationship to your lover, and to the All-Pervading Force Field and Presence of the Radiant Divine Life. In that case, it is not a matter of worrying when subjective forms arise. There need be no such concern. In every moment, simply return with feeling to the present play with Life, and you will see how the inward reflex and its expressions become less and less effective. Thus, over time, the self-possessed phenomena of inwardness and the tendency to betray your lover on your own body will disappear.

T he eyes and the genitals cooperate in sex play. The functional operation or use of each in the actual incident of sexual or psycho-physical intimacy reflects the specific form and level of maturity of one's adaptation to the functional circumstance that is human life.

The eyes may be open or closed. They may guide feeling-attention within or without. They may, if closed, guide feeling-attention to thought, or emotion, or sensation. They may, if open, guide feeling-attention toward one's lover or away from one's lover, and to parts of one's lover or the whole body of one's lover. The eyes may be open, and yet feeling-attention may rest on subjective content—mental, emotional, or physical. The eyes may be closed, and yet feeling-attention may rest in sexual communion with one's lover through feeling and sensation. And in all of these cases, feeling-attention may also pass among views and considerations— the environment, the play, observations, memories, or even concerns that are completely independent of the intimate situation that is supposed to be occupying you in the present.

The play of the genitals is also a sign of the condition of feeling-attention in love play, and the permutations of thought, emotion, and sensation represent the same range in this case as in the case of the eyes. There is the possibility in any moment that feeling-attention may turn within or without, toward one's lover or away from one's lover, into the unobstructed communion of feeling-attention via the sensational intimacy and stimulation—or else away from or counter to the whole process.

What then is the right disposition or use of the eyes and the genitals in sexual communion? It is not a matter of the eyes and genitals in themselves, but it is a matter of feeling-attention itself. Sexual communion is a "yoga," a specific discipline or whole process, an event that is either true and regenerative or false and degenerative.

The process of feeling-attention must be responsibly and consistently available, without obstruction, in the sexual contact between intimates. It is a profound discipline, not a casual opportunity for self-indulgence. It is a rhythmic play of concentration and relaxation, of intensity and diffusion of pleasurably felt Life.

Therefore, the right preparation for the intimate act or process of sexual communion is an openly and consistently intimate relationship, lived as a responsible commitment in time and space. Casual sexual contact with random partners indulges only obsessive sexual fascination. It produces stimulation and concludes it with separation and emptiness. Sexual communion is a <u>constant</u> play of love-desire, lived under the ongoing circumstances of daily life. Periodically, within that continuous pattern of living, moments of profound feeling-attention are expressed in the vital "coil" or lower functional region of the body in the case of both lovers. Such is an appropriate moment for the occasion of intimate sexual communion. It is an expression of profound and unobstructed feeling, or love. It is an expression of clearly absorbed attention towards one's lover, and it is also an expression of intensely stimulated vital desire. Such lovers embrace and yield to one another. And their embrace does not lead to separation or emptiness. It is a regenerative play rather than a degenerative play. It is a paradoxical play of a pair—like the two sides of a single body—rather than of two independent and wholly separate desirers.

309

Such lovers are fully involved with one another bodily, through unobstructed and free feeling-attention. Whether eyes open or close, and whether the genital motion is toward or away, each is in sexual communion with the other, and completely distracted from his or her own independent subjectivity.

Thus, the key to sexual communion is not in the eyes and genitals themselves, but in the relative obstruction or freedom from obstruction in the flow of feeling-attention—both during the genital play and during all the common moments of living in relationship to one's lover. And the relative obstructedness or freedom from obstruction in the present flow of feeling-attention in any individual is described by his or her state of mind (or attention), emotion, and physical sensation.

Sexual communion is a process that is—optimally—free of thinking, reactive or negative emotion, and inhibition of sensation and movement.

T he practice of sexual communion is not an absolute, objective discipline. It is a general or inherent discipline. That is, it represents love rather than self-manipulation. Therefore, it cannot be done merely as an exercise of the bodily and mental functions. It can only be done as an exercise of the whole and entire bodily being in love.

310

Sexual Communion Is the Practice of Whole Body Radiance

I ntense practice of sexual communion must be realized as described, or else it will fail to fulfill its total regenerative function and it will result as well in various side effects that are troublesome and degenerative. Among these side effects is the excessive accumulation of vital chemistry and bio-energy in the lower regions of the body. Another side effect occurs when the whole body conservation of orgasm becomes an end in itself. In that case, the energies are obsessively and mechanically internalized, and the relational radiance of the bodily being is suppressed in an essentially loveless and self-conscious or self-bound ritual.

The whole process must be lived radiantly, in love, as a sacrifice of self-consciousness via relational feeling-attention. If this is not done, the whole affair is little different from conventional degenerative eroticism and sex play. Sexual communion is not, as in the case of Oriental yoga and Tantrism, a process of the exclusive inversion of energy and attention. It is a whole body process—one not determined exclusively by either the left or the right hemispheres of the brain, or by either of the two halves or divisions of the autonomic nervous system. Thus, it is performed as a sacrifice, via feeling-attention, via and in relationship to one's lover, to Infinity (or to the degree of unqualified love of Life and radiance of Life).

When side effects occur, they are a sign that the process is relatively self-contained and self-conscious. These side effects are generally in the form of energy imbalances—such as the feeling of an intolerable excess of energy, or the opposite feeling, either of emptiness or of "deadness" (lack of impulse toward sexual intimacy or ordinary loving contact). Other side effects may include various signs of physical or psycho-physical obstruction, such as body pains, headaches, problems in the region of the sex organs or the reproductive system in general, emotional reactivity, subjective erotic obsessions, pornographic and fetishistic needs, or inclinations toward masturbation, promiscuity, homosexuality (where this is not common for the individual), and so forth. One should not become disturbed by such signs, or indulge them in themselves. Rather, one should consider and correct one's practice as a whole. The beginning of right practice is to "hear" the Teaching of the Spiritual Master relative to the essential understanding of life and its Law. And the first gesture of one who hears and understands is practical and intimate service of others on the basis of devotional surrender to the Spiritual Master and the Divine Reality in Truth. Once there is a return to the intuition and practice of whole body sacrifice, or love, then the truly regenerative process of sexual communion begins to normalize, and the side effects, produced by the failure of the sacrifice, fall away.

The daily rule for dietary discipline is never to eat to the point of fullness. The daily rule for sexual discipline is never to make love to the point of emptiness. Appetite should remain after all vital activities. Otherwise, vital activity enervates, toxifies, isolates, and kills the body and mind.

Food and Sex Are for Life-Assimilation, Not the Casual Indulgence of Hunger or Desire

Sexual communion is not a method for satisfying or eliminating sexual desire itself, any more than food-taking is a method for satisfying or destroying hunger itself. Both sexual desire and food hunger are the perpetual evidence and bodily motivators of activities that serve the body in positive terms. Sexual activity and food-taking both serve a positive and necessary bodily purpose: It is regeneration, or the assimilation of Life, for the purpose of continued growth through adaptation.

Thus, sexual desire and capacity should survive right sexual activity, just as a degree of hunger should survive a meal. The lingering of such desire or hunger is a sign of vitality and of the internal bodily capability to assimilate what has been received through either sexual activity or food-taking.

People tend to eat until sated, and they eat for casual satisfaction of food-desire. Thus, their diet is not a matter of intelligence, but of the indulgence of appetite, without real regard for the regenerative obligation of food. Just so, people tend to indulge sex until exhausted, or until orgasm, and they use sex casually, merely as a method for emptying themselves of the discomfort of desire itself. Therefore, sex is commonly not a matter of intelligence but of the indulgence of the motive force or appetite of desire, without regard for the regenerative obligation of the sexual function.

Both food and sex are means of regenerating the body-mind and permitting it to continue to grow, or adapt beyond its present state. The purpose of daily regeneration is not survival for its own sake, but growth, or sacrifice via the process of higher and also more inclusive structural adaptation. Through such continuous and life-long adaptation, or constant sacrifice of the present state of adaptation, the Divine is allowed to be the always present Realization and ultimate Destiny of the individual.

An important dietary rule is to eat only until perhaps three-fourths full—or clearly less than full. To overeat is to burden the digestive system and cause both toxemia and enervation as a result. To overeat is to serve one's emptiness, not true Fullness of Life.

Just so, the practice of sexual communion should serve the true Fullness of Life. Therefore, frequency must be moderated according to the degree of intensity of feeling and desire, or the living impulse for sexual embrace. To engage in sexual intercourse when tired or relatively disinterested is a way of enervating the body. (Of course, if such disinterest is merely a sign of emotional conflict, the lovers should deal with their love relationship first.)

Just as frequency of embrace should be moderated, or measured according to the degree of love-desire, the length of the period of time given to any such occasion should likewise be measured. If regenerative conservation is truly practiced, and orgasm is by-passed, the physical separation of the lovers should be made at a time when neither is sated, or emptied of desire. Some desire should remain, even as some hunger should remain at the end of a meal.

When the couple separates, the male should commonly or frequently retain an erection, and the female should remain full of Life and even desire. The remaining desire and Fullness is our advantage, our true food. It is the sign that Life has been received and increased, and that it remains available for action, growth, purification, and the natural pleasure of existence. Such Fullness is itself a means of attracting more Life, whereas exhaustion or conventional degenerative "satisfaction" only provides a means whereby we are emptied of Life in every moment of living.

The regenerative conversion of orgasm and of stimulated genital Energy prior to orgasm triggers the nervous system, striking a blow at the brain core, reorienting the brain-nervous system-body complex, and secreting higher chemistry via the entire endocrine gland system that can transform body, vitality, and mental consciousness.

S exual communion is a sacrifice of attention, not a binding exploitation of its sexual tendency.

C oncern about orgasm—either about having it or preventing it—is not appropriate to sexual communion, and it relaxes or falls away when feeling-attention is released via one's lover and into the All-Pervading Radiance of Life.

T he control of orgasm is not the point of sexual embrace. It is simply our responsibility during embrace. Such control is secondary to the motive of embrace, which is love-desire for one's lover. Therefore, the primary disposition of love, expressed feeling, relational attention, and bodily service to one's lover <u>is</u> the <u>means</u> whereby control over orgasm is to be realized.

Control of orgasm is not to become a matter of self-possessed concern, a disturbance in the play of love. We must adapt to it gradually in our loving. Our loving must become the principle of our daily relationship and our embraces before we even begin to adapt to control of orgasm. And that adaptation must necessarily be relatively slow, a living and loving matter, realized by stages.

In any case, control of orgasm is not regenerative to the whole body if done via a self-possessed and mechanical attitude and action. Such an approach naturally creates bodily tension and distracts us toward self via the contraction of love, or the native Radiance of Life.

The sacrifice of self is the human principle, in sexual play and all other forms of experience. And the self is not within. The self is the whole and entire body-mind, obvious and present. Therefore, the sacrifice of self is a moral activity rather than a merely functional one. It is performed through love and service, or free and unobstructed relational attention and action.

In sexual communion, the whole bodily sacrifice of self is realized through consistent feeling, attention, sensitivity, and yielding to one's lover. <u>And the matter of the impending genital crisis is simply managed by periodic, timely, and voluntary relaxation and diffusion of sexual tension.</u>

Sex in love is simply the practice of whole bodily Radiance. It awakens the right hemisphere of the brain and the expansive ecstasy of the entire body. And it communicates Life through the expansive or radiant mechanisms of the whole body. But the regenerative practice of sexual communion does not, therefore, involve exclusive exploitation of the right side of the brain, or the right side of the body in general. Rather, the whole and entire bodily being is awakened to the Infinite Life, through unobstructed feeling-attention, or love, as well as simultaneous conservation of bodily action, bodily chemistry, the impulses of the nervous system, and the stimulated Life-Force. Thus, the left hemisphere of the brain (or the conservative and centering tendency) and the right hemisphere of the brain (or the expansive and relational tendency) are to be in balance, perfectly intensified and whole.

The conventional orgasm is a spasm that releases energy from the entire bodily being via the genitals. It should be controlled through love (not primarily by any mechanical technique) and not indulged more than true and intimate desire proposes.

The process of love in sex play leads toward the blisses of the whole body rhythms of ecstatic Communion with the Divine Life. There even appears a regenerative form of the genital orgasm, in which the usual outward movement of the genitals is naturally reversed, genital tension is relaxed, and a peculiar drawing in and up of energy and genital chemistry is felt. That "drawing" sensation distributes the Life-Force from the genitals to the entire bodily being, without any significant outer discharge of energy or reproductive chemistry from the genital region of the male or the female.

316

The attitudes, positions, and touches—or "asanas"[1] and "mudras"— of sexual communion are forms of circuitry created by the two polarized bodies within the Single and All-Pervading Field of Life-Force. If the lovers are free and intensely involved in feeling-attention for one another—not "seeing," "being seen," and inhibiting one another, but ecstatic and self-forgetful in the embrace—they will naturally and spontaneously choose positions and actions, opening and closing of eyes, and sounds and touches and movements that delight and stimulate one another, and so provide appropriate circuitry for the play of Life they are representing.

The spontaneous and otherwise chosen positions assumed by lovers in the play of sex are always "asanas" and "mudras" of yogic significance. Indeed, the whole play of sexual communion is even preceded by "yamas" and "niyamas" (all the disciplines and restraints of true and loving intimacy) and it includes forms of "pranayama" (functional control of breath and life) as well as "pratyahara," "dharana," "dhyana," and "samadhi" (or the functional disciplines of concentrated attention, leading toward ecstatic absorption).[2]

1. "Asana" means posture.
2. Yama, niyama, asana, pranayama, pratyahara, dharana, dhyana, and samadhi are the disciplines of the eightfold ("ashtanga") process of yoga described by Patanjali.

Thus, sexual communion is a kind of "yoga" in the tradition of Patanjali's ashtanga yoga, and of hatha yoga,[3] kundalini yoga, and Tantra yoga, as well as the yogas of Taoism and all of the ancient practices of truly human and auspicious sexuality. Indeed, sexual communion demonstrates elements of all traditional religious, yogic and mystical approaches to Truth—except that it is not adapted to the conventional dilemma by which men and women pursue Truth, Reality, God, or Happiness as a Goal of striving, but it is a free expression of the priorly Enlightened Way of Divine Ignorance.

This process of sexual communion is not realized by self-conscious control of the sexual play, but by release from the conventional controls—the intentional mind, mental imagery, and obsessive vital desiring. Such release is enjoyed by presuming the whole body disposition of the heart—which is unobstructed feeling-attention, or love—in the play itself, both during genital intimacy as well as in all the moments of the continuing relationship itself. Love does not destroy Life or break its bodily circle. It is itself spontaneous economy of the orgasm, so that its Energy is conserved in the whole body and radiated as the feeling power or sacrifice that is love to Infinity.

In the maturing of the process of sexual communion there is inevitable release of the emotional-sexual locks on the body-mind. Then Life invades the whole body-mind, and Life absorbs the otherwise reactive and self-involved body and mind. Whole bodily feeling-intuition of Life becomes the ecstatic means of contacting Life, which is then able to be conducted to and throughout the

3. "Ha" means sun and "tha" means moon. Thus, hatha yoga is the practice of seeking God-Union through the harmony or balancing of the two opposing or alternating tendencies of the Life-Current (expansion and receptivity) and the two halves of the body, the nervous system, and the brain. Commonly identified today with the systems of physical poses, hatha yoga in its classical form also includes devotional, moral, personal, and higher psycho-physical disciplines of yogic awakening and transformation.

entire body-mind via the breath, in open vital and genital participation, and in relaxation of reactive emotion into love, relaxation of
the entire body, and relaxation of all forms of thought or imagery or
brain contraction. Body and mind must be relaxed into and permitted to engage the Divine Life, primarily through unobstructed
feeling and right breathing.

318
As the process of sexual communion matures, the conventional
genital urge to orgasm relaxes or "inverts," leaving a feeling-sense
of a Current that passes through and pervades the entire body.
Thereafter, genital activity—done with feeling, in Divine Communion, and in conjunction with the breath—acts as a regenerative
process through which Life is Communicated to the whole and
entire bodily being. Higher bodily, emotional, and mental adaptation and growth inevitably follow.

As soon as the genital urge to orgasm "inverts," the sexual
process becomes a form of bodily meditation on the Current
of All-Pervading Life. Thus, sexual activity may be engaged frequently (or infrequently) and for relatively prolonged periods, and it
may also become quickly obsolete. In some cases, a positive regenerative relationship to sex may continue, even throughout the lifetime, or until the body-mind is utterly Absorbed in Transcendental
Ecstasy. In others, it transcends itself quickly, producing a motiveless but Full and loving celibacy. In any case, the original reactive
and mechanical and self-possessed program of degenerate sexual
exploitation falls away in the course of right practice of sexual
communion. And such sexual communion involves whole bodily
Communion with the Divine Life via one's lover and in the Company of the Spiritual Master.

True Desire Cannot Be Satisfied
A talk given by Bubba Free John to his devotees

BUBBA: The satisfaction of desire is always so urgent for ordinary people. The usual man must suddenly satisfy himself and become empty. He cannot tolerate the prolongation of desire itself—in fact, what we call suffering and frustration is the prolongation of desire. The only way the usual man can become satisfied is to get up from the table very shortly after dessert and to have sex to the point of complete emptiness and exhaustion, falling unconscious and waking up the next morning completely dragged out and emptied of desire. Such is the usual man's satisfaction.

All of you have been desirers, but you have only been fulfilled in sudden satisfaction. Satisfaction or emptiness or self-indulgence is your idea of the fulfillment of desire. Thus, desire is a problem. You are always seeking to be stimulated and, when you become stimulated, you seek to be suddenly satisfied. Whereas the uncommon man, the devotee of God, considers the stimulation of desire itself as the occasion of contemplation, Communion, and happiness. For him, satisfaction is not emptiness but occasional, beautiful, and most ceremonious union and pleasure. Such union does not bring an end to desire; rather, it intensifies and reawakens the quality of desire.

Until you become capable of desire, you remain vulgar. The uncommon man, you see, is satisfied by desire itself. He is fulfilled and glorified by it. The common man is satisfied by degenerative contact, by emptiness. Therefore he is always seeking new fulfillment, always looking for stimulation. Then as soon as he (or she) is stimulated, he seeks to feel good through release from stimulation of desire.

320

All of you are involved in this life of relative negativity or emptiness wherein you seek this or that to stimulate you and then lurch upon what is desirable and gorge yourself with it and become emptied by it. Thus, the precise amount of time and space that occupies your literal desiring is very brief. Most of your life is spent in emptiness, seeking stimulation. There are a few moments wherein you satisfy yourself, but most of time and space is totally wasted in you. Most of the time you feel empty, urgent with emptiness and fear and sorrow and anger and doubt, hoping to be awakened into a state of desire, but then, as soon as desire arises, hoping to be satisfied and released from the pressure of desiring. If you are not satisfied immediately, then you become frustrated, and desire itself becomes a principle that awakens negativity in you.

What a puny cycle of craving and frustration! You do not have the slightest trace of exquisite consciousness in you. You are not even barbaric like the Hun, who could at least cut off a head, slice a torso, smash a vein or two, crush a bone, destroy a country, overwhelm a nation! You depend on only the slightest stimulation, some aggravation in your thighs, and two hours later you are either having sex or screaming about the domination of mortality in your life!

Let me tell you that in confrontation in the midst of Infinity with the Force of God, which pervades our very existence, there is not even the slightest trace of satisfaction, not the slightest trace of it. Divine Communion, God-Communion, Love of God, the sacrifice that is native to the devotee, the sacrifice of the whole body, which is a life of devotion to the Divine, is not satisfaction. It is not the ending of desire, but it is the more and more perfect stimulation of desire. As a matter of fact, it is the stimulation of a desire that cannot be satisfied. The communication of the Power of God is the communication of desire, of enjoyment, of contemplation, that is never brought to an end—absolutely never. Therefore, in order to become an uncommon man or woman, we must be able to enjoy desire itself and to abandon the life of the common man, which is only fitted to the urgency of satisfaction.

In our Communion with the Absolute, with Infinity, we are constantly awakened to new levels of desiring through confronting various objects and associations, and we find our satisfaction in union with those objects. This process is active through the six ordinary structural stages of development of the human being, until in the seventh stage of life we realize a condition of desire, of stimulated awakening, of the attraction of our own feeling-attention to Infinity, wherein there is no object that can satisfy. The Way of Radical Intuition, or the seventh stage of life, realizes a Condition of perfect desire wherein we may not be emptied nor our desire brought to an end. Prior to this Realization, in the process of evolution of the being to higher levels of psycho-physical existence, whenever a certain function is stimulated in the structure of our ordinary humanity, the objects that exist relative to that function become available for our satisfaction.

321

At the present stage of your development, you have been awakened principally to the objects of food and sex. Thus, you also enjoy the capacity to be satisfied by the objects of food and sex. Being capable of stimulation or desire relative only to these kinds of objects, you are also moved to be satisfied by these same objects. You are bound to the cycle of the availability of food and sex and of satisfaction by the objects that pertain to these stimulations. Thus it is that, fundamentally, the broadest span of your existence is spent in being emptied of stimulation, emptied of desire, seeking to be stimulated, and, as a consequence of that stimulation, seeking again to be satisfied and emptied.

When you become clarified in your attention and in your understanding of these objects of food and sex, then the more subtle objects to which the structure of our humanity is attuned will arise to surround you, and you will satisfy yourself with these objects. The saints, yogis, and mystics throughout all time and space are examples to you of how an individual can be stimulated to become totally interested in an object higher on the evolutionary scale than food and sex, and then to be moved to satisfaction by such an object. The true devotee, however, is not summarized in satisfaction at any level.

322

At various times in human history certain privileged individuals have been moved into a unique association with food objects, sex objects, mental objects, natural love objects, and psychic objects. Such individuals enjoyed the awakening of desire in association with these objects but were not motivated in the vulgar sense to be satisfied in degenerative union with them. Rather, these extraordinary people remained in the disposition of desire and allowed that desire to be magnified infinitely. The "gopis"[4] in the mythological stories about Krishna, for instance, were not satisfied women. They were women who awakened in desire for Krishna, their lover, but they were not satisfied. Their awakening to desire was intensified from day to day by the various activities of Krishna, to the point that their desiring became ecstasy.

Like these uncommon women, from time to time in human history individuals have appeared whom we call creative and heroic. Their primary characteristic is that they enjoyed the capacity to be stimulated by what is desirable and at the same time they enjoyed the discipline of not having to be satisfied and emptied by what is desirable. Such people are uncommon; therefore, they are also fascinating and worthy of worship in the eyes of ordinary people. But this same disposition is the enjoyment of devotees of God, because God is not One Who satisfies desire. The Infinite is the One Who stimulates desire absolutely and continuously. In Communion with God the stimulations and fascinations of ordinary things vanish, so that ultimately you desire or love to the most absolute degree, and yet you do not at the same time suffer the slightest capacity to be emptied or satisfied.

4. In the allegorical accounts of the life of Krishna, the *gopis* are women who tended cattle in the fields where Krishna wandered. The force of their ecstatic love for the Divine manifest in human form overwhelmed all their worldly attachments, so that they forgot cattle, family, even self in their ecstatic absorption in God.

This is the characteristic of the devotee in Whole Body Enlightenment.[5] Having become so stimulated beyond the capacity to be satisfied, the devotee develops the most infinite capacity for desire, or love, or the magnification of attention beyond oneself. Such a condition is called Divine Translation, which is the condition of Desire beyond comprehension and beyond association with any single human function, the Desire that shatters the entire functional being of man or woman. In such Desire there is not the slightest trace of satisfaction, nor the slightest capacity for satisfaction, here, now, then, elsewhere, in the past, at any time in any space whatsoever.

The devotee who loves God most perfectly enjoys the most infinite and excessive capacity for desire beyond any moment in time wherein he is defined by satisfaction. In our human, loving relations and our human pleasures, we must begin to demonstrate this same capacity for desire, for pleasure, for enjoyment, totally apart from satisfaction, emptiness, and withdrawal into exhausted self-meditation.

True Lovers Feed and Enhance One Another with Life

The timing of inhalation and exhalation during sexual play should be permitted to occur naturally, free of strategic control or emphasis. But sensitivity to the breath cycle, or conscious and feeling relaxation into the process of reception and release,

5. Bubba uses two terms in this paragraph that describe stages in the process of God-Realization. Whole Body Enlightenment is the Realization at the foundation of the seventh stage of life. Divine Translation is the ultimate Divine Realization in the Way of Divine Ignorance, the eternal enjoyment of the mature devotee in the seventh stage of life. Readers who would like to consider Bubba's Teaching on the process of Enlightenment in the higher stages of life are referred to *The Enlightenment of the Whole Body: A Rational and New Prophetic Revelation of the Truth of Religion, Esoteric Spirituality, and the Divine Destiny of Man*, by Bubba Free John.

should become more and more constant. Sensitivity or feeling via the breath cycle should be as profound and ordinary as sensitivity to the genitals and the genital contact.

324

The length of time spent in genital sexual embrace on any one occasion should be determined by the degree of intensity or "excess Energy" felt between the couple at the time.

It generally takes time to adapt to the full responsibility and whole bodily intimacy of sexual communion. Allow it to grow by stages. First become personally responsible for old and childish emotional and erotic patterns, and allow the love relationship to flourish before attempting to integrate with the technical physiological responsibilities for regenerative conservation of the Life-Force.

The practice of regenerative sexual communion depends not only on true feeling-attention, but on actual physical adaptation. Thus, it is best to adapt gradually. First, realize a true and feeling daily intimacy, in which each partner is responsible for emotional reactivity and erotic obsessiveness. Then submit to the regenerative practice merely to the degree of increasing the period of love-making prior to orgasm. When this is natural, go on to limit the number of occasions on which the genital orgasm is permitted. Ultimately, even when genital orgasm is permitted, it should coincide with whole body diffusion and true feeling.

When sex is engaged by lovers as mutual bodily sacrifice and communion with Life, the two become a polarized pair, a machine of electromagnetic energy. Thus, the lovers feed and enhance one another with Life, energizing one another and serving the intensification and the balance or wholeness of the bodily force-fields of each of them. However, individuals who embrace without love, and who intensify the living Energy only to discard it through orgasm, do not enhance one another with Life, nor do they take leave of one another in a more intensified, integrated, and full condition.

Couples should engage in sexual communion only on the occasions of full mutual love-desire. They should not embrace for the motive of repetition of remembered pleasures. Recent memory of pleasurable sex, the imagining of erotic play with others, and ritual eroticism, or simulation of past incidents and roles, should be allowed to pass from one's Life of Love. The play and the pleasure of sexual communion should be an entirely present phenomenon.

Our tendency, in reaction to the relational impositions and frustrations that make up our ordinary experience, is to contract and invert or reverse the flow of the vital currents of Life in the body-mind.

In the natural state, the currents of Life are released whole bodily and radiantly. This should be simply and fully felt, naturally and constantly, under all conditions. Our participation in sexual play, which is meant to realize a harmony that should persist in all relations, is a process wherein the being becomes incarnate, or brought to Life. Therefore, the frequency of our participation must be measured according to the strength and quality of mutual love-desire, and thus it will be limited to fewer occasions than the mere urge to sexual release would dictate. Do not become weakened through excessive indulgence of relational and particularly sexual possibility. Incarnation, or Lawful integration of living structures, is not an end in itself. It is a process whereby there may be the paradoxical Realization of the compatibility of Absolute Oneness and infinite multiplicity. When that is Realized, what is multiple or independent is spontaneously and inevitably Translated into the One.

326

A natural, pleasurable weariness may occur after a prolonged episode of sexual communion. This may occur even when full love-feeling and presently awakened desire (rather than ritual repetition, for the sake of orgasm) have been constant. This pleasurable weariness is not the one of emptiness from orgasm, but it is a sign of the whole bodily release of localized physical, emotional, and mental tension, or contraction of the full feeling of the Life-Force. Such weariness allows the whole body-mind to rest in the generalized intensity of the Life-Force, and so to be regenerated and filled, rather than enervated and separated from Infinity and all relations.

At the end of sexual embrace, lovers should rest in close contact with one another, in magnetic communion with one another and the paradoxical sense of both bodily transcendence and bodily integrity. They should lie together without tension in a kind of "dead pose" (see *Conscious Exercise and the Transcendental Sun*), or, more properly, the "lover's pose" of mutual contact (in any bodily position) and total relaxation. This should continue until both feel fully relaxed, refreshed, and restored to normal equilibrium. Then the two should part affectionately.

S exual communion depends on the full force of both free feeling, or relational and bodily love-desire, and free attention (without the reflex of self-possession in the form of thought, imagery, and the like).

When love is deficient, the Energy awakened and conserved in sexual communion will not rise to pervade what is above the navel, but will only pervade the lower vital region itself.

When the attention is not free and in relationship, but either turns in on internal thoughts and images or else strategically tries to avoid orgasm, then the head becomes hot, the vital region cools, and excitation is achieved only through mental or bodily self-manipulation.

When desire is deficient, the whole process fails to develop sufficient Energy, and happiness in love is frustrated and degraded.

The Regenerative Orgasm and the Thrill of Life

The pleasure of orgasm is casually sought even by true lovers, and this is both a sign and a method of degeneration, conflict, and immaturity in their relationship and in the body-mind of each partner. The conscious and prolonged feeling enjoyment of the regenerative sexual play (either without conventional orgasm or with a transformed engagement of the orgasm) should replace casual sex, oriented toward release of vitality through orgasm.

Just so, those who are addicted to orgasm, and who cannot engage sex as anything but casual erotic stimulation of orgasm, will find themselves making efforts to achieve orgasm even when they are trying to adapt to the process of loving sexual communion. Thus, they may become capable of prolonged and active sexual embrace, but they will feel unsatisfied unless the orgasm can come at the end—or each may feel obliged by the other to have an orgasm, or show signs of an orgasm, or to produce an orgasm in their partner. When such motives arise, the individual will begin to "work" on himself or his partner, in order to stimulate orgasm. The male lover will often seek to arouse himself through internal images.

The female lover will often seek to become aroused through the heightening of physical stimulation, or imagining she is involved in some exciting situation of conflict, such as rape, and so forth. Either partner may do any of these things to himself or his lover, but it is all mere ceremony or ritual, seeking the pleasurable and intoxicating moment of genital orgasm. Whenever such strategies arise in one's own case, they should be observed and, without struggling with these strategies themselves, there should be a return of feeling and attention and fullness of the breath of Life in direct relation to one's lover in the present. In this manner, the ritual forcing of orgasm will naturally come to rest.

Also, those who are beginning to adapt to the process of sexual communion may tend to be self-conscious about their own passion and tendency toward orgasm. As a result they may become involved in self-conscious strategies to prevent obvious passion and to prevent orgasm. Such strategies generally involve either the specific redirection or the casual wandering of attention. The principal method is thinking and imagining of subjects that have no erotic significance. In general, it is the withdrawal of attention from physical sensitivity and feeling in relation to one's lover and fixing attention on one's own and nonsexual subjective contents. In the process, the breath becomes shallow, and sexual involvement or activity becomes generally less intense.

This strategy and method should be observed as it arises, and, without self-conscious manipulation of the strategy or method itself, feeling and attention and sensitivity should be directly returned to Life via one's lover. The transformation and conservation of orgasm is a function of true sexual communion, not of self-conscious manipulation of one's own body-mind. Therefore, feeling, attention, and sexual sensitivity should be constantly maintained in relation to one's lover—not oneself—and, therefore, thoughts and images, loss of feeling, withdrawal of attention, depression of activity or pleasure or breath, and so forth will not characterize lovers who freely and responsibly engage one another.

Conventional involvement in sexual play is an expression of conflict, bodily demonstrated through tension and suppression of emotional feeling. Conventional orgasm is the terminal expression of the increase of tension as Life-Energy intensifies.

Sexual communion is a process in which bodily and psychic and mental tension are released through deep feeling-attention and relaxation into the All-Pervading Life-Energy. This also produces a truly human or regenerative conversion of orgasm, which may occur many times (and even more or less continuously) during sex play. (Indeed, this process is later realized as a continuous process of moment to moment experience, as spiritual responsibility increases in the Company of the Spiritual Master.)

The play of sexual communion grants the whole body orgasm— not only as a transformation of the conventional genital orgasm itself, but throughout the entire occasion of sexual play. It is relaxation and profound breathing and continuous feeling-attention or ecstasy (essentially free of self-reference, contraction, thought, and internal images), in which the thrill of Life is yielded to the whole body and, whole bodily, to Infinity.

In such sexual communion, sexual play is generally prolonged and, although profoundly pleasurable and often excited, it is characterized by a graceful serenity or always present Fullness of Life. There is freedom from obsession, tension, and hurry toward release. There is, instead, love, in embrace and at play, that is not dominated by any end phenomenon or goal.

Lovers in this practice are always balancing and completing one another. And, over time, they individually become more and more stable, open, communicative with true sympathy and feeling, and tranquil in their daily lives and their intimate cycles.

The conventional generative and degenerative exercises of the sexual function exploit all of the mechanisms of the bodily being—including the entire nervous system and the endocrine system—to produce vital release of tension via the genitals.

329

The regenerative process of sexual communion involves all of the mechanisms of the bodily being from beginning to end. Thus, at the point of crisis or orgasm, the genital mechanism is permitted to trigger and awaken every part of the bodily being—including the entire nervous system and the endocrine system.

In the generative and degenerative exercises of sexuality, the entire bodily being yields, to produce genital orgasm. In the regenerative process of sexual communion, the genital mechanisms yield to produce the regenerative Life-Thrill of the entire bodily being.

330

The practice relative to orgasm may include external pressure on the sex organs, but the essential practice is to love and feel <u>continuously</u>, and to release the Energy of the impending crisis to the entire bodily being (using the breath cycle, movement of attention, and general relaxation and cessation of movement, as well as tensing or moving of the body in ways that serve the return of the bodily Energy and the breath cycle to a condition of Fullness and equanimity).

In conventional, degenerative exploitation of the sexual function as a reactive means of discharging the Life-Force, the Life-Force is made to submit to the body. Then, when orgasm occurs, we bodily release and eliminate the Life-Force and chemistry, downward and outward, to our lover and the gross environment. In the conservative or regenerative participation in sexual play as loving communion, the body is made to submit to the Life-Force. Thus, when the crisis approaches (and even on the occasions when it is permitted), the Life-Force and chemistry are released and directed to permeate the whole body <u>first</u>, and then <u>subtly</u> to pervade one's lover and the world to Infinity.

This is the crucial distinction in all our activities. Our lives must become a conscious exercise, in which unobstructed feeling and unobstructed Life become a single Principle, to which the gross or elemental body is submitted, in all relations, under all conditions.

T rue celibacy or "brahmacharya"[6] is not, in principle, merely a matter of no-intercourse or even infrequency of intercourse, but of natural responsibility for the psycho-physiology of the conventional orgasm (discharge of Life-Force via ejaculation in the male and, in both male and female, breaking the cycle of the Life-Force via the descending or local genital discharge at the point of crisis). The energy in sex play must be conserved—that is, not casually eliminated but responsibly conducted in the feeling-breathing cycle of the body. This is a matter of control of motion, breathing, feeling, thought, attention, etc. As long as this discipline is maintained (along with disciplining of the total life of reactivity or contraction) sexual intercourse, frequent or infrequent, is, in principle, a generally positive factor in human and spiritual life. It is a form of "hatha yoga," a natural balance of the two opposing or alternating tendencies of Life (expansion and receptivity) and the two halves of the body, the nervous system, and the brain.

S exual communion is not a method of withholding feeling and Life-Force from one's lover, nor is it a problem-oriented strategy for preventing orgasm. It is simply the true or most perfectly adapted form of sexual intimacy.

6. Brahmacharya (literally, "the study of Brahma, or Truth") has conventionally been equated with the lifelong practice of intentional or motivated celibacy by spiritual aspirants in the Hindu esoteric spiritual traditions. But the term originally dates from the most ancient times in Hindu India, and refers to the "brahmacharya" or student stage of life, generally conceived to occupy the first twenty-five years of life. During those years, the growing individual was formally trained in the Divine Way and Truth of Life. This period generally involved strict celibacy until marriage, or entrance into the householder's stage of life. Over time, the term "brahmacharya" has become essentially a synonym for celibacy itself, even though the ancient practice of brahmacharya encompassed all of the common areas of life, including academic studies, music, art, diet, work, the Scriptures, and so forth.

Neither partner <u>withholds</u> at the point of orgasm, in the manner of ancient practitioners who have been called sexual "misers" by some commentators. Nor is sexual play engaged for the exclusive sake of either partner, as it was in early Taoist practice, where, in most cases, the male alone was engaged in secret understanding of the practice and used the orgasmic energy of the female in a kind of sexual "vampirism." And the esoteric fulfillment of the process is not primarily and exclusively for either partner, or for each independently (exclusive of love-sacrifice), as it was in the case of certain of the cults of Tantric yoga.

In right sexual communion, both partners are equal participants in a mutual sacrifice. It is only that the sacrifice is one of love, or communication of the whole bodily being, rather than any partial or relatively external or superficial sacrifice made by individuals who remain bound into their own independent subjective interior. Thus, <u>orgasm is not to be prevented, but it is to be made a process of the whole and entire bodily being</u>. And its energy is not to be discarded through the exclusive genital spasm, but it is to be conducted equally to every part of the bodily being, and communicated as profound and intense radiation or love-feeling to one's lover and all beings and things to Infinity.

The regenerative orgasm—or the act of conservation of genital discharge—is indeed an orgasm. It is simply conversion of the genital discharge to a whole body profusion of feeling that extends to one's lover and into Infinity. Thus, it is not "control" or any suppressed, "uptight" self-manipulation. It is full, ecstatic pleasure, but one that conserves and radiates the stimulated Life-Energy and chemistry rather than permits it to be discharged and lost.

Thus, sexual communion involves regenerative orgasm rather than conventional or degenerative orgasm. It does not, however, involve the ultimate absence or suppression of orgasm itself. The regenerative orgasm is Life in full communion with its unity with Light and Love.

T he conservation or conductivity of orgasm may not be truly
realized apart from a full relationship of free love-feeling and
complete, whole body submission, or mutual bodily confession,
through open desire and full sensual communication. The conservation of orgasm is not the result of "uptight" control. It is not
produced by mental concern, or anxiety, or self-possession. It is a
natural result of full relational communion, whole bodily, through
communicated love-feeling. It must be added that such love-feeling
must be consistently communicated under all the interim and ordinary circumstances of living.

333

Then the genital sex play will not be initiated by imagery,
memory and the desire for repetition, nor by emotional conflict and
anxiety, nor vital-physical overstimulation. And it will progress
with great pleasure and feeling contact, free of subjective self-
possession, images, and the like. And it will appear wholly natural,
simple, and easy, at the point of crisis, to live it as a whole body
moment of relaxed intensity rather than an aggressive genital effort
to be relieved of the internal pressure of Life.

P rofound and consistent feeling-attention, or relaxation into
radiant love-desire in play with one's lover, is the fundamental sexual discipline. Without it, even the practice of conservation of the orgasm (or enjoyment of the true, whole body orgasm)
described here is a cool and mechanical expression of the antagonism
between the head and the navel.

I f genital discharge is occasionally permitted, it should not
often be a complete permissive elimination of Energy via the
genitals, but it should be done as in the case of the management of
the crisis just prior to discharge. Then the emptying effect will be
minimized. The male partner should observe that in this manner
the process of the emission of semen becomes controllable, and the

degree or quantity of the emission can be minimized even when the discharge is permitted.

The Marriage Relationship
334 | *Is the Yoga of Love*

In the true practice of sexual communion, a kind of etheric[7] resonance typically appears in the case of each of the lovers as they come to rest and hold one another after intercourse. The body feels almost formless. There is a sense of wholeness and fullness, of physical pleasure and harmony, of mental calm, and a sense that emotional and physical feeling is open to Infinity. The internal energies of the bodily being are felt to be balanced (side to side, head to toe, back to front), and the head remains full, equally as sensuous and thought-free as the lower body, but perfectly clear, awake, and aware.

Conventional sexual intimates tend to persist as two self-conscious individuals in, at best, playful conflict—even

7. In the physics of the worlds, ether or functional energy is the senior and most subtle of the gross elements, which also include solid, liquid, fiery, and gaseous substances (the ancient esoteric elements of earth, water, fire, and air). Ether, the most subtle state of gross or material appearance, is the all-pervading element of the physical universe, analogous to space itself. The etheric dimension of force or manifest light pervades and surrounds our universe and every physical body. It is the field of energy, magnetism, and space in which the lower or grosser elements function. Thus, your "etheric body" is the specific concentration of force associated with and surrounding-permeating your physical body. It serves as a conduit for the forces of universal light and energy to the physical body.

In practical terms of daily experience, the etheric aspect of the being is our emotional-sexual, feeling nature. The etheric body functions through and corresponds to the nervous system. Functioning as a medium between the conscious mind and the physical being, it controls the distribution and use of energy and emotion. It is the dimension of vitality or Life-Force. We feel the etheric dimension of life not only as vital energy and power and magnetic-gravitational forces, but also as the endless play of emotional polarization, positive and negative, to others, objects, the world itself, everything that arises.

during sexual activity. They are not by tendency free enough to yield to one another whole bodily, and to become ecstatic (to pass beyond themselves, or to release the hold on the self position). But they must become active as feeling-attention, as movement, excitement, and response, and intensify their embrace mightily, so that each becomes a single, visionless, mindless force, and the two are awakened beyond self-possession to a tacit sense of nondifferentiation from one another and all things and beings. Over time, the frequency of this awakening and the period of its moment will increase. The two will end each occasion by falling from action to rest in one another's embrace or company, and each will rest in a sense of undifferentiated singleness, or tacit identity (as conscious energy) with the totality of existence. In that same moment, the nervous system and glandular chemistry of each of these bodies will be reorganizing toward a fuller and higher level of adaptation.

The regenerative moment of whole bodily diffusion of genital Energy should be prolonged. It is a condition of ecstasy, without thought or contraction toward self and separation. If prolonged, the autonomic nervous system and the right hemisphere of the brain are stimulated and opened into expansive fullness, so that the analytical tendencies of the left hemisphere of the brain and the contracting tendencies of the autonomic nervous system may be balanced and not lead to exclusive and obsessive orientations toward verbal thinking and unfeeling self-possession.

A typical method individuals tend to use during the act of genital sex play, in order to prevent orgasm and what they feel is self-possessed involvement in their own pleasure, is to fix their eyes in open observation of their partner's face. Eventually, this also distracts their partner, who is then forced into a similar gaze, so the two are held eye to eye. This produces self-consciousness in both, and motion and ecstasy tend to come to an end.

This strategy is self-conscious from the beginning. It is a fear reaction that expresses the individual's discomfort with the whole affair of genital intimacy and sexual responsiveness. Even individuals who otherwise enjoy sexual play may use this strategy at times, if they feel in danger of "being seen"—that is, if they feel their intense and free erotic responses are for some reason inappropriate, or a sign of too much self-involvement. In any case, the fixed eyes are not signs of love rather than self-possession. They only pin oneself and one's lover into a fixed self position, unable to respond to the point of ecstasy.

Occasional glances and spontaneous wide-eyed expressions of ecstasy occur naturally in sexual communion. But any strategy of self-manipulation tends to prevent sexual communion—since sexual communion depends on ecstasy, or release of self-possession through feeling, rather than manipulation of physiological events exclusively through self-directed controls.

However, there certainly are many moments of self-aware activity in the play of sexual communion, since only the self first aware of itself can release itself. Indeed, it is confusion over the whole notion of whether any form of self-awareness is appropriate in sexual communion that may lead an individual to the strategy of open staring during the act of sexual embrace. Resistance to self-awareness becomes a motionless state, incapable of ecstatic responses. Likewise, strategic self-manipulation also fails to realize ecstasy, even though it may control orgasm. Only natural ecstatic responsiveness, with full feeling and pleasure, can also realize true regenerative control or whole bodily conservation of orgasm. Such natural participation is, paradoxically, fully self-aware in terms of pleasure, feeling, and physiological responses in general, while, at the same time, it is always oriented to self-release via feeling and bodily responsiveness. Thus, even in the approach of the crisis of orgasm, there is full awareness of one's breath, motion, and so forth. But the control of orgasm is epitomized through feeling responsiveness, and the act that achieves control is itself one in which genital self-possession yields its independent satisfaction to grant the power of Life to the whole and entire bodily being, and, via the whole and entire bodily being, to one's lover, even to Infinity.

Couples who practice this right way of sexual communion should allow it to transform the total pattern of their relationship to one another and to all other beings and conditions of experience. Thus, the process yields gradual transcendence of genital urgency, and reveals whole body wisdom, or true spiritual delight. In this manner, the couple should allow fullness of love and Energy to develop between them and radiate to the whole world to Infinity. Likewise, they should allow a natural serenity to replace their casual obsessiveness and emotional phasing. Also, they should, on this basis, allow the frequency of their actual genital intimacy to attain a gradual and natural economy, so that their relationship is characterized more by love than by rituals of mechanical passion and genital success.

The intimate relationship itself (the mutual polarization of feeling-attention) is the "sexual act" under all conditions. Sexual (genital) play is appropriate when this love is also expressed as intense, imageless (mind-free) vital-genital polarization or desire (without absence of love and without commitment to orgasm as the reason or purpose of intimacy). This rhythm, or the relative strength of love-desire from day to day, determines the appropriate frequency of the occasions for sexual communion.

Intimate and domestic problems may arise when the orientation to vital desire is weaker or less frequent in one partner than in the other, and when the love polarization is not itself strong enough to permit understanding or overcoming of the problem. Polarization itself, or the relationship itself, not genital sex, is the marriage, the constant play of energy, the yoga, the communion. It is thus to be practiced constantly, as feeling and service, even when genital contact itself is, for one or another reason, infrequent.

Too frequent sexual intercourse—even in the form of sexual communion—and especially to the point of genital spasm (whether or not it is converted or suppressed)—tends to devitalize the bodily being, ritualize intimacy, and produce mechanical affections without real feeling or bodily submission. Thus, frequency must be determined by the rhythm of true love-desire, so that sexual communion occurs only at times of great intensity. The rest of the time, serve one another with feeling and enter into the full-time culture of humanizing spiritual practice.

The occasion of sexual intimacy should not commonly be brief. It should be prolonged, like formal meditation, since it has no conventional end phenomenon (such as terminal genital orgasm). The play should continue for a half hour to an hour or even two hours. The lovers may even come to rest in one another's embrace one or more times, and then continue the play of Life again, through active sexual communion.

Therefore, time and place should be set aside and prepared for this profoundly conscious and feeling and sensual and ecstatic enjoyment, or else it will be suppressed and interrupted by the arbitraries and brevities of the daily world, and with the same effect as interrupted meditation.

Individuals who practice sexual communion over time experience many signs of physical, emotional, and mental regeneration and Fullness of Life. Whereas the spasm of release, withdrawal, and even psychological or emotional separation characterize the termination of sex play for most people, those who practice sexual communion identify other signs typical of their unique practice. The urgency of the need and pursuit of orgasm becomes relaxed. The relationship, as well as the sexual embrace, becomes primarily and itself a form of emotional union and mutual sensitivity, in which the mind is calm, attention to one's lover is consistent, and physical sensitivity, as well as responsible awareness of the physiological processes, is most intense. There is a certain gracefulness and steadiness to such lovers as they embrace, but the play itself remains a highly responsive affair, erotic in the most positive sense. And they find themselves adapting to a sexual process in which release is not at all or in general gained, but instead an increase of Fullness or Life is realized.

339

There is no loss of vitality, or clarity, or even desire in the process of sexual communion. Desire, or positive vital attention for one's lover, becomes a natural and more or less continuous factor of one's daily response to Life, and one becomes capable of sustaining the profound Intensity of Life, rather than necessarily becoming motivated to get rid of it, as with the symptoms of a disease. There is a kind of exquisite pain in the sense of continuous and unrelieved vital Fullness, but it is the natural, nonreactive state of the bodily being. Therefore, lovers in sexual communion adapt to this state and learn how to live it positively. As a result, such individuals can become very strong in body, clear-minded, emotionally intense but free of reactivity, and attractive both sexually and in their general person. They enjoy a foundation of human maturity from which to approach the Spiritual Master and begin the fuller adaptation to higher human responsibility.

Couples may do well to "fast," or rest and regenerate, the emotional-sexual function and the marriage relationship itself from time to time. It is simply a matter of abandoning sexual relations for a significant period, perhaps sleeping in separate quarters, and even spending considerable daily time or larger periods of time alone or apart from one another. This permits each individual to regain a certain balance and integrity, outside the "cult of pairs," or the polarized play of their relationship. As a result of such a periodic and purifying fast, the individuals may find themselves strengthened in their vital interest and creative human capability with one another.

L overs should sleep together intentionally, not casually or as a rule. They should not only go to bed with one another on occasions of sexual embrace, but also go to bed together on occasions when they only sleep or rest, and hold one another in the love of Life.

The only way whereby all occasions of literal sleeping together can be a matter of choice is that lovers have separate quarters in which to sleep, or to which they may retire on evenings when they are to sleep alone. Separate beds are not sufficient. It is good that there be times of physical separation and bodily rest, completely apart from the physical and subtle influences of one's lover and all other human beings. And lovers should be sensitive to the cycles of this need. Therefore, they should make love and sleep together by choice, on appropriate occasions, and, likewise, they should be able to choose bodily privacy on other occasions.

340

C ouples should conform their sleeping habits to the simple laws of polarization. The male typically represents the right side, the expansive, active, moving quality or current of existence. The female typically represents the left side, the receptive, passive, inward, inert quality. Thus, if, as a point of reference, we presume the common posture of sleeping on one's back, the woman should generally sleep on the man's left and he on her right.

Bodily Rejuvenation and the Life-Enhancing Chemistry

T he practice of the drinking of one's own urine for health purposes is an ancient and traditional rejuvenating technique, common all over the world until very recently. (See *The Eating Gorilla Comes in Peace.*)

Those who use the drinking of urine, or "amaroli," as an adjunct to general health practice may find it strengthening to drink and gargle with the urine shortly after intercourse, or at the point of the next urination after intercourse. The flow will contain vital chemistry from the sexual organs that the body would do well to retain.

This use of the urine after intercourse applies to both men and women, although those who tend toward high blood pressure, or who are very "yang," "fiery," expansive, or sensitive to salts and biochemical stimulation may find it necessary to moderate or even avoid this practice.

341

The process of sexual communion is not merely one of the retention of Life-Force and the fluid chemistry of the genitals. Rather, whenever the conservative process is animated via the breath and the bodily discipline, the Life-Force is conducted and breathed to the entire body, instead of passing out through genital discharge. In that process, the intensified Life-Force should be made to "strike" against every gland and living center of the body, from toe to crown and crown to toe. When this occurs, the centers and glands so struck or stimulated secrete Life-enhancing chemistry to the entire body. Thus, the body itself is rejuvenated.

The ejaculatory fluid and semen of the male should generally be retained and the rhythmic sequence of discharge bypassed. However, on those occasions where ejaculation is permitted, it should generally be released as an offering to his lover. And just as that substance is precious within the body of the male, it should be accepted as such by the lover who receives it. Most often the ejaculation is released into the vagina, but it may just as well be released into the mouth or even the anus. And, if taken in the mouth, it should not be refused or spit out, but pleasurably accepted and ingested as a carrier of Life and regenerative substance.

The process of sexual communion described here does not involve the effort to release and concentrate the sexual Energy or awakened Life exclusively to the brain, as in kundalini yoga. Rather, the Life is released whole bodily and to one's lover as a Radiance of Love to Infinity.

342

The physical attitudes and postures of lovers in sexual communion should be open, alive, free of self-conscious armoring and contraction. The spinal line should be relaxed, open, and without "kinks." The chest should be open, held up, and full. The pelvis should move freely in all directions. And feeling-energy should be able to move into every area of the body and create Fullness and Pleasure there.

Sexual Communion Is Divine Communion

Conventional sex play is founded on the inward or self-possessed disposition. Such a disposition becomes addicted to the potential pleasures that arise by directing the attention toward the various organs of the body and moving the body into experiences from the point of view of the immediately or strategically chosen organ. This is true of sex and also of the various traditional yogas.

Thus, conventional sexual pleasure, or the spasmodic release of accumulated and pressurized Life-Force, is derived from the fixation of attention (and thus energy or sensation) in the genitals. In the process of sexual communion described in this book, the contracted, reactive, and self-possessed disposition is released, whole bodily, in love and service. And when such lovers embrace, the genital magnet to attention comes under natural control of the whole body. Thus, in sexual communion, the orgasm is converted by a sudden transfer of attention and energy from the genital region to the body as a whole—and from the parts of oneself to one's lover and via one's lover to Infinity (or the state of love without qualification or object or center). Such a process must be felt and enacted and experienced in order to be fully understood.

The significance of the process of sexual communion is that self-possession and bodily contraction are released, and attention, which commonly is directed within the body or from some center or part of the body, is directed <u>as</u> the whole body—as whole body feeling, yielded via and beyond all relations to Infinity. Thus, sexual communion is a kind of initiatory rite, a process of even bodily conversion, from self-possession and inwardness, to sacrifice, through love, into a sense of Radiance or Fullness beyond qualification. One so initiated may eventually go on to animate the responsibilities, equally bodily in character, of the spiritual process of "Breath and Name" in the more esoteric phase of the Way of Divine Communion.[8] The process of esoteric spiritual Communion in the Divine Presence, awakened, intensified, and fulfilled in the Company of the Spiritual Master, is generated on the foundation of the same bodily conversion and awakening of the heart that is realized in sexual communion.

343

Marriage and the Transcendence of Sexuality
A talk given by Bubba Free John to his devotees

BUBBA: Conventional marriages and conventional sex relationships are forms of conflict, acceptance and rejection, contact and separation. They are games of energy and opposition, wherein people

---

8. The Breath of God and the Name of God are the two spiritual or higher psychophysical disciplines of life and meditation in the Way of Divine Communion, the first stage of practice in the Way of Divine Ignorance. The "Breath of God" is the practice of breathing in the Divine Presence, or receiving the Living Power of God whole bodily and releasing all contraction. The "Name of God" is the practice of intuitive whole bodily recollection of the All-Pervading Presence of God.

individuate, then unite, discharge their energy in that union, and then separate again. People become very dependent on the process that uses or consumes Life, not only the physical pleasure of sex and orgasm, but also all the emotional and mental ways of stimulating the body-mind.

344

When the mind and the emotions are obsessively involved with the degenerative play of the lower functions and reactive emotions and the subhuman mentalizing that has to do with ordinary pleasures without God-Remembrance, then the Life-Force in the individual is scattered all over the body. All the parts of the body function in opposition to one another. The body becomes a disunity, a fragmented being that is essentially depressed and not Bliss-full because the circuit of Life in the being is not complete. It is broken. Thus, the bodily being is essentially in trouble all the time, separated from Bliss-fullness, able to realize some semblance of Bliss only in moments of relative unity, when it can exercise its functional capabilities primarily at the grossest level of the bodily being, at the level of food and sex.

For devotees, marriage is itself a way of formally choosing to transcend the periodic and degenerative satisfactions of the subhuman life. When people marry, they are choosing spiritual realization; they are acknowledging that they will not live by exploiting their functions, that a righteous union with one another, dedicated to God, will transcend their ordinary subhuman capacity. The marriage becomes true in the fullest sense when, through the practice of their intimacy (not just their physical, sexual intimacy, but their relationship altogether), they transcend all of the mechanics of satisfaction. The two of them exist then in a God-Realized Condition. They function in the ordinary ways, but they are always already quite happy, and thus they transcend the world.

Such devotees have a different destiny than the usual man. The usual man (or woman) is obsessively oriented toward the satisfaction-release cycle. He has no consciousness, fundamentally, other than his subhuman attachment to the functions of lower organs. Although he always already exists in God, the Eternal Nature, the Eternally Blissful, by association with manifest functions he does not realize

Bliss, but only mechanical association. Such an individual is endlessly reincarnated until at last, having tired of the realm of changes, he awakens. But in the meantime he simply and mechanically fulfills lower bodily possibility. Only those who become responsible at the level of ordinary life transcend the cycle of reincarnation and dullness.

I have told you all a story about a man and a woman in India who were husband and wife. They were traveling on a river when a storm capsized their boat. The husband was terrified that his wife would be killed, and he did everything he could to save her. He struggled for hours and finally was able to pull her to safety on the far bank. He was exhausted and weeping that he was able to save her. But she said, "If you only had one tenth of that enthusiasm for devotion to God, you would realize eternal Bliss. All I am is a bag of excrement. Why are you worshipping me? You should go and give yourself to God." The husband had never heard such utterances before. He was illuminated by her suggestion and he accepted her as his Teacher, because she had spoken the Truth to him. He bowed down to her and then left and became an ascetic.

The life that men and women usually live with one another has nothing to do with such enlightenment. A woman does not want her husband to think that she is a bag of excrement. A woman wants her husband to believe that she is the Goddess incarnate, and that he should worship her genitals and remain enthusiastic for sex with her and be completely attached to her. She does not try to turn her husband to God. She knows very well that her husband is not turned to God, but to her. That is what is going on in the suburbs—wives are trying to keep their husbands fascinated and men are likewise trying to fascinate their wives. Yet the fact remains that all that we are in our manifest appearance is this brief, fleshy thing that has no life of its own. It is only a cycle that rises and falls. It is not absolute in any sense whatsoever.

Yes, your wife is the Goddess in some sense. That is, if you are not attached to her in subhuman ways, you can perceive her to be the Goddess. Spiritual men have acknowledged their wives as the Goddess, not out of erotic fascination or the desire to cling to them in some cultic fashion, but in order to transcend them, to acknowledge the Universal Power beyond the ordinary appearance of the wife.

Just so, a wife must acknowledge her husband as God or Purusha, the Transcendental Consciousness, Siva, not in order to pin Siva into that fleshy shape, but in order to transcend all bodily limitations. Thus, in true marriage, husband and wife acknowledge that the fleshy thing they are has nothing absolute to offer. It is a binding circumstance, especially if it is lived apart from God-Communion. You will not realize the eternal Goddess or God by attaching yourself to some ordinary appearance. You must give up your attachment, give up your soul, and become a sacrifice in God.

Thus, when people marry, they should acknowledge one another in the Mood of God-Communion, and thereby transcend in their consciousness all the limitations of eroticism and subhuman inclination. And then, beginning in the earliest phase of their marriage and always, to the degree that they are sexually active, they should engage in the sexual relationship in the form of sexual communion. Sexual communion is not only the sexual practice of intercourse, but it is also the sexual practice of the relationship itself. Men and women must therefore transcend the eroticism or the play of opposition between them, all of the conflict of ordinary life in which they are not inherently blissful but seek to become blissful through contact with one another. All of that must be utterly transcended. The transcendence of ordinary sexuality is not some superheroic feat that only a few rare souls can realize. It is a very ordinary matter, really, that anyone can realize, through right understanding, through hearing the Teaching, through growing a little bit, through Awakening to Truth while alive.

The general or continuous process of "Breath and Name," practiced by members of the esoteric order of The Free Communion Church,[9] involves the same mechanism awakened

---

9. The obligations of members of the esoteric order of the Church are discussed in "An Invitation" at the end of the text.

through true sexual communion, except that the general process is set in motion more subtly, through intuitive spiritual communion and the simple cycle of the breath, without necessary physical contact with another at any region of the body, and it is lived under all ordinary conditions, moment to moment.

347

Accept this Lawful discipline of sexuality, so that you may be a sacrifice in the play of sex. But in every moment yield the feeling and attention that are distracted by the obsessive need of sexual fulfillment—yield whole bodily in Communion with the Real Divine that is Revealed in every instant of "hearing" the Teaching and of "seeing" the Spiritual Master.

Chapter 16

Sexual Activity Is neither an Obstacle nor an Obligation in the Way of Divine Ignorance

The Ultimate Fulfillment of
Sexual Communion

Sexual Economy and Motiveless Celibacy Are the Natural Consequences of Sexual Communion and the Realization of Whole Bodily Fullness

The child, the younger and sexually naive person, and the individual not yet adapted to existence as Life extended through and via the body as a whole, are adapted and motivated relative to the stimulation, tension, and release exercise of independent bodily functions. The partially adapted individual is primarily limited to the lower functional exercise and to self-oriented exploitation of vital pleasures.

As the individual grows into the disposition of the heart, or the way of love, the lower bodily functions begin to be transformed by a process that relates all independent functions and all life activity to the body as a whole. Thus, as the process of sexual communion matures, the infantile fascination with the independent stimulation of genital pleasure gradually disappears. In place of genital eroticism, the life of human sexual love develops. In that case, genital fetishes, erotic obsessions, and degenerative addiction to the method of orgasm as a means of emptying the body of tension and fear and

Life-Intensity all gradually fall away. The subjective fixation is released, along with the compulsive internalization of sex via thought and imagery.

Thus, over time, and as the higher spiritual adaptation of the body-mind also develops, the individual realizes the native whole body fullness that characterizes the truly human being. When this fullness stabilizes and matures, the specifically genital or conventional sexual motivation of the body-mind also tends to economize itself.

This may be said to be the ultimate bodily realization or level of higher bodily adaptation that is naturally served by the process of sexual communion. Natural sexual economy and motiveless celibacy are both founded in the whole bodily fullness and mental freedom that is native to the pervasive disposition of the heart. But such economy or celibacy is a choiceless bodily event, not a mental strategy or a method of sexual suppression chosen on the basis of self-division, guilt, or a self-possessed intention to attain the illusions produced by the exclusively higher organ stimulations of yoga.

The process of the development of either motiveless celibacy or sexual economy is the simple one of the transfer of the Current of the bodily being from fixation in independent organs to pervasion of the body as a whole. In that process, chronic organ tensions are released, and the body-mind rests in natural fullness, awareness, and feeling, which appears to radiate via the whole bodily being to Infinity.

At first a sense of "inversion" of the sex organs may be felt, wherein tension and energy in the sex organs are felt less often, and less on the basis of arbitrary erotic stimulations of a casual mental or bodily kind. Thus, just as genital tension is released during sexual communion itself, the release of genital tension to the whole body becomes more and more a characteristic of the daily or moment to moment condition of the individual. In place of chronic organ tensions, the individual bodily condition becomes more and more one of whole bodily fullness, in which the bodily Current or Energy is commonly, stably, and naturally or motivelessly sensed to radiate via every cell of the body. Then the common bodily condition becomes the whole body disposition of unqualified feeling, and there is native freedom from self-division and subjectivity or mind.

This realization is the natural consequence or fulfillment of sexual communion over time. It occurs when the common or native condition of the body-mind becomes the one of fullness and radiance rather than tension, contraction upon self and independent organs, and a self-divided sense of separateness. The full realization of whole body fullness, as described, is not realizable via the sexual discipline alone, but it is the natural future of sexuality in the case of those who practice sexual communion as part of the total spiritual discipline of the Way of Divine Ignorance.

351

A true and stable marriage, functioning in the regenerative human manner, is not possible until both partners are emotionally and sexually responsible for the process of sexual communion. In the fourth stage of life, the functions that are below the heart are submitted to the heart (or the feeling dimension of the whole bodily being), and via the heart to the Divine. Thus, only in the fourth stage of life is there full responsibility for regenerative practice in terms of the vital-physical, emotional-sexual, and verbal-intentional aspects of the bodily being. (In The Free Communion Church, the fourth stage of life begins when the individual has attained maturity in the truly religious and devotional life of surrender to the Divine through personal and moral practice. Therefore, marriage is not recommended until the individuals involved have practiced and studied as lay members[1] in the Church and have been fully instructed in the process of sexual communion.)

Previous to the fourth stage of life there is the third stage, which, in The Free Communion Church, is the stage of student religious preparation. It corresponds to the ancient "brahmacharya" stage of life, wherein the individual renounces his parented, childish, reactive, and regressive tendencies, and turns from self to God.

---

1. Please see "An Invitation" at the end of the text for a discussion of the forms of involvement in The Free Communion Church—lay members, novices, and members of the esoteric order.

352

In the third stage of life, the individual should apply himself to intentional and regenerative self-discipline, the practical morality of heartfelt service to others, and study of the religious and spiritual life of Divine Communion. It is this stage that occupies "lay members" in The Free Communion Church, and it is during this stage that the individual becomes increasingly responsible for his human functional conditions, free of self-indulgent and emotionally reactive or regressive habits. The process of sexual communion is studied at this stage. (Members of the Church who are lay members but who are already married are asked to moderate their sexual contact to no more than once or twice per month until they have fully studied the process of sexual communion within the normal sequence of formal study in the Church. Once the fourth stage of life begins, wherein the individual practices as a fully instructed "novice" in the Church, sexual communion becomes a natural and secondary discipline in the religious life, and conventional sexuality, oriented toward degenerative genital orgasm, is gradually and spontaneously economized and transcended.)

The "brahmacharya" or student stage of life (the third of the seven stages, wherein vital-physical and emotional-sexual conditions come under the integrated will and become a matter of whole bodily responsibility) should continue until the fourth stage of life truly begins—wherein the position of the heart or whole bodily psyche, the turning into God-Communion, the devotional or sacrificial relationship to the Spiritual Master, and the assumption of the higher Way and culture of Life are all fully presumed. Thus, marriage should, ideally, not take place until the fourth stage of life begins, or else marriage tends to be devoted to exploitative satisfaction and conflict in the vital-physical, reactive emotional, and degenerative sexual dimensions of life—in which case the fourth stage of life as well as the following stages will be frustrated and prevented by marriage itself.

Sexual Activity Is neither an Obstacle nor an Obligation in the Way of Divine Ignorance

I n the Way of Divine Ignorance, the conversion of conventional sexual activity into the uniquely human process of sexual communion is essential. However, sexual activity is not itself necessary. It is only that the avoidance of sexual activity is neither useful nor necessary in this Way. And most people are likely to prefer to be sexually active, in spite of conflicts and difficulties, rather than choose the strategy of ascetic avoidance of sex. However, in some cases, either the force of sexual motivation is naturally weak or else the Force of Divine Communion itself dissolves the genital game.

In every case, the individual should be made thoroughly aware of the right and regenerative function of sexuality in sexual communion with Life. But some individuals may never enter into sexual intimacy or marriage, or else such an intimate relationship may include little genital-sexual activity, or even none at all.

In any case, whether the individual is sexually active or not, the Way of Divine Ignorance is the Way of total psycho-physical Communion with the All-Pervading Divine Life. And such Communion ultimately becomes functional Transformation by the Power of Life and literal Translation of the body-mind into Life. Therefore, only the Divine is necessary, and only the essential whole bodily disciplines are obligatory. The personal, moral, and higher psycho-physical disciplines that must be applied are the ones that are applied by the whole body-mind and through all the specific functions that are active in one form or another. Thus, genital sexual activity is not itself obligatory, since we can live in Fullness without it. But the sex function must itself be yielded into the Divine Life, and to the degree the individual is sexually active he must convert and adapt that activity into the process of sexual communion.

Any individual who is not genitally active can enjoy the full Realization of the Way of Divine Ignorance, just as any genitally active individual. However, any reactive obstructions that may be preventing or complicating such activity must be released. And the regenerative whole bodily disciplines in general must become the practice of every devotee. But the absence of sexual communion with Life through genital intimacy with a lover is not an inherent obstacle to this Way, since all of the other whole bodily, personal, moral, religious, spiritual, and esoteric yogic disciplines are themselves sufficient.

354

Homosexuality and Whole Body Fullness

It is not necessary to view homosexuality as an inherent problem that we must struggle to overcome. The general taboo against sex itself leads us to exaggerate the negative significance of uncommon patterns of sexual activity.

Homosexual desire appears in one or another form in every human individual. It naturally arises in moments of conflict or psycho-physical imbalance, when the native polarization of the body, male or female, is temporarily suppressed or converted. In the case of most individuals, the extreme forms of such character disability occur in the earlier years of growth, particularly during adolescence. For this reason, and many other reasons, celibacy and adaptation to higher human discipline are essential during the youthful growing years. Just so, it is also essential that the relations between the individual and his intimates, particularly his parents and superiors, be a theatre of love, understanding, right discipline, and creative human demands. Otherwise, aberrations of sexual character, sexual desire, and sexual practice will plague the individual in later years.

The individual is, by virtue of his born sexual type, naturally disposed toward a basic sexual polarization to the opposite sex rather than his own sex. Some individuals may be born with a physiological disposition that runs to one or another degree contrary to his apparent sex. In such cases, the seed of homosexuality may be naturally present in the body. But each individual is also obliged to grow into maturity, and in that process of growth, the structures of the body go through changes that temporarily affect the polarity of the emotional and psychological components of his character. If the circumstances of life are such that homosexual experience is introduced during periods of weakness, inversion, or conversion of the natural sexual character role, then homosexual desire can remain as a fixed aspect of the individual's drives in later life. Just so, if the parental environment does not provide a right balance of experience of sexual roles and of relationships to members of each sex, then the individual may be led to adapt to a homosexual role, or to a complicated or loveless form of the heterosexual role.

Truly, every individual grows in an environment that is imperfect, and very many grow in environments that are a profoundly subhuman kind of school. Therefore, it is very likely that every individual will come to the age of maturity with a sexual disposition that is complicated and even chaotic. Therefore, it is not in itself significant whether one tends to be homosexual, heterosexual, bisexual, asexual, or any other kind of obsessive sexual. Rather, once we enter into the sphere of the common world, we must enter into the School of Life, the Divine Life. If we are fortunate enough to grow up in a truly human culture, full of right testing and higher human influences, then perhaps we have already begun to develop in that School of Life. But most people must discover that School while struggling with the effects and the society of the subhuman schooling of the common world.

The Teaching of the Way of Divine Ignorance is a Communication within the School of Life. And it represents human demands toward Divine Realization. Those who respond to this Teaching must abandon their self-conscious reactivity and enter into Divine

Communion. And an aspect of the discipline of this Way of Life is the responsible practice of sexual communion.

Sexual communion involves, first of all, the demand that the individual enter into a total life of responsible religious, personal, and moral discipline, in which chronic physical, emotional, and mental <u>reactivity</u> is dissolved in responsible or primary <u>activity</u> in self-giving love and service, completely apart from any consolation by the functional pleasures of living, including sexual pleasures. This demand, rather than any problematic or strategic interpretation of one's previously acquired sexual tendencies, is the essential force that must transform one's habits of living, including one's sexual character, desire, and practice.

Some may remain homosexual in orientation, because it is <u>bodily</u> true of them. Others will likely discover that homosexual desire is a reactive tendency in their case, produced by the circumstantial theatre of their earlier adaptation. Therefore, in many cases, homosexual desire and activity will and must disappear, by coming under the control of the fully balanced, nonreactive, whole bodily disposition of primal intimacy with the All-Pervading Life, and with the world, and with the society of <u>both</u> sexes, and with one's own native bodily or structural disposition. In such cases, homosexuality disappears in the same way that masturbation, or erotic heterosexual obsession, or impotence, or frigidity disappears in the case of others. When we awaken whole bodily, from self-possessed reactivity, to Divine Communion and the life of loving service to others, our aberrations fall away.

Members of The Free Communion Church are obliged to adapt in their feeling, whole bodily, to the All-Pervading Life. In the process, they must abandon their loveless and reactive ways, and they must become intelligently responsible as love. Thus, as they grow in this School, they must consider all of their tendencies, and they must change their practice wherever it is not true to Life.

Homosexuality is not considered to be an <u>inherent</u> aberration in the lives of devotees in The Free Communion Church. However, it is presumed that it may very well be an aberration in the factual case of any such individual. Therefore, every individual is obliged to consider his own history and his own pattern of reactivity. Every individual is obliged to adapt to a life of human love, intimacy, and responsible friendship—not only with his sexual intimate, but with all other devotees, male and female. Every individual is obliged to yield his reactive life of self-possession and to love and serve in continuous surrender to the Living God.

Therefore, if each individual does this, then aberration will show itself to be what it is, and right activity will become the natural responsibility. In that case, if a homosexual polarization of character and desire remains, then the practice of homosexual love, in the form of sexual communion, and in an acknowledged formal intimacy (as in the case of heterosexual marriage), is acceptable between members of the Church. If, however, individuals so inclined are not otherwise able to live the happy and full life that obliges devotees in general, their homosexuality is likely to be only a reactive, antisocial, desperate, self-possessed, and degenerative aberration—not different from any other obsession, such as promiscuity, nymphomania, sado-masochism, drug addiction, or alcoholism. And, in that case, the individual must accept disciplines that purify and transform the habits of living and return the functions, with the whole body, to God.

S exual communion may continue as a lifelong practice, until extreme Ecstasy, or Transcendental Dissolution of the body-mind, in the second phase of the Way of Radical Intuition. But the quality of the practice naturally changes over time, as the disposition of the body-mind becomes more and more that of prior Fullness or whole body Radiance. Thus, transcendence of conventional sexuality, either in the form of a profound sexual economy or even motiveless celibacy, becomes the ultimate destiny of human sexuality.

Sexual economy is made of a combination of two practices: (1) infrequency (or natural moderation) of sexual intercourse, and (2) sexual intercourse that is entirely regenerative and nonbinding in its motives or its effects. And motiveless celibacy is simply the continuation of a loving relationship of profound whole bodily intensity, but without sexual intercourse.

In the case of either natural sexual economy or motiveless celibacy, the sex-force, relational feeling, and general Life-Intensity are in no way absent or repressed. On the contrary, the whole bodily Realization of Life and Living Intensity is most profound. And that Life-Force is felt to pervade every organ of the body-mind with blissful energy. It is simply that the functional life-energy is not forced to collect in any organ exclusively, chronically, or problematically. Rather, the life-energy easily and constantly circulates to the whole body, by virtue of the awakened spiritual processes and the functional disciplines, such as sexual communion, that coincide with them. Thus, in the case of mature lovers who have grown in adaptation to the process of sexual communion in the Way of Divine Ignorance, the sex-force and the general vitality of the bodily being constantly pass to all areas of the body-mind, yielding constant Fullness of Life, rather than the chronic need for degenerative release of Life.

The Signs of Motiveless Bodily Transcendence of Genital Orgasm

The process of genital orgasm is transcended spontaneously, naturally, gradually, and motivelessly. It is not truly and positively transcended by problematic and self-possessed effort, mental strategy, or emotional and physical armoring against pleasure. Rather, it is transcended through bodily and sexual surrender to Life, which is Awakened in the native pleasurableness of bodily existence, feeling, breathing, moving, and sexing.

The signs of this natural and spontaneous transcendence of orgasm begin to appear over time in individuals who practice sexual communion with the Living Divine. (Those signs generally do not fully mature until sexual communion is extended into the more esoteric forms of its practice in the Way of Re-cognition. Thus, general transcendence of orgasm appears relatively early, associated directly with the various psycho-physical techniques wherein orgasm is conserved, but motiveless and bodily transcendence of orgasm, more indirectly related to the techniques of conservation, appears only as spiritual practice itself matures most fully. For this reason, motiveless transcendence of orgasm is not likely to appear, in the truest or fullest sense, until general practice matures in the Way of Re-cognition.)

The signs of natural transcendence of orgasm during sexual embrace are primarily these:

1. All genital tension—or the physical genital recoil that eventually leads to genital discharge—relaxes, or is not created. Thus, genital orgasm is made obsolete, since its primary pre-condition, which is genital tension, is not created.

2. General bodily tension and, in some cases, even bodily movements are relaxed or not created, and the sense of the body's form or limits may be temporarily suspended.

3. The breathing cycle becomes naturally relaxed, deep, slow, and may at times appear to have been temporarily suspended.

4. No thoughts or subjective images are generated, or, even when they are generated, they are without tension-creating bodily or emotional effect.

5. Sexual activity remains profoundly stimulating, but the body-mind creates no armor or defense against it. The whole body yields to the Bliss-Full Life-Feeling entirely, and in every functional part, and that Fullness is not isolated in the genitals.

Over time these signs appear spontaneously and more and more often, and other signs, of an esoteric spiritual or yogic kind, may also appear in conjunction with this ecstatic whole bodily submission to the Radiant Life-Power.

There are three phases to the development of the process of sexual communion with Life:

1. The first phase is the initial period of adaptation to Communion with Life through sex. It is the period of transition from conventional erotic exploitation of sexual tension and orgasm and it is the passage to bodily conservation or *conductivity* of Life. Thus, in this period, there is the struggle toward Life-Communion and the psycho-physical exercise of bypassing the degenerative form of orgasm. It is the period of adaptation, or re-adaptation, and initiation into the regenerative function of truly human sexuality.

2. The second phase of sexual communion begins when the bodily and mental strategy toward orgasm relaxes, and the genital motive toward orgasm "inverts." In that case, sexual communion essentially ceases to be devoted toward orgasm, or release of the tension of reactive self-possession via the genitals. Instead, the process becomes one of whole bodily "meditation," or feeling-contemplation, of the All-Pervading Current and Presence of Life. When this "inversion" of the genitals—or the return of the genitals to the whole body—becomes stable, it is then that the truly regenerative function of sexual communion begins.

3. The third phase of sexual communion is begun when the sex function is itself transcended as the necessary medium for Communion with Life and whole bodily conductivity of Life. It begins when sexual activity begins spontaneously to economize itself, making sexual activity unnecessary as a means of bodily Communion with Life, even though the practice of sexual communion in genital embrace may still continue to appear at times. When this phase of sexual communion appears, the esoteric processes of spiritual practice replace or become altogether senior to sexual communion as the Way to Life.

The process of sexual communion described in this book is the Lawful, or natural, human, and sacrificial form of sexual adaptation. It is founded on the basis of <u>positive</u> rather than <u>prob-</u>

360

lematic awareness of human functional and sexual existence. However, it is likewise founded on an orientation toward the All-Pervading Life and Transcendental Consciousness of the Divine Reality. Therefore, it is not a means of self-indulgence, self-satisfaction, or even the satisfaction of others than oneself. Rather, it is simply a process of self-sacrifice in the Divine, or Communion with the Living God through ecstatic bodily surrender.

For these reasons, the process of sexual communion is not in principle ascetic or sex-rejecting, but it is naturally self-transcending and sex-transcending. And, therefore, it naturally and inevitably demonstrates the signs of the bodily and personal transcendence of conventional eroticism and degenerative orgasm.

Those who practice sexual communion as an adjunct of the total practice of the Way of Divine Ignorance see these signs develop as they mature or progress in the stages of our Sacrifice. And devotees who enter the Way of Radical Intuition must have realized the full natural conservative economy of orgasm. Devotees who mature in the Way of Radical Intuition ultimately realize complete sexual self-transcendence, in which a natural and benign sexual economy prevails. This is because their attention is released from the conventional and reactive habits of the independent psycho-physical self, and they are Absorbed in Transcendental Occupation with the Form of God.

361

*The Stages of the Practice of
Sexual Communion*

Sexual Discipline in
The Free Communion Church

1. Sexuality must be realized as a <u>relational</u> and <u>regenerative</u> discipline of body, emotion, and mind, rather than a reactive, self-indulgent, and degenerative exploitation of the body-mind itself. And it must be associated with a whole range of other regenerative personal, moral, and devotional religious disciplines, including dietary and health practices, responsible work, a full life of service, regular study of the Teaching, and general abandonment of casual society.

2. Sexuality must be understood and responsibly practiced as a form of whole bodily Communion with the Infinite All-Pervading Force Field and Radiant Current of Divine Life, rather than a binding form of mutual attachment between two immature individuals. Its right practice, which gradually obliges all members of The Free Communion Church, is described as the process of sexual communion in this book.

3. Therefore, members of the Church should abstain from all forms of casual or obsessive eroticism and promiscuity. They should, during an initial period of celibacy, study and mature in their understanding of sexuality and their emotional responsibility in human relationships. Then they should enter into a commitment of choice in either a heterosexual marriage or, if they are truly so inclined, a formalized homosexual agreement.

4. Sexual intercourse should be engaged only between formally committed partners, and only on occasions of full mutual love-desire.

5. "Lay members" of the Church either must remain celibate or, if already married, must moderate the frequency of sexual intercourse to no more than once or twice per month. Marriages within the Church should generally occur only when both partners have completed formal study as lay members, including full formal instruction in the process of sexual communion. Individuals who regard themselves to be homosexual must abstain from all sexual activity until they have fully and formally completed consideration of the process of sexual communion in the course of study as a lay member. If, after such full instruction, an individual freely chooses a homosexual relationship, then that relationship may be accepted and acknowledged within the Church as one that fulfills all of the conditions of any true heterosexual marriage. Married lay members, or lay members involved in an acknowledged homosexual commitment, may begin to increase the frequency of sexual intercourse once full formal instruction in the process of sexual communion has been received.

6. Once a lay member has been formally and fully instructed in the process of sexual communion, he may engage in sexual relations with his partner as often as love-desire makes appropriate. On all such occasions, the discipline of sexual communion should be practiced. Such lay members soon move on to acceptance as "novices," or fully instructed members of the Church.

7. Novice members of the Church should fully adapt to the practice of sexual communion. In time, the motive of sexual intercourse will gradually cease to be the conventional degenerative genital orgasm. Instead, the regenerative Fullness of Communion with the Divine Life will become the motive and the pleasure of human embrace, and that same Fullness will create a right conservative economy in sexual practice.

8. Those who apply for acceptance as members of the esoteric order of the Church must have matured in their practice of sexual communion, as well as all other religious, moral, and regenerative personal disciplines that belong to the practice of novice members. The practice of sexual communion itself should have matured to the point that the signs of stable bodily transcendence of degenerative

genital orgasm have steadily appeared for a period of at least two months. (Genital orgasm should remain within the capacity of such individuals, and they should be sexually active, but full eliminative orgasm should ordinarily and quite naturally be bypassed, appearing at most perhaps once or twice in a month. And, in the case of both male and female individuals, the regular bypassing (or conversion) of genital orgasm should commonly occur through Fullness of Life-Feeling and easy control of breath and motion, along with alternate tensing and relaxing of the anus-perineum genital region, and random application of finger pressure, generally prior to the actual or full genital crisis.)

9. Members of the esoteric order should continue to mature in their practice of sexual communion, so that native bodily transcendence of casual or degenerative orgasm becomes most profound. When such an individual applies for instruction in the final phase of the Way of Relational Enquiry, a judgment will be made, in conjunction with the Pastoral Service Order of the Church, regarding the special sexual discipline that should formally apply until completion of the Way of Re-cognition.

In some cases, if sexual intercourse is not obsessive or mutually binding, and if the practice of sexual communion can be maintained on a regular basis without the degenerative effects of frequent conventional orgasm, there may be no need to moderate the frequency of sexual intercourse. In other cases, a discipline of moderation may have to be accepted in order to maintain the condition of bodily conservation of bio-energy and internal chemistry necessary for further practice. In still other cases, intentional celibacy, or else extreme moderation, may be necessary, at least until full maturity in the Way of Re-cognition.

10. Devotees who, as members of the esoteric order of the Church, practice the Way of Radical Intuition, must have realized complete transcendence of the obsessive necessity of sexual intercourse itself (as well as conventional orgasm as the motive of sexual intercourse). The Fullness of the Radiant Divine must be sufficient at this ultimate stage of practice. Such devotees must constantly determine for themselves whether sexual activity or celibacy should

characterize their way of life. But as long as they are sexually active, they should practice the regenerative process of sexual communion as the natural convention of daily life.

Devotees who, as members of the esoteric order of the Church, practice the Way of Radical Intuition to the degree of full maturity, are, by virtue of their complete transcendence of the body-mind in the Divine, free of all formal or conventional obligations related to ordinary living. This does not mean that they are likely to engage in self-indulgent exploitation of sexuality, or any other degenerative practices of life. Rather, they have transcended the mechanics of desire in relation to the things of the body-mind. Thus, such devotees, as a matter of daily practice, quite naturally maintain the moderate and regenerative practices that are native to the body-mind in its free state.

365

The difference between such devotees and others is just this ease and naturalness relative to the regenerative exercise of all functions. The lay member and the novice must practice the regenerative disciplines with a certain will or intention that counters the degenerative tendencies acquired from past habits of activity. But the mature devotee in the Way of Radical Intuition, who is fully surrendered in the Living Divine, is free of such subconscious and habitual tendencies toward degeneration, since they are only expressions of self-possessed recoil from the All-Pervading and Radiant Divine.

The Stages of the Practice of Sexual Communion

The practice of sexual communion develops in three stages. The first stage is the stage of transition from conventional or subhuman sexual activity to the regenerative design of truly human sexual activity. It involves intentional practice, or responsible adaptation, to the functional design of sexual communion.

(In The Free Communion Church, such practice truly begins at the "novice" level of preparation for admission to the Company of the Spiritual Master. "Lay members" of the Church are not obliged to practice sexual communion, although they are free to do so, if they are married. The obligation of lay members who are married is to realize their sexuality in an intimate commitment and to moderate their sexual activity through sensitivity to the pattern of true love-desire within that intimate relationship. Those lay members who are not involved in a heterosexual marriage are obliged to maintain total celibacy, including the avoidance of masturbation and erotic amusements, until they are fully and formally instructed, within the education program of the Church, in the process of sexual communion. Once instructed, individuals may then enter into heterosexual marriage or, if they choose, a formally acknowledged homosexual commitment.)

The first stage of the practice of sexual communion functions essentially as a process of initiation into the natural, effortless or spontaneous practice of sexual communion in its fully regenerative sense. Thus, as this first stage develops, the modes of physical, emotional, and mental self-possession, self-division, and separativeness are gradually relaxed. In place of the conventional and reactive tension-release eroticism, a native sense of whole bodily Fullness begins to appear.

This transition develops through ecstatic feeling-submission of the entire body-mind, via one's lover, to the All-Pervading Life, or to the degree of Infinity. The practice matures as prior and natural whole bodily Fullness of Life becomes more common than the reactive motive of genital tension-release of the internal bio-energy or Life-Force. Thus, as maturity in the first stage of the practice of sexual communion develops, it becomes less and less necessary to use forceful intentional control of breathing, bodily motion, attention, lower bodily tension (at the anus-perineum-genital base), pressure on the base of the genitals, and so forth. The crisis of orgasm becomes less and less the motive of sexual activity, and sexual activity itself becomes more and more the simple bodily and feeling Communion with the All-Pervading and Transcendental Current of Life.

Thus, through development of the Fullness of such Communion, the exclusive crisis of genital (or eliminative) orgasm becomes less and less necessary. It is controlled by a more and more simple and less and less exaggerated functional exercise. The process of sexual communion becomes less profoundly associated with control and conservation of orgasm in itself. Instead, it becomes more steadily associated with the intensification of whole bodily Communion with Life, and with continuous simple breathing-conductivity of the intensifying sense of Life during sexual embrace. Ultimately, orgasm becomes obsolete as an automatically motivated necessity. The capacity for genital orgasm remains, but the tendency is naturally, effortlessly, and spontaneously controlled by simple feeling and breathing of the All-Pervading Life.

The second stage of the practice of sexual communion begins when the degenerative tendency and motive of orgasm has become bodily obsolete (not merely controlled by mental strategy). The regenerative conversion of orgasm as well as the generative or reproductive capacity of orgasm remains available at will, but the degenerative tension-release tendency comes under the native control of Life itself via the opened mechanisms of the whole body. The whole bodily realization of feeling-Communion with the Divine Life becomes native whole bodily Fullness of Life, free of chronic reactivity and the motive of tension-release. However, the process of sexual embrace, as sexual communion, may continue as a useful agent for the bodily intensification of Life.

(This second stage of the practice of sexual communion must have begun to show its naturally conservative signs to a significant degree before members of The Free Communion Church may be accepted as members of the esoteric order. And the practice continues to mature in the case of members of the esoteric order, until Feeling Fullness controls and masters orgasm and the practice of intercourse itself.)

368

The practice of sexual communion is essentially mature, or entered into its second stage, when the reactive motive of tension-release, or genital orgasm, is "inverted," or replaced by the continuous feeling-sense of the whole bodily Fullness of Life. Once this becomes the stable disposition in sexual embrace, sexual communion becomes a wholly regenerative process. Then the Power of Life may be contacted and even greatly intensified by the practice of sexual communion, and the intensified Life may also, to a high degree, be made available to the whole and entire bodily being, through the natural conductivity of feeling and breathing, free of the degenerative orgasm (the eliminative discharge of Life).

(This second stage of the practice of sexual communion, with natural "inversion" of the tendency to genital orgasm, must have demonstrated an essential maturity before instruction in the final phase of the Way of Relational Enquiry may be given to members of the esoteric order of The Free Communion Church. And the practice of sexual communion, naturally free of degenerative orgasm, must characterize devotees who practice in the final phase of the Way of Relational Enquiry, or they must otherwise moderate or temporarily abandon sexual intercourse.)

This second stage of the practice of sexual communion is superior to all mental and strategic suppression of the "problem" of sex. It is superior to all conventional or problematically motivated asceticism and celibacy. It allows full and nonproblematic participation in the natural structural function of genital sexuality. And it allows that function to be realized as a fully ecstatic, or self-releasing, process of submission to the Divine. As such, the sexual function, in coordination with the whole bodily conductivity of Life, becomes an actual yogic instrument for the regeneration and higher adaptation of the entire bodily being. True sexual communion, with natural "inversion" of the motive of genital orgasm, is an esoteric form of "hatha yoga" and an instrument of "kundalini yoga" as well as all other forms of the higher psycho-physical adaptation of the body-mind.

(The practice of sexual communion is transformed in various esoteric yogic ways in the later phase of the Way of Relational

Enquiry and in the Way of Re-cognition. Then it may become a useful, although secondary, means for developing higher and higher degrees of available Life-Intensity in the body-mind. In the first two phases of the Way of Re-cognition, this developing Intensity of Life is used in the yogas of higher adaptation, or upward contemplation. Just so, the Intensity or Fullness of Life realized in sexual communion can be positively useful in all of the first three or developing stages of the Way of Divine Ignorance. But the primary personal, moral, and higher psycho-physical responsibilities, and especially the radical spiritual responsibilities of the *conscious process,* serve the same Intensification of Life, even apart from sexual communion, which is a positive but secondary discipline. And as the Way of Re-cognition develops, the higher esoteric responsibilities and the radical spiritual responsibilities become more and more obviously sufficient in themselves. Eventually the process of sexual communion becomes unnecessary as a means of contacting the Full Intensity of Life, since that Full Intensity has become native to the body-mind in all of its natural states.)

369

The second stage of practice of sexual communion is the stage in which the bodily motive of degenerative genital orgasm is effectively obsolete, while the regenerative and Life-Intensifying motive to sexual activity remains. However, this second stage of practice never fully appears unless the whole life of practical, moral, and radical spiritual practice also coincides with it. And the Life-Realization possible in the second stage of the practice of sexual communion matures only in coincidence with the esoteric processes of higher psycho-physical adaptation. Likewise, as the esoteric spiritual processes develop, and as the second stage of the practice of sexual communion matures, the necessity and even the utility of sexual activity as an added means of Life-Intensification becomes gradually obsolete.

Thus, the third stage of the process or practice of sexual communion eventually appears. It is the stage in which sexual activity itself (as well as conventional genital orgasm) has become unnecessary as a means to Life. In such a case, Life-Intensification occurs, utterly and sufficiently, through the native structural disposition and radical spiritual sacrifice of the whole and entire body-mind. Communion with Life is always already absolute at this stage, and neither sexual communion nor any other intentional yogic activity of higher adaptation is necessary for the radical Realization of the Radiant Divine.

370

The Transcendence
of Sexuality

Once native bodily conservation of orgasm is established, and the devotee lives in natural transcendence of mental, emotional, and physical distraction by conventional erotic motives, a unique process is set in motion in the sexual mechanism and the Life system of the body. In that process, the outflowing and outturning tendencies of sexual interest are relaxed, and the Life system inverts or turns around at the point of the sexual center of the lower body. Then the Life-Current and the glandular chemistry of the sexual center begin to be constantly released or absorbed into the bodily system as a whole. This is the secret of bodily transformation in Communion with the Divine.

Sexual communion is not a method of ordinary sexual "fulfillment" or superior sexual indulgence. It is a process of direct Communion with the Radiant Divine via the sexual function. Thus, it naturally, and from the beginning, transcends the self-possessed erotic motive, through love and whole bodily conservation of the biochemical evidence of Life.

And when such transcendence of the erotic or self-possessed sexual motive becomes fully mature, the cycle of regeneration, or bodily Communion with God, begins to appear most profoundly. Therefore, the maturity of the spiritual process also depends on the relative maturity of the devotee in relation to sexuality.

Sexual communion yields, over time, a natural economy of sexual activity and a general relaxation of genital stress, so that the Life-Force and regenerative chemistry of the whole bodily being flow universally, to every part, enlivening the whole bodily being and making its consciousness clearer and its awareness more and more subtle.

Thus, over time, the occasions of genital play become less frequent and certainly less oriented toward genital release. The timing of this process of gradual economization of the sexual process and conservation of the Life-Force, the regenerative chemistry, and the attention or consciousness of the whole bodily being is associated with the four stages of practice in the Way of Divine Ignorance.

Thus, when responsibility for *conductivity* in the later phase of the Way of Relational Enquiry is accepted, the devotee should enjoy complete control of orgasm (that is, full conservation of orgasm in its regenerative form should be common or regular), and engagement in genital relations should have become no more frequent than true love-desire proposes. Such economy is not realized on the basis of any strategic avoidance, but on the basis of natural relaxation of genital stress and continuous enjoyment of the "Breath of God," or the whole body display of energy rather than obsessive and reactive dissipation of energy through independent functional terminals.

In the Way of Re-cognition (as well as in the later phase of the Way of Relational Enquiry) the genital play must naturally be moderated in either its frequency or its effects, because of the quality of the yogic activities that awaken at that stage. The practice of sexual moderation should be continued until the whole bodily being is relieved of all stress and bondage to patterns of thought, reactive emotion, and vital motivation. A primary sign is general withdrawal of exclusive and randomly obsessive concentration of energy and attention in the sex organs—that is, a diffusion of Life-Energy into the whole bodily being creates a motiveless celibacy (or else an easeful economy of sexual desire). Only then can Self-Realization be stable—and only then should the Way of Radical Intuition begin.

Therefore, the beginning of the Way of Radical Intuition should coincide with a Life of Divine Love and universal service, and participation in sexual communion should continue only as a wholly positive and regenerative occasion, free of obsession and self-meditation, and expressing every aspect of the lower and higher structures of the human bodily being. The Way of Radical Intuition is, therefore, the end of bondage to the private life of functional self-meditation, and it is the end or death of Narcissus. The whole bodily being should be relaxed and polarized to the crown, and the force or implications of all differentiation should be dissolved at the Heart. Such is the Way for those who love in the Way of Radical Intuition.

372

When Does Sexual Communion Become Motiveless Celibacy?

In the extreme Ecstasy that appears in the maturity of the second phase of the Way of Radical Intuition, all aspects of the conventional experience of the body-mind are transcended, or Outshined by the Radiance of the Heart of God. It is not that the individual strategically excludes the phenomena of body and mind. They all simply Dissolve in the extremity of Bliss. Therefore, whenever such Fullness appears, at this or any other stage of practice, the devotee may become motivelessly celibate.

Some may become naturally celibate at an earlier stage of practice than the fully mature extreme of the Way of Radical Intuition. Others may maintain the practice of occasional sexual activity (in the form of sexual communion), except for the extreme Events of their own Transfiguration, when not only sex but all conventional activities of body and mind are Dissolved in Transcendental Occupation.

Therefore, devotees in the Way of Radical Intuition may remain sexually active, except when extreme Ecstasy totally Outshines the body-mind with Transcendental Love. As they mature in practice, sexual activity remains regenerative in effect, and it may also become relatively infrequent in practice. Sexual activity may even tend to be more or less confined to occasions when conception is intended. But, at least from time to time, the Mood of Life may demand the loving embrace as the form in which the Divine Ecstasy is expressed. Therefore, even in the Way of Radical Intuition, the practice of sexual communion may continue, except during periods of extreme Ecstasy.

373

Marriage must be founded in devotion to the Living God and the practical disposition of sexual communion. Thus, it is both self-transcending and sex-transcending. The intent of embrace must be that of love in God, not degenerative release through orgasm. Therefore, true marriage is, in its "spirit," chaste, or sexually free. It is characterized either by motiveless celibacy (except where conception is desired) or by sexual communion, free of degenerative and self-meditative motives.

Even frequent sexual communion may have a degenerative effect at last. But occasional or rightly measured sexual communion is not necessarily a negative factor in the life of mature devotees. Therefore, such right sexual practice may be considered to be essentially equal, in its disposition and effect, to a motivelessly celibate practice.

Thus, devotees in the Way of Radical Intuition may maintain either an occasional and Life-conservative sexual practice, or they may remain constantly and motivelessly celibate. Neither practice is necessarily "better," or, as a matter of principle, more appropriate than the other, and neither should be chosen as a strategic or self-manipulative habit. As the body-mind Dissolves in God-Bliss, all conventional activities Dissolve, or come to Life, including sex. At the extreme point of such Ecstasy, motiveless celibacy is inevitable. At all other and more natural times, however, the conservative and occasional practice of sexual communion may be continued.

Thus, it would not be uncommon for devotees in the Way of Radical Intuition to engage in sexual communion in marriage. The frequency might vary, and there might also be prolonged periods of motiveless celibacy. Motiveless celibacy becomes permanent as the

Terminal Ecstasy of Translation through death approaches, but, until then, the conservative and occasional practice of sexual communion may continue to appear, as a very human and loving expression of an otherwise God-Possessed life. Such is the Way for mature members of the esoteric order.

374

After all is said and done about the sexual process, even in its highest form, which is sexual communion, it arises relative to the body, mind, and separate self in this world. It depends on association with this Theatre or Play of Life. It may be realized more and more Lawfully, but, at last, it is utterly without power to bind the Radiant Transcendental Consciousness. It may continue as a conventional practice of devotees, until they are Translated beyond this Play, but it certainly becomes unnecessary, occasional, ecstatic, free, humorous, and only loving.

Chapter 17

Only the Sacrifice Is Guaranteed: Everything Else Must Be Transcended

Sexual Communion and the
Culture of The Free
Communion Church

S ex must be transcended, but sex, even in its common degenerative forms, is not wrong. Sexual awareness and adaptation are simply the beginning of our Transformation into Life. We must first positively adapt to a free, right, and regenerative sexual practice. Then, that very practice will move us beyond sex into whole bodily Fullness of Life.

The same understanding applies to all matters of our social, dietary, intellectual, emotional, moral, religious, and conventional physical adaptations. First we must adapt to regenerative patterns of function in the Spirit of Divine Communion. Then, over time, such functional Communion will itself raise us up, make us whole, and draw us into the Divine Itself.

A n individual who is irresponsible relative to his or her own functional life in general, including personal or bodily functions as well as the common obligations of relational life, will not be able to fully realize the responsibility of sexual communion.

378

Thus, many disciplines must precede adaptation to the process of sexual communion. First of all, the individual should have awakened to the whole body principle of love, or unobstructed feeling-attention, and accepted the foundation discipline of service. The awakening of the whole body principle (which transcends and controls the partial body principles of mind, reactive emotion, and vital movement) is established through "hearing" the Teaching or "argument" of the true Spiritual Master. Therefore, the life of service must also coincide with regular study or application of attention to the Teaching and the Teacher.

From this foundation there follow many personal disciplines that purify and Lawfully readapt the functional being to its appropriate order. There must be discipline of worldly or conventional social involvements, acceptance of responsible and serving work, control of the use of time and space, engagement of an intimate or devotional household situation for daily practice and the focus of daily living, and regular confinement to moderate and vitalizing health practices, including a pure and wholesome and moderate vegetarian diet (with, at most, only occasional and truly celebratory use of such accessories as flesh food, alcohol, and tobacco). Just so, there must be a full, easeful realization of an intimate sexual relationship, founded in love-desire, essentially free of petty conflicts and separativeness, and which includes regular but nonobsessive enjoyment of the ordinary genital orgasm.

Only on such a foundation can the practice of sexual communion be built.

The process of sexual communion is not an end in itself. It is one aspect of a larger and all-inclusive discipline. It represents functional re-adaptation of only one aspect of the whole bodily being. It is only part of a total practice or Way of Life.

The process of sexual communion, in conjunction with all the other disciplines of Lawful human functional readaptation and devotional sacrifice that comprise the entire Way of Divine Ignorance, ultimately yields transcendence, or literal sacrifice, of the whole bodily being at Infinity. Thus, as the devotee matures in the Way of Re-cognition and the Way of Radical Intuition, the attention is liberated from bondage to conventions of not only the lower functional bodily being but of the entire manifest bodily being or body-mind. In that case, sexual activity is transcended. It persists only as a convention of the functional being, without any binding attachment, implication, or dilemma. Right sexual practice matures as transcendence of sexuality itself, or of the binding power of sexual effects on the body-mind.

379

Sexual Communion and the Cycle of Human Adaptation to Be Engaged by Lay Members and Novices of The Free Communion Church

1. The discipline of sexual communion must be adopted as only one of many disciplines and responsibilities within a total personal and relational culture of religious and spiritual Communion with the Transcendental Divine Reality and All-Pervading Force Field of Life. Therefore, the first requirement is true "hearing" and "seeing," or Awakened insight and spontaneous release of the psycho-physical self into the Radiant Divine. This foundation response and Condition is implemented through various devotional practices, in private and in the company of other devotees.

2. Just as the first stage of life involves primary physical adaptation to the Source that Sustains it, the first discipline to which we must adapt in this Way of Life is the discipline of a moderate, pure, and regenerative vegetarian diet.

3. Along with adaptation to the personal discipline of a regenerative diet, we must adapt to the relational discipline of right association, or truly human activity, work, intimacy, society, entertainment, use of energy, use of money, heartfelt service, and

380

regular study of the Way. The relational discipline involves the transformation of our casual, subhuman daily society. The discipline of right association requires adaptation to truly human forms of daily society, within the context of the Way of Divine Ignorance and the community of devotees. Also, within this discipline of right association or right relationship, the primary aspect of sexual communion develops. That is, true, mutually open, and loving intimacy should be established and maintained through mutual feeling-service.

4. Just as the second stage of life involves the adaptation of the emotional-sexual functions, the second primary area of discipline to which we must adapt in this Way of Life is the one of responsibility for emotional reactivity, the positive granting of feeling-attention to others, and the nonreactive bodily participation in regenerative sexual communion with the All-Pervading Life.

5. Once the individual is established in right devotional Communion with the Living Divine, and has implemented that Communion through regenerative dietary and health practice, transformation of his associations, and adaptation to the process of sexual communion, he may begin to grow into the spectrum of higher human functions through whole bodily adaptation to the Living Power of God in the Company of the Spiritual Master.

Social Celebration and Spiritual Maturity

Those who are beginning to adapt body, emotion, mind, and will to a truly religious and moral practice of life may from time to time, once they have begun to make their transition into the fourth stage of life (or been accepted as novice members of The Free Communion Church), celebrate their common humanity with one another. Religious and devotional celebration, both private and communal, should be part of the daily and regular practice of all devotees. But, in the case of novices and some members of the esoteric order, there may also be occasions of conventional social celebration of the pleasurable sacrifice that is human existence itself. On such social occasions, the traditional "sacrifices" may be made. The ancient rituals of celebration included killed food, rich and elaborate meals, alcohol, tobacco, song, dance, and mutual amusements of all kinds.

381

Those who apply for membership in The Free Communion Church must first purify themselves of gross self-indulgent habits. Thus, lay members of the Church abandon all use of the dietary accessories of conventional social celebration. Members in the novice stage may make occasional, brief, and right intimate use of such accessories, with the permission of the Pastoral Service Order, but they must also be free of all commitment to casual self-indulgence of all kinds. And those who apply for membership in the esoteric order of the Church must again freely abandon all use of traditional dietary accessories, except perhaps for rare occasions, with the permission or under the direction of the Pastoral Service Order. (Thus, as a general rule, mature devotees abandon all use of killed food, eggs, unnatural or "junk" food, alcohol, tobacco, and coffee, as well as the previously abandoned social drugs and hallucinogens, and they make only occasional or right use of conventional tea, such as black or green tea.)

The casual use of the "sacrifices" or occasions and methods of social celebration should be eliminated from the life practices of all devotees. The occasions of intentional celebratory use should be infrequent, and they should be maintained for but a short period of hours, perhaps two to four times a year. No degenerative habits or casual attachments to the dietary accessories should be developed or indulged. The motive for celebration should be celebration itself— or expansive, ecstatic self-giving in the company of intimates. And, therefore, such celebration should be made only in the intimate society of one's close friends in the community of devotees. Those who do not accept the "spirit" of celebration, and who cannot celebrate in this manner without forsaking the truly religious and spiritual understanding and discipline of life, should not indulge in the dietary accessories and expansive company that such celebration involves.

Just so, the accessories of celebration should not be indulged to the point of significant degeneration of one's health, vitality, or capacity for creating intimate, pleasurable, loving company with others. And a period of physical purification should immediately follow, even as a period of physical purity or good health should precede such occasions. Some may even prefer, for reasons of general health and well-being, to avoid all forms of the dietary accessories of occasional celebration, although they might celebrate such occasions in a purely social manner, without the traditional accessories.

In any case, as practice in the Way of Divine Ignorance matures, the condition of the individual body-mind becomes gradually transformed, via all of the conditions of practice. The reactive physical, emotional, and mental characteristics that may have been present when practice of the Way began gradually relax into the prior Fullness of the Divine Life. The self-possessed, self-divided disposition, full of chronic tensions and motives toward degenerative release, gradually relaxes into a disposition that is ecstatic, loving, and happy in its native state. Thus, as practice matures, the use of traditional accessories of celebration, along with all attachment to casual degenerative habits, gradually falls away.

The later stages of practice in the whole Way of Divine Ignorance require the body-mind to be consistently stable in its regenerated native state, free of degenerative physical, emotional, and mental reactivity. There must be freedom as well from the effects of both the casual and the occasional self-indulgences that typify the habits of men and women who are not adapted to the truly human and higher human functions of Man. The higher psycho-physical disciplines of the Way of Re-cognition and the superhuman Transformations of the Way of Radical Intuition require the highest degree of psycho-physical balance and Intensity of Life-Fullness. The chemistry of blood and breath, and the processes of all the various bodily systems, must be developed to a degree that permits the subtlest and most highly evolved mechanisms of the body-mind to perform their ultimate tasks.

Therefore, as devotees mature in the stages of practice in the whole Way of Divine Ignorance, they must demonstrate the signs of mature and higher adaptation of every aspect of psycho-physical existence in human form. The Transformation and Liberation of Man is not merely a subjective matter. It is a matter of literal change and higher adaptation of the body-mind and all forms of its activity. Only the Man who is Awake and Whole can be a true and holy Sacrifice in God.

Diet and Sex

Food is senior to sex, just as the first stage of life precedes the second stage. And just as the emotional-sexual stage of life cannot mature until the assimilation-elimination stage is mature, sex cannot be a matter of full and right responsibility until there is full and right responsibility for the practices that relate to diet and general health.

Therefore, dietary and health disciplines, which at first minimize and ultimately eliminate "gross" dietary substances, and then minimize or, in some cases, eliminate "earthy" dietary substances, are essential to right adaptation and eventual maturity in the process of sexual communion.

Conventional dietary and social practices stimulate psycho-physical imbalances of all kinds, and thus support self-possessed eroticism, "confrontation" psychology, and the physical urge toward both sexual excess and the "eliminative" orgasm. Therefore, members of The Free Communion Church are obliged to adapt to dietary practices that gradually eliminate the grossest food elements (such as meat, poultry, fish, eggs, refined sugar, prepared or "junk" foods, alcohol, and tobacco). And their dietary practice gradually matures until there is at most only moderate and/or occasional use of "earthy" food elements, such as milk, milk products, cooked grains (with the possible exception of natural brown rice), breads, nuts, cooked beans, salt, spices, concentrated sweets (such as honey), and the like.

384

When we adapt to such a regimen, the body-mind becomes naturally purified and balanced in relation to the All-Pervading Life. As bodily, mental, and social irritants are eliminated or minimized, there is a freeing up of the obsessive and degenerative sexual orientation. The bio-energies and the glandular chemistry of the bodily being thus move naturally and easily toward a conservative and regenerative pattern of both internal and external activity.

In this manner, frequency of orgasm and frequency of sexual intercourse are naturally minimized toward an appropriate order. Ultimately, the degenerative orgasm, as well as sexual obsession or "irritation" in general, which eliminate both Life and glandular chemistry from both male and female, ceases to be the motive of daily life and sexual embrace. Sexual and emotional ease, psychological balance, and intimate affection become natural to those who practice in this manner. And the bio-energetic mechanisms of the nervous system, in association with the system of endocrine glands, become available for higher psycho-physical development.

Because of this combination of dietary and sexual disciplines, in association with the other devotional, personal, moral, and esoteric spiritual disciplines of the Way of Divine Ignorance, it is clear that a moderate sexual economy, or even a motiveless celibacy, will characterize those who mature in the later stages of the practice. Such is particularly likely at the point of maximum application of the dietary discipline (eliminating all "gross" dietary elements and at least moderating all "earthy" dietary elements) and the discipline relative to orgasm. Therefore, a true sexual economy characterizes devotees in the Way of Re-cognition and the Way of Radical Intuition.

Male individuals will, in the mature stages of practice, observe a clear diminution of the urge toward seminal ejaculation, and female individuals will likely observe signs that the periodic menstrual flow is becoming obsolete, or at least minimal. (The menstrual flow may be regarded as a kind of degenerative or diseased bodily condition, produced by dietary irritation and emotional imbalance, and which can become minimal, or even disappear, if dietary and emotional factors are brought under control. Thus, women who maintain an essentially raw diet, free of excess proteins and acid- and mucus-forming substances, will, if they are also emotionally and psychologically at ease in God and the world, see the menstrual cycle demonstrate conservative signs. And this is a positive indication, much as the conservation of ejaculation in the male individual. In both cases, the critical chemistry of the endocrine gland system is thus made available for reabsorption or direct assimilation into the process of evolutionary or higher development of the body and brain.)

Dietary Discipline in The
Free Communion Church

1. All members must practice fully regenerative disciplines relative to every area of personal functional existence. Thus, each member must strictly practice, as a regular daily discipline, a moderate, natural, and appropriately designed dietary regimen, within the limits of the wholly regenerative vegetarian diet described in *The Eating Gorilla Comes in Peace.*

2. "Novices" in the Church may, if they choose, and with the permission and under the direction of the Pastoral Service Order of the Church, engage in occasional social celebrations with their true intimates. ("Occasional" implies a maximum frequency of perhaps three or four times per year.) On such occasions there may be friendly mutual use (not private, self-indulgent use) of traditional dietary accessories, or the "gross" dietary elements, including meat, poultry, fish, eggs, refined sugar, prepared or "junk" foods, coffee,

386

tea, alcohol, and tobacco. Members of the Church may not, however, use "social" drugs or hallucinogens, or degenerative aphrodisiacs, such as marijuana, LSD, opium, yohimbe, and so forth.
(Such drugs promote a critically deluding effect that lasts beyond
the brief period of any social celebration, and such drugs in fact
prevent truly intimate or whole bodily human and devotional society at the time of their use.)

3. Any novice who feels that even the occasional and moderate
use of the permitted dietary accessories is either too degenerative or
too binding in effect on body, emotion, mind, as well as the
continuity of practice within the Church, should abandon such
accessories entirely.

4. Any novice who makes use of the dietary accessories should,
immediately prior to any such occasion, build up his vital condition
through appropriate dietary preparation. And, immediately after
any such occasion, the individual should purify the body-mind,
restore its balance, and revitalize its general state.

5. Novices who apply for membership in the esoteric order of
the Church should have matured in their daily practice to the point
where it has become quite natural to live without the gross dietary
accessories of social celebration. Thus, such individuals should have
lived completely free of all such dietary accessories for a period of
three months prior to application for membership in the esoteric
order.

6. Members of the esoteric order must strictly maintain practice
of the wholly regenerative diet and health regimen described in *The
Eating Gorilla Comes in Peace*. They must strictly avoid all "gross"
food elements, or dietary accessories, including meat, poultry, fish,
eggs, refined sugar, prepared or "junk" food, alcohol, tobacco, and
coffee, and they must continue to avoid all use of "social" drugs,
hallucinogens, and degenerative aphrodisiacs. They may, if they
choose, make occasional use of conventional tea (such as green or
black tea) as a tonic stimulant when critically fatigued.

Members of the esoteric order may, on certain occasions, be
given permission—or even the recommendation—to make temporary and brief use of some or all of the dietary accessories that are

periodically indulged by novice members of the Church. This might be done from time to time, at least in the case of some devotees, as a means of restoring a natural balance, when prolonged abstinence, coupled with intense practice of meditation and other disciplines, has resulted in symptoms of rigidity, loss of humor or relational feeling, and so forth. Such a departure from the regular disciplines must be done with the permission or under the direction of the Pastoral Service Order, and it would in any case be a rare or infrequent circumstance of practice.

7. The general dietary discipline of lay members, novices, and members of the esoteric order is to eliminate the "gross" elements of daily diet, and adapt to a natural, highly raw, lacto-vegetarian diet, in which only raw milk and raw milk products are used, or else a highly raw vegetable and fruit diet, including seeds, sprouts, and perhaps grains and nuts, and excluding all forms of milk and milk products.

8. The special dietary discipline of members of the esoteric order is to maximize the use of raw natural foods and minimize the more "earthy" food elements—or all dietary substances that represent an excess of protein, or which create an excessively acid or mucous effect in the body. Therefore, members of the esoteric order should minimize or, in some cases, even eliminate the use of milk, milk products, cooked grains (with the possible exception of natural brown rice), and breads. They should minimize cooked food in general, and take care to avoid overeating (as well as undereating). Cooked potatoes and cooked natural brown rice may be found to be sufficiently benign to include in the regular diet, but other cooked grains, and nuts and cooked beans as well, should be used in moderation, and perhaps only occasionally. Grains in general, and beans as well, should be kept in the diet, but most often in raw, soaked, or sprouted form. Salt, spices, and concentrated sweets, such as honey, should also be used in moderation.

9. When a member of the esoteric order applies for instruction in the final phase of the Way of Relational Enquiry, he must have comfortably adapted to a vegetarian diet, mostly raw, excluding all use of "gross" food elements, and at least minimizing use of "earthy"

food elements. Therefore, such an individual should have become habituated, for a period of not less than two months, to a dietary regimen that makes, at most, only moderate or occasional use of milk, milk products, salt, spices, concentrated sweets (such as honey), cooked grains and breads (with the possible exception of natural brown rice, which may be used quite frequently), nuts, cooked beans, and other sources of concentrated protein, as well as any foods or food habits that create overstimulation, constitutional imbalance, acid or mucous effects, or any tendency toward either toxemia or enervation.

388

10. Devotees who, as members of the esoteric order of the Church, practice the Way of Radical Intuition to the degree of full maturity, are, by virtue of their complete transcendence of the body-mind in the Divine, free of all formal or conventional obligations related to ordinary living. This does not mean that they are likely to engage in self-indulgent exploitation of gross dietary accessories, or any other degenerative practices of life. Rather, they have transcended the mechanics of desire in relation to the things of the body-mind. Thus, such devotees, as a matter of daily practice, quite naturally maintain the moderate and regenerative dietary practices that are native to the body-mind in its free state.

The difference between such devotees and others is just this ease and naturalness relative to the regenerative exercise of all functions. The lay member and the novice must practice the regenerative disciplines with a certain will or intention that counters the degenerative tendencies acquired from past habits of activity. But the mature devotee in the Way of Radical Intuition, who is fully surrendered in the Living Divine, is free of such subconscious and habitual tendencies toward degeneration, since they are only expressions of self-possessed recoil from the All-Pervading and Radiant Divine.

The Right Occasional Use of Stimulating Tea

As a daily rule, members of the esoteric order strictly avoid use of the gross dietary accessories. Therefore, even though they continue to engage periodically in mutual celebratory occasions, they generally (except on rare occasions) only make use of the foods that would otherwise be acceptable as a daily rule.

However, members of the esoteric order may make occasional use of conventional tea (such as black tea or green tea), as a stimulating tonic when there is unusual or <u>critical</u> fatigue, from lack of sleep or prolonged labor. On those occasions, if immediate rest cannot be taken, devotees may drink tea as a stimulant (in order to avoid accidents, critical loss of efficiency in necessary and important tasks, and various illnesses that can result from enervation).

Lay members and novices in the Church may also make occasional use of the stimulating properties of tea as first aid for critical fatigue (and, in the case of novices, as an accessory to periodic celebrations). But the practice should not be made frequent or habitual.

Conventional tea is inherently toxifying (a poison) and over-stimulating, and it creates both physical and psycho-physical imbalances. It has an enervating effect on the entire central nervous system, particularly the brain. (People drink tea casually, as a means of stimulating or "waking up" the brain, the adrenals, and so forth. But once the stimulation passes, the same mechanisms are even sleepier.) All of this can be proven by experience. Simply drink tea when you are in a purified and balanced physical condition.

Tea is a conventional dietary accessory, used as a relatively "harmless" or "mild" stimulant by individuals who otherwise also maintain a gross diet, with regular use of other gross dietary accessories, such as killed meat food, alcohol, and so forth. However, such tea may have an occasional right application, in the case of <u>critical</u> fatigue (not simple weariness), and, therefore, it is the only toxic stimulant that is retained for occasional use by devotees in the esoteric order of The Free Communion Church.

Even so, such devotees are advised to limit their use of conventional tea strictly to occasions of <u>critical</u> physical necessity (as a kind of first aid or medical treatment), and to avoid all exploitation of tea for the "high," or the casual and ultimately enervating pleasure of toxic stimulation itself. Although coffee would also provide similar emergency stimulation, it creates much more profound aggravation of the heart and the digestive tract, and so coffee is altogether avoided by members of the esoteric order, while tea is accepted for right occasional use.

The use of conventional tea should be a matter of good judgment, not degenerative permissiveness. Therefore, even though the use of conventional tea is logically permissible for occasions of critical fatigue, many members of the esoteric order may prefer to avoid such teas altogether. They may use other natural and nontoxic teas with a mildly stimulating effect.

Some Natural Stimulating Teas
   Ginseng
   Gotu kola
   Fo ti
   Peppermint
   Sassafras
   Sarsaparilla

Some Stimulating Herbs to Be Mixed in Teas
   Cayenne
   Ginger
   Clove

Ginseng is a general stimulating tonic to the circulatory, glandular, and nervous systems.

Gotu kola has an energizing effect particularly in the brain cells.

Fo ti particularly stimulates the energy in the navel.

Peppermint is a mildly stimulating and refreshing tea.

Sassafras and sarsaparilla are purifying and tend to stimulate energy in the brain. They have a synergistic effect when used together.

Cayenne, ginger, and clove are all purifying, tonifying, and generally stimulating. They can be mixed into any tea and are particularly good combined with honey in peppermint, sassafras, or sarsaparilla teas.

You Must Transcend Everything

Renunciation and Transcendence

Renunciation is a strategic act, motivated by the problems of self, or the independent body-mind in its constant alternations between temporal frustration and fulfillment. But transcendence is a natural process, realized through right application or adaptation of our various functions. Such right application or adaptation is a matter of intuitive sacrifice, or submission to the All-Pervading and Transcendental Divine, via all ordinary activities. Such is the Law of God.

Therefore, transcendence of our functions is a natural, necessary, and inevitable process or event, if we are Awakened to the Way of Sacrifice, which is the Way of Love and Eternal Life.

For this reason, it should be clear that the ultimate result or import of all functional practices of a personal, moral, or esoteric mystical kind that are engaged in the Way of Divine Ignorance is transcendence of all psycho-physical functions, practices, and results of practice.

This Way does not involve strategic renunciation, but it most certainly involves natural and progressive transcendence. This Way is the Way of transcendence and Translation of the separated self, or the disposition of the body-mind, into the Absolute and Eternal Divine, Who is the Transcendental Self and Radiant Person that Pervades and yet Transcends all manifest phenomena and all persons or beings in all worlds.

Thus, as devotees grow and mature in the stages of practice in this Way, they naturally demonstrate more and more of the signs of the transcendence of the separated or conditional self and its functions. This is made clear in my descriptions of dietary and sexual practice, as well as esoteric or meditational practice, relative to the four stages of the Way.

Thus, as devotees mature, their dietary practice first moves away from all gross forms of dietary indulgence—away from such food elements as animal flesh, alcohol, and tobacco. Then, as devotees enter into the later stages of practice, even the "earthier" food elements, such as milk, milk products, cooked grains (with the possible exception of natural brown rice), breads, cooked beans, nuts, salt, spices, and concentrated sweets (such as honey), are used either in moderation or only occasionally (and, in some cases, they are entirely avoided). Devotees thus enter into more and more direct association with the Primary Food Source, which is the All-Pervading Life of God. Eventually, in the Way of Re-cognition and the Way of Radical Intuition, the diet is naturally limited to those substances that serve as a most direct medium of connection or Communion with the All-Pervading Life, and that create the least tendency toward toxemia, psycho-physical imbalance, and enervation. Such is the most perfectly conservative and regenerative dietary practice.

Likewise, as devotees mature in their general practice, including adaptation to the self-sacrificial process of sexual communion, they naturally demonstrate the inevitable signs of the transcendence of eroticism (in thought, desire, and action), including gradual transcendence of the degenerative orgasm. In the Way of Re-cognition, the third stage of practice in the total Way, such signs provide a firm basis for steadiness of attention, breath, feeling, bodily disposition, and the bodily Current of Life-Force. Thus, natural transcendence of the egoic sexual motive gradually produces a native economy in sexual activity, whereby its frequency is moderated and its effects are conserved. And that sexual economy continues in the Way of Radical Intuition.

Just so, the esoteric practices of a meditative kind, which appear in various and progressive forms from stage to stage in the Way, are themselves a form of self-transcending psycho-physical adaptation and sacrifice. Therefore, although various mystical and yogic phenomena are experienced by these means, they are instantly transcended via the *conscious process* (as remembrance of God, enquiry, re-cognition, and radical intuition). In this manner, the stages of esoteric practice are, like those of dietary and sexual practice, self-transcending. And, in the Way of Radical Intuition, all phenomenal exercises of the body-mind are radically transcended in Perfect Absorption in the Absolute Personality that is the Divine Master and Real Self of every individual.

Sexual Communion Is a Spiritual Riddle
A talk given by Bubba Free John to his devotees

BUBBA: Most people are adapted in their self-possessed ways only to the eating and sexing and acquiring of their lower life. Sexuality is for most people the most essential, the most intense, of pleasures. It is the motive that guides them most profoundly. The dimension of food is actually more profound than sex, but the food dimension is easily satisfied in our middle-class life. Thus, we have energy left over for meditating on sex. People who have to struggle just to survive from day to day realize that sex is secondary to food, but once the demand for food is satisfied, and we are established in a more or less safe and continuous daily environment, then we have a great deal of energy and attention for sex. Under such conditions, sex becomes the principle of the social order. It has become so in our worldly and technological society. Sex is the mover.

If you have any powers of intelligence to observe your own life and experience, and the life and experience of others, not just others who are, like you, struggling with the ordinary desires of vital life, but those who have adapted to processes that are higher than the vital, then you may enjoy insight into your motivation, your desiring impulse. Such insight is the beginning of the awakening to spiritual life.

The Spiritual Master appears in the world to communicate right understanding of the causes of experiential existence, and right understanding of motivation, or desire. He lives in order to communicate the process of Real Life, wherein we are happy and free. The essential principle proposed by the Spiritual Master is that feeling-attention is the root and heart of our existence. At the present time, our attention is in the form of mind or desiring only. Attention has assumed the form of mind, the patterns of desire or tendency, fulfilled bodily through the senses. But if we can observe that process of attention, we can see how it arises, and we can intuit its true Condition. The true Way of Life is to realize attention in a form different from desire, or the tendencies toward experience. That form is Divine Communion, or Love-Communion with the Divine Reality. Every moment wherein we exist in Love-Communion with the Eternal Radiant Self of God, we enjoy the transcendence of desire, even of the world. In that moment, we already transcend everything, and we are free and blissful. Thus, the secret of Life is to live in such a disposition of free feeling-attention, or Love-Communion with God in every moment.

In your every moment you are, in the natural course of your life, performing all kinds of action. Therefore, you must find a Way to make all the natural things that you do into forms of Love-Communion with God. As soon as you awaken to this understanding in the Company of the Spiritual Master, you must change your act in general. You must no longer do the vulgar things that characterize one who does not love God, who does not enjoy constant Love-Communion with God. Over time, that kind of responsibility increases. More and more aspects of your life become purified and unnecessary. Even so, all kinds of activities remain that are normal and functionally obligatory. Therefore, through the instruction of the Spiritual Master, you must realize all of your ordinary activities—or all activities which are appropriate activities for a lover of God—as forms of Love-Communion with God.

395

Love-Communion is the transcendence of desire, the transcendence of mind, the transcendence of the body, the transcendence of ordinary existence in Bliss. But the things that you tend to do are generally, ultimately, and absolutely only forms of desiring, motivation, and mind. That is why they exist, even though they may otherwise be natural and apparently harmonious. The only reason natural activities exist at all is that they have been brought into being by desire, the tendency to be born in this psycho-physical condition. Therefore, you must purify your life of the gross lovelessness and self-indulgence that it represents, and then you must perform whatever activities that remain appropriate, but you must always perform them as forms of Love-Communion with God.

One who performs all his actions in this manner is already in a position of freedom, of self-transcendence. He is not truly fulfilling desires anymore. He is, for the time being, engaging in forms of appropriate action, which ultimately are expressions of desire. While this bodily form exists, he performs those actions that are appropriate, but always as a process of literal God-Communion. In every moment of functional activity, his attention is yielded into the Radiant Force and Consciousness of Reality.

Therefore, the devotee who begins this Way of Life is one who has awakened to God through the consideration of the process of attention. He is awake to the nature of desire. He sees how all desire is a self-possessed, fearful motive, based on a feeling of separate consciousness. Therefore, having seen what attention is all about, he must begin to transform his entire life, the entire disposition of the body-mind. Such a devotee begins by eliminating all of the grosser self-indulgence that his old way of life represents. Once he sees what is left over after that, he acknowledges that he must live those activities as forms of God-Communion. If he will do that, then he is always already in a position of transcending all of the things that those activities represent. He naturally transcends all forms of self-satisfaction, all forms of turning away from God, and all forms of the fulfillment of attention, or the desire for experience.

396

From the traditional ascetic point of view, the immediate and strategic renunciation of everything is obligatory. However, spiritual life in Truth is self-transcendence, and mere renunciation is not necessarily an act of self-transcendence. It is, in general, a motivated activity based on mental understanding, without feeling. It is founded in a problem rather than in Bliss. It is as self-possessed as any fulfillment of ordinary desire. It is itself a method of fulfilling another kind of desire. Traditionally, sex is among those things to be immediately renounced. It is true that we must transcend the self-possessed motive in our sexuality, but we will not do so merely by renouncing sexual activity. To renounce sexuality without having transcended it is unintelligent. It is only a degree more intelligent than the decision to indulge yourself in sex. Neither of these gestures—to exploit or to renounce—is truly intelligent. They are equally based on problematic self-possession rather than present God-Communion.

The devotee in the Way of Divine Ignorance abandons his gross orientation toward his sexuality on the basis of truly "hearing" the Teaching. He is converted in his disposition through understanding and insight. He presumes that sexuality is not in principle negative. He considers the process of sexuality intelligently, and he lives as a sexually polarized person. He considers how sexuality may be lived as a form of God-Communion, rather than self-possession, or casual and consoling fulfillment of desire. Sexual communion is, first of all, the living <u>consideration</u> of sexuality. It is not simply a functional practice. It is the consideration of sexuality <u>through</u> practice—through practicing sexuality as a form of God-Communion.

The whole affair of sexuality, in the midst of spiritual life, is a kind of spiritual riddle. Sexuality, as all things in this life, is created through desire, through the movement of attention into an independent self-consciousness. Thus, at first the devotee is oriented to the practice of sexuality through desire. But he is attempting to reorient his sexuality toward God, through God-Communion, through practicing sexuality as sexual communion. Eventually, however, he must awaken to the fact that the disposition that is the true foundation of sexual communion inherently transcends sexuality.

In every moment of God-Communion, attention is liberated from all forms of mind and desire, and the body-mind dissolves in the Blissfulness of God-Realization. Sexual communion is the process of God-Communion as it may be realized in the moments of sexual activity. But if in this moment you are indeed surrendered in your feeling and attention into God-Communion, there is no necessary or binding motive to sexual activity. Eventually, people who practice this process of sexual communion realize that they always already enjoy transcendence of sexuality. They are not obsessed with sexuality, it is not necessary, and there is no longer any negative or self-possessed purpose to sexual activity.

To practice sexual communion is to be already free of desiring. Once you truly awaken to this inherent freedom, the necessity of the conventional sexual game disappears. You realize that you are free of it, that you are not obsessed with sex, that you are not possessed by sex, that sex is not the principal pleasure of existence, and that existence itself is a Transcendental Condition of absolute Blissfulness that has nothing whatever to do with sex or anything bodily or mental.

What is said in the traditions is true: The spiritually realized individual should not practice the habitual desires of the usual man. He should not degenerate himself through sex, he should not be frivolous with diet, he should not be frivolous at all. He should, in other words, show all the outward signs of renunciation—or self-transcendence and self-control. But in the true spiritual practice of life, the only way to be a true renunciate, or a free human being, is to have already transcended the things in life for which you must be responsible, not merely to resist them. The motive of strategic renunciation is false and unintelligent. The individual who has transcended these motivations <u>looks</u> like a renunciate, or a responsible and self-controlled person, because he does not indulge himself. His pattern of living is purified in God-Realization. He is not self-consciously avoiding the conventional objects of desire—in order to look like a renunciate. He is simply Awake in the natural transcendence of experiential desire. Through enlightened understanding, he has become Awakened only to God.

Mature devotees in The Free Communion Church look like renunciates, because they have become literally free of all forms of self-indulgence through the natural disposition of self-transcendence in God. This is not to say that such devotees must also leave the world in order to live in utter solitude. It is not necessary to live in a cave in the world. You must live in God. Then life takes on a natural form, a loving and relational form, a radiant form. Life ceases to be the fulfillment of conventional obsession or self-possessed desire, but simply because you do not indulge the obsessive desires of the worldly consciousness, it does not necessarily follow that you must be a dried-up ascetic living in a dried-up room. On the contrary, such a devotee represents the truest human type, the self-transcending individual who lives in God, who is not manipulating himself, but who is free in God, through the release of feeling-attention in God-Communion moment to moment.

The mature devotee lives a higher human life, a truly human life, a radiant, loving, serving life, in the midst of which he also appears to the usual man to be relatively ascetic. But true devotees do not feel "ascetic." They are perfectly happy. They enjoy their diet, for instance. It happens to be healthful, and it gives the body Life. They enjoy their marriages and their friendships. Their marriages, for instance, are not an endless routine of conflict and erotic obsession and degenerative orgasms. Their married life is a life of love, of mutual service, in which both partners live always in Divine Company, and they are both constantly purified in that Realization. They have no inherent sexual problems, nor any need either to casually indulge the sexual mechanisms of the body or to strategically suppress or avoid the regenerative and pleasurable exercise of their sexuality in relation to one another.

Anybody who must force himself to struggle with sex is not a true renunciate. Anybody who has a great deal of difficulty eating a relatively economized and simple diet is not a true renunciate. He has not transcended his vital desires. The conventional or willful renunciate merely likes the idea of transcending desire. That is why he tortures himself with all kinds of disciplines for which he is not suited. He simply has not yet understood anything. He is trying to approximate the qualities of a true devotee before he represents the mature understanding that is the heart of the devotional Way of Life.

399

In our discussions in the past, those who have come to me as devotees have tended to represent a rather shallow understanding of their relationship to desire. They discussed sexuality as if it were something over which they had no control. Sexuality was viewed as something terribly profound and necessary. Whenever renunciation was considered, it always seemed problematic to them. They always assumed a weak position relative to these desires. "Can I live as a renunciate? Can I do without sex? Can I be free of obsession?" But the principle of freedom from sexual desire is not to decide against sex. The principle of that freedom is in your consciousness, in your understanding, in your present and bodily yielding of attention and feeling into the Infinite Divine.

The transcendence of sexuality involves a profoundly intelligent, clear-minded, mature look at the strategies you embody. You should not talk in precious terms about your desires and wonder whether you can do without them. You have been very aggressive sexually. You have not been overwhelmed by desire. You have overwhelmed yourself with desire. It is not sex in itself that motivates you. Rather, it is because you are so determined to remain self-possessed, to be oriented to your self through accumulation of experience, that you are not living in God. You are living in yourself only. Thus, you require all kinds of desires, all kinds of patterns and habits, in order to satisfy yourself. And you are afraid. You are not inherently blissful and happy.

You acquire moments of pleasure, or pseudo-blissfulness, through satisfaction of desire. But your life is essentially a form of conflict, a form of seeking for permanent satisfaction that never comes. There is no physical or mental exercise of sexuality that will gradually free you of sex. In sexual communion, it is the principle in understanding, the <u>disposition</u>, not the physiological exercise, that transcends sex desire. The physiological exercise will not free you of desire. You will always find some way to satisfy yourself, some way to crave within the practice.

400

The <u>disposition</u> of sexual communion is inherently free of sexual desire. The physiological practice is only the theatre in which that disposition may become active. To mechanically practice sexual communion will not make you a devotee, a renunciate, a free individual who has transcended sex. That is what the mature devotee realizes. When he fully realizes the <u>disposition</u> of sexual communion, then he is already or inherently free in relation to sex. Until then he is merely practicing sexual communion as a process of "consideration," a theatre in which eventually to Awaken to the true and free disposition of the devotee. But the mature devotee is, on the basis of a Divinely Awakened disposition, a natural renunciate, or one who has transcended the conventional motives in all desires.

The true disposition implied in the Teaching of sexual communion is the disposition implied in all descriptions of practice in the Way of Divine Ignorance. It is the disposition of present Love-Communion, the turning of feeling-attention into the Living God. It is Ecstasy, or self-transcendence. Therefore, consider the Teaching relative to sexual communion and all other practices of daily life that are appropriate for devotees. When you Awaken to the disposition of God-Communion, then you will quite naturally be a renunciate, a free man or woman. Then you will no longer need to consult your interior, your desires, to see how free you are today. Rather, you will abide in that disposition that is inherently turned to God-Communion. Whatever casualness exists in the psyche, in the mind, in the world, will be superficial, not worthy of problematic worrying and struggling with motivations. There are no motivations to struggle with. Simply yield yourself in this moment, with full attention and feeling, into the Divine. If you do that, then the content of the body-mind becomes superficial. You will not be reinforcing it, nor will you be bound by it. You will not be motivated to fulfill it. It will all have essentially become obsolete, because you live in God-Communion, no longer in that disposition that makes the body-mind necessary, or that creates it in fact.

Therefore, the body-mind ultimately falls away, forgotten in Bliss. Just as obsessive sexuality falls away when it is transcended, so the body-mind itself falls away in the disposition of God-Communion. There is no body-mind in God-Communion, absolutely nothing of that kind. There is simply absolute Bliss. The body-mind is permitted to fulfill right obligations, pure obligations, as long as it persists, but nothing is done with it or to it to fulfill it, to cause it, or to create an alternative likeness of it in some supercosmic realm. The devotee rests in the Principle that is prior to attention, and the body-mind falls away completely. It is not a matter of migrating to another realm, or of reincarnating in this one. There is no disposition that creates experience. Nor is there the disposition of interiorization or separation from experience. There is simply the Radiant Life, the self-transcending Way of Life. All experiences that persist in the present moment are lived in the Radiance of God-Communion.

If it is in the Will at Infinity to cause lifetimes to continue, then that is the business of God, but the devotee is not concerned about possibility. He is quite naturally mindless, bodyless, ecstatic. The true disposition, the true Ecstasy of the devotee does not necessarily or always appear in the outward forms that people conventionally acknowledge to be ecstatic. It is not necessary to roll the eyes in the head or to roll the body around the floor to be in a condition of Divine Ecstasy. Divine Ecstasy transcends the body-mind. Thus, it is quite compatible with all the ordinariness of the body-mind. The quietness of the body-mind is just as much the vehicle of Divine Ecstasy as its thrills. Ultimately, the Transcendental Ecstasy of the devotee is not truly registered either bodily or mentally. The ecstatic thrills that we associate with mentally intoxicated states of devotional realization do not alone or especially characterize the Disposition of the devotee. This Disposition transcends the body-mind, and therefore the characteristics of Divine Ecstasy may not be identified in any particular form of bodily or mental existence or experi-

401

ence. Rather, all actions and states are expressions of the Ecstasy of the mature devotee. In general, the devotee simply becomes full, radiant, a loving, serving, free person.

Enlightenment and Perfection

The Enlightenment of the Whole Body is not a matter of the perfection or immortalization of the psycho-physical body itself. Rather, it is a matter of the Perfect Transcendence of the psycho-physical body by the Free soul, or the Self in God.

The various disciplines associated with the Way of Divine Ignorance are not methods for the purposeful perfection and immortalization of the body, or even of the psychic being (the soul in its association with subtle phenomena). Rather, they are simply ways of turning each and every function into Divine Communion, or Love-Sacrifice of the soul in God.

The practice of each kind of discipline—such as the regenerative diet, or the process of sexual communion, or the exercise of esoteric meditation after the Awakening of the Life-Current of the body by the Touch of the Spiritual Master—does in fact tend, secondarily, to produce psycho-physical effects, such as purification, harmonization, rejuvenation, and regeneration. Even more extraordinary phenomena may appear, such as enlarged psychic powers, uncommon internal experiences of a yogic kind, and even superior physical states, such as exemplary health, extreme longevity, the transfiguration or infusion of the body by light, and bodily translation into light.

However, such phenomena are merely the caused results of manifest processes in the Realm of Nature, or Energy in Motion. They represent the coverings of the soul, not the Destiny of the soul when Awakened to its Real and Eternal Condition—or the Self Absorbed in God. Therefore, these results are not the motive of practice in the Way of Divine Ignorance. They are secondary evidence or possible effects of the practice, but they are not the goal of practice. Indeed, all such phenomena—all experiential phenomena of the psycho-physical being—must become a sacrifice in Divine Communion.

Therefore, the Principle of all practices in this Way is Sacrifice, or Divine Communion, enacted as a literal discipline in every dimension of the body-mind. Whatever arises as a result of any practice must likewise be made a sacrifice, through insight and the resort to Love-Communion with the Living God.

In any case, the phenomena that are likely to arise will vary greatly from individual to individual. The casings or manifest psycho-physical expressions of the soul are the product of acquired tendencies that have led to the present birth. Therefore, each individual represents different strengths, weaknesses, tendencies, and capabilities in each area of the human psycho-physical structure. Some may never be capable of even superior health, while others may never experience profound psychic phenomena. All, however, must submit each function to the same law, in order to Commune with God through that function, and in order to transcend the tendencies or habit-energies associated with that function. Every one will be given whatever lessons, experiences, successes, and failures are necessary for his or her maturity in Self-Realization and the Ultimate and Perfect Transcendence of attachment or necessity relative to the possibilities of psycho-physical experience, high or low. Therefore, only the Sacrifice is guaranteed. Everything else must be Transcended. And only such Transcendence allows our Sacrifice to be the Realization of the Bliss that Transcends even the attainment of Bliss.

Innocent manipulation of one's own genitals as well as inquisitive inspection of the genitals of others is natural and harmless in the first two stages of life, but sexual intercourse and even masturbatory orgasm would tend to be traumatic and an inhibitor of right psycho-physical development.

In the third stage of life, sexual intercourse and masturbation to the point of orgasm may become fascinating interests. But it is profoundly important at this stage that the individual be instructed and obliged relative to a right and truly human sexual responsibility. Thus, in the third stage of life, the individual should abstain from sexual intercourse and masturbation, and he should become responsible for the control of sexual energy and erotic imagination, or else he will become sexually self-indulgent and tend to be retarded in his heartfelt transition to the fourth stage of life. (In The Free Communion Church, young individuals who are maturing in the third stage of life are instructed in the process of sexual communion—to be fulfilled in later marriage—as well as in the practice of whole bodily diffusion of casual genital energy apart from sexual intercourse, via the special exercise of the breath, which is to be randomly applied even prior to marriage.)

The first three stages of life are essentially a preparatory or foundation period of humanizing adaptation and growth, guided by practical, moral, and rudimentary religious education. In the fourth stage of life, truly human, relational, and self-transcending sexual activity may rightfully appear, in the form of sexual communion in marriage.

The function of sexual communion and all other forms of practice in the fourth stage of life (or in the Way of Divine Communion, the Way of Relational Enquiry, and the first phase of the Way of Re-cognition) is to purify, harmonize, and positively transform the autonomic nervous system (the dynamic descending-ascending or expansive-passive mechanism) and the physical, emotional, and mental conditions of the gross body-mind.

The function of sexual communion and all other forms of practice in the fifth stage of life (or in the middle phase of the Way of Re-cognition) is the redirection of attention and occasional withdrawal of the Life-Current from the gross body-mind and the autonomic nervous system, resulting in confinement of the Life-Current in the central or cerebrospinal nervous system, particularly the brain core.

In the sixth stage of life (or the final phase of the Way of Re-cognition) there is no direct function for sexual communion, but the various specific practices of this stage serve the direct or discriminative intuition of the Radiant Transcendental Consciousness, prior to and exclusive of the body-mind in all of its parts and functions.

In the seventh stage of life there is native abiding in the Radiant Transcendental Consciousness, but the Radiant Transcendental Consciousness remains in free association with the functions of the body-mind (including the central nervous system and the autonomic nervous system). Thus, in the seventh stage of life, or the Way of Radical Intuition, sexual communion and all other right functional conditions or actions of the human body-mind simply express the free and nonbinding association of the Radiant Transcendental Consciousness with the play of psycho-physical experience. This free association remains until Divine Translation becomes Absolute.

Rules of Behavior in the Seventh Stage of Life

The strict maintenance of conservative or regenerative dietary, sexual, and other personal disciplines is necessary for growth in the first six stages of life, once commitment to the self-transcending Way of God-Communion truly begins. This is because the essence of practice in the developing stages is literal and even intentional submission of the body-mind to the Current of Life, rather than to mere experience, or sensual and mental or psychic objects in themselves. However, in the seventh stage of life, such disciplines are no longer necessary—since all processes of the body-mind have ceased to limit or bind the Radiant Heart. Even so, those disciplines have by then become natural, ordinary, and appropriate to the body-mind itself, which is under the Law of Nature. Thus, in the seventh stage of life, the conventional disciplines of the lower functions continue as a general rule—not because they are necessary, but simply because they are natural, ordinary, appropriate, and inevitable. However, the non-necessity of conventions of behavior in the seventh stage also accounts for the sometimes bizarre, unconcerned, unconventional, and even apparently worldly behavior of perfectly Enlightened individuals, particularly in their instructive Play with others.

406

The rule of practice is indeed the conversion and restraint of the tendencies of the body-mind. But the essence of Enlightenment is self-transcendence, or humorous freedom from the conditions of the body-mind. Therefore, even in the seventh stage of life, some individuals have taken occasional exception to the rule through humorously unconventional behavior. Mere self-indulgence is, of course, not the principle behind such behavior. Divine Humor, or Freedom, is the principle, which at times Communicates Itself through the unconventional or paradoxical behavior of Enlightened beings. In general, however, the individual in the seventh stage appears quite austere, pure, and Life-positive in his daily behavior, although he is under none of the restraints of Nature, and his actions are quite spontaneous and Full of Love.

Bodily Transcendence and Sexual Communion

As the devotee matures in the stages of practice in the Way of Divine Ignorance, his practice of sexual communion also matures. Thus, at first he transcends reactive and self-possessed emotional and erotic motivations. Then he realizes regenerative control over the orgasm, so that the energy awakened in the bodily thrill of sexual intercourse is directed toward the nourishment and enlivenment of the higher and the whole bodily functions. Gradually, a natural economy develops in his practice, so that its frequency coincides perfectly with the regenerative needs or patterns of the bodily being.

It can be said that motiveless celibacy is inevitable in the seventh stage of life—or the maturity of the Way of Radical Intuition. But permanent celibacy is only necessary and inevitable in the extremes of bodily transcendence, as in the approach to bodily Translation or bodily release at death. In practice, therefore, regenerative sexual communion may remain as part of the ordinary and humorous play of the individual in the seventh stage of life until the approach of death. (During the lifetime, periods of profound bodily transcendence are inevitable, and motiveless celibacy would pertain during such periods—but sexual communion might be resumed at other more ordinary phases of the bodily play of Life.)

Truly, to transcend the body is not to be bodily inactive. Rather, it is to be in a Disposition in which all bodily activity, including sexual activity, is engaged entirely as a form of Divine Communion, or Transcendental Sacrifice.

The Play of Sex in the Seventh Stage of Life

I n the seventh stage of life, or the Way of Radical Intuition, the experiential conditions of existence, including sex desire, are tacitly and continuously re-cognized to be only modifications of the Radiant Transcendental Consciousness. That is, the Free soul has ceased to feel itself to be either attached and identical to the differentiated conditions of experience or detached from them while abiding in some exclusive Absolute Position. Thus, the Free soul Realizes there is only the Radiant Trancendental Consciousness, and neither objects nor the inner or Free soul are different from That.

Therefore, in the seventh stage of life, the Free soul is simply and profoundly relaxed in the midst of the Realm of Nature, or the endless procession of changes and motivations. The body-mind, and the circumstances of the body-mind, are allowed to be whatever they appear to be, but they are re-cognized, tacitly and in every moment. Re-cognition, rather than any form of reaction or indulgence, characterizes the Free soul's participation in the experiential conditions of existence. The Free soul simply and naturally abides in its own Condition, which is also the Condition of all phenomena.

In this manner, the conventions of mere reaction, indulgence, and, ultimately, even right, ordinary, responsive participation in the conditions of human experience, tend to become obsolete, through non-use. At last, the body-mind simply falls away, Outshined by the Radiant Transcendental Consciousness.

Devotees in the seventh stage of life are naturally Awake in the Radiant Transcendental Consciousness, the Love-Bliss of the Divine Person. However, except in the extreme Moods of Ecstasy, they allow themselves to participate in the natural Play of human events. They participate with ease, until they are finally and bodily Dissolved. They urge other people and all events toward a Lawful turn, but they do not expect experience to achieve a continuous or final perfection of order and fulfillment.

Insofar as such devotees continue to participate in the natural or Lawful order of psycho-physical or human events in general, they may also continue to engage in sexual communion. To the degree that sexual activity continues, it is simply a convention of natural love and affection, not of obsession. Sexual intercourse tends to vary in its frequency in the seventh stage of life. Motiveless celibacy may appear for various lengths of time. Eventually, because the Transcendental Mood or Ecstasy becomes so constantly profound, the Play of sex disappears, along with the body itself.

408

There Is a Right and Occasional Exercise of the Conventional Orgasm

T he entire Way of Divine Ignorance is free and Life-positive from the beginning. Therefore, its practice is not associated with any self-possessed, self-divided ascetic ideal, any more than it is compatible with equally self-possessed but grossly self-indulgent physical habits. The practice is always a matter of total psycho-physical submission to the Blissful Current of Life, which is the Radiant Transcendental Consciousness or true Self of all.

409

Therefore, the practice of sexual communion is simply the Life-positive and relational exercise of the human sexual function. In that practice, the bio-energy and endocrine chemistry of the living body are awakened, intensified, conserved, and communicated to the entire bodily being—rather than thrown off through casual and habitual orgasm of the conventional and degenerative kind.

The practical development of this regenerative sexual capacity has been fully described in this book, but I want to summarize it again, briefly, in order that a right and practical understanding may be brought to the matter of orgasm in particular.

In the first stage of the practice of sexual communion, individuals must deliberately bring body and attention into conformity with the essential psycho-physical process of sexual communion. Founded in awakened insight into the spiritual Truth of Life, the individual must move the bodily processes, via feeling-sympathy, into the Life-positive forms of relationship. And the sexually intimate relationship itself must, in this manner, become free, loving, and a matter of mutual responsibility. Then the practice of sexual communion must be deliberately and rightly practiced over time, until the irresponsible tendency toward degenerative orgasm is replaced by natural and regular responsibility for regenerative conservation of orgasm.

The stage of natural responsibility for the conventional orgasm is the second or middle stage in the development of this practice. It is referred to as the "inversion of orgasm" at various points in this book. During that stage, individuals practice sexual communion in a natural, non-obsessive manner, as frequently or infrequently as is otherwise appropriate in terms of their spiritual practice.

410   The orgasm is, at this stage, naturally or easily conserved, or redirected toward the whole body rather than directed downwards and outwards, through the genitals alone. This does not mean that conventional orgasm (including ejaculation in the case of the male) never occurs during this stage of practice. It is simply conserved as a rule, and without profound effort. But the conventional orgasm may be occasionally indulged, if the bodily conditions are such that the genital discharge will not produce a negative or enervating effect.

Thus, in both the first and the second stages of the practice of sexual communion, there are occasions when the body becomes too right-sided, or physically overstimulated. If this occurs from time to time, it may be found appropriate to indulge the genital discharge during sexual play (while yet practicing all of the other conservative aspects of sexual communion).

Also, for the sake of reproduction, the male body periodically and naturally produces a superfluous amount of seminal fluid, which, if not ejaculated for the purpose of reproduction, would be eliminated via urination. This superfluous reproductive fluid may be observed to appear in cycles, usually every three to four weeks. On those periodic occasions, pressure internal to the sex organs may be felt by the individual, quite independent of any mental or relational arousal of sexual desire. (This internal pressure is not to be confused with any of the common symptoms of sexual arousal. Nor is the natural cycle of this process truly observable in individuals who develop chronic tension or even seminal pressure in the genitals as a result of toxins in the diet, obsessive thought about sexual pleasure, and so forth. It is only in the body of the sexually responsible male individual that the true periodic signs of the superfluous generation of reproductive fluid may be observed.) Thus, responsible male individuals who practice sexual communion may find it appropriate, positively relieving, and quite harmless to indulge the urge to ejaculation on such periodic occasions, with a frequency of perhaps once in every three to four weeks. (Such individuals also, of course, allow the ejaculatory orgasm on occasions when conception is intended, and, on those occasions, the orgasm should be fully permitted and deeply felt, in order to concentrate as much physical and psychic energy as possible into the plane of the reproductive organs of both partners.)

411

Female individuals may find it similarly appropriate to indulge the genital orgasm approximately once each month, timed in association with the monthly reproductive cycle. The biochemical energy of the female body is generally heightened to a degree at the time of ovulation, as a natural gesture or motive toward the generative sexual embrace. But the sensation of superfluous biochemical energy is usually heightened most potently during the eliminative phase of the reproductive cycle, as menstruation approaches, and during the period of menstruation itself. Thus, in the female, the natural periodic urge to orgasm is generally associated with the eliminative urge in the reproductive system, and orgasm during the time just prior to menstruation, or during menstruation, may often tend to calm and stabilize the periodic tension in the individual. (Female orgasm at the time of ovulation is not the most essential or natural moment, since the conventional orgasm is eliminative. However, since the genital orgasm also energizes and rhythmically stimulates the reproductive system, it may be permitted during ovulation whenever conception is intended.)

In any case, whether male or female, indulgence of the conventional or genitally confined orgasm should not be done casually. Rather, this practice should be done intelligently, on the basis of practical self-observation relative to the biochemical phases and states of the body and the general sense of vitality.

Thus, in both the first and second stages of the practice of sexual communion, conventional orgasm is generally conserved, but it may be occasionally indulged, if and when the mature individual makes the judgment that it is an appropriate occasion to do so. That occasion should always be one wherein there is felt to be a superfluity or excess of bodily energy and internal bodily secretions. And, in any case, such indulgence of the genital discharge, or conventional orgasm, should be occasional (generally no more than once or, at most, twice in a month) and it should always be done while yet fully exercising all of the other bodily and feeling aspects of the process of sexual communion. (If the conventional orgasm is permitted more than once in the period of a month, it should generally be done on successive occasions—within a period of two or three days—that is, basically during the same period or occasion.)

The third stage of practical maturity in the practice of sexual communion is the stage of full maturity, wherein neither sexual activity nor sexual communion is either necessary or a hindrance to the regenerative Life-cycle of the bodily being. That is, at that stage, the regenerative "yoga" of the body-mind is spontaneous and constant, so that sexual activity no longer is maintained as a means of regenerative adaptation. Thus, for devotees in the seventh stage of life, sexual activity is ordinary, and unnecessary from the spiritual point of view. Some may come to rest in a motiveless celibacy at this stage. Others may remain sexually active, at least temporarily, but that activity neither adds to nor subtracts from their spiritual Realization of Life. And those who remain sexually active in the seventh stage of life always practice sexual communion, including the regenerative conservation of orgasm. However, they too may occasionally indulge the conventional genital discharge.

Therefore, orgasm is not merely taboo in this Way, nor is a fetish made of the avoidance of the conventional genital discharge. It is simply and always a matter of right and regenerative responsibility. And those whose sexual practice is mature and true should be able to engage the occasional orgasm, or genital discharge, in a Life-positive and ecstatic manner. However, if any individual observes that even moderately occasional indulgence of orgasm creates urges to habitual indulgence, or intensifies sexual obsessiveness, or creates bodily signs of enervation, or intensely distracts the mind, or interrupts the emotional harmony of the sexual relationship, or in any other way creates significant negative effects, then the practice should either be engaged extremely infrequently or else abandoned altogether. The occasional enjoyment of the conventional orgasm (within the general context of sexual communion) should be a matter of good judgment and feeling sensitivity, not periodic degenerative permissiveness.

413

The Regenerative Response
*A talk given by Bubba Free John
to his devotees*

BUBBA: We must be careful not to view the outward conservation or prevention of orgasm as an end in itself. In that view our disposition toward sexuality becomes negative, as when we strategically prefer celibacy to sexual activity. The true conservation of orgasm is not equivalent to the suppression or elimination of orgasm. The purpose of sexual communion is not to eliminate the orgasm, not to deaden the response that produces orgasm in the usual man, but to transform the orgasm. The response that ultimately produces orgasm in the usual individual is as much a part of sexual communion as it is of conventional sexual activity. Without that response, the regenerative usefulness of right sexual activity is lost. In sexual communion we are not trying to bring an end to the sexual Life-response. That response must be conserved, or preserved, transformed, and positively aligned to the Life-Current. A deadening of the response that would otherwise produce orgasm prevents the positive transformation of the orgasm. The deadening of the sexual response is a deadening of the natural yoga of the body. Merely to be celibate, you see, merely not to have sex, or merely not to have an orgasm, is not a regenerative practice. Merely not to have sex or merely not to have the orgasm has no ultimate yogic or spiritual value. Sexual communion is a process of right participation in sexual activity and right use of the tendency of orgasm, through conversion of our Life-responses, or heartfelt surrender and Divine Communion.

There are two forms of this awakening of the Life through sexuality. One is degenerative—it throws off the Life. The other is regenerative—it conserves or surrenders to the Life. The regenerative process does not eliminate the orgasm; it transforms the orgasm. Thus, the response that would otherwise produce the orgasm must continue to be present in sexual communion. Through right participation in the ecstatic or overwhelming pleasurable response, something occurs in the body that is regenerative and that serves the awakening of the higher functions of the brain. True yoga is not about avoiding sexuality or eliminating the orgasm. It is the process whereby attention in the Life-Current in the body is reversed, or made Life-positive. The true yogi, whether motivelessly celibate or sexually active, is "urdhvareta"—he has turned about or converted the motion of the sexual energy. He has not ceased to experience the sexual energy, nor has he merely or strategically deadened his sexual response or his Life-response; but, rather, he has turned it about. The Blissful Current of Life is fully active in the true devotee or yogi.

The regenerative thrill of orgasm is natural to sexual communion. It vibrates throughout the body and stimulates the glandular centers all over the body, including the centers of the brain, releasing the "soma," the higher chemistry of the body, and enhancing and enlivening the entire body with the Light of Life. Thus, devotees in the Way of Divine Ignorance do not try to avoid sexual activity, but engage it Lawfully, so that the regenerative orgasm (not the degenerative orgasm) is produced, and so that the regenerative thrill is magnified throughout the body and via the body, in love, to all relations, to the degree of Infinity.

Without this conservation of orgasm or positive bodily surrender to Life, we remain obsessed with the degenerative play of sex and all the moods and habits of separation and emptiness. As people mature in the practice of sexual communion, the response that would otherwise produce orgasm is intensified in sexual play. It is not suppressed or minimized, nor does it disappear. Thus, devotees

414

of the Living God continue to engage in sexual activity, because it has a positive value. Our point of view is not: "Since you are so obsessed with sex and cannot restrain yourself, then you may continue to have sex, as long as you will engage it in this conservative way and not have orgasm." No, our point of view toward sexuality is that sexual activity is essentially positive, both in bodily and human terms and in higher human and spiritual terms, if it is engaged as mindless bodily submission to the All-Pervading Current of Life.

415

Sexuality has a real and ultimate function, which we must value. That function is activated through a Life-positive sexual response, which does not deaden or suppress the response that would otherwise produce orgasm, but rather intensifies it, surrenders it to Life, and also conserves it within the body, so that the Life is not thrown off, but is made to vibrate throughout the body. That process is the function of sexual communion. Thus, the practice of sexual communion is different from the ascetic view of sexuality or the conventional religious and spiritual view, which are essentially motivated by the conceived dilemma of Life, the problem and solution games of negative Life-conception and negative views toward the functional Play of Life itself.

As people mature in this practice, then, the orgasm is converted, but it is not suppressed. Those who truly practice sexual communion do not lie with one another and have mechanical sexual intercourse with no responses of energy or feeling. On the contrary: All of the normal and pleasurable responses occur, but they are transformed through a different kind of attention than is brought to sexual activity by the usual man. Therefore, as people mature in the stages of practice in the Way of Divine Ignorance, their practice does indeed transcend sex, but it is a matter of transcending the negative, self-possessed, or anti-ecstatic activities and the degenerative effects of conventional sexuality. Sexual play becomes essentially a Life-positive, ecstatic, and regenerative practice. Devotees in the Way of Divine Ignorance may thus very well remain sexually active at every stage of practice, except perhaps for periods of time wherein certain states of functionally absorbing yogic transformation are in evidence (in which case it is natural to relax sexual activity for a period of time). When the bodily evidence of Divine Translation begins to appear in the maturity of one's spiritual life, one may or may not become immediately or permanently celibate. But the bodily mechanism that is otherwise active in sexual communion remains active even in the case of such celibacy, without the necessity of sexual contact.

416 Although devotees may become motivelessly celibate in the course of practice, factual celibacy is not itself the inherent sign of the transcendence of sexuality. Rather, the conversion of the movement of attention in the Bodily Current of Life is the sign of the transcendence of sexuality. That turnabout of attention and feeling in the Current of the body-mind, so that it serves the regenerative function, can occur even though conservative sexual activity continues. Thus, the majority of devotees in the mature stages of this Way are likely to remain occasionally sexually active, always engaging the regenerative or conservative flow of the Life-Current. By "conservative" I do not mean anything negative. I mean regenerative or Life-positive, rather than degenerative and Life-negative. Mature sexual activity is, likewise, not frequent but occasional, the frequency being determined by the qualities of the individuals involved.

Periods of natural or motiveless celibacy also appear in the case of all devotees in this Way, because of the heightening of the natural yoga and self-transcendence of the body-mind in the mature stages of practice. But there is no sex-negative point of view hidden in this Way of Life. It is quite natural that motiveless celibacy appear, at least periodically. And even those who remain sexually active are not obsessed with sexual activity. Thus, there naturally are periods of weeks or months from time to time when there is no sexual intercourse. In some cases it may become very natural at some point not to engage in sexual intercourse at all, except perhaps to conceive a child. In other cases, it is equally natural to remain sexually active in this Life-positive manner. Such Life-positive sexual activity can remain a natural attribute of the life of devotees as long as it is true, wholly regenerative, and ecstatic, or surrendered to Life, even in the higher stages of practice.

The right question is not, "Are you or are you not having sex?" but, "Is your participation in sex Life-positive or is it Life-negative?" To remain sexually active in this Life-positive way is not to be attached to mortal destinies in this world—as the conventional ascetics believe—because the devotee does not engage in sexual activity for its own sake. The sexual activity of devotees is a form of God-Communion. They need not stop being sexually active in order to be free. Their sexual activity is itself a form of freedom. It is not binding—it is self-transcending. It is not obsessive, nor is it degenerative. It is ecstatic participation in the positive, inherently pleasurable, or Blissful activity of the Life-Current. And it has even bodily virtues: It intensifies the amount of available or unobstructed Bio-Energy and regenerative blood chemistry, and it sends the vibratory effects of the Life-Current into all areas of the body.

Enlightenment Is a State of Body, Not of Mind

Enlightenment is not a higher state of mind. It is not a glorified state of the inward or subjective being. Enlightenment is a bodily Condition. It is a matter of the transcendence of mind, all inwardness, and all illusions of independent existence. It is a matter of relationship, not inwardness. It is a matter of the conversion of attention from exclusive fascination with the objects, states, desires, and mental reflectiveness of the subjective disposition. It is a matter of the dissolution of attention in the Transcendental Reality, the Living God. In this manner, Radiant Life Transfigures the body, and the mind is Dissolved in Transcendental Consciousness. Enlightenment is Love.

Therefore, the Way of Enlightenment is not a Way of bodily asceticism, separative inversion, chronic inwardness, problematic self-manipulation, concern for the attainment of internal and mental states of experience, and so forth. Rather, it is a matter of the bodily conversion of attention. The objects and conditions of our various relations, gross and subtle, are not abandoned or even embraced for their own sake. Rather, all experiential relations are engaged as a medium of Love-Communion with the Living God. The experiential play of relations and actions is responsibly engaged by the true devotee. His actions are made to conform to the Lawful pattern wherein Life is always enhanced and Love is glorified. But all of his actions are engaged as instants of bodily Love-Communion with the Living God.

Thus, the true devotee is neither an ascetic nor a self-indulgent individual. His actions are right, but they are also essentially ordinary, natural, and regenerative, or Life-positive. The key to his actions is not the inversion of attention and the strategic avoidance of relationship. Rather, the key to his actions is the conversion of attention in the midst of relations—or the intuitive conversion of bodily participation in the All-Pervading Life. It is not a matter of the strategic control of body by mind and desire—but it is a matter of the transcendence of mind and desire in bodily Love-Communion with the All-Pervading and Transcendental Reality.

Therefore, devotees in the Way of Divine Ignorance are first purified in their disposition and activity through true "hearing" and "seeing" in the Company of the Spiritual Master. But then they are regenerated, even bodily, in Love-Communion with the Living God.

In the process of purification, the conventional and obsessive disorder of the body-mind is transcended. Thus, the devotee transforms his participation in the patterns of relations, of food and sex, and so forth. But, beyond such purification and transformation of his action, his action does not become less and less. That is, after an initial period of purification and responsible change of habits, the process of the Way is simply one of the conversion of our functional processes, not their suppression.

Thus, for instance, devotees in the Way of Divine Ignorance do not pursue an intentional celibacy. Celibacy is merely the non-use of the sex-function. Rather, devotees in this Way become responsible for the obsessive and self-possessed pattern of mind and desire in relation to sex. Then they freely engage in the regenerative sexual process—wherein neither sex nor orgasm is avoided, but wherein both are converted. Only the conversion of sex and orgasm serves a right and regenerative purpose. Mere celibacy, without the natural yogic conversion of the bodily participation in Life, is a form of Lifeless self-possession. The suppression of sex is a habit devoid of Bliss and the Lawful valuation of Pleasure or Radiant Love.

419

Devotees in the Way of Divine Ignorance may thus remain sexually active even in the stages of highest spiritual maturity. Their sexual activity is a form of surrender to Life, in which orgasm is converted from an eliminative and degenerative discharge of Life to a bodily regenerative Communion with Life.

Likewise, devotees in this Way are Enlightened bodily in every function. Thus, body, not the mind, is the place of true Enlightenment. And only the bodily Enlightened devotee is in a position to transcend the body in Transcendental Ecstasy, in which the body itself follows the mind and is Dissolved in the Radiant Bliss of God.

Therefore, in the Way of Divine Ignorance, devotees do not first abandon the body and then glorify the mind. Rather, they first transcend the mind (or the process of experiential attention) and then the body is glorified by the Love-Radiance of Life. Then the body itself Dissolves in that same Radiance or Love wherein the mind is first to fall.

Transcendence of the Mind Is Enlightenment of the Whole Body

The mind is not out of control. The problem is that thought, which is a superficial reflection of the body-mind as a whole, appears to be independent of the body. We think that thought is the

420

mind. But the mind is actually beyond conception. The mind is simply motives, or unspoken desires, produced by past associations. The mind is directly manifested only as the body itself. Therefore, the body is the past. The past cannot be controlled. The mind cannot ultimately or finally be controlled. The mind survives while trying to control itself, functioning through thought, as if independent of the body, and as if independent of the Radiant Transcendental Consciousness. Therefore, the independent mind must be constantly transcended, or else there is no Realization beyond desire and the results of desire, or bodily existence as mind. But if the mind is transcended, then the Living Consciousness is Revealed, and all conditions of existence, high and low, are transparent in that Consciousness, while they are also clearly and presently perceived, prior to thought (which is present and chronic differentiation from the Absolute).

The mind, or desire, seems to cause physical or bodily action. But in fact the body is not other than the mind. Action is not caused by mind. Action is itself mind. It is only thought that seems to be separate from the body and to cause action. But thought is only a superficially differentiated part of mind, or the body-mind as a whole.

Because of the relentless continuation of thought and desire, the constant repetition of similar experiences and the chronic conflict between desires seem to be eternally caused, or necessary forever. Therefore, blaming the independent mind, we seek to control it. But this effort fails to dissolve the mind, since the body remains. Therefore, we seek to control the actions of the body. But the motives of the mind remain hidden behind all our self-control. Truly, body and mind are simultaneous with one another, and equally coincident with the Radiant Transcendental Consciousness. The body is only mind, and the mind is not other than the body. To play one against the other is frustrating, and fruitless, and an illusion founded in thinking, or disembodied mind. Therefore, at last, it becomes clear that the Way is not self-control any more than it is self-indulgence. Such efforts are forever founded in the conflict or separation between body and mind. The Way is total self-transcendence, or the Present and Ecstatic Surrender of the whole and entire body-mind into the Condition in which all of it is arising.

The self is not transcended in the control of body or mind. The self is transcended only in intuitive surrender of the body-mind as a whole into the Radiance of the Transcendental Divine. The self, or body-mind, is transcended only in Ecstasy, wherein the entire body-mind is entered into God-Communion. The body-mind must be constantly yielded into present God-Communion, wherein body and mind are simultaneously surrendered into Transcendental Consciousness and Radiant Life, or Love. The body-mind as a whole must be surrendered into Radiant Consciousness, or the All-Pervading Life, which is the Condition of Love.

If this is done moment to moment, via every function of the body-mind, in all relations, under all circumstances, and through every action, then the self is constantly transcended, the mind is constantly transcended, the body and all its conditions are constantly transcended. Then the strategy of self-indulgence and the strategy of self-control are both equally dissolved in a natural economy of existence, and mere existence is always transcended in Ecstasy, prior to thought, prior to desire, and prior to the body.

If thought and desire are stilled, the mind appears to have been transcended. But such is the illusion of mystics and yogis. The mind is transcended only if the body is made transparent in Consciousness. Therefore, if the true mind Dissolves in Radiance, even the body is Enlightened. And true Enlightenment is bodily Enlightenment.

When mind is transcended in Transcendental Consciousness, the past is Dissolved in Bliss. In that instant, the body is mindless, free of the past. Indeed, when the body is free of mind, the body is not created. Therefore, the body also Realizes the Radiance that is prior to self-definition and self-division, or the differentiation of the mind, wherein thought, inwardness, or subjectivity stands over against the body. The body becomes Transfigured in that Ecstasy. And then the body, in the same instant in which the last trace of self-differentiating mind is transcended in Consciousness, also Dissolves in the Radiant Bliss or Love wherein desire and thought and mind and self first appeared. The body is first and last.

The Way of Renunciation and the Way of Ecstasy

I f anyone renounces sexual activity, he discovers the mind in its place. The mind is all desires. Even if all desires are renounced, the mind remains. The mind is attention itself. But even if attention is renounced, the mind is victorious. The mind is the root of attention. It is the ego, Narcissus, the self-enjoyer, who renounces every one and every thing, for the sake of his own immunity from the threat in all relationships.

But if anyone truly transcends sexual activity, then he also transcends the mind. He transcends all desires, every gesture of attention, and the recoil of self from Infinity. Such a one transcends the person and the motive of Narcissus. Such a one has chosen the Way of Ecstasy rather than the Way of Renunciation. Such a one is Awakened to the true Self, through Eternal Communion with the Master of Love.

Therefore, renounce no thing and no one, but transcend every thing and every one. Do not struggle with the Force of desire and self-definition. Rather, be Awakened. Be turned about in your attention, your feeling, and your action. Let every moment of attention, feeling, and action be a moment of Ecstatic Love-Communion with the All-Pervading Radiance and Eternal Consciousness of the Living God, the true Self of all.

The Householder's Destiny and the Illusions of Traditional Holiness

T o choose to be an ascetic, to distinguish between the inner and the outer Man, to choose not to live and work and act and enjoy and even suffer in the world, is a frivolous decision in a society wherein there is no practical and cultural accommodation or necessity for such a habit or method of existence. Every individual must accept practical responsibility for himself as long as he lives. Even to choose not to marry is an uncommon and, in general, socially inauspicious choice. In the Way of Divine Ignorance, as well as in the common world, there is no special usefulness either in asceticism or in non-marriage. Rightly managed, marriage and regenerative sexual activity are parts of the ordinary and ecstatic enjoyment of Life. Therefore, marriage and sexual pleasure are not avoided by members of The Free Communion Church. And the Church and its culture benefit from the direct participation of every one of its members in the God-Realizing Way of Life.

Our Church has no priestly or monastic class. The complete Teaching and all of its practices are available to all members, and each one is directly responsible for Communion with the Spiritual Master and the Living God. Each one has the same range of practical possibilities and responsibilities, including personal, bodily and moral disciplines, service to the world, and service in relation to intimates and other members of the Church in general. And each one must also establish regular times of seclusion and privacy, in which to engage in devotional and spiritual practices of the highest or most perfect kind. We do not require a unique class of individuals who, more than anyone else, or instead of everyone else, live the Way of Life in God.

Such priestly or monastic classes do exist in almost all extant traditional sacred societies. The Roman Catholic Church, for instance, supports celibate priests and nuns who serve in the outer community, and it also supports celibate monks and nuns who live entirely in seclusion. The institution does not support such people on the basis of pity or indulgence. Rather, it is presumed that lay members of the Roman Catholic Church benefit from the life of prayer and seclusion of "holy" individuals—that is, individuals who are "set apart" to perform sacred activities in the name of the Church community as a whole.

424

The traditional presumption behind "holy vocations" is that individuals who work and enjoy in the world are to be permitted only indirect responsibility for religious and spiritual activity, because of their inherent worldliness. And they, therefore, need to support a priestly and monastic class that has direct and even proprietary access to the means of salvation. Thus, over time, the "holy classes" begin to signify the only true Way of Life, while to live and love in the world signifies a secular and even "unholy" career, in which salvation is made possible only by institutional fiat, or the vicarious association with "holy substitutes." Thus, the "holy activities" of priests replace or at least supplement the true and higher wisdom and morality of the lay membership, and liturgies and ritual sacraments replace actual mystical and spiritual Realization in the case of "ordinary" people.

The traditional model of "holy" versus "ordinary" roles within the sacred community need not pertain when every member is obliged to enter into a right, full, whole bodily understanding of human existence. The Free Communion Church is founded on that understanding. Thus, it is not simply the householder life or the sexual conditions of marriage that characterize devotees in this Way —it is the acceptance of all the natural cultural or broad social and relational obligations of one's birth as the framework within which to live the God-Realizing practice. To choose God, to choose a life totally devoted to God-Realization, no longer means that you must drop out of the world of conventional human relations. That is the choice one makes in the extant and less ancient traditional societies, wherein the spiritual vocation is commonly associated with subjective inversion and "holy" other-worldliness. But from our point of view the choice of the God-Realizing life is not a matter of psychic inversion and other-worldliness, nor is it a matter of obsession with the ordinary or vulgar things of this world. It is a matter of Realizing the Living God as the Truth of Life, and God-Communion as the Way of Life. And it is a matter of Awakening to the insight that the functional conditions of relationship, the natural and psychic conditions of one's birth, are the theatre within which one must live the God-Realizing Way of Life.

One must realize a non-problematic orientation to one's ordinary functional existence. One must become committed to the condition of relationship, rather than exclusive or subjective inversion. One must simply devote oneself to God through the natural form and purify the body-mind of all of the reactive and self-possessed habits that became associated with it prior to one's direct commitment to God. All of the forms of self-possession that have become part of the ordinary conditions of the body-mind must be overcome. But, the ordinary phenomena of human experience need not, in principle, be avoided or abandoned. We should not become other-worldly while transcending our worldliness. Thus, in The Free Communion Church, we do not set apart a professional vocation of asceticism, or seclusion of a few for the sake of all. In general, devotees accept the conditions of the householder, or the married person, and everyone is responsible for the most sacred or "holy" vocation—not symbolically or nominally, but literally and fully.

By avoiding marriage one does not get closer to God—one only avoids marriage! There is no special pleasure in avoiding sex or marriage. Thus, in most cases, devotees in The Free Communion Church marry. But to marry is not just to choose to live in sexual intimacy with another person. It is to choose the householder's destiny, and to choose that destiny from a spiritual point of view. When one marries, one acknowledges and accepts right responsibilities of service to God and humanity. One chooses the relational life of self-transcendence in the midst of activity, rather than the self-bound life in the seclusion of subjectivity. Such responsibility must be understood to be inherent in the decision to marry.

Many "holy" people today advocate psycho-physical inversion, asceticism, and the avoidance or suppression of sexuality. And because of the self-divided, guilty orientation people commonly have toward sex, they tend to become fascinated and impressed by this argument. Sometimes "holy converts" give up sex for awhile, but celibacy is very troublesome for them. Usually they abandon that determination eventually—but they remain self-divided and all the more guilty about sex!

The many swamis, religious monks, nuns, and yogic ascetics who travel about trying to persuade people to abandon or "sublimate" sexual activity represent a conventional point of view that is not necessary to the Fullness of Life in Truth. Mere asceticism is nothing more than another form of self-possession. The "holy" aura that surrounds self-denial and inwardness seems to indicate some kind of unique closeness to God. But it is only an aura granted by our childish self-doubt. In Truth, it is not such "holiness" that Realizes God, but only Ecstasy Realizes God—and Ecstasy requires the transcendence of the self-possessed motives of both introversion and extroversion.

Asceticism does not necessarily have anything at all to do with God-Realization. A person can be a fierce ascetic and a passionless invert and be just as far from God-Realization as any libertine. Therefore, discriminate between your various persuasions. And be wary of the instruction promoted by professional ascetics, just as you should be wary of the deluded fancies and dogmas of conventionally self-indulgent or worldly people. The professional ascetic has chosen a vocation that may be logical within his or her traditional culture, but the method of "holy abandonment" is becoming both culturally and personally untenable, as a result of the greater Communication of Truth in the world. Your own fascination with the idea of asceticism and inversion is simply part of your own guilt, your own self-division. It is not necessary or useful to abandon sexuality in order to Realize God. Abandoning sexuality yields no such result. One surely must become responsible for one's sexuality, and one must transcend its self-possessed and self-possessing force in any case. But the question is not whether to have sex or not.

The modern advocates of asceticism in general even argue from a non-traditional point of view relative to the decision to be ascetic. Modern advocates argue against sex itself, as if they themselves were immune to all pleasure. But the more ancient or orthodox traditional reasoning for not having sex was not based on a negative attitude toward sex in itself. Rather, it was based on an understanding of what human life is altogether. There is no convincing argument against sexual pleasure in itself. It is what it is. The more ancient or orthodox traditional argument against sex was not based on a conviction that sex is in any sense pleasureless. Some of the consequences of sexual indulgence may be pleasureless or painful, but what was criticized from the orthodox ascetic point of view is the total affair of life in the world—the human, bodily-born, social life. The classical orthodox ascetic was not avoiding sexual pleasure especially, but he was avoiding being married, having children, having to have a job, having to be at work in the world. The orthodox ascetic fears and wants to avoid such responsibilities—all of the implications of what it is to be married, all of the attachment and responsibilities that marriage, householding, and social responsibility represent.

When the orthodox traditional ascetic chooses the inverted life, he is not choosing to avoid pleasure. Rather, he is choosing to avoid pain, the pain of born and social existence, and he therefore chooses not to marry and not to be sexually active. In contrast, the conventional advocate of the ascetic life today wants people to abandon sex because he thinks there is something wrong with sexual pleasure itself. Such a person plays on the guilt and negativity and self-doubt of ordinary people, including himself. And, in any case, human beings in general have no business giving up sex, or marriage, or social responsibility, or sacred devotional and spiritual practice. In Truth, we must be transformed in our understanding of the body-mind, our relationship to the natural world and the human world, and our relationship to sex and to pleasure in general. We have no business giving up the world, but, rather, we need to be transformed in our relationship to the world.

"Ordinary" people need to become oriented toward God-Communion in the form of all of their activities. They need to Realize the holiness that is native to human existence, not the deluded "holiness" of inversion and seclusion, in which Man is denied or, in some cases, glorified, but not transcended. The question is not, "Shall I perform the activities of ordinary, worldly life or not?" but, "What is the right relationship to them? What is the right use of every human possibility? How are common activities transformed into forms of God-Communion?" That is the consideration you must bring to the ordinary things of human experience.

Therefore, the vocation of the professional invert has become obsolete in our Church. It is obsolete from the point of view of the Divine Truth and the Way of Divine Ignorance. The strategic life of the professional invert is not a generally appropriate or necessarily spiritual response to the conditions we encounter by birth. It is not that we must not enter into the highest or most profound reaches of spiritual Realization. Yes, we must also be responsible for the dimensions of experience that the ascetic encounters in his inwardness. While participating in our responsibilities at the ordinary human level, we must also be responsible for the subtler dimensions of our experience, and we must likewise transcend them. We who are Free as Man do not even choose the phenomena experienced within the highest plane of the psyche. The ascetic chooses them, but we are Free to transcend them. We are Free to transcend the body-mind entirely and not to pursue any aspect of our experience as the Goal of spiritual practice. We are obliged to transcend every aspect of experience at every moment through Love-Communion with the Living God.

The Ascetic Problem and the
Freedom of True Devotees

The world-renouncing ascetic considers his born existence to be a problem. He feels himself always confronted by two great alternatives: Sex and God. He feels obliged to choose one or the other. He struggles to choose God. But the God he chooses is only an aspect of his own experience, a modification of his own body-mind. It is the God who is the opposite of sex, the alternative to sex, at the opposite terminal of the body.

The ascetic suffers himself as a problem. He considers his own body to be structured like a problem. There is sex, or the experience of the world, at one end. And there is God, the inner and higher mind, or the brain in itself, at the other end. He chooses what is within and above, and he abandons what is below and without. He is at war with himself, and even what he chooses as God is only a part of himself.

But the self-transcending devotee of the Living God is Awake to the Truth that precedes all problems, all solutions, and all experiential choices. He enjoys insight into his own dilemma, his own motivations, his own strategic efforts. He is free of the alternatives that troubled ascetics see mapped in the body-mind. He has realized that the truly Great Alternatives are not two forms of experience or two aspects of the body-mind. The Great Alternatives that truly confront him are not Sex and God, but self and God. And the consideration of these Alternatives does not produce a dilemma or division in him. The two Alternatives are not within himself. Rather, they are the two possible orientations of himself. He may turn upon himself by exploiting his relations, for the sake of the pleasures of such experience. (Such is the choice of the libertine.) Or he may turn upon himself by strategically renouncing his relations, for the sake of the pleasures of inwardness. (Such is the choice of the ascetic.) But the ultimate Alternative to both of these choices is self-transcending Love-Communion with the All-Pervading and

Transcendental Divine. And such is the free choice of the true devotee.

The true devotee is free of the double-bind of problematic choices. He is not obliged to renounce the world, nor is he bound to exploit the world. Rather, he may surrender himself into God-Communion via all of his true relations. Thus, the true devotee need not choose between Sex and God. Sex is ordinary to those who love God. The true devotee lives his sexual possibility as a form of Spiritual Worship, or self-transcending Love-Communion with the Living God. Likewise, all of his functional possibilities, high or low in the structure of the body-mind, are engaged or lived as forms of that same Love-Communion. The true devotee does not choose among his own parts. He does not suffer doubt of the world, or the body-mind, or experience. Rather, he is liberated by insight into his participation in the world, or the body-mind, or experience. Therefore, he neither chooses nor abandons the world, or the body-mind, or experience. He simply surrenders as the body-mind in the world, and via every kind of fundamental and right experience, to the Living God. He surrenders as himself. He does not renounce himself or any part of himself. He transcends himself through surrender, or Love-Communion with the Living God, via every function, through all his relations, under all conditions. Therefore, he is always already free—neither bound by the choices of the libertine nor deluded by the choices of the ascetic.

This Way of the true devotee is the Way of Divine Ignorance. And when that Love is Perfect in the seventh stage of life, then where is God and where am "I"? Where is a place? Where does experience happen? When all arising is Realized to be only an unnecessary and temporary modification of Radiant Consciousness, then even the motive is understood as That. Such is the Free Disposition in which even the body Shines with a mindless Shout and Dissolves in Happiness.

430

Epilogue
Love of the Two-Armed Form
(*a free rendering of portions of the*
***Bhagavata Purana*),**[1]
by Bubba Free John

I

Your Master speaks:
I will tell you a parable of ancient understanding.

Imagine a deer in a garden of flowers, his attention caught by a female in the garden. Therefore, his senses are swooning in the fragrant maze of grazing grass, humming aloud with honey bees, where she moves. Thus distracted, he does not taste the scent of wolves, that wait ahead of him, hungry for blood. Nor does he hear the arrow at his back, that kills him at the heart.

Need I say it? The deer is Man in the ordinary way. He is the soul, involved with mind and senses. Flimsy passion wanders in the company of thighs. But lovers are like flowers. Their blossom is sudden, and suddenly it is gone. Attention wanders in the garden of the senses. Therefore, Life Itself is spent, in payment for exaggerations of taste and touch. But all our superficial pleasures and all our moving desires are themselves nothing more than the mechanical achievements of vagrant attention. A lifetime is nothing more than

1. The *Bhagavata Purana* (also commonly referred to as the *Srimad Bhagavatam*) is rightly esteemed as the most complete and authoritative exposition of ancient knowledge in the literature of the Hindu tradition of spirituality. Its roots are in ancient oral traditions, but it may have been put into writing between the fifth and tenth centuries A.D. The author is purported to be Vyasa (Krishna Draipayana), a contemporary of Krishna. This "Purana" is the ultimate text of spiritual science, or the Way of Devotional Sacrifice of Man into God. It extols the Virtues of the Divine Person, principally in the form of Krishna, and communicates the esoteric secrets of the Way in which we may Realize that One.

self-illusion, a temporary and troubled distraction from the Bliss of Eternal Transcendence.

While the soul sleeps in an unmindful state, attention wanders into realms of possibility. Now we are absorbed in sexual love, clinging to the household sounds of lovers and children. Like the deer in the garden, our ears are occupied with creaturely conversation, and our senses are fixed upon the taste and odor of the petty object we are born to Idolize.

Thus exiled in our dreamy houses, the years of days and nights pass unnoticed in their suddenness. But we are always fed upon by search and satisfaction, as by wolves in secret, unconscious, unobserved in our deadly meditation. Suddenly, the garden is undressed. Suddenly, the eloquent weapon of our devourer, who always followed us, is felt within the heart, heard within the mind, and all this Life is stolen in a moment.

Consider this well in the lesson of your own desiring. Bring the motive of the senses to rest in the mind itself. Convert the Current of Life from its worldly course, and surrender bodily, toe to crown. When the mind is thus made Full of Life, surrender it also, in the Heart.

Abandon the "married" disposition. Awaken to the Disposition of a devotee. Exceed the company of ordinary desirers, who only talk of food and sex and casual amusement. Yield attention to the Life and Self of all. Be Absorbed in the Living God, and thus transcend every kind of experience.

(Book 4, chapter 29, verses 52–55)

II

Thus Awakened, the true man says: I am amazed! This soul, the King of the World and the Master of Man, gave itself up to the mind of desires, and thus played into the bodily trap for years and years. I became nothing more than the pet deer of a childish woman.

I deceived myself. For what is there in common between a woman's body (full of excrement and bad smell) and the imagery of flowers, such as fragrant purity and eternal beauty, which I attributed to her? I saw in her body what I only had in mind. A man thus becomes attached to the dying flesh of a woman, praising her in his heart: "Oh, how I love this face, this shapely nose, this goddess of smiles." But, at last, what is the difference between a man whose principal delight is in a woman's body—made of skin and flesh, blood, fat, nerves, bone, and marrow—and a worm that loves to luxuriate in excrement, urine, and pus?

435

Through the senses of the body, attention comes in contact with the various objects of desire. The mind arises and moves when there is contact with the world of experience. But no one is disturbed by what he cannot see or hear or touch. Therefore, a man may transcend the play of desire by turning his attention from things in themselves, and yielding all attention to the Divine Person, through Love-Communion in the Good Company of the Spiritual Master. In this manner, a man's mind becomes tranquil and clear. Then he may give up even his mind to the Radiant Self, the Master of the heart. When a man is thus free at the heart, he may live in the world as long as it is given, but he will only Exist in the Domain of God.

(Book 11, chapter 26, verses 7–26)

III

Thus Awakened, the true woman says: O Master, what mortal woman Awakened to this understanding of Life could surrender herself to any ordinary man, who is always meditating on the great fear? The Master of the heart is the Domain of everything auspicious and wonderful. Those who surrender to the Divine Person are liberated from all experience by Transcendental Love. Awakened to my true need, I surrender only to You, the Radiant Self of all beings.

The body of a mortal man is an odorous corpse. It is nothing more than flesh and blood and bones, full of excrement, mucus, and wind, held together with a little skin and moustache, with nails and hairs from head to toe. Only a stupid woman, who has not Realized the Bliss of surrender in Your fragrant Company, would make a mortal man the Husband of her heart.

(Book 10, chapter 60, verses 42–45)

IV

Thus Awakened in the garden of the world, the lady surrenders to the Master of the heart, Who Abides Eternally in Radiant Bliss. And the Master gives Himself up to loving conversation with her, in the manner of a man. In that same Eternal Moment, the All-Pervading Master of Man appears simultaneously in the households of all devotees. In the form of His own devotees, male and female, husbands and wives, who transcend the garden of desire through Love-Communion with the Living God, the Eternal Master is occupied in all the two-armed ordinariness of humanity.

(Book 10, chapter 60, verses 58–59)

APPENDIX
Physical Exercises Related to the Process of Sexual Communion

Those who practice sexual communion should be in generally good physical condition—as strong, healthy, and physically flexible as possible. The diet should be wholly regenerative, as described in *The Eating Gorilla Comes in Peace*. In general, all should practice the foundation disciplines of standing, sitting, walking, and breathing, the exercise routines of calisthenics, hatha yoga, Surya Namaskar, and pranayama (control of Life in breath), and the sitting postures for meditation, work, or repose, as presented in *Conscious Exercise and the Transcendental Sun*. (*Conscious Exercise and the Transcendental Sun* is Bubba's essential text of instruction on the psycho-physical culture of love and whole bodily Communion with the All-Pervading Energy of Life.)

Bubba has also specified a number of exercises of particular use to those who practice, or are preparing to practice, sexual communion:

A. "Emergency" Procedures for Restoring Whole Body Equilibrium in Life when Casual Sexual Desire Arises

    1. Restoring the Whole Body to Life

    When casual sexual desire arises, whole bodily equilibrium should be reestablished, or else the body-mind will become obsessed, contracted, and separated from Life. The cause of sexual desire is genital tension, supported by contraction of breathing and feeling, and mental dwelling on memories, images, and imagination. Sexual desire may be obviated by relaxing genital tension, engaging in full breathing and feeling, and relaxing the brain-mind into the Life-Force. The process of sexual communion is itself a realization of this entire cycle.

a. In moments of casual sexual desire and distraction, allow full feeling in the genitals. (Genital tension-desire is the result of partial genital feeling and exclusive localization of bodily feeling. Thus, first relax into feeling completely with the genitals.)

b. Then inhale fully to the genitals, abdomen, solar plexus, middle and upper lungs.

c. Feel fully, whole bodily, into the All-Pervading Force of Life, from the genitals.

d. Retain the breath briefly, while continuing to feel with the genitals.

e. Then exhale, allowing the Force of Life to pass from the genitals, filling the entire body.

f. Feel the Force of Life to the tops of the ears, and allow the entire brain to relax and feel into the Force of Life.

g. Relax with profoundly open feeling into the All-Pervading Force Field of Life, which is communicated in the body as a blissful Current of Energy. Feel this Current in every part, head to toes, and radiate its blissful Energy to all relations and to Infinity.

h. Then breathe normally, but with full inhalations and exhalations. And feel into the All-Pervading Force of Life with the whole and entire body, releasing all tension of body, emotion, and mind into the unobstructed Feeling of Life.

Do this any number of times, until natural equilibrium and Fullness of body and emotion are restored, and the mind is clear and awake as thoughtless attention in the All-Pervading Field and Force of Life within which all phenomena are arising.

2: Breathing with Lower Body "Locks"

At random moments of stimulation, during sex play or otherwise:

a. Relax and release the concentration of energy that is in the genitals.

b. Exhale the free energy to the whole body (then radiating it whole bodily to Infinity).

To aid this exercise:

c. First inhale fully to the vital or lower region of the body.

440

d. "Lock" the lower body with physical contractions below, at the bodily base, which is the total or continuous area of the urethra, sex organs, perineum, and anus.

e. Then exhale and release energy, feeling, and attention from below to the whole body (aiding this release by either steady or rhythmic contraction of the bodily base).

B. Exercises for Learning and Adapting to the Physiology of Sexual Communion

1. Tension-Release Cycles

Rapid or slow tension-release cycles of the bodily base while sitting or standing (also occasionally during elimination[1] of urine and faeces), feeling the "flow" of energy all over the body.

This exercise may be used in sex play also, prior to orgasm and after the orgasm tendency passes (but not during the orgasm).

These tension-release cycles generate energy throughout the nervous system and control the tendency of the lower organs to function as continuous, low-grade outlets or leaks for the Life-Force. They serve the process of whole bodily reception (or *conductivity*) and conservation of Life.

2. The Breath Cycle of Sexual Communion, with Tension of the Bodily Base, to Be Practiced at Random

---

1. We unconsciously and chronically throw off Life-Force via the lower body. Practice of tension-release during elimination is simply a way of becoming aware of, and thus more responsible for, this leak.

Assume a comfortable sitting posture and practice the following simple exercise of breath and feeling:

a. Inhale to the vital center of the body (extending between the solar plexus and the anus), tensing the bodily base as the end of inhalation approaches.

b. Exhale to the entire body (or to the ears) while still tensing the bodily base.

c. Relax the whole body at "kumbak" (the brief period of "retention" of exhaled breath) before the next inhalation.

d. Repeat this as many times as desired.

Do all this with Life-Feeling, Radiant at the heart, solar plexus, and brain.

3. Shooting Life to the Whole Body

While sitting or standing:

a. Slowly inhale Life to the vital center.

b. Contract the bodily base as you become Full, and slightly contract the abdomen.

c. Exhale slowly, releasing (even shooting) Life to the whole body, with slight emptying and shooting contraction of bodily base and abdomen.

Do several times, and at random.

4. Tensing of the Sexual Organs (Vajroli Mudra)

Sit in any comfortable seated posture:

a. Place the hands on the knees and close the eyes.

b. Breathe easily, relaxing the whole body through feeling into the All-Pervading Life.

c. While exhaling, draw the sexual organs upward by pulling and tensing the lower abdomen and contracting the entire urinary system (or the bodily base as a whole).

d. Hold for as long as you comfortably can, then relax and breathe easily.

Repeat several times.

C. Breathing Exercises

These breathing exercises are to be done at random, apart from sexual intercourse—but as a preparation for and duplication of the process there. (These exercises are directed toward feeling, ecstasy, and opening and relaxation of the Life-Force to the whole body and thence to Infinity; rather than armoring, contraction, self-meditation, shallow inhalation, and bad exhalation.)

The following six practical principles of breathing exercise duplicate the process of breathing and whole body Fullness that devotees engage in the Way of Divine Communion, as described in *Breath and Name: Bodily Worship of the Living God.* The formal devotional practices in this Way are themselves exercises that prepare the devotee whole bodily for the intense feeling-surrender to God awakened in sexual communion.

1. Take fewer but deeper breath cycles per minute.

2. Pay particular attention to full exhalation-permeation.

3. Work the breath and Life-Energy to and from the base of the lungs and abdomen, then to the middle and the upper lungs and body, including the head.

4. Relax the heart and feel (rather than think) into the world. Feel as the total bodily being, toe to crown.

5. Relax into whole body Fullness through feeling to Infinity, allowing tension and self-contraction to dissolve, along with erotic obsession and all goals of release. Fullness replaces release.

6. The Principle of Reception-Release:

Orderly, full, deep reception-release of Life-Breath, as described in *Conscious Exercise and the Transcendental Sun:*

a. Breathe via the nose, with the mouth closed.

b. Initiate the breath from the heart (the conscious, feeling, psychic core of the bodily being)—that is, initiate the breath with the power of emotion, or whole body feeling—through and with the throat, to the navel.

c. When you inhale, draw in, relax into, and conduct the Life-Energy of the universe with the whole being, even through the entire skin surface of the whole physical body, head to toe, down to or into the vital center, the great life region, whose felt center is behind and below the umbilical scar. Feel the Life-Energy at and from this life center, radiating through the whole being as fullness.

d. Inhale fully, with deep feeling of heart and body, completely filling the lungs with air and the whole body with Life-Force. As the Life-Force moves through the body with the inhalation, it is first sensed in the soft-life region of the solar plexus. As it is drawn downward, it fills and expands the lower body, even the genitals and then the legs and feet. You may also feel a slight tingling sensation at the perineum, which is the lowest or terminal point of the etheric "pathway" of the bodily being. Then the chest and upper regions of the body open, including the neck and head, and the entire body from the crown to the perineum, even to the toes, is tangibly permeated with vibrant energy.

e. When you exhale, do not discard the energy itself or allow it to dissipate, but release and relax all hold on it, allowing it to radiate, from the vital center and the whole body. Allow and feel the pleasurable force of life to be pumped by the heart through the entire body (the limbs, the belly, the sex organs, the head, the teeth and hair and nails, etc.) and the universe. Exhale fully, and with deep feeling of heart and body. Let the energy pervade the whole body and the universe to Infinity, and release, via that radiating and expansive energy, all accumulated conditions, positive or negative, so that inhalation may bring what is new and thus become an instrument of change and refreshment.

444

NOTE: The assumption that heavy breathing and strenuous physical exercise are altogether beneficial and create longevity is false. In fact, those practices tend to enervate the body-mind. Rapid intake of oxygen in the body creates excessive carbon dioxide, which requires increased energy for its elimination and leads to enervation. Obstruction of the Life-Force and the desire for stimulation lead to hyperventilation and strenuous activity, both in forms of physical exercise and in sexual play. Establishment of a right and graceful relationship to the Life-Force is the truly regenerative practice.

About The Johannine Daist Communion

The Johannine Daist Communion represents a complete culture of spiritual practice.

The Laughing Man Institute is the first form of participation. In addition to its educational programs for the interested public and formal friends of the Institute, it serves an important role in preparing the beginning student for the "hard school" of practice that follows in The Free Communion Church. Study or "listening" to the Teaching of the Adept is the primary form of involvement at this stage.

The Free Communion Church is the educational and cultural body for maturing and advanced practitioners. It has six stages of membership corresponding to degrees of maturity in spiritual practice.

The Crazy Wisdom Fellowship. Entrance into The Crazy Wisdom Fellowship is coincident with Enlightenment or Sahaj Samadhi. The ultimate Yoga of Enlightenment is naturally Awakened, and the signs of Transfiguration and Transformation, leading to Indifference and ultimately to Divine Translation in Bhava Samadhi, appear.

An Invitation

If you would like to know more about the study and practice of the spiritual Teaching of Master Da Free John or about how to begin to practice the Way, please write to:

THE LAUGHING MAN INSTITUTE
750 Adrian Way
San Rafael, California 94903

The Books of Master Da Free John

SOURCE TEXTS

THE KNEE OF LISTENING
*The Early Life and Radical Spiritual Teachings of
Da Free John*
$8.95 paper

THE METHOD OF THE SIDDHAS
*Talks with Bubba [Da] Free John on the Spiritual Technique of the Saviors
of Mankind*
$8.95 paper

THE HYMN OF THE MASTER
*A Confessional Recitation on the Mystery of the Spiritual Master based on
the principal verses of the* Guru Gita *(freely selected, rendered, and
adapted)*
$8.95 paper

THE FOUR FUNDAMENTAL QUESTIONS
*Talks and essays about human experience and the actual practice of an
Enlightened Way of Life*
$2.95 paper

THE LIBERATOR (ELEUTHERIOS)
*A summation of the radical process of Enlightenment, or God-Realization,
taught by the "Western Adept," Master Da Free John*
$12.95 cloth, $6.95 paper

THE ENLIGHTENMENT OF THE WHOLE BODY
*A Rational and New Prophetic Revelation of the Truth of Religion,
Esoteric Spirituality, and the Divine Destiny of Man*
$14.95 paper

THE TRANSMISSION OF DOUBT
*Talks and Essays on the Transcendence of Scientific Materialism through
Radical Understanding*
$10.95 paper

SCIENTIFIC PROOF OF THE EXISTENCE OF GOD WILL SOON BE
ANNOUNCED BY THE WHITE HOUSE!
Prophetic Wisdom about the Myths and Idols of mass culture and popular

religious cultism, the new priesthood of scientific and political materialism,
and the secrets of Enlightenment hidden in the body of Man
$12.95 paper

THE PARADOX OF INSTRUCTION
An Introduction to the Esoteric Spiritual Teaching of Bubba [Da] Free John
$14.95 cloth

NIRVANASARA
Radical Transcendentalism and the Introduction of Advaitayana Buddhism
$9.95 paper

INSPIRATIONAL AND DEVOTIONAL TEXTS

CRAZY DA MUST SING, INCLINED TO HIS
WEAKER SIDE
Confessional Poems of Liberation and Love
$6.95 paper

FOREHEAD, BREATH, AND SMILE
An Anthology of Devotional Readings from the Spiritual Teaching of
Master Da Free John
$12.95 cloth

REMEMBRANCE OF THE DIVINE NAMES OF DA
One Hundred Eight Names of the Divine Reality and the Radiant Adept
Master Da Free John
by Georg and Pat Feuerstein
$4.95 paper

GOD IS NOT A GENTLEMAN AND I AM THAT ONE
Ecstatic Talks on Conventional Foolishness versus the Crazy Wisdom of
God-Realization
$6.95 paper

MANUALS OF PRACTICE

THE FIRE GOSPEL
Essays and Talks on Spiritual Baptism
$8.95 paper

COMPULSORY DANCING
Talks and Essays on the spiritual and evolutionary necessity of emotional
surrender to the Life-Principle
$3.95 paper

THE ADEPT
Selections from Talks and Essays by Da Free John on the Nature and
Function of the Enlightened Teacher
$4.95 paper

THE WAY THAT I TEACH
Talks on the Intuition of Eternal Life
$14.95 cloth

THE DREADED GOM–BOO, OR THE IMAGINARY DISEASE THAT
RELIGION SEEKS TO CURE
A Collection of Essays and Talks on the "Direct" Process of Enlightenment
Taught by Master Da Free John
$9.95 paper

BODILY WORSHIP OF THE LIVING GOD
The Esoteric Practice of Prayer Taught by Da Free John
$10.95 paper

"I" IS THE BODY OF LIFE
Talks and Essays on the Art and Science of Equanimity and the Self-
Transcending Process of Radical Understanding
$10.95 paper

THE BODILY LOCATION OF HAPPINESS
On the Incarnation of the Divine Person and the Transmission of
Love-Bliss
$8.95 paper

THE GOD IN EVERY BODY BOOK
Talks and Essays on God-Realization
$3.95 paper

LOOK AT THE SUNLIGHT ON THE WATER
Educating Children for a Life of Self-Transcending Love and Happiness
$7.95 paper

DO YOU KNOW WHAT ANYTHING IS?
Talks and Essays on Divine Ignorance
$6.95 paper

PRACTICAL TEXTS

EASY DEATH
Talks and Essays on the Inherent and Ultimate Transcendence of Death
and Everything Else
$10.95 paper

CONSCIOUS EXERCISE AND THE TRANSCENDENTAL SUN

The principle of love applied to exercise and the method of common physical action. A science of whole body wisdom, or true emotion, intended most especially for those engaged in religious or spiritual life.

$8.95 paper

THE EATING GORILLA COMES IN PEACE (rev. ed., forthcoming)

The Transcendental Principle of Life Applied to Diet and the Regenerative Discipline of True Health

$12.95 paper

LOVE OF THE TWO–ARMED FORM

The Free and Regenerative Function of Sexuality in Ordinary Life, and the Transcendence of Sexuality in True Religious or Spiritual Practice

$12.95 paper

COMMENTARY ON THE TEACHING OF DA FREE JOHN

HUMOR SUDDENLY RETURNS

Essays on the Spiritual Teaching of Master Da Free John—A Scholarly Tribute, edited by Georg Feuerstein

$8.95 paper

PAMPHLETS

THE TRANSCENDENCE OF EGO AND EGOIC SOCIETY

$2.00 paper

A CALL FOR THE RADICAL REFORMATION OF CHRISTIANITY

$2.00 paper

SPIRITUAL TRANSMISSION AND SELF–SURRENDER

$3.00 paper

SCIENCE, SACRED CULTURE, AND REALITY

$2.50 paper

FOR CHILDREN

WHAT TO REMEMBER TO BE HAPPY

A Spiritual Way of Life for Your First Fourteen Years or So

$3.95 paper

I AM HAPPINESS

A Rendering for Children of the Spiritual Adventure of Master Da Free John, edited by Daji Bodha and Lynne Closser from
The Knee of Listening *by Da Free John*

$8.95 paper

PERIODICALS

THE LAUGHING MAN
The Alternative to Scientific Materialism and Religious Provincialism
4 copies (quarterly) $18.00

CRAZY WISDOM
The Monthly Journal of The Johannine Daist Communion
(Available only to Students and formal Friends of The Johannine Daist Communion)
12 copies $48.00

The recorded talks of Master Da Free John (each $9.95):

UNDERSTANDING

THE FOUNDATION AND THE SOURCE

THE YOGA OF CONSIDERATION AND THE WAY THAT I TEACH

THE BODILY LOCATION OF HAPPINESS

THE TRANSCENDENCE OF FAMILIARITY

A BIRTHDAY MESSAGE FROM JESUS AND ME

THE PRESUMPTION OF BEING

THE GOSPEL OF THE SIDDHAS

THE COSMIC MANDALA

THE ULTIMATE WISDOM OF THE PERFECT PRACTICE

PURIFY YOURSELF WITH HAPPINESS

THE ASANA OF SCIENCE

FREEDOM IS IN THE EXISTENCE PLACE

DEATH IS NOT YOUR CONCERN and THE RITUAL OF SORROW

WHAT IS THE CONSCIOUS PROCESS?

FEELING WITHOUT LIMITATION

CHILDREN MUST BE LIBERATED

THE BRIDGE TO GOD

TRANSFORMING SEX AND EVERYTHING and THE ADDICTION AFFLICTION

KEEP ATTENTION IN THE SACRIFICE

THE ULTIMATE MUDRA and YOU CAN'T GET THERE FROM HERE

THE KNOWLEDGE OF LIGHT

Other cassette tapes:

CRAZY DA MUST SING, INCLINED TO HIS WEAKER SIDE
Da Free John reads his Confessional Poems of Liberation and Love
$9.95 cassette

OF THIS I AM PERFECTLY CERTAIN
Ecstatic Readings by Da Free John
$9.95 cassette

DA BELLS
Tibetan "singing bowls" played by Da Free John
$9.95 cassette

HEAR MY BREATHING HEART
Songs of Invocation and Praise Inspired by the Teaching and Presence of Da Free John, by The First Amendment Choir
$9.95 Dolby stereo

TRUTH IS THE ONLY PROFOUND
Devotional readings from the Teaching of Da Free John set to a background of devotional music and songs
$9.95 cassette

THIS IS THE HEART'S CONFESSION
Devotional singing by students of the Way Taught by the Western Spiritual Adept, Da Free John
$9.95 cassette

THE HYMN OF THE MASTER
A confessional recitation of Da Free John's The Hymn of the Master *by a devotee*
$9.95 cassette

VIDEOTAPES

THE BODILY LOCATION OF HAPPINESS
A consideration by Da Free John
$80, 56 minutes, VHS format

THE FIRE MUST HAVE ITS WAY
A consideration by Da Free John
$80, 57 minutes, VHS format

Classic Spiritual Literature

THE SECRET GOSPEL
The Discovery and Interpretation of the Secret Gospel According to Mark
by Morton Smith
$7.95 paper

LONG PILGRIMAGE
The Life and Teaching of the Shivapuri Baba
by John G. Bennett
$7.95 paper

THE DIVINE MADMAN
The Sublime Life and Songs of Drukpa Kunley
translated by Keith Dowman
$7.95 paper

THE YOGA OF LIGHT
The Classic Esoteric Handbook of Kundalini Yoga
by Hans-Ulrich Rieker,
translated by Elsy Becherer
$7.95 paper

A NEW APPROACH TO BUDDHISM
by Dhiravamsa
$3.95 paper

VEDANTA AND CHRISTIAN FAITH
by Bede Griffiths
$3.95 paper

FOUNDING THE LIFE DIVINE
An Introduction to the Integral Yoga of Sri Aurobindo
by Morwenna Donnelly
$7.95 paper

BREATH, SLEEP, THE HEART, AND LIFE
The Revolutionary Health Yoga of Pundit Acharya
$7.95 paper

THE SPIRITUAL INSTRUCTIONS OF SAINT SERAPHIM OF SAROV
edited and with an introduction by Da Free John
$3.95 paper

THE SONG OF THE SELF SUPREME
Aṣṭāvakra Gītā
Preface by Da Free John
translated by Radhakamal Mukerjee
$9.95 paper

SELF–REALIZATION OF NOBLE WISDOM
The Lankavatara Sutra
compiled by Dwight Goddard on the basis of D. T. Suzuki's rendering from the Sanskrit and Chinese
$7.95 paper

These books and tapes are available at fine bookstores or by mail order from:

THE DAWN HORSE BOOK DEPOT, Dept. L2
750 Adrian Way
San Rafael, CA 94903

Add $1.50 for the first book or tape and $.35 for each additional book or tape. California residents add 6% sales tax.

Index

abortion, 48f.
absorption, 89, 143, 316, 318
Adam and Eve, 27
Adept. *See* Spiritual Master
adolescence, 26f., 135ff., 138, 211
"Alternative Reality," 289f., 299
amaroli, 340f.
antisexuality, 29, 36f., 46, 64, 289f., 292.
    See also asceticism
aphrodisiacs, 222, 224, 226
Arjuna, 189
asana, 316
asceticism, 47, 212, 291ff., 361, 396,
    398, 409, 417f., 423–28, 429f. *See
    also* antisexuality
ashtanga yoga, 317
attention, 303, 326f., 394
Awakening, 43, 54

betrayal, 134f., 138ff., 211, 221, 285,
    307
Bhagavad Gita, 11, 13–15, 13n, 189,
    195f.
Bhagavata Purana, 433n, 433–36
birth, 50
birth control, 49, 226
Bliss, 92, 128, 160, 203, 298, 344f., 401,
    421
body, viii–ix, 406f., 419ff., 435f.
body-mind, 53, 61
brahmacharya, 331, 331n, 352
brain, 210, 211, 281, 313, 335, 342, 389
brain core, 313
breath, 58f., 211, 233ff., 236ff., 249–58,
    283, 305, 368, 323f., 347, 442ff.

celebration, 380–83
celibacy, 40, 331, 413, 418, 424
    motiveless, 7, 205, 318, 350, 358,
    372f., 407, 408, 416
change, secret of, 109
chemistry, sexual, 29, 235f., 240f., 414
    conservation of, 125, 232, 239ff.,
    254–64, 265, 293ff., 299, 315, 340f.
childhood, 25, 36f.
childishness, 25f., 86, 134ff.
    and betrayal, 139

and consolation, 86, 123
and jealousy, 132
and marriage, 146
and religion, 36
and responsibility, 35f.
and sex, 78, 80, 145, 211
and the true man, 138
Communion, Divine, 22, 51, 92, 136f.,
    143f., 298, 318, 353, 394f., 401, 421,
    429f.
    and desire, 127, 158f., 320ff., 395ff.,
    400
    and Enlightenment, xxii
    and "I am the body," 18
    and reactivity, 100f.
    and self-possession, 117ff.
    and sex obsession, 47
    as "conscious exercise," 202
    conductivity in, 104
    transcends sex, 94, 370
    via sex, 85
community, xxiv, 449f.
Condition, 18, 93, 125, 137
conductivity, 104n, 285, 299, 317, 360,
    371
confession, 150f.
conscious exercise, 43, 202, 233, 271
*Conscious Exercise and the
    Transcendental Sun*, 57, 202, 233,
    237, 250, 268, 326
Consciousness, 21, 92
consciousness, 92
conscious process, 202n, 393
"consideration," 1–4, 396
contraceptives. *See* birth control
conversion, 139ff., 22, 418
cult of pairs, 155, 339
culture and sex, 166ff., 168ff., 172f.

Da (Bubba) Free John, xi–xxiv
death, viii, 111f., 132, 145, 300
desire, 158f., 186, 312f., 319–23,
    393–402, 433ff.
    and attention, 394
    and mind, 420f
    and orgasm, 128, 211
    and promiscuity, 148
    infinite, 322f.
    in marriage, 337
    mastered by love, 124
    not satisfied, 114, 312f., 319–23
    objects of, 321f., 433ff.
    transcendence of, 397ff.

true, 127
Desire in Enlightenment, 323
Devil, 26, 28, 31, 33
dharana, 316
dharmas, 189
dhyana, 316
diet, 58f., 311ff., 379, 383–93
dietary accessories, 381f., 385f., 389f.
disciplines, 90f., 94, 131, 311, 362–65, 378, 379f., 383–88, 402f., 405f.
Divine Communion. *See* Communion
Divine Domain, 43, 112
doubt, 61, 146, 157, 289ff.
Dracula, 27f., 33f.
dualism, 17

Eating Gorilla Comes in Peace, The, 57, 340
economy, sexual. *See* sexual communion
Ecstasy, 105ff., 120, 121, 373, 374, 400, 421
 and experience, 124f., 401f.
 and pleasure, 105ff., 113, 122f.
 and politics, 44
 and renunciation, 422
 and sacrifice, 99f., 120
 and sexuality, 64f., 65ff., 105, 113, 121, 134, 304, 318, 357
 of Light, 88
Eden, 27, 39, 42
education, 27, 36–37, 77, 225
ego, 139, 422
energy, human, 23, 293
Energy. *See* Life-Current
Enlightenment, 87, 139, 323, 402, 406, 417ff.
Enlightenment of the Whole Body, The, 41
emotion, 92, 140f., 213ff., 219
erection, 303, 313
erotica, 48, 68f., 223ff.
eroticism, 48f., 67ff., 130, 151f., 153, 157, 167, 169f., 228f., 325, 349, 392
 and death, 216
 and incest, 150
etheric body, 334, 334n
evil, 26, 28, 33, 42, 44
evolution, 53f.
eyes, 308f., 335f.
experience, 124f., 203

faith, 58

fear, xix, 44f., 118, 146, 224
feeling, 45, 91, 104
feeling-attention, 19, 23, 39, 91, 249f., 303f., 308f., 317, 333, 394
female character, 164ff., 173ff., 176ff.
fetishism, 65ff., 349
"flesh, the," 32, 37, 345, 435
food, 58f., 74f., 76f., 312f., 321f., 383, 393
Frankenstein, 27f., 34
freedom, 125, 126, 329, 406
free rendering, defined, 11
"Free Standing Man, The" (free rendering from *Bhagavad Gita*), 195f.
frustration, 98ff., 320, 325, 391

genital discharge, control of, 239ff., 255ff., 258ff., 265f., 293f., 303, 333f.
God, 21, 429
God-Communion. *See* Communion
Goddess, wife as, 345
God-Realization. *See* Enlightenment
gopis, 322
guilt, 39, 42, 65, 224
Guru. *See* Spiritual Master

happiness, 208
hatha yoga, 293, 317, 331
hearing, 19, 81, 118, 204, 217, 247, 311 347, 379, 396, 418
heart, 80, 90f., 93f., 181ff., 207, 215, 232, 270, 299, 301, 302f., 317, 349, 351
 regulates sexual communion, 302f., 317
"heat," 205
holiness, 424ff.
homosexuality, 50, 311, 354–57
humor, 406

"I" am the body, 17f., 41, 62
Ignorance, 104
imagery, 221, 223ff., 307, 317, 327f., 333, 359
immortality, viii, 290, 293, 300
incarnation, 19
incest, 133, 150
intimacy, 50, 132, 133, 185f., 208, 309, 337
 and "heat," 205
inversion, 290f., 310, 417, 426, 428
 of sex organs, 350, 360

inwardness, 307, 417

Jahan, Shah, viii
jealousy, 115, 132f., 183f.
Johannine Daist Communion, The, vii, 447

karma, 125
Krishna, xxiii, 189, 322
kumbak, 252
kundalini, 241, 317, 342

Law, the, 40, 42, 74f., 93, 99, 117f., 125, 181. *See also* sacrifice
Life, 85ff., 101, 134ff.
   and sex, 111, 297, 317f., 325
   is Loved-One, 130f.
   surrender to, 92f.
Life-Current, 58, 325
   and higher stages, 71f.
   and sex, 85ff., 104, 213, 244ff., 292, 297, 302f., 318, 330, 350, 416f.
   and Spiritual Master, 51
   as Food, 58, 213f.
Life-Energy. *See* Life-Current
Life-Force. *See* Life-Current
Light, 145, 189, 211
longevity, 293
love, xx, 41, 137f., 181ff., 208
   and Communion, 137f.
   and desire, 124, 128, 158f., 226
   and genital sexuality, 219, 250, 286f., 297, 300
   and jealousy, 132f.
   and marriage, xvii
   and mortality, viii, 297
   and pleasure, 115
   as "conscious exercise," 43, 202
   conventional, 128
   "I is the body" is, 17ff.
   masters desire, 124, 226
   whole bodily, 315, 317
Love-Communion. *See* Communion
love-desire, 64, 128f., 186, 221, 223, 243, 251f., 285, 302, 309, 323, 326f., 333, 338
Love of the Two-Armed Form, purpose of, 1-5, 20, 30, 44, 45, 64
"Love of the Two-Armed Form" (free rendering from *Bhagavata Purana*), 433
lust, 127

madness, 45
male character, 164ff., 173ff., 176ff., 289ff., 294
man, superior, 25ff.
marriage, 48f., 146, 147, 148ff., 198, 337, 343-46, 351f., 373, 423, 425, 427, 434
   and the State, 148
   preparation for, 152f.
   sleeping position, 340
   sleeping separately, 154f., 339, 340
masturbation, 65ff., 214, 224, 225, 227ff., 403f.
materialism, 17
menstruation, 29, 31f., 384f., 411
mind, 419ff., 422
monogamy, 148ff.
mortality, viii, 135
mudra, 316
mudra, genital, 244ff.

Narcissus, xviii-xx, 140, 144, 196, 227, 301, 372, 422
"need connection," 138ff.
nervous system, 210, 232, 236, 253, 295f., 310, 313, 315, 335, 389

object. *See* desire
Old Testament, 34
orgasm, 102f., 124, 125, 126f., 212f., 214ff., 327f.
   adaptation to, 213f.
   and breath, 236ff., 254ff.
   and desire, 79, 102, 120, 124, 211
   and diet, 383f.
   and loss of chemistry, 216, 234, 293ff., 330
   and reactive emotions, 214ff., 218
   and relaxation, 244f.
   and Taoism, 293f.
   and thought, 281f.
   and whole bodily thrill, 49, 69, 295, 329, 343, 406, 414
   as proof of "good sex," xvii-xviii, 153, 209
   concern about, 314
   conservation during, 266ff.
   conservation of, 6, 103, 239ff., 254-65, 275f., 293f., 314ff., 331ff.
   control by finger pressure, 258ff., 293f.
   control by tension, 244ff., 259f., 293

458

control through love, 315
dependence on, 64, 327
during menstruation, 411
East and West, 216f.
inversion of, 292f., 318, 368
Oriental view of, 216f.
regenerative, 238, 240, 272, 332
right exercise of, 409–13
sign of eroticism, 69
superficial, 49
throwing off energy in, 114f., 185,
211, 214, 216, 234f., 236, 293, 296,
330
transcendence of, 283f., 285f., 358f.,
367f.
Western view of, 217
Oriental disposition, 216f., 290, 310

Paradox of Instruction, The, 41
Patanjali, 1, 316f.
physical exercises related to sexual
communion, 438–44
physics, 51, 141, 204
pleasure, 105ff., 113ff., 122f., 323
and death, 216
and ecstasy, 105ff., 122f.
and sexuality, 46ff., 78f., 113ff., 298,
304
and tension-release, 105
anti-, 46
genital, 61, 62f.
native, 298
polygamy, 148ff.
practice, spiritual, 85, 90f.
practices, esoteric sexual, 51
pranayama, 316
pratyahara, 316
priests, 423f.
promiscuity, 3, 64, 148f., 150, 184f.
and boredom, 152
and marriage, 146f.
and polygamy, 149
as anxiety, 147
as defense, 165f.
desire for promiscuous partners,
157f.
psyche, 183
Purusha, 346

Radiance, 21, 307, 421
reactivity, 92, 97f., 118, 183, 309, 380
and passion, 100f.

and sex, 229
and tension-release, 105ff.
root of conflict, 154
root of degenerative sex, 212, 214f.
Reality, 136f.
reception-release, 59n, 323
relationship, 19, 66ff., 120, 425
religion
and love, 144, 181
and sexual communion, 85
conventional, 136
true, 4, 90
renunciation, 391, 396ff., 422
repetition, urge to, 105, 122, 124, 159
reproduction, 50
responsibility, 35, 40, 304f., 377
romanticism, 130, 148f., 185, 218

sacrifice, 40, 90f., 93, 119. *See also* Law,
the
and love, 112, 227
and self-denial, 126
and sexual communion, 20, 125, 310,
332, 360f.
as worship, 90f.
sahasrar, 188
samadhi, 316
samyama, 1–4
seeing, 118, 247, 347, 379, 418
self-denial, 126, 182
self-indulgence, 46f., 204, 395, 398, 406,
409
self-transcendence, 47, 53, 99, 395
semen, 341
separation, 181f., 305ff.
separation anxiety, 305ff.
service, 311
sex
and death, 216
and emotion, 213ff., 219
and social order, 393f.
and thought, 306
as attention, 159
as conflict, 153f.
as riddle, 396f.
as "sin," 289f.
control of impulse, 40ff., 399
end of play, 274
generative, 198, 207, 235, 329f.
key to Divine Life, 85
necessity of, 353f.
play of opposites and likenesses,
274f.

polarization, 163, 166
problem of, 121f., 219, 360f., 429
regenerative, 187f., 217, 238, 274,
    295f., 300, 318, 329, 330, 332, 335,
    357, 413–17
ritual, 113ff., 221, 328
roles, 164f., 170f., 173ff., 185
transcendence of, 206f., 217f., 369f.,
    370, 374, 377, 379, 396f., 399, 407,
    408, 416
sexual character, 33, 63, 164ff., 169,
    173ff., 176ff.
    female, 164ff., 173ff., 176ff.
    male, 164ff., 173ff., 176ff., 289ff., 294
sexual communion, 6f., 18ff., 39, 49, 94,
    110, 129f., 156, 158, 196ff., 201,
    231–87, 305, 310, 329, 338f., 343
    adapting to, 243, 262ff., 271f.,
        278–83, 324, 440f.
    and conservation of orgasm, 6, 129f.,
        187, 265f., 244ff., 258ff., 304, 314,
        410f.
    and genital mudra, 244ff.
    and homosexuality, 356
    and human growth, 80f., 207, 229,
        299
    and love-desire, 128f., 325, 339
    and marriage, 351
    and sexual economy, 110, 129, 155f.,
        156f., 198, 235f., 317, 350, 357f., 370,
        406
    and stages of life, 76, 81
    and transcendence of desire, 397, 400
    as "conscious exercise," 233, 237ff.,
        307
    as sacrifice, 131, 197
    as truly human sexuality, 49, 79, 130
    as worship, 93
    basic instruments of, 264f.
    before marriage, 152
    concentration and relaxation in, 277f.
    defined, 6f.
    disposition of, 400
    etheric resonance, 334
    frequency of, 338
    length of occasion, 324, 338
    nondifferentiation in, 335
    not a method of Realization, 88, 201,
        203
    not opposition, 153
    physical exercises related to, 438–44

preparation for, 338, 378
self-consciousness in, 328, 335f.
side effects of, 310f.
spread of awakened energy, 270, 341
stages of, 6f., 18ff., 360, 365–70,
    409–13
use of eyes in, 308f., 335f.
use of breath in, 236ff.
weariness after, 326
sexual intercourse, 113, 125, 295f., 403f.,
    408
sexuality, genital, 43f., 48, 61, 110, 210,
    219, 342
"Shakti" in polygamy, 149
shame, 65
Siamese twins, 133
sin, 31, 40, 82, 97f., 205, 289
Siva, 31, 346
social order, 168ff.
"Song of the Heart of God, The,"
    13–15
Spirit, 90
Spiritual Master, 51f., 107f., 137, 142f.,
    159, 160, 181, 298, 311, 318, 347, 394
    as Agency of life, 51
    as lover, 128, 436
    preparation for, 52, 137
stages of life, 71ff., 321
    first three, 75ff., 86, 151, 181, 351f.,
        403f.
    fourth, 74ff., 181, 207f., 215, 287,
        351f., 404
    fifth, 404
    sixth, 405
    seventh, 321, 405f., 407f.
stimulation, 113f., 126, 209, 218, 227,
    319f.
Stoker, Bram, 31
stress, genital, 273
subhumanness, 26, 51ff., 74f., 80, 98f.,
    109, 146, 167, 345
subjectivity, 163f.
"suitcase" stories, 110f.
superior man (human being), 25ff.
surrender, 92f., 129f., 358, 430, 435f.

taboos, 29, 36, 66f., 130, 307, 412
Taj Mahal, viii–ix
Tantrism, 240f., 240n, 289–300, 310,
    317, 332
Taoism, 240f., 240n, 289–300, 317, 332

tea, stimulating, 389–91
Teaching, 136, 140
tension, 244ff., 259f., 293, 301, 329, 359
tension-release, 65, 100ff., 105ff.
thinking, 92, 309
thought, 76, 281f., 306, 419ff.
thrill, whole bodily, 49, 69, 295, 329,
    406
transcendence, 391f., 397ff., 403f., 406f.,
    421, 422
Transfiguration, 51f., 105, 402, 421
Transformation, 47, 52, 105
Translation, 43, 47, 51f., 82, 87, 94, 105,
    112, 189, 323, 374, 402, 416
Truth, 18, 70, 88f., 90, 156
two-armed form, xv, 4

Upanishadic period, 291
Upanishads, xix
urine, 340f.

verbal mind, 81, 305

Way, 87, 90f., 138, 294f.
Western view of orgasm, 217
will, 76
wisdom, 188ff.

yamas and niyamas, 316
yang, 341
yoga, sexual, 6, 32, 45, 120, 242, 291ff.,
    300, 308, 317
Yoga Sutras, 1

461